Deterrence Now

Patrick Morgan's authoritative study revisits the place of deterrence after the Cold War. By assessing and questioning the state of modern deterrence theory, particularly under conditions of nuclear proliferation, Morgan argues that there are basic flaws in the design of the theory that ultimately limit its utility. Given the probable patterns of future international politics, he suggests that greater attention be paid to "general" deterrence as opposed to "immediate" deterrence and to examining the deterrent capabilities of collective actors such as NATO and the UN Security Council. Finally, he contends that the revolution in military affairs can promote less reliance on deterrence by retaliatory threats, support better collective management of peace and security and permit us to outgrow nuclear and other weapons of mass destruction. This new major work builds upon Patrick Morgan's landmark book, *Deterrence: A Conceptual Analysis* (1983).

PATRICK M. MORGAN holds the Thomas and Elizabeth Tierney Chair in Peace and Conflict Studies and Professor of Political Science at the University of California, Irvine. His published books include *Deterrence: A Conceptual Analysis* (1983), *Strategic Military Surprise* (with Klaus Knorr), *Regional Orders* (with David Lake), *Security and Arms Control*, Vols. I and II (with Edward Kolodziej) and *Theories and Approaches to International Politics*.

Deterrence Now

CAMBRIDGE STUDIES IN INTERNATIONAL RELATIONS

Series list continues after Index

Deterrence Now

Patrick M. Morgan

University of California, Irvine

CAMBRIDGE
UNIVERSITY PRESS

PUBLISHED BY THE PRESS SYNDICATE OF THE UNIVERSITY OF CAMBRIDGE
The Pitt Building, Trumpington Street, Cambridge CB2 1RP, United Kingdom

CAMBRIDGE UNIVERSITY PRESS
The Edinburgh Building, Cambridge, CB2 2RU, UK
40 West 20th Street, New York, NY 10011-4211, USA
477 Williamstown Road, Port Melbourne, VIC 3207, Australia
Ruiz de Alarcón 13, 28014 Madrid, Spain
Dock House, The Waterfront, Cape Town 8001, South Africa

http://www.cambridge.org

First published 2003

Printed in the United Kingdom at the University Press, Cambridge

Typeface Palatino 10/12.5 pt   *System* LATEX 2$_\varepsilon$ [TB]

A catalogue record for this book is available from the British Library

Library of Congress Cataloguing in Publication data

ISBN 0 521 82257 2 hardback
ISBN 0 521 52969 7 paperback

To Thomas and Elizabeth Tierney,
whose heads and hearts are both in the right place

Contents

Acknowledgments

As the words pile up so do the debts. To start with, I must thank Thomas and Elizabeth Tierney. I wallow in the luxury of an endowed chair they created at the University of California, Irvine, and its resources were crucial in sustaining me on the sabbatical leave during which the initial work on the book was completed and over the rest of time it was refined. They made this book possible. Their extraordinary generosity sustains many people at my institution and the surrounding community and it is always a great pleasure for me to say so.

That year on leave was spent primarily as a visiting faculty member at the Department of War Studies at King's College London. It was a great treat intellectually and personally. When the department was designated as the strongest in international relations research in the nation by finishing first in the quadrennial competition for government research funds, I even imbibed a memorable amount of free champagne. Especially helpful in all things was the head of the department, Professor Lawrence Freedman. A better scholar and friend could not be found, particularly on anything to do with deterrence. I learned much from others in the department: Jan Willem Honig, Jo Spear, James Gow, Beatrice Heuser, and some outstanding graduate students.

Terry Terriff at the University of Birmingham stoutly upheld his end in vigorous discussions at shifting venues from which I learned much. Eric Herring at the University of Bristol and Yuen Foon Khong at Oxford invited me to try out ideas on skeptical faculty members and probing students, as did T. V. Paul and colleagues at McGill University in Montreal later on. I benefitted very much from laying out central elements of the book at the National Defense College in Tokyo at the invitation of a delightful friend, Yoshihide Nakamura, at the Strategic Command in Omaha, at the University of Washington – thanks to

Acknowledgments

Christopher Jones – and at the Battelle National Laboratory in Richland, Washington.

Much of the initial writing was completed at the Rockefeller Center at Bellagio, a place which offers an extraordinary experience. Charming and indefatigable hosts seat you in the lap of luxury, catering to every need and confident that you will feel driven, out of quiet guilt feelings that you can't possibly deserve such treatment, to push resolutely through the task at hand. It is a winning concept applied with brio in a setting of unparalleled beauty.

At home, graduate students who worked on library materials in my behalf included Mark Bretches and Brenda Seaver. They alerted me to sources I should have known about, and tracked down ones especially hard to obtain, working pleasantly for a pittance. I am steadily grateful, and happy they have gone on to good things. Ted Gaulin generously offered to tackle the index and did a fine job – as a graduate student, he could have found better things to do with his time.

John Haslam, one of the finest of editors, was commendably patient with my delays. Trevor Horwood, my copy-editor, was excellence personified.

I make the usual apologies to my wife for uncivilized behavior in getting the damn thing done and taking too long at it, but also note that anglophile Marilyn had wonderful fun in Britain and that there are worse places to be dragged off to for a summer month than the Italian Alps.

Abbreviations and acronyms

BMD	Ballistic missile defense
CFE	Conventional forces in Europe
C³I	Command-control-communication-intelligence
DEFCON	Defense condition
EMP	Electro-magnetic pulse
EU	European Union
ExCom	Executive Committee (of the President)
GPS	Global positioning system
GRIT	Graduated reduction in tension
IAEA	International Atomic Energy Agency
IISS	International Institute for Strategic Studies
JCS	Joint Chiefs of Staff
KLA	Kosovo Liberation Army
LOW	Launch on warning
MAD	Mutually assured destruction
MID	Militarized international dispute
MIRV	Multiple independently targetable reentry vehicles
NATO	North Atlantic Treaty Organization
NPT	Non-proliferation Treaty
NSC	National Security Council
OSCE	Organization for Security and Cooperation in Europe
PGM	Precision guided munition
R&D	Research and development
RMA	Revolution in military affairs
RoK	Republic of Korea
RV	Reentry vehicle
SAC	Strategic Air Command
SALT	Strategic Arms Limitations Talks

List of abbreviations and acronyms

SAM	Surface-to-air Missile
SIOP	Single Integrated Operations Plan
SOP	Standard operating procedure
START	Strategic Arms Reductions Talks
WEU	Western European Union
WMD	Weapons of mass destruction
WTO	World Trade Organization

Preface

I wanted to write this book because of several developments in the wake of the Cold War. First, the end of that era produced a profound adjust-ment in political relations among great states with nuclear arsenals, in spite of the continued existence of reciprocal threats of vast magnitude. They began to act, in many ways, as if those arsenals did not exist and in other ways as if those arsenals permitted relations on a friendlier basis than would otherwise have been possible. Thus most of them announced that they were significantly reducing their strategic nuclear arsenals and their nonstrategic nuclear forces and, on the other, that they had no intention – for the time being at least – of eliminating nuclear weapons because they remained important for security. I hope to show how this indicates that a number of things often taken for granted about nuclear weapons – and thus about nuclear deterrence and often about deterrence without nuclear weapons – are not necessarily true, and that certain other things that have been asserted about nuclear weapons and nuclear deterrence (and deterrence at other levels) are indeed correct. The end of the Cold War and the years since have been very illuminating and it is instructive to consider how.

Second, debate about deterrence, and related things such as threats, continues to churn in the academic and policy oriented literature, and it seems appropriate to reconsider the issues involved.[1] The debate is often about fundamental matters: whether deterrence works, how it works (if it does), and how to find out. With such basic questions still on the agenda we don't seem, at first glance, to have learned much. After more

[1] Examples, not always cited in the rest of the book, include Bracken 1991 (on coming threats to American deterrence from the Far East); Manwaring 2001; several articles in *Journal of Strategic Studies* 2000; Freedman 1996; Cimbala 2000; Joseph and Reichart 1998; Payne 1996, 2001; Huth 1999.

than five decades of experience with, and thinking intensively about, deterrence in the shadow of nuclear weapons, these are the same questions we faced when we started. Surely we ought to have answered at least some of them or the worth of the enterprise is in question. I first wrote about these sorts of questions years ago and I wanted to see how the subject had turned out – to do an update on deterrence and deterrence theory as the best way to tackle the current questions/debates about deterrence now. I attempt to assess what we know and, where there are significant limitations along those lines, try to explain why progress is slow. An underlying question is: how useful is deterrence theory? Since the theory, from its inception, was meant to shape the development of effective strategy in the practice of deterrence, conclusions on the utility of the theory are highly pertinent. Even if we don't have reliable conclusions about the utility of the theory, that would be important.

Third, some years ago I introduced the distinction between "general" and "immediate" deterrence and I wanted to examine general deterrence more closely in view of the altered international situation after the Cold War. An immediate deterrence situation is one in which an actor realizes that another specific actor is seriously contemplating attacking and undertakes to deter that attack. During the Cold War the study and the practice of deterrence was dominated by the image of immediate deterrence, by the conception of deterrence as designed to cope with a pressing threat or one that could become pressing at almost any time. I suggested that this was not altogether wise, that immediate deterrence was relatively rare and that more attention be paid to general deterrence in theoretical and strategic analysis. That had almost no impact, and general deterrence has received little attention down to the present day. General deterrence has to do with anticipating possible or potential threats, often hypothetical and from an unspecified attacker, and adopting a posture designed to deter other actors from ever beginning to think about launching an attack and becoming the "potential" or "would-be" challengers so prominent in deterrence theory. In theory, general deterrence has been given little systematic attention by me or anyone else, but it is where most of the practice of deterrence is lodged most of the time. It is worth trying to remedy this. The end of the Cold War eliminated the urgency and intensity from deterrence among the great powers, placing them more clearly in a general deterrence posture vis-à-vis each other. For many other states now immediate deterrence is less relevant than it was, and general deterrence considerations dominate security planning. At the same time, many states now frequently confront issues of broad security management in a regional or the global system – issues pertaining to conflict prevention, peace enforcement, and collective security which require taking general deterrence considerations into account. This is worth exploring too.

Fourth, the end of the Cold War led to considerable speculation about the utility of deterrence, literature on how the US or the West now has to confront opponents not easily deterred – terrorists, rogue states, fanatical ethnic or religious movements, intensely insecure smaller states. The fear is that these opponents will be difficult to understand, inclined to be uncompromising, likely to take high risks and pay a high price in pursuit of their goals, and possibly irrational; as a result deterrence will not work well, if at all. There is a related concern that the US or the West will not be able to deter these actors and others effectively because Western states will not accept the associated costs. They might be unhappy about maintaining the necessary forces without a clear and compelling threat. Or the level of effort and related costs they are willing to bear in specific confrontations is declining so that, having forces for a militarily effective response, they won't use them. Or the ability of potential attackers to inflict harm, such as via weapons of mass destruction, will rise to where they deter the deterrers. And in all these situations Western states, even if willing to act, would have a serious credibility problem, the bane of any deterrence policy.

There is also the suggestion, widespread in discussions on nuclear proliferation, that regardless of the future effectiveness of American or Western deterrence there will soon be confrontations between other actors in which deterrence will fail. There is fear of confrontations between nuclear-armed states quite inexperienced in managing nuclear deterrence postures – in comparison with the Cold War superpowers – and concern about a breakdown or failure of deterrence at a crucial point. A related worry is that a confrontation will involve nuclear-armed states with unstable deterrence postures in that they actually increase the incentives to resort to force. (This might be due to inexperience or the result of other factors, so this is not the same concern as the previous one.) Also noteworthy is uneasiness about confrontations between governments, leaders, and movements that are irrational, leading to failures of deterrence. This is exacerbated by the prospect that one or both parties will be armed with weapons of mass destruction.

The burden of these views is that if deterrence is less reliable then the international system, or its subsystems or regional systems, are much less safe. A standard theme is that at least the Cold War, whatever its deficiencies, imposed a degree of stability and prevented warfare between the two blocs while curbing their appetites elsewhere and prevented, repressed, or contained violent conflicts among other states, while providing a framework within which the horizontal proliferation of nuclear weapons was contained. When examined closely, these assertions almost always ascribe this stability to deterrence and trace the coming decline in stability to the deficiencies in deterrence that are emerging. If deterrence is less reliable international politics is less safe. That is certainly not a comforting prospect. The traditional concept of security, which highlights clashing human values pressed to extremes and the deliberate harm done as a result, remains relevant. Military threats are still important, as are military responses to them. Military capabilities remain vital in any current or prospective international security arrangement. Deterrence needs tending and maybe pruning, especially nuclear deterrence. One study cites some thirteen schools of thought now about how to ease our reliance on nuclear weapons (Howlett et al. 1999).

Fifth, concerns about the usefulness of deterrence feed directly into a subject that is already a major element in international politics, will be more so in the years ahead, and thus deserves greater attention: how collective actors, representing our interest in the stability and security of an international system (regional or global), practice deterrence. Actors such as NATO when conducting peacekeeping or peace enforcement or peace imposition, or the UN Security Council, or an ad hoc coalition. We have seen several relevant instances – Bosnia, the Gulf War, Kosovo – and it is appropriate to ask whether the theory and strategy of deterrence need adjusting to encompass such actors. After all, the theory developed, and the variants of deterrence strategy were designed, with individual states or traditional alliances doing the deterrence. The theory and strategy were also conceived with individual governments as targets, not a collective actor. Does it make a difference to shift the nature of the deterrer or the target in this fashion?

Still another impetus for the book is the surging interest in the "revolution in military affairs," as already upon us or as something that has not yet fully taken hold but is on the horizon. Revolutions in military affairs do not come along often so it is important to ask whether one is indeed brewing now. More important, however, is the impact such a revolution might have on deterrence. After all, the last revolution – the coming of nuclear weapons – generated successive waves of deterrence thinking during the Cold War and was the primary preoccupation in the variants on deterrence strategy that emerged. It seems reasonable to suppose that a new revolution could have major implications for deterrence in theory and practice so an investigation, however speculative it must be, of the possible implications is in order.

Finally, it should now be apparent that deterrence is not going to disappear just because the Cold War is gone. It is the underlying basis of most prospective or plausible regimes for the management of regional or global security. This includes regimes for preventing proliferation and upholding arms control agreements, so the impact of deterence reaches far beyond prevention of military attacks and war. We continue to have much at stake in deterrence. It is not simply a way of trying to force others to behave; it is woven into many elements of foreign and national security policy. For instance, deterrence in place remains a political prerequisite for *cooperation with adversaries or potential adversaries* – for making meaningful and risky concessions, pursuing "engagement," and reaching many types of agreements. (Everyone wants to negotiate from at least this much strength.) And if we are to build successful international communities, general deterrence will play a role comparable to police protection in fostering domestic society.

Yet deterrence remains an important tool for *failed* relationships and communities – it is not ideally our first choice, but more like a recourse. And it remains a flawed policy instrument, often uncertain or unreliable in its effects. Having to use it is always somewhat tragic. It should be used only with care, with ample appreciation that it is shot through with limitations. We must understand it as best we can, therefore, and that is what I have tried to do.

The book has the following plan. It opens by reviewing our Cold War experience with deterrence, setting off a discussion that is theoretical in nature and requires linking ruminations about the key elements of deterrence theory and how they developed to the theoretical problems that emerged years ago and still persist in the analysis of deterrence today. The idea is to see what can be said about those problems in the light of, on the one hand, our experience with deterrence in practice and, on the other, the work that has been done on them and on this basis to offer suggestions on how to think about them now. Added to this are theoretical reflections, and practical observations, on the nature of general deterrence in contemporary international politics. All this takes several chapters.

Then there is a review of empirical findings about deterrence in practice, complete with a discussion of the problems in such studies – deterrence is devilishly difficult to study. But the studies continue to pile up and no book like this would be complete without at least an attempt to assess them. There is also a chapter on collective actor deterrence which cites recent experience in constructing hypotheses for shaping future studies on how this sort of deterrence will go. Left until late in the book is discussion of the "revolution in military affairs." While there are concrete things to say about what makes a revolution like this and the new and prospective developments that are shaping it, the core of what is offered is very speculative – musings about the probable impact of these developments on the nature of future warfare and how changes of that sort will affect deterrence as a tool of statecraft.

Then the last lengthy chapter turns to the concern about whether deterrence will remain reliable or is increasingly unlikely to work. This involves bringing considerations raised and findings elaborated in the rest of the book to bear on the question of how useful deterrence is now and will be in the future. A brief concluding chapter summarizes the others.

All this makes for a lengthy and complicated book. My thanks to you in advance for proposing to wade through it.

1   History: deterrence in the Cold War

Deterrence is an old practice in international politics and other areas of behavior. It has been given plenty of thought and study, yet is not easy to understand or explain. The onset of the Cold War provoked enormous interest in deterrence because its role in international politics, particularly at the global level, promised to be critical. However ancient it is in some ways, the greatest part of what we think we know about it was gleaned in the last six decades of systematic thinking and research on deterrence. I won't inflict a lengthy review of its modern history. However, certain comments about deterrence theory and deterrence during the Cold War will be useful for what comes later. I briefly outline what we thought we were doing in managing the Cold War via nuclear deterrence and assess, briefly, the actual role it played in preventing another great war. What the parties *thought* they were doing was not always what they *were* doing and the role of nuclear deterrence was not entirely what it seemed. For those familiar with all this, apologies and a request that you grimace and bear it.

The origins of Cold War deterrence

The essence of deterrence is that one party prevents another from doing something the first party does not want by threatening to harm the other party seriously if it does. This is the use of threats to manipulate behavior so that something unwanted does not occur: "...the prevention from action by fear of the consequences. Deterrence is a state of mind brought about by the existence of a credible threat of unacceptable counteraction" (*Department of Defense Dictionary* 1994). This is fairly straightforward and refers to behavior practiced by nearly all societies and cultures at one level or another.[1] Thus it is hardly surprising to find it used in international politics. However, there the concept came to be applied explicitly, and narrowly, to threats for *preventing an outright military attack*. In a technical sense deterrence is used in international politics in far more ways than this, but forestalling attacks became the focus. Thus a more elaborate definition would be that in a deterrence situation one party is thinking of attacking, the other knows it and is issuing threats of a punitive response, and the first is deciding what to do while keeping these threats in mind (Morgan 1983, pp. 33–42).

Deterrence is distinguished from *compellance*, the use of threats to manipulate the behavior of others so they stop doing something unwanted or do something they were not previously doing.[2] As with deterrence, in security affairs a compellance threat also normally involves military action and often the unwanted behavior to be stopped or steps to be taken involve the use of force, e.g. stop an invasion that has begun, pull out of an occupied area. The distinction between the two is quite abstract; in confrontations they are often present together and virtually indistinguishable. Nevertheless, we attend to the distinction because analysts consider compellance harder than deterrence – it is more difficult to get people/governments to stop doing something they are already doing, like doing, and prepared carefully to do. We now think this is because people tend to be more reluctant, under duress, to take a loss – to give up a benefit in hand – than to forgo seeking an additional benefit of equivalent value. Also, using force to maintain the status quo often seems psychologically more legitimate (to the parties involved and observers) than trying to change it.

---

[1] Other definitions: "persuasion of one's opponent that the costs and/or risks of a given course of action he might take outweigh its benefits" (George and Smoke 1974, p. 11) – a very broad definition covering almost all forms of influence; "discouraging the enemy from taking military action by posing for him a prospect of cost and risk outweighing his prospective gain" (Snyder 1961, p. 35) – narrows what is to be deterred; "... the effective communication of a self-enforced prediction that activity engaged in by another party will bring forth a response such that no gain from said activity will occur, and that a net loss is more probable" (Garfinkle 1995, pp. 28–29) – a very precise, rational-decision conception somewhat at odds with threatening under *nuclear* deterrence to blow the enemy to kingdom come, a real "net loss"; "... the absence of war between two countries or alliances. If they are not at war, then it is reasonable to conclude that each is currently being deterred from attacking the other" (Mueller 1989, p. 70). This makes deterrence ubiquitous – everyone is ready to attack everyone else if not restrained – which is not rewarding analytically.
[2] A recent work on compellance, where the distinction is reaffirmed, is Freedman 1998a.

In practice the two overlap. For one thing, they involve the same basic steps: issue a threat, the credibility of which is vital; avoid having the threat make things worse; and thus compel the other side to behave itself. However, parties to a conflict often define "attack" and "status quo" differently, so they disagree over who is attacking whom. When the US threatens military action to halt North Korea's nuclear weapons program is this *deterrence* of a provocative step (a kind of "attack" by the North), or *compellance* of the North to get it to stop what it is doing? And is the US defending the status quo (in which the North has no nuclear weapons) or aggressively threatening the North, which has not directly attacked the US or its allies? The parties in such cases disagree on the answer. If compellance is harder than deterrence then *it matters what the opponent thinks is the situation* since that is crucial to his reaction to the threat. In the example both deterrence (in the US view) and compellance (in North Korea's view) are present.

Thus we should put less emphasis on the distinction between deterrence and compellance and instead treat them as interrelated components of *coercive diplomacy*, the use of force or threat of force by a state (or other actor) to get its own way. This book is about deterrence but assumes that an overlap with compellance is often present and that the two can and must often be discussed interchangeably when examining real-world situations.

In settled domestic societies, deterrence is a limited recourse, used only in particular circumstances and rarely expected to provide, by itself, a viable way to prevent unwanted behavior. In international politics it has had a more pervasive presence. Used primarily as a *tactic*, it has also had a role as a strategic behavior within the jockeying for power that preoccupies states. However, while it was a popular recourse of those fearing attack, it was not the only or even the predominant one, and was not thought of, in itself, as a true strategy.

Without nuclear weapons and the Cold War deterrence would have remained an "occasional stratagem" (Freedman 1996, p. 1). After World War II, for the first time, deterrence evolved into an elaborate *strategy*. It eventually became a distinctive way of pursuing national security and the security of other states or peoples. Nuclear weapons forced those who possessed them, particularly the superpowers, to turn deterrence into a new and comprehensive strategy that touched, shaped, and coordinated many policies and activities. It came to seem intrinsic to international politics, an omnipresent, natural, and continuous recourse in a dangerous environment, something governments engaged in as a regular feature of their existence.

In addition, however, deterrence by the superpowers and their blocs was gradually developed further into *cooperative security management* for the global international system. The superpowers began with unilateral steps to keep safe via deterrence, but the interactions between their deterrence postures soon constituted an elaborate deterrence structure (a "regime"), which constrained them and their allies in numerous ways (not always to their liking) and eventually impelled them into joint efforts to better manage this structure. This had the effect, intended or not, of producing a large increment of security management for the system. Deterrence became a cornerstone of international politics, on which virtually everything else was said to depend.

Thus deterrence came to operate on three levels: as a tactic, as a national security strategy, and as a critical component of security for the international system. Of these the last two made it a suitable subject for theoretical analysis, but it was deterrence as a *national* strategy, in particular within a mutual deterrence relationship, that provided the basis for the theory and became its central focus.

The theory was developed initially to prescribe. The initial question was not "what factors are associated, empirically, with success or failure in deterrence?" but "what are the requirements for a credible deterrence policy?" The straightforward answer (Kaufmann 1954) was to persuade your opponent

(1) that you had an effective military capability;
(2) that it could impose unacceptable costs on him; and
(3) that you would use it if attacked.

The goal was to assist governments to survive in the nuclear age, to conduct an intense conflict without a catastrophe. The stimulus was the appearance and proliferation of nuclear weapons, but in a larger historical context development of some sort of deterrence theory was overdue. Many elements of deterrence thinking appeared before World War II (Questor, 1966; Overy 1992) and important concepts in arms control applied under nuclear deterrence theory were widely discussed after World War I. Nuclear deterrence is best understood as a solution to a fundamental problem of long standing. The evolution of military and other capabilities for war of major states had, well in advance of nuclear weapons, reached the point where great-power warfare, particularly on a systemwide basis involving most or all of the great powers, could be ruinously destructive. One element was the rising destructiveness of weapons. Artillery became extremely accurate at ever longer distances, rifles replaced muskets, machine guns appeared. Other capabilities of military relevance were greatly enhanced. Vast increases in productivity, combined with new bureaucratic and other resources, gave great states huge additional capacities for war. They acquired greater abilities to sustain and coherently manage large forces and exploited the breakthroughs in communications and transportation. Nationalism added the collective energies of millions, whether for raising armies and money or for production of everything those forces needed (Levy 1982, 1989b). Great states became capable of huge wars – in size of forces, levels of killing and destruction, duration, and distance. This was foreshadowed by the Napoleonic Wars, displayed by the American Civil War, and grasped in Ivan Bloch's penetrating analysis at the turn of the century of what the next great war would look like (Bloch [1899] 1998). All that was missing was a graphic example, which World War I supplied. It had become possible to conduct "total war."[3]

It is important to understand just why this was *the* problem. For practitioners of international politics it was not war itself. Particularly for great powers, war had always been a central feature of the international system, a frequently used and legitimate tool of statecraft, the last recourse for settling disputes, the ultimate basis for the power balancing that sustained the system and the members' sovereign independence. It had also been fundamental in creating nation states. "From the very beginning the principle of nationalism was almost indissolubly linked, both in theory and practice, with the idea of war," and thus "It is hard to think of any nation-state, with the possible exception of Norway, that came into existence before the middle of the twentieth century which was not created, and had its boundaries defined, by wars, by internal violence, or by a combination of the two" (Howard 1991, p. 39). It was difficult to imagine international politics without war since it seemed an inevitable adjunct of sovereign autonomy. War had last threatened to get completely out of hand during the Thirty Years War (1618–48) and states

---

[3] Vastly destructive wars are not unique to the twentieth century (Ray 1989; Mueller 1989, pp. 3–13). But beginning in the nineteenth century the capacities for destruction, even in a losing effort, expanded rapidly with the developments listed above and others (such as conscription) which "... served to make it much more likely that war, when it did come, would be total ... The closely packed battle, in which mass is multiplied by velocity, became the central feature of modern European military thought. For the first time in history, governments were coming into possession of constantly expanding means of waging absolute war for unlimited objectives" (Dougherty and Pfaltzgraff 1981, p. 195).

had responded by setting the Westphalian system into operation partly to get it under control. In the twentieth century the system was again being overwhelmed by war. Detaching sovereign rule, which is highly prized, from the rampant use of force for selfish purposes is the ultimate security problem of international politics, and now it threatened to destroy everything.

The development of deterrence was driven by a particularly onerous alternative solution that had emerged some time earlier to the threat of great-power war. Confronting the distinct possibility that the next war would be enormously destructive and costly, states worked hard to devise variants of a *cheap-victory strategy*. The idea was to ensure that the great costs, destruction, and loss of life would fall mainly on the other side. This was foreshadowed in Napoleon's shattering victories via single grand battles that collapsed the opponent. It dominated Prussia's wars against Denmark, Austria, and France in 1862–1871, wars so successful that such strategies have shaped military planning ever since. The Prussian approach involved diplomatically isolating the opponent, then utilizing industrial-age resources and nationalism to mobilize rapidly and throw huge well-coordinated forces into the initial battles to overwhelm the opponent, inflicting a complete defeat to end resistance. As a result, the major states approaching World War I had plans for rapid mobilization and decisive offensive thrusts to overwhelm the opponent in the opening battles, forcing the enemy to collapse in just weeks before intolerable casualties and costs were incurred. The Schlieffen Plan sought a cheap victory, as did the French Plan 17, the prewar plans of Russia and the Austro-Hungarian Empire, and British plans for fighting with Germany on land. Hitler sought to recapitulate the Prussian approach by isolating the target state and inflicting a (blitzkrieg-style) defeat so as to avoid a long and costly war. The point of the French Maginot Line was to fight a cheap, minimal-casualty war by exploiting the superiority of settled defenses (supposedly demonstrated in World War I) to wear down the attacking Germans; eventually France would push into a gravely weakened Germany and impose defeat at little cost. Japan's attacks at Pearl Harbor and elsewhere in late 1941 were meant to establish an impregnable defense far from home that would wear out the Americans and bring a settlement on terms favorable to Japan, producing victory at low cost.

Cheap-victory solutions influenced the development of deterrence theory in two broad ways. In the twentieth century these strategies were terrible failures in the world wars. Often initially successful, in the end they failed and the resulting wars were dreadful even for the winners, making the problem of great-power warfare clear to everyone. Another approach was obviously needed. In addition, cheap-victory solutions – which often turned on winning quickly – could be highly destabilizing because they usually required striking by surprise or before the other party was fully prepared. Thus once a war looked quite possible they could have the effect of initiating it.

Making interstate war virtually impossible by either fundamentally changing international politics or abandoning it was difficult to contemplate. Neither seemed remotely feasible so serious thinking shifted, almost inevitably, toward how great wars might be deterred, temporarily or indefinitely. The first effort along these lines was the formation of the League of Nations. It was meant to provide *collective actor deterrence* – deterrence by the entire membership against any member thinking about attacking another. In addition, components of what would become deterrence theory began to emerge in the 1920s. Analysts began to describe certain forces and capabilities as dangerous because they made war by surprise attack or on short notice plausible. Hence the ban on conscription imposed by the winners on the losers after World War I; the absence of masses of trained men, plus limits on the size of the losers' professional forces, would – it was hoped – prevent the quick mobilization of vast armies to achieve a cheap victory. Analysts began to characterize offensive, as opposed to defensive, forces and postures as too provocative. The British eventually developed strategic bombing as a deterrent, with preliminary thoughts on how key targets might be industrial and military or the will, politically and psychologically, of the enemy to continue to fight, foreshadowing the distinction between deterrence via defense (war-fighting) and deterrence via punishment (retaliation). US military thinking was similarly interested in deterrence through the threat of strategic bombing (Overy 1992).

What drove these efforts to coalesce into a theory was the coming of nuclear (particularly thermonuclear) weapons and the emergence of more than one national nuclear capability, especially when linked to ballistic missiles. Those weapons seemed ideal for achieving a cheap victory and thus were regarded (by thoughtful scientists even during their development) as very destabilizing. And they promised destruction at even higher levels.

Nuclear deterrence was the ultimate in threatening awful consequences to prevent wars. It had been known for years that great-power wars could be awful, so threatening one was not, in itself, new. The

7

innovation lay in using nuclear weapons to *strip any cheap-victory strategy of plausible success*, to leave an opponent no reliable way to design a great-power war in which it would suffer little and gain much. As this is important for the discussion later on it is worth emphasizing. It was not that nuclear weapons promised so much destruction that made them crucial in deterrence, it was that they made this destruction seem virtually *unavoidable under any plausible strategy*. This was the crux of the "nuclear revolution" (Jervis, 1989a) in statecraft.

The essence of deterrence theory

In discussing the *theory* it is important to distinguish it from deterrence *strategy*.[4] Deterrence strategy refers to the specific military posture, threats, and ways of communicating them that a state adopts to deter, while the theory concerns the underlying principles on which any strategy is to rest. Failure to keep this in mind is largely responsible for the frequent but mistaken suggestion that there are many theories of deterrence. Mostly there are different strategies, not theories. The strategies vary in how they operationalize key concepts and precepts of the theory. As for alternative theories, they are mostly theoretical fragments, not theories.[5]

The key elements of the theory are well known: the assumption of a very severe conflict, the assumption of rationality, the concept of a retaliatory threat, the concept of unacceptable damage, the notion of credibility, and the notion of deterrence stability. Examined briefly here, each is of importance later in considering whether deterrence has changed since the Cold War.

Severe conflict

Since deterrence theory was developed to help states cope with the Cold War, the nature of that struggle had great impact on it. The most

---

[4] Standard works on deterrence theory are: Freedman 1981; George and Smoke 1974; Jervis 1979, 1984, 1989b; Morgan 1983; Powell 1990; Questor 1986; Maxwell 1968; Wohlstetter 1959; Brodie 1959; Kahn 1961, 1965; Schelling 1960, 1966; Snyder 1961; Mearsheimer 1983; Jervis, Lebow and Stein 1985; Lebow and Stein, 1989, 1990a, 1994; Lebow 1981; Stein 1991.
[5] Escalation dominance/war-fighting was not a different theory, as is sometimes suggested. During the Cold War it presented a different view of what generates stability and credibility, what was unacceptable damage (particularly for Soviet leaders), and how to cope with deterrence failure. Colin Gray (1990, p. 16) says "theories of deterrence – or approaches to theories – are the product of their time, place, and culture," but the operationalization shifts more than the theory itself.

important feature in this regard was its *intensity*. To both sides it was total and ultimate, with the future of the world at stake. Both considered war a constant possibility; the enemy would not hesitate to attack if a clear chance for success arose. Thus deterrence had to be in place and working all the time, every day. The necessary forces had to be primed and ready to go. All that was keeping this conflict from turning into a war, probably total war, was deterrence. It stood between the great states and Armageddon.[6]

Years ago I devised the distinction between "general" and "immediate" deterrence. In general deterrence an actor maintains a broad military capability and issues broad threats of a punitive response to an attack to keep anyone from seriously thinking about attacking. In immediate deterrence the actor has a military capability and issues threats to a specific opponent when the opponent is already contemplating and preparing an attack. Thus an immediate deterrence situation is a crisis, or close to it, with war distinctly possible, while general deterrence is far less intense and anxious because the attack to be forestalled is still hypothetical. For years the Cold War was conducted as if we were on the edge of sliding into immediate deterrence. The attack-warning systems operated continuously, weapons and forces were on high alert, and there were elaborate calculations as to whether the opponent could pull off a successful preemptive attack or had programs under way to produce such a capability. It seemed that a crisis could erupt quite suddenly and lead to war, and there were very strong threat perceptions. One Strategic Air Command (SAC) commander testifying in 1960 on why his bombers should be constantly on airborne alert said: "... we must get on with this airborne alert to carry us over this period. We must impress Mr. Khrushchev that we have it and that he cannot strike this country with impunity. I think the minute he thinks he can strike this country with impunity, we will 'get it' in the next 60 seconds" (Sagan 1993, p. 167).

This was a distorted and distorting perspective. Seeing the opponent as just looking to attack, as "opportunity driven," was a Cold War political assessment of a particular challenger. There is no necessity to start with this assumption – we did so because that is where, at the

---

[6] In the Soviet bloc the stakes seemed just as high, the enemy just as ruthless and willing to use war, but war seemed much less likely to come at any moment. Soviet strategic forces were less often on alert; political portents of a Western attack were expected to provide enough warning in advance. Only under Yuri Andropov, confronting the Reagan Administration, did Moscow consider an attack at almost any moment a real possibility.

time, deterrence *strategy* had to start. The theory worked outward from considering how to cope with a war-threatening confrontation, a worst-case analysis, rather than with general deterrence and working down to the rare and extreme situation of an impending war. Immediate deterrence was the primary consideration, dominating most thinking even about general deterrence. This was awkward because much of the theory, therefore, particularly in connection with arms control, came to be concerned with stability in situations in which neither party wanted a war. Refinements emphasized, in spiral-model fashion, the existence of a conflict and the nature of military plans and deployments as potential causes of war in themselves, and not only the machinations of an opportunistically aggressive opponent.[7]

This had a strong effect on theory and strategy. It is hard to imagine the theory as we know it ever having emerged if each side in the East–West dispute had felt the other had little interest in attacking. The theory could operate as if deterrence was critical for preventing an attack. It did not explore what the motivations for war might be (and thus whether they were always present). It simply took as its point of departure a conflict so intense that the two sides would likely go to war if they thought they could get away with it. Hence the recurring concern in the US that deterrence was delicate and could easily be disturbed by developments that might seem to give the other side a military advantage. Deterrence strategy, as Lebow and Stein (1990a) emphasize, came to view the occurrence of war as related to windows of opportunity generated by a flawed deterrence posture. More precisely, theory and strategy operated on the expectation that each side must assume the other would attack if a suitable opportunity emerged. (Actually, the theory did not have to do this – it simply concerned what to do to deter if and when a state faced a possible attack.)

This was why the theory paid little attention to other ways of preventing war, such as by seeking to reconcile differences or offering reassurances and incentives. Efforts to suggest how deterrence might be used in conjunction with other approaches to peace were never incorporated; instead, it was about preventing a war when these other approaches had failed or could not be expected to work. In one sense this was fine. The theory was not held to be comprehensive or depicted as the only route to security under any circumstance. It merely

---

[7] Thus Jervis (1976) contrasts a "deterrence model" with a "spiral model" when the theory embraced both.

explained how deterrence produced security under very unpromising conditions.

In another sense, however, this was not fine because the theory paid no attention to the effect deterrence might have on the *utility* of other approaches to peace. In the politics of national security adherents of deterrence tended to emphasize how alternative approaches could damage it (inviting advocates of other measures to do the same in reverse). In the terms supplied by Robert Jervis (1976), those attached to a deterrence model not only rejected the perspective of spiral-model adherents but regarded their prescriptions – don't think the worst of the other side's motives, seek détente, look and be cooperative so as to not incite the opponent's suspicions and insecurities – as a recipe for disaster because too little would then be done to maintain a robust threat.

This was related to shifting deterrence from a tactic to a strategy. As a tactic deterrence would obviously not be suitable in itself for managing national security – it was just one policy option, sometimes useful and sometimes not and never the sole recourse. Elevated to a strategy, deterrence could be viewed as suitable on its own for security. And the Cold War made it appear necessary not just for dire straits, when all else had failed and war loomed, but all the time.[8]

Assuming the existence of a strong conflict not only matched the preoccupations of policy makers, it was very attractive for constructing a theory. It allowed analysts to simplify the description of state preferences and the calculations of unacceptable damage (only the costs and benefits of an attack would really matter in enemy decision making). It simplified the construction of deterrer priorities – deterrence was the prime objective – everything depended on it, and it was easy to arrive at a conclusion as to what prevented war (deterrence did).

The assumption of rationality

There is extensive discussion about this assumption and its effects on the theory in the next chapter so discussion here is brief. Deterrence theory was developed to prescribe. Since another great war could be absolutely dreadful, deterrence had to be practiced as effectively as possible. For purposes of the theory "effectively" was initially equated with "rationally," and this became the point of departure. The aim was to help decision makers understand what a rational actor would do in immediate deterrence situations or in preparing to best handle those situations;

---

[8] This was how American security studies came to be "militarized" (Baldwin 1995).

the initial assumption was that *both parties* would be rational. Rationality, in turn, was defined as gaining as much information as possible about the situation and one's options for dealing with it, calculating the relative costs and benefits of those options as well as their relative chances of success and risks of disaster, then selecting – in light of what the rational opponent would do – the course of action that promised the greatest gain or, if there would be no gain, the smallest loss.

This predilection stemmed in part from the precedent and influence of the realist approach, which insisted that international politics imposed on a state a preoccupation with conflict, the expectation that others were prepared to use force, and readiness to use force oneself. Deterrence was a component of this, one of the objectives and consequences of a balance-of-power system, and could not be ignored because other strategies for influencing the choices of opponents were seen as having limited utility. Realists saw themselves as assisting the policy maker (plus elites and citizens) in understanding the rational way to cope with the constant concern about security. Deterrence theorists set out to do the same, particularly because deterrence within a balance-of-power framework had an uneven record in preventing war and similar results in the nuclear age would mean catastrophe. However, deterrence theory was not equivalent to realist thinking. After all, it presumed war (at one level at least) could be avoided indefinitely, concluded that hostile states could cooperate in arms control endeavors, and anticipated that they could cooperate in managing security in crises or controlling conflicts at lower levels, etc., activities for which realists held out little hope of persistent success.

Another contributing factor was the normative and psychological appeal of rationality. "Irrational" was a pejorative term, and the nuclear age invited fears that irrational impulses and actions might kill everyone. Deterrence theory and deterrence had appeal if described as rational in conception and action. (So did criticisms of it – hence the recurring charge that relying on deterrence through vast nuclear arsenals was absurd, insane, criminally stupid.) A third element was the powerful inclination in the social sciences to model behavior in rational decision terms, as the best route to a strong theory. Analysts from these fields were prominent in development of the theory and it showed. For many analysts assumed rationality is intrinsic to theory building: "If expectations about benefits and costs do not shape behavior, what does?" (Downs 1989).

In principle, however, figuring out rational behavior for the deterrer did not require assuming the other side was rational. It would have been possible, say, to describe rational behavior for a defender uncertain about the rationality of challengers or to specify what would be rational behavior in response to specific patterns of nonrational behavior by challengers, but this was a road not taken. It was also possible to develop a theory in which both deterrer and the challenger were not altogether rational or one in which the attacker was rational but not the deterrer. These were also neglected in the original design. Instead, elements of them later crept into refinements of the theory and into specific deterrence strategies in the Cold War; they became adjuncts to, not the point of departure for, the theory. As a result deterrence was virtually *conceived in terms of application by a rational deterrer against attacker rationality*. It was not threatening an opponent so that he would behave; it was conscious, calculated threats to adjust the challenger's cost–benefit calculations so he saw attacking as nonoptimal.

Assuming rationality opened the door to a rigorous, parsimonious, abstract theory. In conjunction with assuming survival as a universal goal, which greatly simplified the estimation of actor preference hierarchies, that theory generated interesting and sometimes nonevident conclusions and prescriptions about how to conduct deterrence.

The concept of a retaliatory threat

Freedman (1996) has pointed out how it is possible to deal with a threat of attack by militarily eliminating it via a preemptive attack, or containing it by a vigorous defense. Deterrence theory proceeded as if neither was likely to be as effective, or as appealing in terms of comparative costs and harm, as deterrence. The proper goal was to prevent a war, not start it or fight it effectively. Prevention was to be achieved via manipulating the opponent's thinking, making deterrence a *psychological* relationship. To militarily eliminate or contain a threat would be a *physical* relationship, so deterrence was quite different in nature. The manipulation comes by means of the threat of very painful consequences via either defense or retaliation. The conception of deterrence via retaliation owed much to the presence of nuclear weapons. There would have been little surprising or useful in conceiving of deterrence as saying, in effect, "if attacked, we'll fight" or "if attacked we will win and then exact a nasty revenge." With nuclear weapons a state could say "if attacked, whether we are able to fight or not, and whether we win or not, we will do terrible things to you." One could conceive of pure retaliation or a combination of retaliation and fighting as reactions, as opposed to simply fighting. Nuclear weapons made pure retaliation plausible. It was also welcome as a recourse because of the possibility that a state attacked by nuclear weapons would suffer so much damage that it would shortly collapse or disappear – retaliation might be the only way an attacker would suffer. Thus deterrence was not equivalent to defense. They overlapped because one could deter via a threat to defend vigorously or by a threat to both defend and punish. But it was also possible to deter simply by a threat to punish, and this came to be seen as the ultimate, essential basis of deterrence in the nuclear age – after all, the goal was to never have to defend.[9]

This represented an important advance and reflected both the experience of war earlier in the century and the presence of nuclear weapons. One way to seek a cheap victory, displayed in both world wars, was to attack first either by surprise or by mobilizing and moving to the front more rapidly than the opponent. A state with this sort of military capability could deter only by promising to fight effectively, putting a premium on gaining a better war-fighting capability than the opponent and being ready to go to war quickly. Deterrence via retaliation meant being able to wait until the attack had started or later before doing anything. This made it possible, in theory, to try to rule out preemption. The challenger would have no incentive to attack and nuclear weapons would make a prospective war too dreadful for the deterrer to want to initiate it as well.

It was simultaneously a retrograde development. To deter via threats of retaliation alone came to mean a threat, as the ultimate resort, to devastate the core elements of the enemy society. Throughout the century it had become steadily more attractive to attack civilians but at least the point was supposedly to inflict a *military* defeat by disrupting the civilian base. Pure retaliation could mean attacking civilians with no military purpose at all (only the *threat* of it had a military purpose) and that is what all the great powers (and certain other states) threatened to do. Deterrence became hostage-taking on a vast scale.

The concept of unacceptable damage

How much prospective punishment was enough to deter? Assuming rationality provided an outline of an answer. If the opponent was rational

---

[9] Analysts and officials realized that in practice it could be hard to distinguish defense from deterrence due to severe collateral damage in fighting or treating civilians as a war-making resource to be targeted accordingly, making defense look a lot like retaliation.

then the prospective punishment needed was that which pushed his costs of attacking too high to make it worthwhile, so that the total costs outweighed the total benefits because an alternative course of action offered a better payoff. The key to success was to be able to threaten the opponent with unacceptable damage (via defense, retaliation, or a combination of the two).

The key question became: how much harm would be unacceptable? This clarified matters by highlighting the importance of understanding the opponent's cost–benefit calculations.[10] But it did not provide instructions on just how to gain such an understanding. However, nuclear weapons made it relatively simple to prepare a level of harm – destroying much or all of the enemy as a viable twentieth-century society – which was presumed to be unacceptable to any rational government. At lower levels of response, however, it was hard to figure out what would be unacceptable. It is a difficult concept to operationalize.

The idea of credibility

Credibility quickly became one of the two central concerns and problems in the theory and practice of deterrence. (Stability was the other.) Establishing why and how credibility was important was a major contribution of deterrence theory because many of the conclusions that followed were not intuitively obvious. Credibility is the quality of being believed. Deterrence theorists led the way in appreciating that it was not a state's capacity to do harm that enabled it to practice deterrence, it was others' *belief* that it had such a capacity. What deterred was not the threat but that it was believed. While this is not startling, governments had often simply assumed that if they had a significant military capability and issued threats the other side would get the message. Officials were now told to reexamine this, for it became clear that there were many ways a challenger might not get the message so proper crafting of a deterrence posture and effective communication of threats might be quite difficult. (After all, *conclusive* evidence for the attacker that the threat must be taken seriously would be available only when the defender retaliated.) It became apparent that deterrence had an intrinsic *credibility problem*, one with many facets.

Having to practice extended deterrence drove this home. Directly attacked, a state was quite likely to respond militarily. It was less apt to

---

[10] Critics have charged that deterrence theory is insensitive to this, which is incorrect. Officials practicing deterrence have sometimes ignored the opponent's perspective on costs, but the theory does not encourage this.

do so if a third party was attacked instead, no matter how closely it was associated with that party's welfare, because a military response would be costly and risky and it had not yet actually been attacked itself. Hence the threat to respond to such an attack was less credible.

There were other, nontheoretical, concerns. In the US in particular, concern about credibility rested in part on fears that its opponents were rather primitive, imperfect, or irrational in assessing the will and intent of the US and the West.[11] What should be credible to a rational opponent might not be so for them. This also encouraged considerable uneasiness as to just when one had achieved sufficient credibility, as illustrated for example by the nervous American reactions, from JFK on down, to the Kennedy–Khrushchev summit in Vienna in 1961. Both considerations incited the desire to overcompensate, to reinforce credibility via everything from the scale of the destruction promised to the size of the defense budget to endless reiteration of American and Western commitments (Morgan 1985).

Some elements of this problem could be dealt with directly, others were impossible to resolve conclusively in the theory and remain conundrums to this day. To have credibility it was necessary to be able to do unacceptable damage, to have proper forces for that purpose, and have the opponent conclude that you had the will to carry out your threat. Having the necessary forces was achieved by great powers during the Cold War by extremely destructive weapons – even a few could do extraordinary harm; also via redundancy – having several times the minimum forces capable of doing unacceptable damage; and by giving great attention to their survival in an attack via hardening, hiding, mobility, and high-alert status.

For credibility the opponent had to know about these military capabilities. Initially, governments had to consider how far to go in making the necessary information available. Under the logic of deterrence, conveying some information to the challenger with great clarity, especially about one's military capabilities, is beneficial. In the long run the burden of what to convey and how was eased by the growth in surveillance capabilities.

If what was important was not capabilities but being *perceived* to have them, then it was also possible to bluff. This was important at times. The Russians bluffed about their capabilities several times in the 1950s

---

[11] For instance, in ExCom discussions during the Cuban missile crisis (May and Zelikow 1997, p. 700; Blight 1992, pp. 79–83).

and 1960s to enhance their deterrence credibility, and the US did the same in the 1980s concerning its prospective ballistic missile defense capability. Eventually improvements in surveillance made this more difficult, linking credibility more closely to actual capabilities (see, for example, "Report: Russia..." 1998).

Credibility also meant effectively *communicating* one's commitment. Deterrence could fail if commitments were not clear. The outbreak of the Korean War drove this home to Americans, leading the Eisenhower Administration to specify US commitments through formal alliances. Deterrence could also fail if it was not clear just what actions by the opponent were unacceptable. However, clarifying commitments and expectations was never complete, because rarely in politics is it appropriate to say something exactly and leave no room for later adjustments. There is also an inhibiting element in ambiguity which can be exploited to achieve deterrence. Debate continues as to whether an element of ambiguity about commitments and prospective responses to an attack enhances or detracts from deterrence.

Emphasis was also placed on ensuring that the opponent knew you were quite *willing* to do what was threatened. This became a driving concern during the Cold War, one lesson the US took away from the Korean War. Conveying intent and will was clearly more difficult, on reflection, than conveying capabilities and commitments. Governments could deceive others about their intent and will, and often did; officials could change their minds when the need to act arose, which they often did too; or they could be unaware when they promised that carrying out the promise would seem unwise if the contingency arose. A would-be attacker suspecting that any of the three was true might not believe the deterrence threat.

This brought strong interest in demonstrating intent and will directly in extended deterrence by giving commitments elaborate publicity (mortgage national honor), by highly visible statements of commitment and intent (mortgage the president's honor), and by suggestive military maneuvers (like the Team Spirit exercise in Korea each year – display plans to do what you have promised). It was also pursued *indirectly*, by acting in other situations so as to strongly suggest that if a situation you were concerned about ever arose you would do what you threatened to do. What might convey this? Perhaps fighting/retaliating when lesser commitments were challenged would create and sustain a reputation for upholding them. Or placing one's forces where they would be in the line of fire in an attack on an ally; maybe delegating the decision to fight to commanders of those forces if they were attacked; or making – in advance – arrangements so the decision to fight/retaliate was virtually automatic once an attack was under way or about to occur. All this was so policy makers would seem to have little choice in the matter. And there were costly investments in forces – why buy so much if you were reluctant to use them? All were used at times during the Cold War. Thus the government study NSC-68 in 1950 rejected a posture of no-first-use of nuclear weapons because to opponents and allies this would signal weakness, that the US would not fight. This view is still held by the US, and is one reason Russia now has a posture of possible first use too.

However, these adjustments could not resolve the credibility problem. In *nuclear* deterrence, there is no necessary connection in logic or in fact between upholding lesser commitments (successfully or not) and what the deterrer will do later on a commitment that would involve vastly intolerable costs to uphold. Even the loss of some of your own forces could not be expected to justify upholding a commitment that would mean losing your society. If it would be irrational to uphold a major commitment, neither prior preparation to uphold it nor prior fulfillment of lesser commitments (no matter how consistently done) can make it fully credible under a theory that envisions rational decision makers (Freedman 1981, p. 397).

Hence it appeared that the best way to convey intent and will, assuming rationality, was to *demonstrate that a forceful response or retaliation was rational*. This turned out to be very difficult. The primary solution proposed but never fully implemented was a combination of flexible response and escalation dominance. It was claimed that multiplying your options for responding to an attack would enhance credibility. Who would want to set off a general nuclear war, and thus who would be believed in threatening that? Better to have effective responses at many levels of fighting – then you could threaten to respond not apocalyptically but sufficiently. This became one justification for a war-fighting flexible response doctrine and capabilities. And at each level of fighting the deterrer would seek to be able to do better than the challenger (escalation dominance) and thereby discourage the challenger from escalating.

However, this has inherent limitations. First, deterrence was to *prevent* an attack. Once one occurred the situation would change, making it necessary to reconsider what to do. Retaliation then might not make sense. It might be costly by causing the attacker to escalate the attack and his objectives, or counter-retaliate, very painfully. In effect, in contemplating retaliation the deterrer became the prospective attacker and its urge to respond might be deterred by the prospect of retaliation. This was where Khrushchev landed in October 1962. He sent missiles to Cuba to deter a US attack on the island, but once it became clear the US was going to attack if they weren't removed, he had no stomach for retaliating.

It also seemed that credibility was particularly difficult to achieve in practicing extended deterrence because it would be harder to make a forceful response rational. If State A has an alliance with C and C is attacked then C is already suffering, but A is not yet suffering and may not have to if it chooses not to uphold its commitment. It could be argued that such a commitment to retaliate must be upheld because this has implications for the future effectiveness of deterrence (by impressing future enemies) and this makes it rational to respond. The immediate costs would be high but the long-term costs would be lower. This was a popular argument during the Cold War and had enormous impact, but there are problems with it. The costs of retaliating now are real, will be borne immediately, while the costs of not responding are hypothetical, pertaining to scenarios that might never arise. Of course, it is always possible that retaliating will not lead the attacker to redouble his efforts or to counter-retaliate – the attacker might decide to quit. But that is unlikely – few states start a conflict planning to quit at the first sign its opponents intend to fight.

The other major problem was posed by nuclear weapons. Retaliation against a nuclear-armed state (or one of its allies) might set off a nuclear war and *cancel the future* – your society and state could disappear. There would be no point to retaliating to prevent future attacks. So why defend or retaliate? On what rational basis could it be justified? This spilled over into maintaining credibility for commitments at the conventional (nonnuclear) level. If you knew a conflict would remain nonnuclear then it could be rational to defend/retaliate so as to forestall future attacks. But if the conflict might well escalate into even an all-out nuclear war, then it would make sense to not retaliate.

These considerations undermined the appeal of flexible response. In the past retaliation could be assessed in terms of the immediate outcome it could produce and the favorable effect it could have on future confrontations. But with extremely high levels of actual or potential destruction risking national survival, and when no precise calculation can be made of the probability of disaster, retaliation is not made more rational (even at lower levels) by multiplying available options.

This was sticky because if it is irrational to retaliate then the attacker can attack with impunity, making deterrence unreliable. There is no ready answer to this problem within the confines of deterrence theory based on rational decision making. The only answer is to retreat from the assumption of rationality, which is discussed in the next chapter.

The problem of stability

Paralleling credibility was the other core problem in Cold War deterrence. Analysis of the stability problem started with the most severe test of stability, the crisis where an attack is primed and ready to go and deterrence is used to bar a final decision to carry it out. In such situations, the deterrer might take steps that looked to the opponent like plans not to retaliate but to attack and, concluding that war was unavoidable, the opponent could conclude it had better launch the planned attack. The steps taken to deter would further incite the attack – in terms of preventing war deterrence would be unstable. It would be even more serious if, in a *mutual* deterrence relationship, each side feared it could readily be attacked and each side's last-minute efforts to deter might lead the other to decide war was inevitable. Then deterrence would really be unstable because it would make both sides strongly predisposed to attack. Given the stakes, the goal had to be to keep nuclear deterrence stable.

Analysts also asked about the implications for stability of preparations taken by one or both sides to cope with a deterrence failure. How did they expect to fight a war? If they believed the war could best be fought by attacking first to gain a crucial advantage, then once war seemed likely the incentive to attack would be immense. This would be one result of striving for a "first-strike capability" to conduct a successful preemptive attack. The military preparations undertaken at least partly with deterrence in mind would make it unstable.

There was also the matter of escalation. If fighting broke out it would be important to avoid all-out warfare, in part by threatening to retaliate for any escalation. But if each side was prepared to fight primarily in ways that made escalation a deliberate or inevitable choice then instability would be severe. Analysts also worried about the vulnerability of command-control-communications-intelligence complexes as well – if they were highly vulnerable to disruption by an initial attack, then this provided a great incentive to attack first, but destroying them risked having the opponent lose control over nuclear and other forces early in the fighting and be unable to control escalation.

These hypothetical situations concern deterrence stability in a crisis or a war. Of equal interest was the possibility that even if existing deterrence postures did not invite a war, serious mistakes in the application of deterrence could cripple its effectiveness and cause its collapse – like the deterrer not effectively communicating its capabilities or credibility, or the opponent somehow not getting the message and understanding it. Deterrence would be unstable because it was improperly applied.

Then there was the notion that in constantly refining their military forces and plans states might deliberately or inadvertently make deterrence more unstable. If a state suddenly achieved a technological or other breakthrough that made attacking first very attractive then deterrence could collapse. The breakthrough might lead it to attack, or lead the other side to fear that an attack was inevitable and think seriously about at least getting in the first blow. Thus the two parties could repeatedly provoke each other into a lather over current or prospective developments in their forces, increasing each other's fear of attack and tendency to attack first – instability due to the arms race their relationship involved.

There was also the unique fear in the nuclear age of a war by accident or, more broadly, through a loss of control. Since strategic weapons took only moments (hours at most) to arrive, deterrence postures were taken to require having numerous weapons on high alert with governments primed to act within moments. Worry developed that a malfunction within a warning or weapons system could lead to a launch when it was unauthorized or need not have been authorized. There was concern that a launch could occur if, without authorization, people in charge took steps, irrationally or by wrongly reading their instructions, to fire the weapons. Or if, in a crisis, unauthorized behavior by lower-level officials, officers, or units conveyed the wrong (highly threatening) message to the other side, provoking a mistaken decision for war.

If the stability problem afflicted relations between the superpowers, it was certain to be larger with more states involved. In a crisis the superpowers might behave circumspectly only to have allies behave provocatively. They might take steps to avoid crises yet be drawn into one by their allies or others in a region in which they had important stakes. Also, the more states with nuclear weapons the greater the chances that some would be fired accidentally or in some other unauthorized fashion. Thus nuclear proliferation could disturb deterrence stability; so could the proliferation of other kinds of weapons, as could the outbreak of wars or confrontations.

Finally, it was suggested – particularly by critics – that each side would see efforts by the other to sustain or reinforce deterrence as actually signs of hostile intent, of seeking to be in a position to attack with impunity. The deterrence relationship itself could poison political relations between the parties, heightening fear and hostility. Deterrence stability called for balancing threats and conflict with steps that avoided provocation, so as "to instill caution without raising tensions" (Gjelstad and Njolstad 1996, p. 7), but it was hard to be confident of success.

In the 1950s the stability problem(s) spurred development of the modern conception and theory of arms control. The arms control branch of deterrence theory concentrated on preemptive attack or loss of control as likely routes to deterrence failure: governments should act rationally to avoid irrationality or flaws in self-control which threatened stability. Distinguishing arms control from disarmament, in that arms control sought a stable relationship in spite of – and via – the parties' military forces, was a product of the preoccupation with stability. So was the notion that disarmament could make war more likely, something arms control could avoid. Related was the conclusion that arms control was more feasible. Even in a serious conflict, the parties would have a common interest in deterrence stability but would be unable to agree on disarmament.

Theory asserted that concerns like these were appropriate for a rational deterrer and it was incumbent to deal with them; in a mutual deterrence relationship both parties had to explore how *mutually* to deal with them. Theory described what could be done (such as guarding against accidental launches of weapons), helped assess the relative virtues of various military postures in terms of stability, suggested the sorts of agreements that might be devised to forgo destabilizing behavior or curb proliferation, and so on.

The core political/policy debates

The fundamental debates on deterrence during the Cold War can be briefly summarized. We can encompass the political and policy struggles, for nearly all the major powers (China is a partial exception), within four broad schools. (For an alternative classification see Glaser 1990.) We can call one the *Rejection School* – those vociferously opposed to seeking security via deterrence in the nuclear age.[12] In their view, piling up

---

[12] This included many peace activists, governments that condemned nuclear deterrence as irresponsible, analysts like Linus Pauling, Andrei Sakharov, Jonathan Shell and the

vast destructive capabilities constantly on alert was absurd or foolish – definitely not rational. They stressed the limitations of the deterrence enterprise: the internal inconsistencies in the theory, the record of past failures, the defects in governments and leaders who had to operate deterrence, the nefarious motivations behind the arms race, the heavy economic burdens involved, the intensification of insecurity through the interacting tensions and hostility mutual deterrence provoked, the immorality of holding whole societies hostage, and the blunting of human (particularly official) sensibilities in the everyday planning of obliteration. Even a limited use of nuclear weapons would be an unprecedented disaster so there was no reason to be concerned about what would constitute unacceptable damage. The unacceptable possibility of utter disaster far outweighed concerns about credibility.

To the *Minimum Deterrence School*,[13] the security deterrence supplied could be obtained with only a few nuclear weapons. Being able to destroy cities and kill millions of people was enough to deter any government that was deterrable; that required delivery of a few hundred nuclear weapons at most, maybe as few as ten. Credibility was not a problem; just the remote possibility that an opponent would retaliate on such a scale would daunt any challenger. This eventually became a relatively widely accepted view. "By 1990 the consensus appeared to be that deterring total war required no more than a palpable risk that nuclear weapons would be used, and that this was virtually guaranteed simply by the existence of the weapons" (Freedman 1996, p. 6). Just a small nuclear arsenal gave a state an inherent or "existential" deterrence credibility. Minimum deterrence also curbed the stability problem. Properly practiced, it would eliminate the need for large nuclear arsenals and major arms racing, would minimize crises and confrontations, would discourage seeking a preemption capability.[14]

The *Massive Destruction School* believed that nuclear deterrence was effective and stable when the threat posed was the complete destruction

Canberra Commission, plus retired military officers from many countries, such as George Lee Butler in the US, who campaigned for nuclear disarmament.
[13] Britain, France, and China were adherents in terms of how they expected their deterrence postures to work (Johnson 1998; Grand 1998). It is a view any new or would-be nuclear weapons state will endorse. Analysts associated with it included McGeorge Bundy, John Steinbruner, and Kenneth Waltz.
[14] The one caveat might be on nuclear proliferation. Waltz argued that minimum deterrence was so stable that nuclear proliferation was good – longstanding conflicts would be stabilized. Others in this school, and most analysts, have regarded proliferation as destabilizing.

of a challenger (its society, state) and, if necessary, its allies.[15] The threat worked in two ways. First, it would deter nearly any leader or government – no matter how frantic or zealous, angry or frightened – by making it clear that an attack would be suicidal. Hence the level of challenger rationality required was modest. Second, fear of a war escalating into massive destruction would deter lesser attacks. No challenger could be sure, in starting a lesser conflict with a state with a huge nuclear arsenal, that escalation to its own complete destruction would not occur.

Hence credibility was not a problem. A state with massive destructive capabilities primed and ready to go could not be dismissed as bluffing, discounted for lacking the will to retaliate, or counted on to avoid escalation, because an attacker making a mistake on this would be committing suicide. Stability was not a problem either, at least in the central deterrence relationship – offsetting capabilities for total destruction in the Cold War made deterrence profoundly stable. That is why it was not seriously disrupted by surprise technological breakthroughs (Sputnik), large numerical imbalances in nuclear weapons (favoring the US in the 1950s and early 1960s), fears of missile gaps, intense confrontations (Berlin, the Cuban missile crisis), the defection of major allies (China, Iran), even the collapse of one superpower! Where stability was problematic was that there were always pressures to develop first-strike, counterforce capabilities or effective strategic defenses, and a tendency to worry too much about this. The answer was arms control to keep those pressures restrained. There was also the possibility of unauthorized use of nuclear weapons or provocative warning system failures. Minimizing these sorts of errors required additional arms control efforts plus redundant controls on weapons. Help came from the massive stability of huge invulnerable arsenals which permitted states to avoid panic-stricken responses to false warnings. There was the problem of horizontal proliferation, with nuclear weapons in states which had not yet, or could not, set up stable deterrence postures, and this had to be contained through cooperative nonproliferation efforts.

The fourth approach is often called the *War-fighting School*.[16] Its adherents found the credibility and stability problems in nuclear deterrence

---

[15] Adherents included analysts like Dagobert Brito and Michael Intriligator (1998), Charles Glaser (1990), leaders like Khrushchev and Eisenhower, McNamara in his later Pentagon days, and West Europeans in helping shape NATO's deterrence.

[16] This included Herman Kahn and adherents of flexible-response variants like Colin Gray, Keith Payne, James Schlesinger, Paul Nitze, and Harold Brown. Also advocates of preemption capabilities and preemption planning in the Soviet General Staff.

very serious. A threat to fight/retaliate was credible only if it looked rational to carry it out, so fighting back or retaliating had to be made rational. This required being equipped to *fight and win* at any level: very capable sub-conventional and conventional forces, plans and forces to fight limited nuclear wars, even the capability to fight and survive an all-out nuclear war. What deterred was not the threat of physical destruction so much as lowering enemy chances for military success and political survival. The Soviet government, for example, did not care about the costs to its people as long as it was successful – only the threat of losing the war or losing its power would deter it. Preemptive strike capabilities, strong counterforce targeting, missile and bomber defenses, and a wide range of theater and lesser nuclear capabilities had to be given priority. Otherwise, clever and daring challengers would exploit gaps in credibility, or enlarge a war if their initial military efforts were frustrated, or constantly seek to gain military superiority through arms racing. And if deterrence broke down anyway, a war-fighting capability was a hedge against the worst effects because it might hold the destruction of one's society (and allies) to an acceptable (or at least survivable) level. A war-fighting posture was good for deterring a rational opponent and having to fight an irrational one.

One thing to add is that each school found the others irresponsible and dangerous, willing to pursue policies that increased the dangers in nuclear deterrence, raised its costs, and increased the destruction if deterrence failed. They shared a general conception of what deterrence was all about but disagreed about what it took to deter (what was unacceptable damage), the degree to which deterrence was credible and how to keep it so, the nature of the stability problem, and the role of rationality.

We can also briefly summarize the debates about what was needed, in association with nuclear deterrence, for deterrence on the conventional level. Three positions emerged: deterrence by a capacity to fight then escalate, by a capacity to deny, and by a capacity to defeat. The first was the NATO doctrine and posture from the latter half of the 1960s on. NATO promised to put up a good fight on the conventional level, and that if and when it began to lose (which it expected in a war with the Warsaw Pact) it would turn to nuclear weapons. This was also the position in Korea – the US and RoK were prepared to fight a major conventional conflict but would respond to losing by escalating (to the US stockpile of nuclear weapons there). An important question was how likely or inevitable to regard escalation. Eisenhower assumed any significant East–West war would become all-out, and that this was good for deterrence – a view that survived in the mutually assured destruction (MAD) approach. NATO allies took roughly the same view about deterring conventional attacks but were less certain that escalation would occur unless Europeans were themselves able to provoke it. The Soviets saw escalation as very likely – analysts and planners came to accept that it might not happen but this never dominated Soviet deterrence. Most nuclear armed states preferred to approach deterrence of conventional attacks by other nuclear powers as an extension of nuclear deterrence.

Next, the US and its allies were prepared to deter by the threat of denial and demonstrating the capability for this. The US tried this in Vietnam in sending military advisors and combat units. The UN and US started out to do this in the Korean War and they settled for it after the Chinese intervention. Finally, there was the threat to defeat the attacker and bring about a surrender. This was what the UN and US switched to in Korea after the Inchon landing success and before China's intervention, what the Soviets sought in Afghanistan, what the US threatened in the Cuban missile crisis if the missiles weren't removed, and what the Soviets did in Hungary to deter others from trying to leave the Soviet bloc. For years some American critics of NATO wanted NATO to be able to defeat the Warsaw Pact.

There were endless debates in US and Soviet circles about the relative merits of these postures in terms of credibility. The most significant ones concerned whether any threat of nuclear escalation in Europe was credible, and whether a significant conventional war capability was really necessary – the threat of escalation being sufficient to deter even a conventional attack.

Deterrence, deterrence theory, and the end of the Cold War

Recent developments require that we reexamine things long taken for granted about deterrence because it now appears that some are confirmed and some are not. Sorting them out is important for learning properly from the Cold War about the utility of deterrence today and in the future. If we look back at how that conflict ended, and at changes in nuclear postures adopted since, the following lessons emerge.

First, *the Cold War ended in spite of nuclear weapons and nuclear deterrence.* They did not bar a massive political reconciliation that resolved the crucial longstanding issues of the division of Germany and Europe and the competition of contrasting ideological-political-economic systems. Old arguments that the nuclear deterrence version of the security dilemma, the poisonous effects of nuclear weapons on political relations, and the way deterrence postures automatically reinforce political conflict turned out not to apply in 1990, however much they might have earlier. Nuclear weapons did not *create* a security dilemma that barred high levels of cooperation when governments were so inclined (and if ever there were weapons that should have produced such a security dilemma it is these!). Thus they did not displace the primacy of *politics*. "We should recognize that the danger of war stems from the adversarial nature of the Soviet-American relationship, and not from their nuclear arsenals" (McGwire 1985, p. 124).[17] Intense political conflict dictated the Cold War, not the arms race or the balance of terror. The Cold War was about politics. It is also clear that nuclear weapons did little to create the opacity that afflicted each side's efforts to ascertain the other's political intentions. The Cold War collapsed when the two sides' preferences overlapped considerably *and this could be clearly understood*. Politics was much more responsible than nuclear deterrence for the lack of transparency.

In fact, nuclear weapons and nuclear deterrence seem – if anything – to have *facilitated the end of the Cold War*, including the departure of Soviet forces from eastern Europe and the dissolution of the Soviet Union. They provided insurance against attack no matter how much the Russian state lost ground in Europe, providing confidence that weakness or conciliation would not mean attack. This allowed Soviet leaders to accept the loss of their security glacis in eastern Europe and even dissolution of the Soviet Union itself (White, Pendley and Garrity 1992). Yet even here their impact was not the central factor. More important was the

---

[17] Lebow and Stein (1994, 1995) correctly note how American actions to shore up deterrence set off a spiral that culminated in the Cuban missile crisis – the strategy of deterrence undercut the political stability it was supposed to create (see also Lubkemeier 1992). But was *deterrence* at fault? This was the improper conduct of general deterrence, the Soviets by deliberately exaggerating a supposed missile advantage and pushing hard in this context on Berlin, the Americans by hugely overreacting and building a true missile advantage. US actions were readily misinterpreted as plans to attack Cuba, provoking intense Soviet efforts to deter, while Moscow failed to face the fact that sending missiles to Cuba would be terribly provocative and that neither missiles nor Cuba could be protected from a determined US attack. This was governments making errors of the sort deterrence theory was supposed to help them avoid. They eventually escaped the Cold War with nuclear deterrence in place; deterrence was not destabilizing per se. Their political conflict was the problem.

confidence Gorbachev and his colleagues had that the West would not attack. Nuclear deterrence was insurance against only a very improbable contingency, so improbable it could no longer serve as the basis of Soviet foreign policy. States can define threats not in military capabilities but in the internal political nature and external political objectives of others.

A second point is that *nuclear weapons did not a superpower make*, contrary to a standard view in the study of international politics. Despite neorealist insistence that bipolarity arose from the existence of those vast arsenals, it vanished with the Cold War while the huge gap between the nuclear strength of the former superpowers and other states remained and alongside their rough nuclear balance. Bipolarity involved a dominant political conflict which divided the world and mobilized the other capacities (economic, political, etc.) of the two largest states – to which their huge forces were in service. Without the conflict and the other capacities the weapons meant (mean) little in terms of power and stature.

We can also conclude that *nuclear weapons contributed much to making the world safe for the Cold War*. (A related argument is in Gaddis 1992). Only within a pervasive fear of another great war could the intensity of that conflict have been sustained so long with neither war nor détente.

> By claiming to have solved the problem of nuclear weapons, deterrence dogma dissipated the sudden urgency that this devastating capability had brought to the search for new ways of managing interstate relations. The pressure for a new approach had been building up for fifty years and more. But the steam was let out of the movement by the promise of deterrence.　　　　　　　　　　　(McGwire 1985, p. 121)

By the end of the Berlin crisis in 1961 and the Cuban missile crisis in 1962 both sides grasped the fundamental limits imposed by fear of another vast war, fear imposed in part via nuclear deterrence. They were then free to press their competition into many other areas, as they repeatedly did, without really risking another great confrontation and a global war. (The October 1973 confrontation in the Middle East was largely artificial.) Nuclear weapons induced great powers to tolerate "a haphazardly designed, awkwardly configured, and morally questionable status quo" (Gaddis 1996, p. 42).

Yet another conclusion, settling an old argument, is that *the weapons in superpower arsenals were grossly excessive*. By some estimates the Soviet Union eventually had at least 34,000 in 1989 and the US over 22,000 (a cut from some 32,000 in the early 1960s).[18] (See also Senate Armed Services Committee 1992, p. 124.)[19] There was no radical shift in primary targets after the Cold War, no end to nuclear deterrence, no official redefinition of how much is enough to deter. Yet deterrence rested on far fewer weapons – half or less of the strategic arsenals at their peak with plans for cuts to about 2,000. Britain cut its nuclear weapons by close to 70 percent, and France made significant cuts as well. Greater transparency is a factor, of course, but slicing away many of the weapons began even before transparency improved.

A severe conflict presumably makes parties more willing to fight; it alters their preferences to make their level of unacceptable damage higher so it takes more to deter them. A severe conflict expands the parties' emotional intensity, making rational calculation less likely or appealing, and that can make them harder to deter. Or a severe conflict may heighten the belief of each that the other is eager to attack, provoking reliance on a much higher threat of destruction to deter than needed. Even so, the response to the Cold War in nuclear weapons was silly. If a severe US–Russian political conflict emerges once more each will be confident its arsenal can deter the other without racing frantically back to Cold War levels, which is why plans to store many of the nuclear weapons cut are wrong-headed. Nuclear stockpiles did not shrink earlier, not because of the dictates of deterrence, but because the domestic and international political situation was not supportive and because military planners sought so much preemptive attack capability.

The overkill capacity that resulted invites another conclusion. Many analysts now look back on Cold War era deterrence as qualitatively different because each superpower faced an opponent it understood, both lived with rules that provided a framework, and their long experience enabled each to understand the other's interests and perspectives. *This is mostly nonsense.* For the most part, the US did not understand the Soviet Union well at all, and vice versa. Studies expose their interacting misperceptions, particularly in the Korean War, the Taiwan Straits crises, the Cuban missile crisis, the Soviet occupation of Afghanistan, etc. As

---

[18] The Brookings Institution (Schwartz 1998, p. 23) estimates that as of 1998 the US had spent approximately $5.5 trillion on nuclear weapons and had some 15,000-plus strategic nuclear weapons late in the Cold War, having produced nearly 40,000 nonstrategic nuclear weapons. The estimated Soviet totals: 12,000 and 35,000, respectively.

[19] Apparently the SIOP in 1991 still had 12,500 targets, one to be hit by sixty-nine nuclear weapons. This was the Soviet General Staff's main command post and the very low probability that one weapon would destroy it led planners to simply pile on weapons until the statistical probability of destruction reached over 90 percent. See Hall 1998; Butler 1998.

one analyst puts it, their emotional responses produced reciprocal reinforcing misperceptions, with tendencies to:

overestimate the other side's military strength and improvements;

overestimate the other side's willingness to run risks for its purposes;

base planning on worst-case analysis;

see the other side's planning, control, and organization as near perfect;

exaggerate the opponent's adherence to a long-term strategy;

be preoccupied with fantasy fears of gaps, windows of vulnerability, and impending attacks (Van Benthem van den Bergh 1992, pp. 61–62)

During the Reagan years the Andropov government ordered its embassies and the KGB to be alert to early signs of a preemptive American attack. Meanwhile, that administration rested its foreign policy on conceptions of Soviet strength and durability that were ludicrous; a Soviet Union depicted as ten feet tall soon collapsed. Gorbachev had long since shifted the entire basis of Soviet foreign policy but the new Bush Administration took months to perceive this and begin to respond.

Debates about how best to pursue deterrence were endless because the US had no real certainty (a) that the Soviet government really needed deterring or (b) what would constitute unacceptable damage to that government (some analysts insisted it would readily accept World War II-scale losses again). MAD was not based on a calibration of unacceptable damage. It was designed to cope with the *inability of the US to know what it would actually take to deter*. Calculations of unacceptable damage ranged from 20–30 percent of the Soviet population and 50 percent of Soviet industry to hitting 200 Soviet cities with nuclear weapons to ten bombs or fewer on ten cities (Gjelstad and Njolstad 1996, p. 27; see also Schwartz 1998, p. 23). Flexible-response variants rested, to a great extent, on misplaced fear that the other side might be irrational enough to attack and this was particularly true of the most elaborate proposals for war-fighting such as ballistic missile defense. Debates flourished about what affected the US image for resolve: Weapons decisions? Interventions? Defeats? Rhetoric? Defense budgets? The US lacked a good grasp of what shaped Soviet estimates of American credibility (Hopf 1994). It eventually pursued "essential equivalence" because just a *numerical* imbalance in strategic forces *might* have an unfortunate effect.

Analysts now claim that for today's irrational or hard to understand enemies we need to focus on what will specifically deter each opponent and, particularly for rogue states, threatening leaders' political and physical survival. But the US in the 1970s targeted the Soviet leadership on exactly the same grounds. Secretary of Defense Harold Brown said:

> "We need capabilities convincingly able to do, and sure to carry out, under any circumstances what the *Soviets* consider realistic, whatever damage the Soviets consider will deter *them*. Put differently, the perceptions of those whom we seek to deter can determine what is needed for deterrence in various circumstances."

But no one knew what would deter Soviet leaders. Late in the Cold War it was still true that "much of what passes for nuclear knowledge rests upon elaborate counterfactual argument, abstractions or assumptions about rational actors, assumptions about the other nation's unknown intentions, and simple intuitions" (Nye 1987, p. 382).

We can also say something pertinent about the fit between deterrence in theory and the practice of deterrence. To begin with, *governments often did not behave responsibly in terms of deterrence theory* and thereby brought themselves and others closer to disaster than necessary. Is this surprising? In what area of policy do governments rigorously prevent ignorance, political calculations, biases, routines, and similar factors from distorting decision making? All wars depart from the optimum in terms of what is believed known. By building far more nuclear weapons (and chemical weapons) than needed, the superpowers increased the difficulty of keeping their arsenals under complete control. Civilian officials exercised little control over the size of superpower nuclear arsenals or on many conventional weapons developments. Top officials almost never carefully examined their national plans for a nuclear war (for Britain see Twigge and Scott 2000) or for maintaining control over nuclear weapons in a grave crisis or war, or tried to ascertain the specific consequences that nuclear wars would entail. "Deterrence failed completely as a guide in setting rational limits on the size and composition of military forces [resulting in] ... the elaboration of basing schemes that bordered on the comical and force levels that in retrospect defied reason [with] ... war plans with over 12,000 targets, many struck with repeated nuclear blows, some to the point of complete absurdity" (Butler 1998; Nolan 1999). Leaders lacked real understanding of what it meant to put forces on a higher level of alert. Thus they had little basis for deciding whether arrangements for crisis stability, devolution of authority to use nuclear weapons, or escalation control were sufficient to keep things in hand; in confrontations "civilian authorities did not thoroughly understand the military operations they were contemplating" (Sagan 1985, p. 138), because "statesmen do not understand what their state's armed forces do when they go on alert" (Jervis 1989b, p. 89). They did no real cost–benefit calculation as to the virtues of deterrence with nuclear or conventional forces, not just because there is no ready way to do this but because even the necessary information was not gathered (Schwartz 1998, pp. 18–21). They lacked the prerequisites for calculating the full costs and benefits of competing policy options – limits on their ability to make rational decisions they themselves created.

South Africa developed nuclear weapons with no conception of who it would use them against and no strategy for their use – it hoped they would induce the US, out of concern for instability, to come to its aid in a crisis (Reiss 1995, pp. 28–30). Just as Truman took office with no knowledge of the atom bomb project, Lyndon Johnson came abruptly to power with no prior briefing on the "black bag" that accompanied him everywhere thereafter. When civilian decision makers tried to intervene to alter the plans for a possible nuclear war, the armed forces strongly resisted – planning a war was their responsibility and civilians were to keep out (see Feaver 1992; Nolan 1999). The main responsibility, very jealously guarded, rested by default with the armed forces and they were never comfortable with deterrence theory. Their objections started with mutual deterrence, leaving security in the hands of the enemy, then went on to how the theory made little provision for surviving a deterrence failure – instead, it proposed arrangements that would cripple the chances of gaining the best possible outcome in a war. True to their major responsibility, they prepared not just to fight but to win, to enable their societies to survive. As a result, the superpowers consistently groped for a counterforce capability close to successful preemption (Glaser 1990, pp. 246–248, 365–367).[20] Hence Eisenhower was appalled at the first version of the Single Integrated Operations Plan (SIOP), McNamara's effort to adjust it came to little, Schlesinger and Kissinger never succeeded in getting it fully altered as they wished, nor did the Clinton Administration (Nolan 2000). George Bush Sr. achieved significant shifts in the SIOP targeting but simply went around the Pentagon in promoting

---

[20] Not that civilians played no role; they ultimately approved basic targeting doctrine in the US, for instance. See Mlyn 1995.

strategic arms cuts. In theory, this was a serious mistake because the services' efforts could have been very destabilizing, particularly in a crisis. We needed a supplemental theory that said: "in the inevitable competition between what seems rational to keep deterrence stable and what seems rational for hedging against a deterrence failure, the latter will be compelling to the armed forces and drive them to undermine the former." This better fits how the superpowers behaved than deterrence theory. Fear of instability never matched or exceeded the fear of lacking a possible war-survival advantage if deterrence failed.

Deterrence theory strongly suggested avoiding what resulted: desire for a preemption capability and fear that the other side might have one led both governments at various times to install a launch-on-warning (LOW) posture or something close to it. In both there was also considerable pre-delegation of authority to use nuclear weapons in the event of war. (On the US see Pincus 1998a, 1998b; Pincus and Lardner 1998.) In the Cuban crisis Kennedy had to insist specifically that in a clash in Europe the American forces there were not to implement standard plans that included using nuclear weapons.[21] In deterrence theory anything like a hair-trigger posture or automatic resort to nuclear weapons, especially if mutually installed, invites disaster.[22] Both superpowers also flirted with the idea of a preventive attack on China (the US in 1964) to prevent its emergence as a nuclear power, which could have been catastrophic. (See, for example, Mann 1998, which reports on a study by Jeffrey Richelson and William Burr.)

Arms control thinking reinforced the emphasis in the theory on avoiding moves and conditions that could undermine crisis stability. Nevertheless, the various nuclear establishments experienced close calls or accidents that sharply increased the possibility of disaster and war. Nuclear weapons fell out of planes, fires occurred in missile silos, false alarms moved weapons to high-alert levels, some weapons were temporarily stolen, highly threatening steps were taken by armed forces elements during crises in ways unknown to and not authorized by their civilian superiors, etc. Just the reported accidents involving nuclear weapons in 1945–1980 came to over 100 (Canberra Commission

---

[21] Paul Nitze, in the ExCom crisis deliberations, noted the services' resistance (May and Zelikow 1997, pp. 222–223). See Kaiser (2000) on the US readiness to use nuclear weapons in the 1950s and 1960s.
[22] With this history we can see why Russia is now in a LOW posture (Nunn and Blair 1997; Hoffman 1998; US Information Agency 1998).

1996, p. 12). There were instances of warning systems reacting incorrectly including, during the Cuban missile crisis, a radar warning system incorrectly reporting a Soviet missile on its way from Cuba (Sagan 1993, pp. 3–10; he offers many other examples, as do the Cockburns 1997). During the missile crisis Soviet generals in Cuba shot down a U-2 without permission; the head of SAC ordered US forces to go to DEFCON II in the clear – without permission – and some air force units went to a higher level of alert than authorized, Castro used troops to surround missile batteries to try to keep the Soviet Union from removing them. In the 1973 Middle East War the US and Soviet navies in the Mediterranean were in very close contact while on extremely high alert, with hair-trigger status for their nuclear weapons, inviting war through a very small misstep (Lebow and Stein 1994). When the Russians downed a Korean airliner in 1983 six F-15s were ordered to loiter near Sakhalin Island to lure a challenge by Soviet interceptors and shoot them down – a provocative step which lasted until American military headquarters in Tokyo learned of this. And in 1983 a Soviet satellite detected five Minuteman missiles supposedly launched at the USSR (it was actually detecting reflected sunlight off the clouds) (Hoffman 1999a), while in 1980 a SAC headquarters computer reported an incoming Soviet attack and bombers went on alert as missile solos were opened until the mistake was detected (Sauer 1998, p. 25).

If nuclear deterrence worked during the Cold War it was not because we developed a neat theory and implemented it precisely. The Cold War is not a consistently favorable illustration of the utility of deterrence in either theory or practice. This makes it hard to believe that something implemented in such an uneven, at times incompetent, fashion was primarily responsible for the absence of World War III. The history invites looking elsewhere, resisting the widespread inclination to conclude that nuclear deterrence obviously worked and did so because we learned a lot and became quite good at it.

The next comment must be that, despite all this, it is probably correct to conclude, as many do, that *nuclear deterrence did indeed work, to a point.* To quote some of its severest critics:

> Over the period of the Cold War, deterrence proved to be an open-ended, highly risky and very expensive strategy for dealing with the reality of nuclear weapons in a world of nation-states with enduring, deep-seated animosities. Conversely, given the origins and peculiar ideological character of the East–West conflict, the extreme alienation of the principal antagonists, the vast infrastructure put in place and the

sense of imminent mortal danger on both sides, deterrence may have
served to at least introduce a critical caution in superpower relationships.   (Canberra Commission 1996, p. 14)

Nuclear deterrence has been given credit for the "long peace" after
1945.   (Gaddis 1991)[23]

From this perspective it worked, which means it works and thus the
theory is correct. Jervis (1989b, pp. 23–45) argues that unlikely developments in international politics we would expect nuclear deterrence to
generate did, in fact emerge: no wars among the great powers, limited
peaceful change that the great powers disliked (a point outmoded now),
the near disappearance of grave crises among great states, governments
behaving as if a small chance of total disaster is too great to risk, and a
tenuous link between the distribution of military power among states
and the outcomes of their political contests.

But there is a plausible contrary view, that deterrence, at least nuclear
deterrence, was largely irrelevant. There was little chance of another
great war and thus nuclear deterrence was not necessary to prevent
it. Neither view is entirely correct. I suggest deterrence, particularly
nuclear deterrence, contributed to preventing World War III but also
made another great war much more likely than otherwise. We can take
up each side of this in turn.

Seeing deterrence as responsible for escaping World War III rests on
several contentions. One is that wars are inherent in international relations. If great powers have always been prone to war, a long period
without great-power wars is so unusual one looks for an exceptional circumstance to explain it and the obvious candidate is nuclear deterrence.
The trouble is that the *frequency* of great-power wars has been markedly
lower in the past two centuries, with systemwide wars clustered in
the Napoleonic era and 1914–1945. So many years without great-power
wars, particularly systemic wars, since 1815, mostly without the presence of nuclear weapons, call the importance of nuclear deterrence into
question.

A more impressive argument is that wars are not inherent – the nature of international politics contributes to the incidence of wars, particularly through its limited restraints on war, but is not responsible in

---

[23] Numerous analysts reached the same conclusion: Bundy (1984; 1986); the Harvard
Nuclear Study Group (1983); Questor (1986); and Tucker (1985). Others are listed in Payne
1996, pp. 40–41.

itself. Something else is responsible, and that something is severe political conflict. Wars become quite plausible only when states are caught up in a deep conflict. Such conflicts among great powers have been a recurring feature of international politics and there was certainly one at the heart of the Cold War, so severe that a US–Soviet war seemed a logical outcome. This is why the absence of World War III is an anomaly that needs explaining, not the existence of a long peace per se, and nuclear deterrence lends itself to this. I like this because it calls attention to the severity of the Cold War conflict. Each side thought the other capable of the worst behavior, and each saw the conflict as fundamental – about basic values, the future, life and death. Each prepared extensively for a war. Under these circumstances the probability of war escalates. Wasn't nuclear deterrence responsible for the fact that no great war occurred?

Despite its appeal, this is not completely convincing. After all, the superpowers won the last great war and had greatly benefitted in terms of their postwar stature in world politics and, especially important to them, in European affairs. This made them status quo powers in some ways, more preoccupied with preventing losses than taking big risks for gains at the other side's expense (Lebow and Stein 1995). Wars among winners of the last great war have historically been uncommon for a lengthy period thereafter – they are normally more concerned about the losers who want to get back what they lost. In addition, the US and USSR had no long history of conflict with each other, their peoples had no longstanding mutual dislike. They had no territorial disputes, which are the most common issue in wars (Vasquez 1991).[24] The Soviet archives have revealed that the Soviet Union had politically expansionist objectives but not a strong bent for attacking the West.

Thus two partly status quo states came into serious conflict and began developing hard-line images of each other. This can be traced specifically to Stalin's policies, and to the way in which Soviet and American approaches to international and domestic affairs had revolutionary implications even if their governments were not given to imperial expansion. It also stemmed from fear that not looking sufficiently tough would encourage nasty behavior by the other side. Given these reciprocal images and Stalin's mania for a harsh foreign policy and a totally closed society, minor clashes readily escalated, significant disagreements became tests of resolve, and deterrence seemed very important (though it

---

[24] Colin Gray: "it would be difficult to find a plausible nuclear-armed opponent of the United States less inclined toward nuclear adventure than was the USSR of most of the cold war years" (1992 p. 261).

seldom was). When no attacks occurred deterrence was taken as work-ing (though outright attacks were rarely intended), so the mutual threat system was very self-sustaining politically. This is a haunting picture of what probably occurred, because the Cold War consumed much that was good and decent in its world.

Unlikely parties for a great war were caught up in a conflict so severe that they thought seriously about fighting for over a generation. They had confrontations and numerous incidents which might have blown into confrontations. War was plausible. While not all aspects of their relationship and their positions in the world drove them toward a great war, their relationship encouraged one and they prepared mightily for it. Something must have worked to prevent it. It is implausible that nuclear weapons had no effect in encouraging greater caution, serving as "an important source of restraint" (Lebow and Stein 1994 p. 355). Nuclear weapons *did not prevent a war one or both governments wanted*; but they did help prevent the war the Cold War made plausible.

Then there is the contention that great-power warfare became obsolete early in the twentieth century, so nuclear weapons were not necessary for avoiding World War III (Mueller 1989). Wars became far too destructive to serve as rational instruments of policy long ago, experience was a good teacher, and by 1945 the great powers had absorbed the lesson. Michael Howard's (1991) version cites the decline of an era of intensely ideological and teleological nationalism in Europe, the fading of warrior societies plus the decline of territory as a prime source of national wealth and power as leading to the marked drop in the bellicism of developed countries that is observable today.

The argument is correct but needs some revision. If the sheer destruc-tive potential of great-power warfare is to effectively foreclose such wars several other things are necessary. Also required is elimination of the idea that war, at least on such a large scale, is *inevitable*. Otherwise states will prepare for and engage in it. This was roughly where the great powers were in approaching World War I. Officials knew a great war could be terrible, but there was no credence given to the idea that it could be avoided forever. In fact, important elements regarded warfare as necessary for the tempering of nations and selection of the fittest – great wars were not only unavoidable they were functionally necessary and valuable. Here Howard's argument becomes quite important. The falling off of bellicism and an extreme nationalism, and the emergence of alternative routes to national power (Rosecrance 1986), have done much to make great-power wars today highly implausible.

Another very important requirement is *negation of cheap-victory strategies*. It is possible to respond to the horrific damage another war might produce not by concluding that war is obsolescent but by vigorously designing ways to conduct wars so that the enemy bears most or all of the costs. This is imperative if another great war seems unavoidable or highly plausible. In the past two centuries we find repeated examples of the great powers spotting and using what they took to be cheap-victory strategies. The nuclear age was no different. Superpower forces repeatedly sought ways to win a nuclear war with acceptable casualties, either by a preemptive attack or effective defenses against nuclear forces, or a combination of the two (Questor 1986; Glaser 1990, Jervis 1989a). This fit badly with the theory of deterrence (see Glaser 1990) but was quite consistent with having to prepare for a possible collapse of deterrence.

By 1945 the great powers knew great-power wars could be intolerable; in some ways they knew this by 1815. Nuclear weapons (especially the hydrogen bomb) certainly made this even plainer, less disputable, and thus contributed to this aspect of preventing great power wars. But World War II was probably enough to do this; nuclear weapons were icing on the cake. Where they really made a difference was *in canceling cheap-victory strategies*.

However, even here their contribution was qualified. After all, the most realistic prospect for a great-power war lay in US–Soviet relations. The most fearsome strategic problem in a great-power war is to inflict a convincing defeat, at low cost, on a large and distant great power. A disturbing feature of the international system in the past two centuries was that the leading powers were geographically small and neighbors. They could readily be reached and overrun and thus possibly be cheaply defeated. This was conceivable even for the Soviet Union in 1940 because it could be reached from Germany and because the heart of the country lay in a small part of its total area.

The United States and Soviet Union, on the other hand, were not next door to each other (except in the North Pacific where they could reach each other but for no serious strategic purpose). With strictly conventional forces, they would have needed a vast military effort just to get to each other with serious ground units, much less force a victory. The attacker faced the need to project power over vast distances, with the prospect of large casualties, huge costs, and the likelihood an all-out war would drag on for years. Using conventional forces there was no plausible recipe for a cheap victory, and thus nuclear deterrence *was probably never needed to prevent it being devised*.

What made the relationship fraught with the possibility of war was nuclear weapons. They made possible a cheap victory against a vast state half a world away. The real contribution of nuclear deterrence was to cancel this, to *void the utility of cheap-victory strategies* based on nuclear weapons. The route to achieving this was laid out by the conception and theory of nuclear deterrence. It was not the presence of nuclear weapons per se that made World War III unlikely, it was the gradually developed understanding of just how they could be arranged so as to have this result.

Lest this be thought of as knowledge inherent in the presence of nuclear weapons and quickly grasped, we must note that real understanding of how deterrence might work was slow to develop. The armed services did not initially regard nuclear weapons as truly different, just bigger, and trying to treat them as just larger conventional weapons lasted well into the 1950s in both East and West. Full appreciation of the stability problem did not develop until the late 1960s; before then there were deployments that practically invited a first strike in a grave crisis, insufficient controls against accidental or unauthorized launches, weak civilian understanding of SAC's nuclear war plans which amounted to a preemptive strike (Trachtenberg 1985). Strategic arms control, like forgoing defensive weapons, was a hard idea to sell to, and in, the Soviet Union. It remained difficult to get Congress to accept arms control agreements when US–Soviet political relations were at a low ebb, regardless of what the theory said about cooperation for mutual benefit. And always there was the pressure to strip the opponent's deterrence by preemptive attack capabilities.

Thus nuclear weapons and deterrence theory did make a notable contribution to the avoidance of World War III. However, they did not prevent an almost certain war; both governments had good reasons not to want one. Nuclear weapons certainly contributed to suspicion and fear – neither superpower would have faced a serious security threat after World War II for years, had it not been for nuclear weapons and intercontinental delivery systems. This made East–West cooperation more difficult and incited plans for war. Yet, as noted earlier, it is difficult to believe they were responsible for the depth and intensity of the Cold War.

As for deterrence, nuclear weapons reinforced what would have been a very strong reluctance of the superpowers and other great powers to fight another major war. They led these states to carry that reluctance into lesser confrontations, probably more often or more extensively, out of fear of escalation. In the few grave crises that emerged, nuclear deterrence worked through a combination of existential deterrence and a strong fear of losing control (see Blight 1992). In the Cuban missile crisis, for example, the parties were most impressed by the threat of massive destruction in general without calculating just how a nuclear exchange would go.[25] This was suggested as the relevant explanation for how deterrence works years ago (Morgan 1983). However, the real contribution of nuclear weapons was to negate their potentially awful impact. For avoiding another great war we would have been as well off with no nuclear weapons around. But they *were* around and they had the capacity to make another great war more likely. Something had to be done to offset this, but the fit between the theory and practice, and between nuclear deterrence in practice and the actual prevention of World War III, were far from exact.

We can also note that nuclear deterrence did not prevent any and all wars between nuclear powers. The 1969 Sino-Soviet clash over Damansky Island in the Ussuri river is a standing rebuke to that idea in that two nuclear powers moved into fierce military activities with significant casualties. Little of the careful behavior in the Cuban crisis was apparent there, except that nuclear weapons restrained the fighting and encouraged negotiations. Even strong Russian hints of escalation did not get the Chinese to back down (Karl 1995).

Nuclear deterrence did not prevent fighting between nuclear and nonnuclear powers either. Always cited on this are the Korean and Vietnam wars, even the Soviet war in Afghanistan, but there are other relevant examples. Vietnam refused to back down to very serious threats from China. China in turn launched an attack on Vietnam in spite of Hanoi's alliance with Moscow. In 1973 Egypt and Syria attacked Israel, as did Iraq in the Gulf War, despite Israel's nuclear arsenal. Argentina fought with nuclear-armed Britain. Again, this casts doubt on the existential or inherent deterrence supposedly attached to nuclear weapons. Nuclear deterrence did not prevent wars in all cases, whatever its success in the Cold War (Sagan and Waltz 1995, pp. 127–130; Paul 1995). In fact, profound concerns for maintaining credibility to keep deterrence effective actually helped stimulate the war in Vietnam.

Finally, arguments about the utility of nuclear deterrence in preventing World War III are largely speculations about *general* deterrence, which is notoriously difficult to detect and assess in terms of impact.

---

[25] Lebow and Stein 1994; May and Zelikow 1997.

As for immediate deterrence, there were mercifully few occasions when it was called upon to prevent the outbreak of general war. Thus we are trying to gauge the impact of a phenomenon when its existence, much less its effects, is difficult to pin down.

Conclusion

We are left with the overall conclusion that nuclear deterrence was a relatively peripheral, and relatively flexible, factor in the rise and decline of the Cold War. Nuclear weapons and nuclear deterrence did not cause the Cold War or end it, nor did they end with it. They did help contain the Cold War but also helped sustain it longer than it otherwise would have existed. They helped the superpowers to get out of the Cold War but only by providing insurance, a favorable background condition for steps toward cooperation. They were not irrelevant, but their main contribution lay in heightening incentives for war avoidance that would have been very strong in any case, promoting caution in a very severe political conflict, and voiding the appeal of cheap-victory strategies which nuclear weapons themselves made possible. Their chief contribution came at the level of general deterrence – rarely were the superpowers drawn into confrontations that constituted grave crises, despite our focus on crises in devising conceptions of how deterrence worked. We imagined immediate deterrence far more than we experienced it.

2   Deterrence and rationality

While much has been written about deterrence theory, satisfaction with it is very uneven, which suggests we might better leave it alone. However, deterrence remains important and many issues turn on whether it can be a reliable instrument of statecraft today. It helps to consider how useful the theory can be, and the place to start is with rationality because much recent discussion about deterrence, weapons of mass destruction (WMD) proliferation, and other aspects of security has been stimulated by concern about actor rationality. Thus the subject of this chapter (and the next) must be bearded with energy, though enthusiasm comes hard. Deterrence theory has been called one of the most influential products of the social sciences (Achen and Snidal 1989). This is true but misleading. In various ways it is also a case study in how not to design a theory, test it, or apply it.

It is fairly clear how the theory came to be closely associated with rationality. The Cold War put the emphasis in thinking about deterrence on competition and strategy, on making the best moves. The very high stakes reinforced this. We needed instruction on how to do our best, to be rational, to avoid disaster but not lose. Finally, nuclear weapons and the Cold War seemed to simplify matters greatly, to force on actors a set of overriding preferences which could serve as the starting point for a rational decision approach.

With this in mind, the theory has been expected to perform three services. One is to *describe* what takes place in deterrence situations. The second is to *explain* how deterrence works, specifying what determines the outcomes of deterrence situations. The third is to *prescribe* good behavior for governments/decision makers in deterrence situations, maximizing their ability to secure the outcomes they (or the analyst) desire. In a sensible world these would overlap. Description would culminate in, and confirm, explanatory generalizations and help generate effective advice for policy makers. Or a powerful explanatory theory would drive refinements in the description of deterrence situations and guide policy makers. Unfortunately, in the exploration of deterrence the three functions have not overlapped all that much, which is not healthy.

Work continues on development of the theory with an eye to both explanation and prescription by means of a deductive approach resting on the assumptions of rationality and of states as unitary actors. Theorists display uneven interest in actor behavior in actual, as opposed to hypothetical, deterrence situations. Some claim that if descriptions of what happens were developed properly, they would nicely fit the theory.[1] Others contend that descriptions of deterrence situations should be expected to fit the theory in only a limited way; description has little relevance for explanation and perhaps even prescription (Achen and Snidal 1989; Wohlforth 1999).

Extensive description of deterrence situation behavior has been primarily the work of analysts highly critical of deterrence theory. They display uneven interest in rational deterrence theory, sometimes using it for guidance but often finding it partially or largely irrelevant. They nearly always assert that the theory must largely fit the observed behavior of decision makers and governments in decision making to be valid and to serve as a reliable basis for policy.

A desire to prescribe, plus uneven policy-maker desire for advice, provided impetus for development of the theory. In turn, unhappiness with the prescriptions (or official versions of them) has stimulated explorations of deterrence situations by the critics. That also accounts, in part, for the intensity of the debate between rational deterrence theorists and critics, the latter often strenuously objecting to uses of the theory in shaping policies and policy debates.

The theme of this chapter and the following one is that deterrence theory cannot now, and will not in the future, resolve the difficulties, in the abstract and in practice, that we regularly encounter with deterrence. There are flaws in the design of the theory that limit its utility. The problems spill over into flaws in deterrence as a strategy. Contrary to many post-Cold War commentaries, these problems are not due to deterrence having become much more complicated now so that the theory

---

[1] An illustration of linking such analyses to description is Wagner 1989. Or see Zagare 1987.

43

provides less effective guidance. It was not all that effective during the Cold War either, for reasons that apply now as well.

Rationality and the conception of deterrence

Sometimes deterrence is defined simply as threats of a forceful response to prevent some unwanted action, usually a military attack. However, *for purposes of theory building* deterrence has generally been conceived as an effort by one actor to convince another to not attack by using threats of a forceful response to alter the other's cost–benefit calculations. Looking back at the components of the theory set out in the preceding chapter, it is clear that the *conception* of deterrence concerns an effort to prevent an attack by threatening unacceptable damage so that *in the attacker's cost–benefit calculations* the best choice is not an attack. This presumes a rational challenger. The point, particularly when the theory is used for devising a strategy, is to figure out what would be the most rational thing for the deterrer to do in a deterrence situation or in preparing for one. This presumes a rational deterrer. Thus the definition itself explains how the threat can have the effect sought, or rather it contains guidance on how to most effectively model the impact of the threat for purposes of theory. The outline of the theory is implicit in the conception of deterrence used. Hence it is regularly cited to illustrate the use of rational decision assumptions in the social sciences. Many problems with the theory can be traced to this initial starting point. Deterrence was not considered a phenomenon in its own right to which one could apply notions of rationality to see how helpful they might be; deterrence was *conceived* in terms of actor rationality. This resulted in any number of difficulties because the concept of rational decision making fits deterrence situations very awkwardly for explanation (including testing), description, and prescription. As a result there are internal inconsistencies in the theory and a mismatch with the nature of many deterrence situations.

The theory was constructed in an odd way. When we look closely, the emphasis on rationality often seems inappropriate or unwise. In fact, the theory does not rest on the rationality assumption in a normal way. While it detected certain difficulties with deterrence in operating in this fashion, it neglected others. It was based on the assumption of rationality,[2] but analysts tried also to respect the utility of irrationality

---

[2] Russett 1963; Kugler 1984; Huth and Russett 1984. On the use of rationality assumptions see Lebovic 1990, pp. 144–185; Downs 1989.

and the complications posed by limits on rationality, and they also had to adjust the assumption to resolve one of the central problems in deterrence. Thus the theory became something of a hybrid, based on rationality but skewed by the varying presence and impact of something less.[3]

It is easy to see why the rationality assumption was used, but it is not a necessary assumption. It is not necessary to assume rationality to model deterrence for description, explanation, and prescription. Alternative conceptions of decision making exist. (Zey 1992; Friedman 1995a) Assuming rationality is an attractive strategic simplification but there are alternatives for this too.[4]

In principle, defining rational behavior for the deterrer did not require assuming that the challenger was rational. A theory was possible given pervasive uncertainty about attacker rationality or in response to specific patterns of nonrational attacker behavior, but this was a road not taken.[5] Deterrence was virtually defined in terms of attacker rationality and the response of a rational opponent. This opened the door to a rigorous, parsimonious theory but we have never arrived at a fully satisfactory one. In conjunction with assuming survival as a mutual goal, which simplified the estimation of preferences, the theory generated interesting and sometimes nonevident prescriptions but these often had little to do with rationality.

To assume attacker rationality was to be at odds with the way deterrers sometimes, perhaps often, feel about opponents (often seen as irrational) and thus at odds with one reason officials use deterrence. Analysts have never systematically considered whether deterrers think they are confronting rational opponents and whether this might matter. Assuming rationality also meant having a theory at odds with the way deterrence often is practiced. The superpowers constructed overwhelming arsenals

---

[3] Many see it as a model of a rational actor approach; see Allison and Zelikow 1999, pp. 40–48.
[4] For example, seemingly complex decision processes can be modeled with simple equations. A graduate admissions committee, for example, considered reams of information but its decisions could be predicted via an equation using three variables: "... a simple linear equation ... is an extraordinarily powerful predictor. If one can identify and measure the clues that judges consider, then one can mimic their summary judgments quite well with simple modes that combine those clues in ways bearing no resemblance to the underlying cognitive processes" (Fischhoff 1991, p. 122).
[5] An early discussion is Dror (1971). He stressed how irrationality makes deterrence problematic and called for constraining "crazy" states because deterrence would not work on a state not instrumentally rational. Contemporary modeling is often prescriptive on coping with uncertainty or limited rationality or severe limits on, for example, perception.

in part so, it was hoped, even a marginally rational opponent would be deterred, while consistently trying to design around each other's deterrence postures in ways the theory described as quite dangerous (destabilizing) and thus perhaps irrational. Finally, the assumption of attacker rationality made the theory difficult to test.

Inconsistencies

We will start with difficulties internal to the theory under the assumption of rationality: some internal inconsistencies.[6] When a rational decision maker attempts to deter, he must start by doing a cost–benefit analysis of deterrence versus other available options. To opt for deterrence he must find that:

(1) implementing the threats will not be more costly than other effective alternatives; or

(2) carrying out the threats, though costlier now, will have future benefits – such as a reduced likelihood of being attacked because credibility is bolstered – that offset those costs better than other options.

If neither applies, then retaliation or fighting defensively after an attack is not rational. If so, threatening either response is not likely to be credible and deterrence won't work against a rational opponent, unless he can be fooled into thinking one of the two conditions actually applies.

If the rational challenger can see this, so can the rational deterrer. Thus the initial difficulty is explaining how the two parties ever get into a deterrence situation. No rational challenger would carry a conflict to the point of attack knowing that the deterrer could inflict unacceptable damage and would find it rational to do so – and no rational deterrer would bother mounting deterrence threats an opponent knows would be irrational to carry out. To quote an eminent authority well known to me: "our entire notion of deterrence must rest on the existence of great uncertainty in the world and considerable imperfection in its decision makers" (Morgan 1983, p. 83). It must take significant ignorance and uncertainty to bring about deterrence situations. Therefore, if careful case studies often find the initiator surprised by the other side's making strenuous effort to deter and not backing down so that war occurs, or that

---

[6] For critiques stressing internal inconsistencies: M. Williams 1992; Deutsch 1987; Zagare 1996.

the defender surprises itself by in the end backing down or deterrence fails to prevent a war, this is about what we should expect. If rational actors were involved, they would reach agreements that preclude the need for deterrence.[7]

This gives us the first inconsistency – assuming rationality cannot easily account for the need to practice immediate deterrence. So we have to shave the rationality of the parties (or at least one), or their ability to make the most rational choice (due to lack of time, relevant information, etc.), to begin to explain how deterrence situations arise. Once one has arisen, if the prospective cost of deterrence is too high then it should not be chosen as a policy, unless the deterrer thinks highly of bluffing.

Even when a bluff is preferred, however, in many instances credibility should be hard to come by – an effective bluff should normally be tough to make. Why? To defend or retaliate is to *attack the attacker*. But if the attacker, prior to when the crisis arose, was able to inflict unacceptable damage as part of its own deterrence posture then the deterrer who responds militarily to an attack risks much more damage than can be tolerated. It would be irrational to react militarily unless not responding would bring at least as much harm as responding, so deterrence should collapse. Thus the second inconsistency: assuming rationality generates a serious credibility problem for deterrers in mutual deterrence relationships, making for difficulty in explaining how deterrence works.

Deterrence would also collapse if, under mutual deterrence, two parties were constantly poised to attack and one realized that the worse pressure to avoid disaster will always fall on the party which, after a series of confrontations, is attacked in a limited fashion. Then the defender is put on the spot, forced to try to practice compellance to reverse the challenger's initiative and facing the risk that its forceful reaction will produce disastrous escalation. A suitably driven leader would exploit this, as Hitler did in the 1930s and Khrushchev tried to by sending missiles to Cuba. Why wouldn't both parties be so inclined, making mutual deterrence inherently unstable?

---

[7] A parallel argument in Fearon (1995) traces wars among rational opponents to private information making both optimistic about how a war will go. Each has incentives to withhold such information or to cheat on any war-avoiding bargain reached (Powell 1990). In Snyder and Diesing (1977, p. 290): "some differences in images, if not theories, is probably essential to the occurrence of a crisis. If two states could agree on each other's relative capabilities, willingness to take risks, interests, and intentions, there would be little to bargain about." Many analysts trace wars to miscalculations and misperceptions (see Arquilla 1992; White 1987; Lebow 1981; Blainey 1973).

Inconsistency applies on unilateral deterrence too. In some conflicts, retaliation cannot be readily carried out if needed when the punishment would not fit the offense. In effect, imposing excessive costs on the attacker does excess harm (in the negative reactions of third parties or its own citizens) to the defender! Retaliatory threats are then not credible despite ample capacity to carry them out. This has dogged nuclear powers in dealing with nonnuclear states, making them vulnerable to attack by less powerful ones. On the other hand, if the threatened response seemed proportional credibility would not necessarily be a problem. If the costs are acceptable, the deterrer could retaliate or defend with impunity. But then why would a rational opponent attack? Why would a deterrence situation emerge? Of course, if the conflict is severe then, as rational actors, all parties should move vigorously to give themselves, at a minimum, capacities to retaliate or defend strongly. Even though mutual deterrence makes the credibility problem severe, it is almost certain to emerge *eventually* among conflictual rational actors.

A possible resolution is that the costs and benefits of carrying out a threat change for the deterrer *once an attack takes place*, making a punitive response more attractive, so threatening one is more effective. For example, if in attacking C state A thereby weakens its ability to harm C's allies for coming to C's aid, state B can better "afford" to retaliate for A's attack on C. But it would be odd for a rational attacker to put itself in a position where it could no longer impose unacceptable damage on B, particularly via an attack B had been trying to deter and would therefore probably respond to. It is also more likely that the preference shift after the attack is not rational but arises out of reactions like rage, hatred, or a desire for revenge.

Another example would be that the attack shifts B's preference structure in favor of a military response. This is plausible. B may have been uninterested to ever attack A partly out of fear that A would harm C; now that C is being attacked, B may want to attack too. Or B may have never wanted to harm A because it believed that fundamentally A was not hostile, but now revises its image of A because of the attack on C. But there are difficulties here. One is that a rational actor analysis is tricky when preferences can readily change – it becomes next to impossible to detect irrationality reliably and thus to falsify the analysis. The other is that if states revise their opinions of each other as threats, due to their behavior, fairly readily and commonly (as some studies of crises and confrontations maintain), then it should be something that rational actor A will take into account.

Deterrence theorists early on perceived the gravity of the credibility problem in mutual deterrence, particularly extended deterrence. The problem drove Western thinking about deterrence thereafter. One major response was the strategy of flexible response which, in various guises, became the dominant "official" approach for the superpowers. The justification was that if a retaliatory or defensive response to an attack was limited, perhaps matching the nature and level of the initial attack, then it could defeat that attack without provoking escalation into mutual disaster. That would make it rational to respond, the challenger would know this, and deterrence credibility would be maintained – or the challenger would attack and deterrence would be upheld at acceptable cost, establishing the credibility of the deterrer's future threats.

This was not, alas, a reliable solution. Europeans suggested that in pressing hard for flexible response the Americans were announcing that they were really scared of ever having to retaliate at the nuclear level, eroding their credibility. A more worrisome difficulty is that while there is logic in retaliating when the immediate cost–benefit ratio is unfavorable, because the retaliator hopes thereby to enhance its credibility and forestall future attacks, it is a defective solution. Analysts emphasized that the deterrer could not control the end result or calculate the probabilities of really awful outcomes following retaliation, and as a result fear of escalation would make even a limited military response irrational. During the Cold War retaliating to be credible in the future risked canceling the future. Henry Kissinger once told the European allies to stop 'asking us to multiply strategic assurances that we cannot possibly mean or if we do mean, we should not want to execute because if we execute, we risk the destruction of civilization' (Kissinger 1981, p. 240).

Another view was that European security "rests on an American threat to do what American strategic thought has concluded and American statesmen admitted would be irrational" (Lawrence Martin, in Heuser 1997, p. 17). De Gaulle argued that no one "can be sure that in an hour of peril a President of the United States would . . . risk having New York or Chicago destroyed in order to save Hamburg or Copenhagen" (Fontaine 1972, pp. 33–34).

Even in situations without the immediate threat of nuclear destruction, there is an equally fundamental difficulty. How do we calculate the utility of a plan to avoid events yet to occur? If a nuclear war (since 1945) has not occurred how do we calculate the probability of one if South Vietnam is not defended or West Berlin not sustained? How does a decision maker know that not fighting a small war today means more will break out tomorrow? (See, on this problem, Rapoport 1995, pp. 279–285.)

Another way of dealing with the credibility problem, suggested by Schelling, became an axiom of American foreign policy. Since credibility could come from a reputation for upholding commitments, the deterrer should treat commitments as interdependent. Upholding each was vital, even if not advisable in immediate cost–benefit terms, because this would bolster the credibility of the others (Hopf 1994; on this thinking applied to Vietnam see Winters 1997). This reasoning was eventually extended. Other things were seen as affecting the national image for being resolute – level of defense spending, language and demeanor, willingness to develop new weapons. Almost anything could be found relevant.[8]

The defects here are ample. It is open-ended in the requirements imposed for the sake of credibility. Making all commitments of equal importance is a recipe for exhaustion in upholding lesser ones and thereby *losing* credibility on others. This happened via the Vietnam War: officials wanted to bolster the credibility of other commitments but the war had the opposite effect. An additional defect is that it is hard to convince others – they may well assume that the credibility of a commitment rests on its intrinsic worth to you (Maxwell 1968), that anything else would be irrational. It was impossible for Britain and France to convince Hitler in 1939 on Poland, for the US to convince Aidid in Somalia, for Britain to convince Argentina over the Falklands – commitments upheld in part out of reputational concerns. Upholding commitments not worth the effort in themselves, when it is not clear that some larger commitment will ever be saved from challenge as a result, is irrational because future costs and benefits cannot be calculated. Thus you aren't believed on lesser commitments, and you end up fighting hard in response, to sustain a credibility for your major commitments which should be much less in doubt.[9] It would be better to ignore unimportant commitments and defend intrinsically valuable ones unless failure to uphold a lesser one is almost always followed by another challenge.

---

[8] Top policy makers early on felt that *just fighting* in Vietnam was vital, winning less so (McMaster 1997, pp. 180–237, 332). A bad mistake! The real danger to US credibility was to fight and lose.
[9] Mercer (1996) argues, from findings in psychology, that rationality does not apply; credibility is easy to sustain with opponents and difficult to maintain with allies because of how the mind explains others' behavior.

Another problem is that there is no logical reason why someone should uphold a commitment at great cost just because less burdensome ones have been upheld earlier – the negative cost–benefit calculation would apply irrespective of earlier behavior in other cases. A rational opponent will see this and not be deterred. Thus the notion that a commitment of dubious credibility can be strengthened by upholding lesser commitments requires that the deterrer, confronting a rational opponent, demonstrate a robot-like consistency, not action based on rational calculation. This may be reinforced because an attack often *reduces the incentives* for a rational deterrer to respond, making the response politically hard to sell. After all, B's deterrence threat was intended to prevent an attack; now that it has taken place that motivation has evaporated. Moreover, the challenger has just demonstrated its willingness to fight, making a cheap retaliation look much less plausible. A rational calculation in this situation may lead the deterrer to not respond, and the challenger may have counted on this.

In fact, as implied by the reaction of some Europeans to flexible response, going to great lengths to sustain credibility may have the opposite effect. Jervis argues that to go to extra lengths to make a commitment look credible can readily suggest that you are doing so only because it isn't really solid after all – you really might not uphold it (Jervis 1997, pp. 146, 255–258).

A final difficulty with this solution is that treating commitments as interdependent so others do is not something you want to encourage. That would make opponents strongly resist conceding anything lest you think them soft; you would want them more flexible than this on many matters.

Another popular solution during the Cold War – made prominent by Herman Kahn – was to escape from mutual deterrence: be prepared to retaliate and suffer the consequences because you have made sure they will be acceptable. Even for nuclear deterrence, this meant being able to cripple the challenger's retaliation or withstand it – being able to fight and win a nuclear war.[10] On this basis the deterrer could credibly threaten and effectively deter. This applies to nonnuclear deterrence too. It is the unilateral deterrence argument again – you may have no credibility problem if deterrence is unilateral – and, once again, it contradicts the initial assumption that *all* actors are rational. No rational state in a

---

[10] China may currently believe that the key to deterrence is willingness to fight a nuclear war to the point where the other side's cost tolerance is exceeded.

severe conflict and relying on deterrence can allow itself to be put in a position where it cannot inflict unacceptable damage. If this starts happening it will make every effort to strengthen its military capabilities. In trying to escape from mutual deterrence B will incite redoubled efforts by A to sustain it. A may even attack, lest it be attacked once it is deterrentless. Thus this solution, which appears rational, invites an attack or an intensified arms race, neither of which makes sense.

Hence, trying to escape from mutual deterrence could readily exacerbate the stability problem. This brings us to another inconsistency in the rationality of deterrence in theory and practice – *steps to bolster credibility can be irrational in terms of deterrence stability*.[11] If the point is to deter an attack, and stability rests on each side being confident it can deter, then one side's determined effort to gain the capacity to fight and win for the sake of credibility will breed deterrence instability. The theory has rationality dictating incompatible policies.

The urge to escape from mutual deterrence may arise for another reason that exacerbates the stability problem. It is difficult to keep mutual deterrence stability – resting on mutual vulnerability – compatible with a rational response to a deterrence failure. Deterrence is not guaranteed to work. If fear of what could result can be exploited by a daring opponent to make significant gains, then it seems rational to take precautions by escaping from mutual deterrence to either face down a ruthless opponent or win the resulting war at acceptable cost. The superpowers installed counterforce postures bordering on preemptive strike capabilities, hardly rational in the theory but attractive if deterrence is not guaranteed to work and a preemptive capability can be achieved. The major criticisms were that this was dangerous to attempt and would not succeed, not that it was foolish to want to be invulnerable if the balloon went up.

Thus mutual deterrence seems rational and stable yet can breed rational efforts to escape from it that cause its collapse. Unless calculations about how reliable mutual deterrence is under various conditions can be performed and it appears reliable, the relationship dictates contradictory policies. In addition, the gains in defecting from mutual deterrence normally cannot be calculated – each party can only estimate what they might be in deciding what to do so there is no way to predict what choice the parties will make and thus whether deterrence will be sustained or abandoned.

---

[11] Advocates of war-fighting capabilities argued (and still do) that deterrence was unstable anyway – it could easily fail so an ability to fight successfully was sensible (Payne 1996).

If fear of deterrence instability breeds R&D aimed at counterforce capabilities or effective defenses then a mutual deterrence relationship virtually *requires an arms race* to maintain stability (either in fact or in the perceptions of the parties). Severe conflict will incite fear of deterrence failure and lead to efforts to cope with this which undermine mutual deterrence stability unless the other side races to do the same and offsets any progress made.[12] Unless both sides always get it right, the result is regular fear of instability.

We can add another problem. The tensions between divergent inclinations to live with mutual deterrence and to escape from it led to strenuous political debate in the US (perhaps at times in the USSR). The result was a compromise. The US did not put maximum effort into its war-winning capability but did not ignore it either. The superpowers curbed delivery systems in SALT I, then installed multiple independently targetable reentry vehicles (MIRVs) that greatly expanded their counterforce capabilities. This is about what we would expect it takes politically to get a semblance of a policy and SALT I ratified. This did not fit deterrence theory but did fit the logic of domestic politics. Is that rational? British decision makers were divided on whether to rearm and confront Hitler or limit arming and seek a deal. The government pursued both: some rearmament (like a big air force) plus alliances for possible confrontations, while limiting other defense spending and negotiating with Hitler, a policy compromise. It did roughly the same on Italy (Post 1993). It might be said that this is not an inconsistency, just an additional set of preferences the theory was not intended to comprehend. But what is the theory if not an explanation as to how rational decision makers act based on their preferences, *whatever those are*?

The dominant solution to the credibility problem was to relax the assumption of rationality. There are several ways to do this. One is to assume that a challenger is irrational enough to let the deterrer achieve unilateral deterrence – the deterrer is rational in trying to escape mutual deterrence while the challenger is irrational enough to let this happen. The obvious criticism: why should the distribution of irrationality be so congenial?

The favored variant was asserting that states are just not always rational, particularly in grave crises or under attack, and can do things a fully rational actor normally would not. One actor could credibly promise to

---

[12] Buzan and Herring 1999, p. 127 – they cite Hoag 1962; McGuire 1965; Mandelbaum 1981; and Thee 1986, among others.

retaliate even if it would suffer unacceptable damage, because it might be so angry, or frightened, or lacking in control that it would do it. Since retaliation would cause unacceptable damage the challenger cannot ignore that threat. Today, maybe China relies on the fact that there could be no certainty that it would behave as if it were a rational actor if attacked.

This is one basis for the suggestion that nuclear weapons, in particular, generate an "existential" deterrence. If nuclear-armed governments were not certain to be rational in confrontations, they would do well to avoid those situations or treat them with extreme caution. If nuclear armed governments were not guaranteed to be rational once war started, when retaliation and escalation could produce disaster, they would do well to not start a war. Lebovic (1990, p. 193) says: "The existential deterrent acquires its power from the nonrational world of fear, psychological bias, and uncertainty and not from the rational world of deduction and mathematical precision." The eventual conclusion was that nuclear deterrence is basically stable, relatively easy to operate. It was not affected by major shifts in the strategic balance once even the "inferior" state could do catastrophic damage after being attacked (Bundy 1984; Intriligator and Brito 1984). With stable nuclear deterrence in place conventional deterrence was also stable: to launch a conventional war would risk a disastrous escalation. Thus deterrence was not sensitive to ups and downs in the conventional military balance. Even below the conventional level, fear of escalation helped induce great caution so that even the local military balance in a conflict or in a crisis might not be decisive. That is why the Cuban missile crisis was handled so gingerly.[13] The working rule in superpower relations came to be: avoid *deliberately* killing each other's citizens, regardless of the provocation.

This had enormous impact. It was the basis for the MAD analysis and resisting efforts to rest credibility on a war-fighting capability instead. It shaped NATO's posture – Europeans resisted having enough conventional forces to defend themselves, preferring to allow fear of escalation (NATO promised to escalate soon after war broke out), and fear that NATO would do this even if it seemed irrational, to deter the Soviet bloc.[14] That large impact makes its defects all the more disturbing. The flaws start with the fact that we can't presume irrationality

[13] Lebow and Stein (1994) and Blight (1992) show that in the crisis many American officials displayed great fear and caution in their comments despite the enormous US military advantage (see also May and Zelikow 1997). But not all felt this way.

[14] A 1995 US Stratcom report argued that the US could deter adversaries by appearing "irrational and vindictive" as part of "the national persona we project to all adversaries" (Diamond 1998).

afflicts only the deterrer. That is possible, but it is an unwise basis for theory or strategy. Instead, if the deterrer might be irrational in such a way as to retaliate, the challenger might be so irrational as to attack. The proper conclusion should have been that mutual nuclear deterrence has an *existential instability*.

Embracing irrationality as beneficial is the closest we have ever come to devising a truly different theory of deterrence. Yet in the end it was not different, because it assumes attacker rationality; at the crucial moment in an encounter the deterrer's capacity for irrationality and the *attacker's rational appreciation of it* make deterrence work. Thus during the Cold War, "those who emphasize credibility in policy create another logical paradox: they assume that a 'nonrational' U.S. policy stance will be met with a rational Soviet response" (Lebovic 1990, p. 185).

This envisions a rather selective irrationality. During the Cold War, for instance, its champions presumed that governments *are rational about the fact that they can be irrational*; they appreciate their limitations and act accordingly. There is something to this. I find it attractive for explaining how deterrence works, when it works (see Morgan 1983). But it is unclear how to conclude that deterrence *will* work, which is what the policy maker wants. The amended theory seems better for explaining that deterrence is imperfect, sometimes benefitting from actor irrationality and sometimes not. To deal with this problem some analysts argue that decision makers aren't given enough credit:

> The theory . . . postulates that the adversary is a rational decision maker and can be rationally deterred, but it does not attribute to this rational decision maker sufficient reasonableness to recognize the vast uncertainties, unknowns, risks, and dangers associated with initiating a nuclear attack. (Deutsch 1987, p. 150)

But we would do better to drop assuming rationality and attribute sufficient "reasonableness" to decision makers *sometimes but not always*, to explain why deterrence works and highlight the fact that enough sense for that is unevenly present. Then we could stop thinking that deterrence works because we "understand" it and governments are rational practitioners of it, and also avoid sentiments such as these:

> In thinking about the role of nuclear weapons today and in the future, one must remember that, even at the height of the Cold War, no one possessed an exact understanding of how deterrence worked. In the end, it may have been the very uncertainty that surrounded the nuclear enterprise – the how, the when, and the where of our response up to and

> including strategic nuclear strikes – that imbued it with the greatest
> deterrence value. (Joseph and Reichart 1998, p. 19)

If we don't know how it works how do we know that the only serious uncertainty is about when we might use it? And why entrust so much to such a sometime thing?

Left unexplained, therefore, in MAD and related explanations is why deterrence is not inherently unstable. An answer of sorts was offered by Kenneth Waltz (Sagan and Waltz 1995) in suggesting that nuclear deterrence works (1) because almost anyone knows not to take chances with utter catastrophe:

> A little reasoning leads to the conclusions that to fight nuclear wars is
> all but impossible and that to launch an offensive that might prompt
> nuclear retaliation is obvious folly. To reach these conclusions, compli-
> cated calculations are not required, only a little common sense.
>
> (p. 113)

and (2) because the prospect of a gross disaster makes governments behave very sensibly:

> Who cares about the "cognitive" abilities of leaders when nobody but
> an idiot can fail to comprehend their destructive force? What more is
> there to learn? How can leaders miscalculate? (p. 98)

The former asserts that governments are rational enough to handle nuclear deterrence, and the latter that nuclear deterrence makes them rational enough, a neatly circular argument. Related is the suggestion that nuclear deterrence works because little rationality is needed to react properly – officials know not to challenge it just like people know not to play with dynamite (Mueller 1989). The concept of "existential deterrence" also rests on governments being rational enough to not risk disaster and to appreciate that they can be irrational or lose control if pushed too far. Governments are *rational enough* to get by. Sure.

It is never clear why the limited rationality nicely fits the requirements of deterrence or, to put it another way, why the limits on rationality are only beneficent. Why can't governments be irrational in that a deterrence threat provokes nasty emotional reactions, fiery resentment and a rising willingness to challenge and take risks? Why can't irrationality show up as certainty that God or fate is on our side so great "risks" can be run with confidence?[15] We lack a model in which the rationality to make

---

[15] "[T]here is nothing in rational choice theory, in models of limited rationality, or in the theory of deterrence itself that tells us when human beings are likely to be rational rather

deterrence work is present in challengers while the irrationality needed is infrequently but sufficiently present in deterrers, no doubt because it is impossible.

I have heard distinguished analysts assert that no one ever depicts a plausible route to a nuclear war and disaster; governments will simply stop short of such awful steps. Governments are rational enough. It is really troubling that this view is offered after a century especially rich in instances of governments consciously taking awful steps into immense disasters. There was, for instance, no plausible route to a civilized society's government deciding to eliminate Europe's Jews.

The ultimate drawback of the Cold War version of the nuclear age was that everyone had to take comfort in resting security on a batch of recognizably imperfect governments capable of killing vast numbers of people almost instantly.[16] If, in retrospect, this is nonetheless deemed acceptable then nuclear proliferation into major trouble spots, as Waltz has proposed, makes sense (Sagan and Waltz 1995).[17] The flaw is in presuming that imperfect governments and officials can manage nuclear deterrence to perfection indefinitely, instead of trying to minimize chances of destruction by curbing their ability to generate catastrophe – limiting arsenals of nuclear and other weapons of mass destruction and eying their eventual elimination.

Clearly, the theory does not rest on the assumption of rationality in a normal way. It tends to require a departure from that assumption in order to have confrontations to analyze; it has difficulty explaining how deterrence works without departing from that assumption; and it cannot avoid conflicting guidance as to whether a preemptive strike capability is rational. The application of the theory for explanatory purposes varies sharply in its conclusions when we shift among these starting points:

(1)   Each actor behaves rationally, and acts from roughly similar preferences.
(2)   Each actor behaves rationally, and acts from quite different preferences.

than irrational. Why assume human beings are rational in initiating war but irrational in responding to attacks? Why not the reverse, for example" (Achen 1987, p. 96).
[16] "What are the implications of basing defense of one's civilization against nuclear war on a theory that assumes a high degree of rationality in order to work and then at a critical juncture recommends irrationality to solve a tactical problem?" (Vasquez 1991, p. 210).
[17] Various analysts believe in nuclear proliferation: Bueno de Mesquita and Riker (1982); Mearsheimer (1990, 1993); Feldman (1982); van Crevald (1993); Berkowitz (1985).

(3) Each actor does not behave rationally – sometimes/mostly the challenger does not.
(4) Each actor does not behave rationally – sometimes/mostly the defender does not.
(5) No actor behaves rationally.
(6) Threats and risks can induce considerable rationality.

Deterrence theory starts out stressing (1) and ends up relying on (4). Critics tend to stress (2) and (3) and are not averse to (4) and thus (5). Governments are particularly interested in (3) and (6).

Why associate deterrence with rationality?

We opened this discussion by tracing the connection between the initial development of deterrence theory and the assumption of rationality, then moved on to see how problematic it is to keep the theory consistent and retain confidence in deterrence. On further thought, the close association of deterrence and how it works with the assumption of rational decision making looks steadily more peculiar. We really can't talk about deterrence situations between fully rational actors – we have to start with actors that are somewhat irrational, not capable of being wholly rational, or lacking sufficient time or information to be rational. And there are other reasons deterrence might be better depicted as involving nonrational or irrational actors.

For one thing, many irrational or nonrational creatures, including human beings, can be readily dissuaded by threats – deterrence can be quite effective with little or no rationality to target. Creatures like this can still readily respond to pain and threats of more and be deterred. This is true of children, animals, the mentally ill. Even extreme irrationality does not necessarily place someone beyond deterring. And practicing deterrence sometimes incites irrationality. In ordinary confrontations a threat is often the spark that sets off a mêlée. This sometimes seems to happen internationally too. Deterrence can incite hyperreactions to hypothetical dangers, an irrational preoccupation with "image" and credibility, and overblown conceptions of threats.

Next, the parties in crises sometimes don't see one another as rational. This is not always apparent. After all, opponents often depict each other as crafty, having clear goals and being organized and calculating about how to achieve them (Jervis 1976). If so the proper basis for deterrence is clear; ascertain the opponent's preferences, perceptions and information, and the specific factors used in calculations of costs, benefits, risks, and chances of success. This means breaking into the opponent's cognitive world to figure out how the opponent thinks. Then design and communicate threats to penetrate that mindset which are compelling in the adversary's cost–benefit calculations. Occasionally there is evidence of all this. Recent studies of the Cuban missile crisis trace each side's efforts to explain the other's motives, goals and probable reactions as a rational actor.

But consider an alternative picture. When a confrontation emerges we find ourselves uneasy about the opponent's perceptions and calculations, not just because they are difficult to grasp accurately but because we suspect they are not very rational. Why? Because the opponent just hasn't been reasonable about the conflict; his *extreme* positions and demands are the reason the situation has deteriorated. Thus in the missile crisis Khrushchev and his colleagues felt the US was disrespectful, insensitive, and arrogant in neglecting their concerns in Berlin and elsewhere while putting missiles in Turkey. US leaders felt Khrushchev was weird to be challenging the US in its backyard despite express warnings about this, and worried about his hotheaded recklessness. Often the opponent is seen as out of touch with reality. Of course efforts can be made to get inside his thinking but they aren't promising because comparisons with rational governments would be misleading – his behavior is hard to predict other than that it is likely to be extreme. Instead of tailoring threats to fit the opponent, threats become a way *to simplify that communication process*, cutting through the complexities of trying to figure the opponent out – threats are needed that work even when he can't be understood.

We hope the threats will bring the opponent "to his senses," leading him to reevaluate his situation and turn back. Deterrence is used not because the opponent is rational but in hopes of shocking or scaring him into doing the right thing – "force is the only thing he understands." The threat substitutes for approaches one would normally make to a rational opponent or to one, rational or not, well understood. It reflects the fact that you haven't gotten into the challenger's mind and never will, and is a way to manage dealing with a somewhat irrational opponent.

There are elements of this in history. British analyses of Germany and Italy in the 1930s cited irrationality: "Hitler and Mussolini were sometimes described in clinical terms as irrational, sometimes paternalistically as unruly children or unpleasant boors who violated proper standards of international decorum" (Post 1993, p. 11, also pp. 6–10).

Americans said similar things about Japan. While opponents look calculating and crafty, they are also seen as fanatical, blind, or pig-headed.[18] This is not always inappropriate. Some cultures and individuals, in certain situations, do not particularly value rationality. They believe in fate or God's protection or intuition. In some cultures, when honor or being suitably decisive is at stake elaborate calculation is unacceptable. Seeing the other side this way is particularly likely when the parties are sharply different ideologically or culturally, or have a long, highly developed hostility: "the problem in a situation of high hostility is that the assumption of rationality is weakened, because if hostility is extremely high, then irrational behavior, almost by definition, becomes more plausible" (Buzan 1994, p. 31). The enemy is alien or primitive; it takes threats to get through to him. Then rationality does not capture the selection of a deterrence policy or its application. George Lee Butler (1998) explains the Cold War nuclear arsenals this way:

> I have no other way to understand the willingness to condone nuclear weapons except to believe they are the natural accomplice of visceral enmity. They thrive in the emotional climate born of utter alienation and isolation. The unbounded wantonness of their effects is a perfect companion to the urge to destroy completely. They play on our deepest fears and pander to our darkest instincts. (p. 4)

Hence nuclear deterrence was born of a "holy war" mentality.

This can readily describe the challenger's view. "After all, the defender has been unreasonable despite the justice of our case, is irrationally thinking he can win the war that looms or can deter the attack his unreasonable attitude has incited. His deterrence threats reflect a poor grip on reality" (p. 4). Examined in detail, perhaps this is the ultimate in careful analysis but it is more likely half analysis and half hype (or hope). So if the deterrer thinks the challenger isn't fully rational he may be right. Do we then benefit by describing deterrence, for purposes of analysis, as an encounter of rational actors?

There is another problem in depicting deterrence this way. Rationality is not necessarily the key to who "wins." Early analysts realized that an irrational government or leader might have an advantage. Deterrence

---

[18] This odd combination reflects a cramped notion of rationality. Many observers say North Korea is rational, despite policies that brought the economy, society, and state to near collapse, because it is sly, determined, and purposeful – its behavior has explicable patterns. These are silly indices of rationality – they can appear in willful children, the mentally ill, compulsives, etc. – yet are often cited nonetheless.

theory does not say that deterrence works *only* when actors are rational (though many people think it does), it just explains how deterrence works and fails when they are. It also says that *sometimes irrationality helps*. Schelling noted the utility of appearing to be, or being, somewhat irrational in making deterrence commitments credible or making even the determined deterrer back down. He referred to "obvious reference points" around which cooperation coalesces, including an agreement with enough credibility for effective deterrence, even though these points are "obvious" only in some cultural context. Schelling suggested that, with mutual disaster looming, the party that could commit first and leave no room to retreat would leave the opponent the last clear chance to avoid disaster and compel a compromise in its favor. If it is irrational to carry out your threat but you arrange that it will be carried out automatically, the threat is effective even if irrational because you have suspended your capacity to decide and act rationally. Lest this be seen as cleverly rational, try imagining a situation in which – if you didn't win you would be killed – you would readily use it. You can't calculate the odds it will work and thus it is hardly a rational choice on which to stake existence if other alternatives are not fatal. However, someone irrational enough to do it might well benefit.

In the same way, it was eventually concluded during the Cold War that to make American commitments credible it was helpful that the US could not guarantee to be rational if challenged. In particular, that was a justification for continuing to rely on nuclear deterrence. This was not a rational selection of the best basis for deterrence, merely a rationalization of the only promising basis available.

Meanwhile, asserting that commitments be treated as interdependent to sustain credibility puts a rational gloss on a contention resting on irrationality. Building a reputation by always upholding commitments, no matter how onerous the task or unimportant the commitment, sounds clever. But since some commitments are normally not worth fighting for, to fight for all of them would convey *irrational* consistency. Advocates in the Cold War hoped that by implacably upholding minor commitments credibility would be firmly attached to the ultimate US commitments which would be irrational to uphold. The US was to deter by demonstrating that it wouldn't think when challenged, just react automatically.

The same applies to the falling-dominos argument – failure to uphold a commitment will lead allies and enemies to conclude your will and determination are failing (Hopf 1994). This presumes only limited rationality at work in others' assessments of your credibility and your rationality. With rationality present, if my interests dictate upholding a commitment, it is credible even if I didn't uphold another one where they were not engaged. By the same token, rational decision makers elsewhere will not be influenced by my prior actions unless they assume I am not rational. (Or if they have only my prior actions as evidence as to how I perceive my interests.) The US operated in the Cold War as if assessments of its commitments would be shaped by things that should have had little effect for rational observers or because those observers might assume the US was not rational about commitments.

The same occurred on measures of the strategic balance. There was no agreement as to the importance of "superiority" however defined – numbers of strategic reentry vehicles (RVs), throw weight, megatonnage, etc. But it became important to be seen to be equal, or ahead, in such measures. Why? Not because "equality" or "superiority" clearly shaped the credibility of commitments and the effectiveness of deterrence, but out of fear that people (publics, allies, enemies) would irrationally think that simple numerical equality or superiority mattered, that nonrational elements (the "image" of being behind) might shape their perceptions and decisions.

Expectations of irrationality apply not just in peripheral matters but to the essence of some deterrence situations. The US was capable of wiping out the Soviet presence in Cuba during the missile crisis and had strong incentives to do so. What it lacked was confidence the Soviet Union would not be provoked into an irrational response, or confidence that both governments could avoid being caught up in a process they could not control that led to widespread destruction. A blockade was not the optimal choice for rational governments in Washington and Moscow, but it was appropriate if there was a distinct possibility that one or both might not be rational.[19] More recently, North Korea has been a porcupine bristling with threats, with an uncertain capacity for carrying them out yet taken seriously for fear that it is no paragon of rationality.

In another illustration, theory suggests that ample information conveyed with clarity is good for deterrence, allowing the opponent to rationally decide it would be too costly to attack. However, the opponent only has to *believe* that you would carry out your threats. It does not matter whether such a belief is correct – deterrence works just as well whether it is or is not. And deterrence can fail if the threat is not

---

[19] American military leaders thought the blockade was silly – it didn't eliminate the missiles and left the US vulnerable. But JFK kept insisting on it due to possibilities of irrationality or loss of control (May and Zelikow).

believed – whether it is sincere and feasible to implement does not matter. A deterrer must concentrate on manipulating the challenger's perceptions, and analysts noted that sometimes this can be done by being misleading or ambiguous, by a bluff or by being obscure – the challenger is unable to calculate that an attack is worthwhile and thus is deterred.

This set off a debate, never resolved, about whether clarity or ambiguity is best, including whether deterrence works better if a government is opaque or ambiguous about having weapons of mass destruction. This was raised repeatedly in studies about Israel, India, and Pakistan practicing "opaque deterrence" (Hagerty 1993; Cohen and Frankel 1991). Japan has what Daniel Deudney has called "recessed deterrence" via a "virtual nuclear arsenal" (Mazaar 1997), an existential deterrence not unlike the argument (by Jonathan Shell and others) that states without nuclear weapons deter if they can readily build them.

The Eisenhower Administration was quite specific about US commitments (via alliances) but settled for being vague about what it would do to uphold them. First Stalin (Holloway 1994, p. 267) then Khrushchev tried to deceive the West about Soviet nuclear weapons in the 1950s, practicing deterrence by bluff. Sometimes ambiguity works. In other cases it has not prevented an attack, as Israel found in 1973. In the Gulf War Israel's threats to possibly retaliate with nuclear weapons if attacked by Iraq did not keep Scud missiles from landing there, but perhaps the threats dictated that only conventional warheads exploded. Was this success or failure? In sum, it is impossible to specify the relationship between availability of information and success or failure of deterrence – sometimes a lot helps and sometimes it doesn't.

There are other ways irrationality can increase the chances of deterrence success. If a challenger sees almost any confrontation by another as a credible threat, this could be irrational – something like paranoia. But deterrence is more likely to succeed if the challenger is primed to see others as credibly threatening harm. Perhaps the challenger has a fear of risks that goes beyond any evidence that serious harm will result. To deter someone who is deathly afraid of heights from approaching a cliff is easy. Some national leaderships are deeply afraid of even modest risks of defeat or casualties. This was the Guatemala government during the CIA-organized ouster of it in 1954; just a mob at the dock deterred the first Clinton effort to intervene militarily in Haiti. Such irrational calculations make the challenger easy to deter; success results from challenger irrationality.

Is there a consistent connection between rationality and the outcome of deterrence situations? If we knew one or both actors was not rational, what would that tell us – by employing the theory – about the likelihood deterrence would work? Consider some possibilities among nuclear-armed states. State A rationally practices deterrence but B does not decide rationally. A constructs a credible threat of nuclear war and effectively communicates it but B is so angry or distraught that it barges ahead anyway. War results and both are badly damaged or destroyed. In case 2, State A strongly suspects that State B is irrational in disturbing ways. A carefully constructs a nuclear deterrence posture but in a crisis finds it really doesn't want to rely on deterrence to avoid disaster and abandons the commitment. The challenger's irrationality determines who wins.

There are cases in which it looks like two parties had significant misperceptions but they were compatible with deterrence success. There are instances in which one side had a window of opportunity to attack when the other was badly prepared to respond effectively, but the rational choice was not adopted (Lebow 1984). In some circumstances the chances of success can be enhanced if the deterrer locks into a position and makes retaliation automatic, although analysts have always worried about a crisis in which both sides used this tactic. However, case studies show that leaders normally refuse to limit their options so drastically. And why have nuclear powers not used those weapons against nonnuclear opponents, even when this meant accepting a military defeat? Why do states that "should" acquire nuclear weapons (because of their security situations) abjure them and a capacity to attack successfully or to deter? It might be that preferences of the states in question were responsible, but it is at least as likely that they were being irrational and that this strongly affected how well deterrence worked.

Rationality is an inconsistent guide to how deterrence turns out. This is true whether it succeeds or fails, for individual instances and over the long run. It is easy to show that rationality does not maximize a player's result in every situation, but we assume that over the long run rationality does best. I don't think it is possible to show this to be so with deterrence. As a result, perhaps a fully capable theory must rest on other conceptions, or on more than rational decision conceptions. By the same token a fully capable theory cannot be constructed on a nonrational decision maker basis either until we have evidence that in deterrence situations actors are never rational or their rationality never is crucial to the outcome. But there is real difficulty in developing a theory that assumes rationality but tries to encompass the impact of irrational elements, and in using theory to explain how any individual deterrence situation will work out or on how to operate deterrence in general. It seems impossible to associate deterrence solely with rationality – it is not only rational actors that have to be deterred and can deter, it is not only among rational actors that deterrence works, it is not always better to be rational in deterrence situations, and there is probably no consistent link between what works in general and in individual instances.[20]

Rationality and deterrence in practice

The assumption of rationality is troublesome for deterrence not only in theory but also in practice. What is rational for an actor depends on the actor's preferences. In designing a deterrence strategy, it is difficult to assess a target's rationality on the basis of its actions without knowing its preferences. But knowing preferences is not necessarily enough. People often fail to distinguish between the notion that what is rational depends on the initial preferences of the actor and the fact that someone can look rational but not be rational. Rationality is not simply acting out one's preferences or objectives – it is arriving at that action by choosing in a specified way. Otherwise a seemingly rational act could come from drawing straws. This gives us several ways to detect irrationality. A government may pursue manifestly inappropriate objectives for manifestly improper reasons; it may pursue actions clearly at variance with its objectives; or it may make its decisions in an inappropriate manner. The trouble is that detecting these things can be terribly difficult, making irrationality (and rationality) very hard to detect.

It is commonly believed that deterring the irrational is very difficult, but if a government cannot tell for sure what would be rational behavior for its opponent, how will it know if there is a lot of it around? Nor can analysts help; we cannot readily tell the difference, particularly if it is sometimes useful for challengers to feign irrationality. It might be possible retrospectively to determine whether the opponent was rational, but for *practicing* deterrence actors probably must use intuition. The concept of

---

[20] Davis and Arquilla (1991) suggest that prior to the Gulf War the US needed two models of Saddam, as rational and less so (more intuitive), to compare against incoming data. The latter model is necessary because "There is a deep-seated reluctance on the part of Westerners to recognize and appreciate the behavior patterns and motivations of conquerors, ideologists, and revolutionaries. Our tendency is to assume a degree of pragmatism and incrementalism ..." (p. 77).

rationality does not help in diagnosing the nature of the situation and the opponent and therefore does not help much in figuring out what to do. In addition, if what is rational depends on preferences then to maximize chances of success deterrence must be tailored to opponent preferences. If those are misperceived: (1) deterrence may be practiced unnecessarily, (2) it may be practiced incorrectly – punishment is threatened when an opponent's chief fear is defeat, or defeat when the chief fear is death, etc., and (3) regardless of the outcome, it is hard to determine if deterrence worked, or why, and thus whether the strategy was correct. Unfortunately, governments rarely know enough about others' preferences. Information is insufficient, ambiguous, contradictory, and unreliable. Leaders aren't consistent; they shift preferences or their relative importance and often suspend the comparative weighting of preferences until forced to do so. Asking leaders what they want, specifically and with possible outcomes ranked in relative appeal, is seeking knowledge they themselves often lack. And government preferences readily shift. Sometimes this is because of changing circumstances, including deterrence threats. In addition, preferences are normally a collective product so coalition shifts alter the relative weight assigned to them – and the political complexion of coalitions shifts frequently in some circumstances. Hence the profile of opponent preferences used for designing deterrence can readily be wrong or unreliable.

Designer deterrence, tailoring threats to the opponent's history, culture, leaders, and domestic politics is frequently impossible.

> Not all actors in international politics calculate utility in making decisions in the same way. Differences in values, culture, attitudes toward risk-taking, and so on vary greatly. There is no substitute for knowledge of the adversary's mind-set and behavioral style, and this is often difficult to obtain or to apply correctly in assessing intentions or predicting responses.
>
> (Craig and George 1995, p. 188; see also Vasquez 1991;
> Deutsch 1987; Kolodziej 1987)

After all, people *inside* societies who share a culture, history and language regularly misread their compatriots' intentions or risk-taking propensities – as studies of internal insurrections indicate. Thus in stressing rationality deterrence has to rest on the assumption either that the international system *simplifies* the parties' imperatives and preferences so they can be reliably ascertained, or that deterrence threats simplify by *dictating* the opponent's preferences.

The same problem applies to suggestions that theorists and governments refine their images of the challenger for deciding when to use deterrence. Lebow and Stein (see Stein 1991) distinguish confrontations where misunderstanding is crucial from those where incompatible goals are responsible and the opponent deliberately seeks a big gain at the deterrer's expense; deterrence is likely to work in the latter but is inappropriate, may even make things worse, in the former. They are probably correct, but how can governments know which situation exists (Kolodziej 1987)? That can be difficult to determine for historians. Stein (1991, p. 24) writes that "In the late summer of 1914, deterrence was inappropriate as a strategy of conflict management." But how were the parties to know this and how can we be sure even now given continued debates about some actors' motivations? Once again, actors may see deterrence, implicitly or explicitly, as useful because it cuts through such complexities – simplifying sufficiently to permit action. The problem would be not that deterrence is sometimes inappropriate but that not knowing when is likely to drive decision makers to use it as the safest choice.

A theory on how to behave rationally in a rational world is nice, but decision makers often want to use deterrence to override the complications of a somewhat irrational one. They probably prefer a "one size fits all" concept of deterrence meant to work on almost any government, whatever its preferences and whether it is rational. They may want deterrence to scare the daylights out of a crazy government and make irrational leaders "come to their senses."

Rationality and the theory revisited

To this point we have considered various ways it is awkward to associate deterrence with rationality; inconsistencies emerge which are reflected in difficulties with deterrence as a strategy. This recapitulates complaints about rational decision models in the social sciences that: their use is not matched by serious empirical tests (Green and Shapiro 1991); governments, organizations, and decision makers are not consistently rational (Simon 1985; Halpern and Stern 1998); alternative approaches better explain decisions, like prospect theory (Farnham 1994; Levy 1992a, 1992b) or cognitive process theories (Mercer 1996).

On the other hand, it is difficult to just abandon the theory or the rational decision approach. We need a theory because deterrence plays a central role in national and international security. We need a rational decision approach, among others, because deterrence is also a strategy, making it vital to probe the underlying logic of competitive situations and figure out how to align one's efforts with that logic. This may call for going beyond a rationality assumption, but that starting point can help frame analysis, provide insights, and produce a model of ideal behavior against which to compare the real thing. But to use a rationality assumption well we must determine how far it takes us.

The ideal solution would be to put the rational decision assumption to the test, directly or indirectly, so as to determine the fit to deterrence situations. For instance, it might be that getting angry after an attack and retaliating almost blindly is more daunting to a potential attacker than cooly calculating the payoffs from retaliating and other options. If so,

> human beings following their emotions will lack the full range of strategies to pick and choose optimally . . . [and] deterrence will often work in the fashion everyone believes it does . . . There is no necessary reason why evolution should favor perfectly rational behavior. Hence, there is no reason to imagine that human beings necessarily will exhibit it.

Then rational choice models won't fit deterrence situations (Achen 1987, p. 102). We need a better notion as to when the rationality assumption applies to real decisions, and how.

Testing deterrence theory to determine this is inherently difficult and assuming rationality does not help. In fact, as presently designed rational deterrence theory is very difficult to test, directly or indirectly. To begin with, the theory abstracts from reality (Achen and Snidal 1989):

> Rational deterrence is very much an ideal-type explanation. No sensible person pretends that it summarizes typical deterrence decision making well, or that it exhausts what is to be said about any one historical case.   (p. 151)

As a deductive theory it can be tested for internal consistency, for whether it has "logical cohesion and consistency with a set of simple first principles" (p. 151), and in this chapter I have tried to suggest how it lacks logical cohesion. It can be tested indirectly by seeing whether hypotheses derived from it are compatible with appropriate evidence, and this raises problems. There is no consensus on the details of a rational theory of deterrence, no fully effective operationalization of the key concepts, just a general sense of what one might look like

(Achen and Snidal 1989; Downs 1989; Jervis 1989a). As a result, there are many hypothetical variants. Needless to say, this is a complication for testing.

More important is whether the theory applies if the actors are not rational; if not, then whatever the outcome the theory cannot be expected to explain it and is not tested by that case. Some think the theory explains failures of deterrence where the actors were irrational (because irrationality produced either the improper practice of deterrence or an improper reaction by the challenger), but this is not so. The theory does not say deterrence works *only when the actors are rational*. It tells us, in an initial way, how deterrence works when they are rational. It only *implies* that deterrence will not work, or not work as well, when they are not rational, so we cannot conclude that a deterrence failure must be due to irrationality. In fact, theorists treat irrational behavior as sometimes useful in deterrence.

One might think that if, in many or most cases, actors are not rational the theory is incorrect, but that is not necessarily so. First, it may just be irrelevant, not incorrect. It explains behavior among rational actors. Unless we knew that actors were almost never rational we could not decide whether the theory is incorrect or irrelevant. The question would be: how do we tell, how does an actor tell, when the theory does not apply? Since we cannot say, without detailed information about preferences, whether actors are rational, the applicability of the theory is impossible to determine precisely. What compounds the problem is that the evidence is normally indirect; it pertains not to actor cognitive processes but to behavior that *may* imply something about cognitive processes. But behavior is unreliable for such inferences. If the challenger attacks after being confronted with a deterrence threat this could mean that:

he valued the objective more than the probable costs of attack (he was rational);
he valued the objective enough to take the chance (also rational);
he misperceived the cost–benefit ratio, or miscalculated it, even though he then made a cost–benefit based choice (maybe rational, maybe not);
he felt he had no acceptable alternative (rational);
he was irrational.

The evidence will normally not tell us in a convincing fashion which was the case.

Second, it may be that the theory applies, but not *descriptively*. Rational decision theorists have argued that what matters is whether the predicted outcomes accord with the evidence; if they do, the theory is fine even if, when examined closely, the actors don't appear to have been rational.[21] As a result, evidence of nonrationality or irrationality is not evidence the theory is incorrect. It can't be tested by process tracing.

This is an important claim; if it is true, then we can never test a rational decision theory of deterrence other than for internal consistency or the fit between predicted outcomes and evidence. However, this conflates two ways of employing rational decision analysis that should be considered separately. The first is its use as a short cut to arrive at an abstract outcome (i.e. this is how specified deterrence situations will come out) or to develop a hypothetical outcome to see if it fits the real one. The theory fits the real outcomes, i.e. it "explains," regardless of what real decision making looks like, and that is all we care about.

The second approach uses it as an explanatory tool *because rationality itself makes a difference in the outcome*. This is often said or implied. We often associate rationality with effectiveness and expect different decisions from rational than from nonrational processes. For instance many explanations of the behavior of economic interest groups on foreign policy predict the positions those groups take on issues as rationally reflecting the costs and benefits involved (Milner 1997; Friedan and Rogowski 1996). This is how rationality has often been used in the study of deterrence. Individuals can arrive at the same specific decision whether they are rational or not, but can't do this effectively over a range of decisions; eventually gambling by the odds is better than gambling by intuition. We expect actors who are rational to make better decisions overall than those who aren't – that seems inherent in our conception of rationality. If rationality doesn't affect outcomes of decision processes, why assume it to explain behavior? That is why a rational decision theory is used, in deterrence and other matters, to assist people to maximize payoffs with their choices. But if rationality affects behavior, how can assuming rationality produce a theory consistent with actions produced by a nonrational decision process? If rationality means anything, a rational decision process has a different outcome from a

---

[21] This argument is usually traced to Friedman (1953). On deterrence see Achen and Snidal 1989. For general discussion – Green and Shapiro 1994, pp. 20–23, 30–32.

nonrational/irrational one yet here, it is said, the results are, in important respects, the same.[22] How can assuming rational decisions produce a good prediction of the choices made in deterrence situations while not describing the process of making those choices?

To determine which approach fits deterrence it seems that for purposes of testing we need a more elaborate theory when it is constructed by assuming rational actors.

> [I]f a model is to tell us something we did not already know about some historical situation, it is important that its conclusions not require that states in that situation either be able to do things that they could not in fact do or [be] unable to do things that they could in fact do.
>
> (Wagner 1994, p. 604)[23]

The theory might assert that decision makers are rational, either individually or collectively – the starting assumption captures reality. However, most analysts of deterrence who proceed by assuming rationality describe the assumption as convenience not reality.

That would mean treating a rational decision approach as an ideal type, leaving open the question of how well it fits any particular case for investigation. Because it will fit only a limited number of cases we fully expect to be employing others as well (see Friedman 1995a, "Introduction," on such theories). To assist in determining when and how a rational decision conception should fit we need a further elaboration of the theory. If governments are not rational, in important respects in some instances, why should the theory fit? To assert that actors deficient in rationality will produce outcomes "as if" they were rational requires additional explanation specifying why this occurs, so that it can be tested.

To explain why this happens there are, I think, just four possibilities.[24] The first is that conditions exist, and can be identified by the analyst (and perhaps by actors), within which certain behavior is more rational – it

---

[22] Snyder and Diesing (1977, pp. 332–337) describe a rational leader in a crisis as having doubts he understands the situation, searching for more information, and looking carefully at the opponent's behavior, while an irrational one has rigid beliefs and great confidence he understands the situation and the opponent, and thus is less open to reconsidering his views and plans.

[23] Or, "Very few theories ... have emerged triumphant when propelled by demonstrably incorrect assumptions that have a large effect on the predictions they generate" (Downs and Rocke 1990, p. 195). They assert that the rationality assumption is accurate for governments (pp. 92–96).

[24] For suggestions that rational decision theories need more elaboration (unrelated to deterrence) see Green and Shapiro 1994, pp. 23–30.

carries greater payoffs in terms of actors' prime values. Rationality comes to apply *over time*, not necessarily because actors are rational but because actions that accord with rationality are the most beneficial and thus, over time, actors behaving as if they are rational flourish while others don't. Eventually, all actors might come to behave as if they were rational. Perhaps over time they learn what works and what doesn't, with no initially rational grasp of why, so their behavior more steadily resembles what it should be if they were rational. Or maybe they are just socialized into doing what works.

In effect, the rationality assumption captures a "hidden hand" at work, compelling contextual features to which actors respond unanalytically (even unconsciously). The theory just puts into consciously rational terms behavior actors are forced to display. Examples of such analyses can be found in evolution studies, sociobiology, the effects of markets, and the impact of anarchy in international politics. We can proceed as if a conscious rational decision maker is at work because over time the results conform with what rationality dictates whether a rational actor is available or not. Actor appreciation of what is rational is unnecessary. In one evolutionary approach to deterrence, learning that boosts the success takes place over time so that deterrence is best studied via cases of extended rivalry.[25] The contention is that during a series of nasty encounters the deterrer gradually drives home the point that its commitments should be believed. Deterrence frequently fails early on but works better over time, and the eventual outcome resembles rationality at work.

There might be something to this. Still, it is not without problems. We have to confront evidence, such as from studies of crises, that compelling features often incite irrational, not rational, behavior. Maybe painfully accumulated lessons about what works are overridden in the heat of the moment. That still leaves unexplained how actors nonetheless end up producing outcomes that fit the theory's predictions. Another problem (with the Liberman analysis) is that there is no reason why the challenger is the learner. The defender could gradually learn that the opponent's impulse to attack is too strong so that the eventual decline in deterrence failures is due to a decline in deterrence attempts – some other policy is adopted instead. As a result, a decline in crises would not provide lessons about the effectiveness of deterrence. Only a close examination of the rivalry might help.

[25] On extended rivalries see Goertz and Diehl 1992, 1993.

One might also hypothesize the reverse – deterrence works at first but produces so much frustration that over time it breaks down. With successful deterrence steps are not taken to ameliorate the conflict, storing up frustration that culminates in a later collapse. George and Smoke (1974) suggested this years ago in assessing the utility of deterrence in crises. To decide that the theory of deterrence (or deterrence itself) works on the basis of the initial encounters would be incorrect. But to decide after a later failure that it is incorrect would also be wrong, because the failure came from a side effect of the earlier deterrence success – in rational decision terms, the theory would not be invalidated by the later failure. This would also mean that clustering cases for statistical analysis would mask the differences among them that bear on deterrence effectiveness.

A *second* option, a variant of the first in that preset conditions shape behavior, is to suggest that rationality most likely applies when the objective is clear and narrowly specified, especially if this objective and the process for securing it are repeatedly present (see Ferejohn and Satz 1995; Kelley 1995; Taylor 1993). This makes rationality a narrowly focused instrument and very powerful, especially if the goals are important. It is actively at work in war and military operations, sports, election campaigns, business behavior, etc. The objective is to win or achieve something that can be clearly specified as can the conditions under which the effort is conducted, including the nature and objectives of the opponent. When deterrence can be reduced to a highly instrumental activity a rational decision maker model readily applies, and this is most likely when deterrence is repeatedly pursued.

This is one basis for game theory approaches to deterrence. In a game the objective is clear, as are the conditions under which it is pursued (the rules, similarly motivated opponents, payoffs, possible strategies). When uncertainties are introduced to model situations in ways that more closely resemble reality, the uncertainty concerns information about possible risks and payoffs of the strategies or about the other side, not about the basic objective and conditions. Serious uncertainty about the latter would damage the use of game theory itself. The closest we get to introducing these larger uncertainties is in analyses citing difficulties in determining just what game is being played (Snyder and Diesing 1977) – once that can be figured out then the analysis can proceed.

The difficulties with this version of how rationality applies are as follows. The most important is that we would expect rationality to apply to the selection of deterrence over other options and its overall design, not just when those things are already settled and a concrete case with specified objectives, enemy preferences, etc. appears. The same applies to the attacker. Japan in 1941 was an attacker highly rational about *how* to initiate war against Western states that were collectively far superior militarily, but far less rational about *whether* to mount such an unpromising venture. Deterrence is about shaping these larger decisions too, so explanations about why the theory works should apply to them.

A second difficulty is that it may be hard to link instrumental rationality to the real world. How to deter the Soviet Union? The answer eventually was very highly detailed plans for many kinds of nuclear strikes – each a nice demonstration of instrumental rationality at work once a specific objective (hit cities, hit elite headquarters, etc.) was specified. But American officials had no idea which were necessary for deterrence and which were irrelevant in terms of what would properly deter – it was not even certain the Soviet Union needed deterring.

The *third*, and very interesting, option is to suggest that training intervenes. Rationality applies unevenly and slowly but cumulatively in producing decisions and actions – behavior learned or inculcated achieves good results but not in any one instance in a strictly rational process. An outcome in a particular situation may fit a rational decision model when the decision process does not, because actors' behavior results from a long chain of experience and training that is cumulatively rational in effect – like the automatic responses of an athlete. What is rational can be gradually figured out in principle. People who don't or can't figure it out end up through training acting as if they were rational. Their behavior is equivalent to a rational decision maker's though they are inconsistently rational. A decision maker might be inconsistently rational inherently, or from lack of time to explore possible strategies and their effects, or because there are a range of situations to confront and it is impossible to keep track of what is rational when. Training and/or experience makes the rational response routine, by preparing the decision maker to apply simple rules, react to standard cues, and select/implement a reaction without much thought.

There are descriptions of some deterrence situations and other, somewhat parallel, situations that depict a rationality that works unevenly and slowly but cumulatively. One implication is that over time in successive situations actors would look progressively more rational.[26] This

[26] Janis (1982) finds this in comparing US missile-crisis decision making with that preceding the Bay of Pigs invasion.

is an alternative way, referring to the prior discussion, to expect more effective deterrence over time in enduring rivalries. David Ben-Gurion thought in terms of:

> Cumulative deterrence: namely, that an evolving Israeli track record of successfully confronting the Arabs and defeating their efforts to destroy the Jewish state would eventually produce an Arab perception that Israel could not be defeated militarily and must be accommodated politically. (Feldman 1982, p. 67)

This can readily explain rational choices from an imperfectly rational actor. The key, of course, is whether the trainer (theorist) can determine what is rational as the basis for the training. This could be done via theoretical understanding or past experience. In either case, appropriate learning and programmed action can make behavior consistent with rationality more widespread, and analyzed as rational even if little rationality really existed.

The problem? Experience is not always a good teacher, practice breeds routines that suppress creative or flexible thinking, and longstanding conflicts sometimes suddenly burst into violence as if any accumulated learning has been forgotten or ignored. For example, it is easy to imagine decision makers deterring the last war or the last threat and thus failing to contend with the current one. In addition, there is no guarantee that a decision maker has had the appropriate training or experience, or is willing to be guided by those who have. Top positions turn over, often rapidly, and many are distributed on a political basis or for reasons that have little to do with demonstrated knowledge, talents, or experience.

This suggests the *fourth* option. Decision makers desire to learn how best to perform, to maximize success, and thus are able to act rationally if and when they, or others, have figured out what would be rational under the circumstances. Maybe the actor often can't do that personally, but can benefit from it once someone else does. When someone discovers a correct way to position a candidate to appeal to voter preferences it is widely used – rational behavior results even though the actors initially lacked the capacity to know, on their own, what it is. This learning is what a good theory assists, serving as a short cut or more effective route than experience. One implication is that a well-crafted deterrence theory can contribute significantly, as a short cut or substitute for accumulated experience and training. Nye (1987) suggests that this is how the Soviet–American relationship developed during the Cold War, with learning aided by theory making deterrence safer, more stable and effective.

Generally, this means that what is rational is not intrinsic but learned; in the absence of a suitable theory it may not be displayed. This is what deterrence theory was developed to provide. It has often been observed that "deterrence theory probably has had more success than any other social science product in influencing American foreign policy" (Hopf 1994, p. vii). However, DeNardo's research (1995) finds that the central maxims of deterrence theory are not intuitively appealing, even after considerable exposure to the theory. Without deterrence theory people would probably not have intuitively adopted or applied its maxims. Achieving rationality may require considerable ongoing assistance. This would explain why the US and Soviet Union often readily departed from the theory's prescriptions, or why an experienced leader like Yitzhak Rabin could assert that for Israel there was no contradiction between forces for deterrence and forces for a quick, decisive victory if deterrence fails, flatly ignoring the stability problem. DeNardo concludes that we are all amateurs in this sense – limited in the rationality deterrence theory suggests we display. In some cases rationality has to be theory-induced and theory-inculcated.[27]

This view might be a useful adjunct to a rational decision theory of deterrence, but it cannot be taken on faith. Absorbing a good theory can be very uneven, as DeNardo found, so it might then be misapplied. During the Cold War we learned, it was said, from Munich that aggressors must be deterred, not appeased. Then we learned, it was said, from Korea that it was important to make commitments clear. And we learned, from Kennedy's summit in Vienna, that to convey weakness is to incite challenges. The "lessons" from these historical analogies steered American foreign policy on to the rocks in Vietnam (Khong 1992). The evidence is ambivalent on the learning of Cold War decision makers. Often, lessons were taken to heart or applied in ways at variance with rationality. Deterrence theory was ignored or only intermittently followed in the development of weapons systems and the design of deterrence postures. In short, even with a respectable theory available, decision maker behavior may not be consistently rational. If so,

---

[27] DeNardo rightly proposes that we accept the existence of the untheoretical notions – theory can't fully install rational decision making. But note that his subjects most readily used intuitive notions where deterrence theory is weak – on what it takes to deter or the opponent's character and preferences.

assuming it is should result in predictions somewhat at variance with reality.

These four options may overlap, of course, with several operating together in the same case or with the appearance of one connected to the incidence of another. For instance, learning what is rational in theory and wanting to act accordingly may be combined with training to maximize its application.

What are the general implications for deterrence theory of this discussion? A theory built on the assumption of rational decision making cannot be relied on, where there is considerable evidence of irrationality, without an explanation (or elaboration) as to how the behavior of irrational actors can resemble that of rational actors. If we think rationality is dictated over time by encounters with powerful conditions to which actors adapt, then we can't expect actors to produce decisions in keeping with the theory until they have had lots of experience or those conditions have had time to weed out those who behave inappropriately. The theory would apply in some cases and not others. If we think rationality is normally displayed only in a highly instrumental fashion, then the theory will not apply when the actor lacks clearly specified or specifiable objectives, the rules are vague, available strategies and their effects are not clear, etc. If proper training is the key then the theory applies only when it has taken place. If people need theoretical guidance, then the theory will apply only if it has been absorbed.

Thus the rational decision approach ought to culminate in specifying how the capacity to produce "rational" outcomes operates. That would generate a much more precise explanation. Without it, in testing we can't get much beyond detecting a correlation between what rationality dictates and the behavior that is studied, which is inadequate (particularly if theory development is conditioned by prior knowledge of a set of events or is even designed to fit those events). This is really a problem if deterrence works unevenly. Are the failures due to irrational behavior or to our failure to grasp the real preferences and perceptions of the actors so that the theory would fit if we could correctly apply it? Without specifying how actors can produce behavior that fits rationality without being rational we can't indicate the limits to applying the theory. Otherwise analysts will suspect that the difficulty of detecting rational behavior accurately has produced a theory that survives because it cannot be sufficiently tested.

It is not clear which of the alternatives deterrence theorists think is operating. They seem never to have systematically addressed this, which is troubling.[28] For instance, a hidden-hand approach implies that all deterrence situations might be much the same, while the slow-motion view implies that participants in one situation are much better equipped to produce a "rational" outcome than those in another because they have more of the relevant experience and training.

It doesn't help to conceive of the rationality necessary for deterrence, such as nuclear deterrence, as quite limited, asserting that an outcome fits a rational decision model because actors are "rational enough." The theory should explain why and how they can be rational enough, and never in the wrong way. Otherwise the theory can't cope with the criticism that imperfectly rational governments will sooner or later make mistakes that produce disaster. Opposition to nuclear proliferation asserts that governments often don't behave like rational actors in deterrence situations and therefore proliferation is dangerous. Without specifying how governments can be sufficiently rational, and in the right ways, we cannot readily reject this attack on deterrence strategy and, by implication, the theory behind it.

Conclusion

This chapter has reviewed difficulties associated with thinking about deterrence in rational decision maker terms. I have tried to address not only contradictions within the theory but whether deterrence is normally associated with rationality either by the deterrer or in terms of how the deterrer sees the challenger and thus how the function of deterrence is perceived by the deterrer – asking whether deterrence is seen as appealing to a rational opponent or as needed precisely because the opponent is not very rational. I have suggested that deterrers are apt to be irrational and that this is sometimes associated with success. I have also questioned the feasibility of tailoring deterrence to the opponent. I stop short of dismissing rational decision approaches, but it is inappropriate to treat complaints that the behavior assumed is often not present as irrelevant. Needed instead is a more extensive explanation, part of or

---

[28] Achen and Snidal, for example (1989, p. 164) depict decision makers as driven by constraints to instinctively do the rational thing: "decision makers need not calculate. If they simply respond to incentives in certain natural ways, their behavior will be describable by utility functions." But they disagreed about whether decision makers really calculate along rational lines.

auxiliary to the theory, as to why deterrence theory constructed in that fashion will be accurate anyway. This would enhance testing the theory, thereby possibly better meeting or coping with major objections by the critics.

This is also necessary because the theory is used in the design of strategy. Without some explanation along the lines suggested, the strategy will be constantly bedeviled by complaints that some or all of the participants in real deterrence situations are not rational and therefore the theory is not of much help.

3 General deterrence

We have an additional theoretical topic that is relevant for the ensuing chapters. Having explored what can be learned from the Cold War and from analysis of deterrence as a rational activity, we turn to *general deterrence*. I define it as what is present where (a) relations between opponents are such that at least one would consider attacking if a suitable occasion arose, (b) the other maintains forces and offers warnings of a forceful response to deter attack, and (c) the first party never goes beyond preliminary consideration of attacking because of the threat from the second party. General deterrence is to ensure that thinking about an attack never goes very far, so crises don't erupt and militarized disputes don't appear and grow. It is also used to avoid being coerced by threats – you look too tough to be pushed around (Morgan 1983, pp. 42–44; Huth 1999).

General deterrence is complicated and ambiguous, hard to analyze. It covers matters rarely referred to as part of deterrence, yet its main elements play a central role in security policies of states and in security management for any international system. The concept is widely mentioned in the literature, sometimes outlined, but rarely given further consideration:[1] "General deterrence is among the most important and least systematically studied phenomena of international politics" (Huth and Russett 1993, p. 61). I am partly to blame; I intended to say more about it years ago but never did. I introduced the concept to distinguish it from immediate deterrence. The latter is highly episodic, associated with crisis and confrontation. But deterrence is far more ubiquitous than this, so it seemed important to have another term – hence

---

[1] Important exceptions are Freedman 1989; Huth and Russett 1993.

"general deterrence."[2] Here the analysis offered by deterrence theory is not always pertinent because the theory uses immediate deterrence as its reference point with analysis proceeding by imagining a looming attack, by a specified opponent, all laid out in some detail because much is specified about the situation and the target. General deterrence is harder to pin down. The potential attack is more distant and less defined, even hypothetical, while the components of the deterrence posture are less specific. Immediate deterrence is usually linked to specific military capabilities and the threats built on them; general deterrence is an outgrowth of an overall military posture and the broad image it conveys.

A major confrontation is when deterrence is most needed but also when the strain on it is most extreme. By contrast, general deterrence comes into play where two or more actors have a potential for significant conflict so the idea of war is not irrelevant or farfetched. The US–China–Taiwan tangle offers good examples. Each is trying to deter at least one of the others in hopes of preventing confrontations and crises – trying to deter not only preparations for an attack but provocations or political bullying. In turn, each also wants deterrence to be nonprovocative, compatible with good relations with the target, particularly economically. In these examples general deterrence has specific targets, but often the target is any potential attacker.

In deterrence theory general deterrence was commonly explored only as an extension of immediate deterrence. For instance, if credibility in a crisis depended on how you had reacted to prior challenges, upholding commitments when challenged was important not only for deterrence in that crisis and future ones but to forestall the emergence of challenges, i.e. general deterrence. Flexible response doctrine posited that for a Soviet attack with conventional forces the US and the West should respond conventionally – it envisioned immediate deterrence scenarios and the best response – but the resulting posture was meant to inhibit the emergence of such situations by preventing Moscow from thinking conventional attacks could offer significant gains.

The demand for a *prescriptive* theory put particular emphasis on crises reflecting an intense Cold War with serious crises, some large East–West regional wars, and a plausible threat of nuclear war. However,

---

[2] Bar-Joseph (1998) says Israel's "cumulative deterrence" is "the long-term policy which aims at convincing the Arab side that ending the conflict by destroying the Jewish state is either impossible or involves costs and risks which exceed the expected benefits." This is general deterrence.

deterrence theory prescriptions have much greater impact on general deterrence. It is unwise to focus mainly on conceptions of crisis situations because governments spend much more time practicing general deterrence, and it is also unwise to confine our understanding of general deterrence to a Cold War context when grappling with contemporary challenges.

Several things are immediately apparent about general deterrence. One is that general and immediate deterrence clearly are hybrids of the same basic phenomenon and have much in common. The fundamental mechanism for producing results is the same – persuasion via threat. In both, the distinction between deterrence and compellance breaks down under close examination. As noted in chapter 1, if the US sounds menacing to try to prevent nuclear proliferation – general deterrence – and then uncovers North Korea's nuclear weapons program and begins to apply pressure and threats, is this deterrence or compellance? North Korea would describe it as compellance; its programs on nuclear weapons and missiles never constituted an attack on the US (deterrence was never called for), just a reaction to American domination. As Richard Betts has noted about nuclear deterrence, the threatened party *always sees the threats* as blackmail – *a kind of compellance* (1987, pp. 4–6).

There is also no reason to associate general deterrence with rationality. Deterrers often do not see possible challengers as rational and may not see their own military preparations as appealing to the rationality of potential attackers. General deterrence may not be practiced in a rational way either – a case in point being North Korea, which has looked irrationally belligerent for years. China's rigid position on Taiwan, to bolster its general deterrence, often seems irrational in terms of the risks it runs.

On the other hand, the two differ in many ways. Immediate deterrence is brief and rare, general deterrence can go on indefinitely. The target in a crisis is clearly, at that moment, an *enemy*, but the targets of general deterrence need not be enemies at all. Immediate deterrence involves assessing a particular opponent's calculations and plans at a particular time; general deterrence tackles these tasks far more broadly. Immediate deterrence is conveyed through specific, detailed communications, military postures, etc., while general deterrence threatens more diffusely. Analysts often stress the importance of clarity in threats, but general deterrence threats can be quite vague, even unvoiced. Though not always. Prior to 1914 Britain said clearly (to Germany) that violating

Belgian neutrality would be a casus belli while for years NATO clearly said that an attack on one member would mean war with all them – general deterrence can be pretty specific or very broad.

General deterrence is not usually tailored to only one opponent or contingency. Because of this, there is a good possibility of a gap emerging between a state's general deterrence posture and what it needs for deterring a particular actor. In fact, it can be hard to see how overall military power is made relevant for general or immediate deterrence in specific cases. The US has faced this in trying to deter terrorist attacks by nonstate actors.

It is also inherently more difficult to prevent general deterrence from failing. For one thing, the general deterrence has a long-term focus but may be undone because of a challenger's compelling short-term considerations. A possible example: the US wants general deterrence to shape its long-term relationship with China over Taiwan, but Beijing is periodically enraged or provoked by short-term developments or domestic political pressures into thinking seriously about military action – a partial failure of general deterrence even if each time China drops such plans.

More crucial is that, in contrast to immediate deterrence, the promised retaliation is usually *not directly connected to a challenge*. Rarely is a threat offered to the effect that "if you even think about attacking you're going to get it." It can happen, such as when I think broadly about an attack and you respond with sanctions, or a new alliance, or an arms buildup. But often the only response to such thinking is to reaffirm the general deterrence posture (a heightened alert or a tough verbal stance), and even those may be slow in coming. Thus there may be no serious cost if a challenger contemplates or even initiates long-term plans for an attack. Often failures are initiated secretly, provoking little or no reaction and penalty. Leaders can then shelve thoughts of attacking if the prospective outcome never looks feasible and appealing, with no painful response incurred.

Thus general deterrence is very vulnerable to probes by opponents undecided how far to go.[3] It is vulnerable to challengers who make menacing moves to see if they can't induce the deterrer to strike a bargain. This is how the Russians exploited the West's vulnerability in Berlin for years and it had an effect. By 1960 the allies were contemplating neutralizing the city, and during the missile crisis concern about a Soviet

---

[3] George and Smoke anticipated this year ago.

reaction in Berlin helped to make attacking the missile sites or invading Cuba unattractive.

This means general deterrence works primarily through hypothetical threats of harm if an attack ever occurs, not real threats to hurt someone for thinking about an attack. It is a second-order phenomenon, derived from promises of immediate deterrence in a crisis or the implementation of immediate deterrence threats, and is not as readily sustainable through direct threats on its own. This makes it a deterrence that can fail with no corresponding punishment attached. No wonder it is problematic.

For taking timely steps to prevent failure it doesn't help that an outcome is even more difficult to spot than in immediate deterrence. Failure is easier to track than success but is not always apparent. Extended general deterrence may be discounted by opponents because the commitment is not clear (prior to the Korean and Gulf Wars) or because its connection to a particular case is not readily apparent. Success is much harder to identify (Lebow and Stein 1990a). As with immediate deterrence it is hard to know why something doesn't happen; the "something" can be as amorphous as "contemplation" which, when detected, can be portrayed as plans for contingencies. For years the Japanese navy conducted elaborate war gaming on attacking Pearl Harbor; only once was this a US general deterrence failure. (The US now does war gaming vis-à-vis China, which is not a failure of China's general deterrence but someday could be.)

Tracking success is also hard because general deterrence may work not to prevent fighting but to significantly restrict it.[4] Thus one observer's failure (the outbreak/existence of fighting) could be another's success. General deterrence didn't prevent all East–West wars but may have prevented direct US–Soviet combat and is often given credit for there being no World War III. While nuclear deterrence sometimes kept crises in hand, nuclear weapons made major war so unappealing that little real thought was given to starting one.

A second broad difference is that general deterrence is basically more important. The security achieved is greater. Deterrence fails first as general deterrence. Immediate deterrence situations are threatening, nerve-racking, dangerous. Fending them off instead is better, particularly if, as is widely believed, it is harder to get a government to reverse a course it

---

[4] Bar-Joseph (1998) cites this general deterrence function as one use of Israel's "specific deterrence."

has initiated. It may be hard to keep general deterrence from failing but if this is detected early enough then deterrence may yet take hold before a decision to attack is taken. Hence the difficulty of detecting failures of general deterrence is a serious problem.

General deterrence is also vital as the context for developing the deterrence capabilities for confrontations. It is for general deterrence that alliances are constructed, armaments purchased, forces prepared, basic deployments made. It is within general deterrence thinking that critical assessments emerge about when, where, and how confrontations could arise, affecting how well actors cope with crises. Unanticipated threats from unexpected opponents can make life very difficult.

Immediate deterrence draws primarily on military resources – other elements are introduced essentially as supplements. General deterrence, however, embraces a broader range of military-related activities and is readily employed in tandem with other conflict management tools. Thus deterrence theory and nuclear deterrence gradually extended into arms control, which was primarily associated with general deterrence: avoiding destabilizing weapons and deployments, containing arms race costs, curbing proliferation. In the same vein, general deterrence/compellance capabilities are used in conjunction with or to backstop diplomacy and, more recently, peacekeeping. This makes it hard to separate from other broad components of national power and the many other uses of military power. Its success has broader and deeper roots than the raw compelling threats of immediate deterrence.

General deterrence has always been a central element of balance-of-power relationships and systems. It took on more distinctive characteristics when it became associated with concerns about avoiding a great crisis that could lead to a nuclear war and became one of the keys to national survival. During the Cold War there was little confidence in other routes to peace and security; often they were pursued with deterrence in mind. Détente was sought largely for stabilizing deterrence; "reassurance" measures were regularly used in part to solidify deterrence as part of crisis management, and to sustain alliances.

By contrast, the end of the Cold War has seen a sharp decline in great-power conflicts. Their improved relations often now make even general deterrence more like a fall-back position. They rely less on even general deterrence for security and it is less salient; only in the Sino-American relationship is it still central. In great-power relations with lesser states and other actors, however, general deterrence remains very much in play, particularly for the US, and is of great concern to many other states worried about attacks. It is important to collective actors maintaining regional or global peace and security, and to governments with responsibilities in that endeavor. It is important because we can now plausibly prevent crises and outright fighting from dominating global and national security agendas. Therefore, it deserves more extended theoretical treatment.

At best we have fragments of a theory of general deterrence. Some elements of deterrence theory are relevant. So are aspects of theory about how power balancing works – in conceptions of hegemonic stability and analysis of multipolarity and bipolarity or how a concert or collective security system works. We lack good theoretical treatment of how to move from one variant of general deterrence to another, or of how one variant can be less satisfactory than another (as in debates about the general deterrence effects of nuclear proliferation), and of exactly how to shift away from deterrence-based security arrangements, toward something like a pluralistic security community in which deterrence is irrelevant, in the face of fears that some states will eventually defect. We lack a good theory on how to build a deterrence-based international system in other than a balance-of-power or Cold War configuration – we don't really know how to build a concert or a collective security system, which rest on deterrence; we just know what they look like.

While deterrence always rests on the existence of conflict, we can think about general deterrence in the absence of *intense* conflict. We can apply the notion of a stability problem but the threats to stability are broader in nature for general deterrence. We must attend to broader elements that contribute to or detract from a stable general deterrence for a system, alongside the familiar fear that steps to achieve deterrence will provoke hostility and threats of war instead. The credibility problem also applies to general deterrence, for states and larger systems.

In short, we need a theoretical perspective on roles for general deterrence in any international system and the factors that condition how well those roles are played. We need emphasis on how general deterrence functions within a context of other tools of statecraft and must be integrated with them. (The more immediate the deterrence situation, the greater the dependence on/reliance on deterrence – and vice versa.) We need to return to questions of how an international system can become unstable in hopes of better using deterrence in the design of durable stable systems. All this is a tall order and well beyond what can be attempted here. But I have some preliminary comments, speculations, and propositions about many of these matters.

Variants of general deterrence

There are three variants or patterns of general deterrence. One is pursued by an individual state (or a tight cluster of states – like a strong alliance) on its own behalf – we should call it a *single-actor pattern* – leading to either unilateral or mutual deterrence relationships. It seeks to ward off the emergence of direct threats by looking tough enough to nip thinking about attacks in the bud. While deterrence theory has always stressed retaliation capabilities, for most states general deterrence means having forces for a vigorous defense; they seldom rely on retaliation. For many it means alliances. Both are popular in tough neighborhoods, particularly with states that were attacked in the past and face real hostility – Israel, for example. The alternative is to forgo deterrence. The modern history of Czechoslovakia encompasses both. In the late 1930s Czechoslovakia worked hard at general deterrence – a strong army, major fortifications, alliances. This did not prevent Germany from invading, of course. In the late 1960s Czechoslovakia discarded general (and immediate) deterrence, in hopes of avoiding invasion from its neighbors. This also failed. (It *really* was a tough neighborhood.)

General deterrence should not be confused with the capabilities and preparations needed to practice it. It exists when there is a notable level of conflict, and is not present in efforts to sustain military capabilities when there is no conflict present and none on the horizon – the US and Canada do not deter each other.

In writing about general deterrence initially, I suggested that it is not always mainly threats but can be something where "arms and warnings [of states] are a contribution to the broad context of international politics, to the system within which the state seeks its security" (Morgan 1983, p. 45). This needs considerable elaboration now to better understand the relevance of general deterrence today. The second pattern of general deterrence is *inadvertent systemic* in nature. The term is meant to capture the way general deterrence for a system can emerge from the interactions of single-actor deterrence (and other) efforts.[5] The actors arm and threaten, huff and puff, seek to expand and to curb others' expansion, and what results are *systemic* constraints that help deter thinking about the use of force, restraints only partly planned if at all, but sometimes effective. An example is the deterrence exerted by a balance-of-power system that emerges out of states' competitive interactions. A would-be

---

[5] For a rich discussion of unplanned effects of actions in systems see Jervis 1997.

attacker faces deterrence from the target (and its allies) and from possibly hostile reactions of others who could feel damaged or threatened by the attacker's success. The system deters, not just the deterrer. Deterrence without a deterrer? Yes, since the system effect is embodied in the plausible forcible reactions of other actors. A parallel example is how myriad drivers create a traffic system that helps constrain how each drives.

Analysts disagree as to how reliable this deterrence is, or about which configuration of the power of states is most likely to curb warfare in a system. The point is that the deterrence offered by the efforts of individual states is supplemented by the collective arrangement of their capabilities those efforts generate. This inadvertent deterrence might linger almost indefinitely.

In chapter 1 I noted that the East–West, particularly US–Soviet, deterrence relationship eventually constituted a global security management. An important component was this sort of general deterrence. Superpower rivalry and power projection efforts often inhibited the development of crises. This was much of the stability Waltz (1979) referred to, citing bipolarity or nuclear weapons. One analyst refers to the "common deterrence" that arose (Van Benthem van den Bergh 1992).[6] General deterrence operated to keep some conventional wars limited, restrained the incidence or scale of superpower interventions in trouble spots, produced pressures against nuclear proliferation, and so on. What drove this was fear that lesser conflicts might escalate and draw the superpowers in. East–West deterrence as security management elevated many "local" conflicts into concerns at the highest level and made the management a multilateral endeavor involving cooperation among friends and enemies alike. Nuclear deterrence on a suitable scale became the basis for the great powers' stature as great powers and their elaborate interdependence. Often the Cold War system is described as a bipolar, balance-of-power operation, classic international politics. Actually it was not a balance-of-power system but a deterrence-dominated system, in which war was no longer normal behavior among the great powers. It was a very distinctive general deterrence at work.

Hence the preoccupation with sustaining their nuclear weapons of the British, French, and Chinese. It is often said that their underlying objective was (and is) "prestige," a special "nuclear power" status. That

---

[6] Systemic general deterrence generated from a balance of power differs from general deterrence in Cold War bipolarity in usually being reinforced by periodic clashes – war is part of how actors are constrained. With nuclear deterrence the point was always to prevent *any* major war.

trivializes their intent. If general deterrence based on nuclear weapons provided a security management for the system, then what they sought was a voice, a seat at the table, in helping shape it, and that comes to a good deal more than prestige.

Inadvertent systemic deterrence, of whatever sort, is unevenly available to many system members. Because no broad planning or central design drives it, because it arises from the self-interested efforts of actors, its operation and impact can be highly unpredictable. The uncertain security in balance-of-power systems, particularly for smaller states, is typical. In general deterrence systems some states benefit because they are important enough in nature or location to warrant attention and support, like Yugoslavia and Sweden during the Cold War. But others become pawns or targets in great-power rivalries instead, often a terrible fate. It happened to Koreans after 1945 and they are still trapped in the results. It happened at one point to Ethiopia and then to Angola, with dreadful consequences. Then there are countries not important enough to get protection from the system security management. This is what Lebanon experienced, as did Cambodia after the Vietnam War. And a distribution of power in the system good for some members' security can suddenly dissipate, leaving them bereft.

No wonder there is considerable interest in the third pattern, *deliberate systemic deterrence*. Here general deterrence exists for a system because of deliberate steps to create and maintain it – a variant of extended deterrence that is linked to the difficulties and complexities associated with deterrence by a collective actor.

This comes in various forms.[7] One is a very deliberately designed and maintained power balancing. The members believe that offsetting power for any significant concentration of power in the system is good for everyone's peace and security. General deterrence efforts consist of steps to generate or maintain that offsetting power. The Chinese and Russians talked this way after the end of the Cold War.

Another version is a great-power concert. Here the great powers shrink the necessity for general deterrence among themselves by reducing their rivalries. While this might take the form of a deliberate, cooperatively managed balance of power, typically some relaxation in their power balancing takes place to permit more cooperation. (Hence some analysts describe the Concert of Europe not as a retreat from

---

[7] The complexities of various systemic arrangements are explored in Snyder and Jervis 1993.

power balancing but its collective operation.) A concert can also produce great-power agreement that security for other states is their collective concern, and that they should maintain order in the system for the general welfare. A concert has ample strength for discouraging (non-great-power) violence and this may produce a settled and stable system.

The obvious concern of smaller states is that the concert not operate at their expense. An example would be a concert of states engaged in parallel aggrandizement or exploitative spheres of influence – the kind Hitler offered Stalin in seeking Soviet membership in the Axis. This concern influenced the design of the UN Security Council, where the great powers and a larger set of voting members are a concert charged with enforcing peace and security for everyone, hopefully via deterrence. It is dubious that this forestalls collective great-power hegemony, and some smaller states fear the Council is dominated by not only the great powers but by the US as their leader. In the 1990s antagonism among several great powers led the US and its allies to go around the Council, so another concern for smaller states is that a concert may not always deter the threats they most fear.

A recent concert variant, quite hegemonic, is the regional security management provided by NATO. I call it a variant because it is management which includes all states with major relevant military capabilities (the true great powers) and augments that power with ties to many other states. The critical roles in NATO decisions are played by the great-power members, with Russia as an adjunct. But all members have a say and a vote (NATO acts only if all members agree) and nearly all attempt to participate in the military activities involved in security management, as do the NATO associates. The great powers normally carry the others with them when they agree, though having such a broad base adds important psychological and political weight to deterrence so lesser members cannot just be ignored. For states that are not members or associates there is often no influence on the decisions and actions taken. On Kosovo NATO ignored the Russians, other Security Council members, and unassociated nonmembers.

If security management includes *all* system members and the focus is on security *within* the system then we have general deterrence via collective security. (If it is also for protection from outside threats it is collective security plus an alliance.) Using force against another would provoke a military response from all the members. Its proponents after World War I were confident this would be a powerful deterrent to war. If it works it can cancel security dilemmas among the members, solving a perennial difficulty when states practice deterrence on their own. The closest thing to collective security these days involves states that have almost no fear of war among themselves and thus constitute a pluralistic security community. Over the years some states belonged to NATO in part to be safe from some of the other members. Some new members have joined with this in mind as well. However, the members today see little possibility of going to war with each other and are not geared to prevent that – it is not really a collective security system and its security-related institutions are not designed to protect members from each other. Maybe true collective security will someday emerge in Europe if Russia and the remaining eastern European states join NATO.

All these arrangements rest on deterrence; they are variants of general deterrence and can be evaluated as such. They appeal particularly to states that fear they cannot sustain deterrence on their own or that they will incite security dilemmas if they do. The collective approaches (a concert, a collective security system, and NATO's in-between system) are the most striking and innovative approaches to deterrence today, but are rarely analyzed in this fashion. (Chapter 5 is devoted to collective actor deterrence.) They contrast with a pluralistic security community or the use of a moderate level of integration where security is achieved with no recourse to deterrence.

In deliberate systemic deterrence hard questions must be faced. What arrangements best provide deterrence and do existing arrangements measure up? (Can any gap be closed?) What is the scope of the general deterrence arrangements – what challenges are covered, what exactly is deterrence supposed to prevent? What role does deterrence play in comparison with other elements of security management in the system? Finally, what about going from general to immediate deterrence and beyond – how is that supposed to work?

Experience with deliberate systemic deterrence is modest. In Europe after the Cold War, only the first question got much attention, and while this led to maintaining a healthy NATO it left non-members uneasy. That is, the question was only partially answered; the second question was neither asked nor answered, and it was here that serious problems soon erupted. To answer it the first question had to be reopened and it proved impossible to get a region-wide consensus. The resulting general deterrence arrangements have had to be repeatedly adjusted, and some uneasiness remains. It is also not clear how the critics of what emerged propose to answer these questions. For instance, as Europeans now move to adjust the arrangements again, via creation of an EU intervention force within NATO, how would we evaluate these plans in terms of the four questions?

As with individual-actor deterrence, there is a built-in escalatory mechanism in defining threats (operationally) which must be dealt with: over time, it is easy to conjure up more threats of an ever more hypothetical nature. As in individual actor deterrence *there is no natural boundary* to threat perceptions, and political dynamics inside the community can readily press perceived threats into unanticipated areas. This can be put as a series of speculative generalizations.

(1) The more well developed the sense of community among members, the broader the conception of security.

In a well-developed and deepening community the things to be protected from (through collective efforts) inherently expand. When threats to these additional things emerge, there are complaints that the security management is not working, needs further development. And this is just for cases where *force* is the presumed recourse.

(2) Hence, the broader the conception of security the broader the definition of "attack."

As a result the burdens on general deterrence expand: an arrangement meant to prevent interstate wars will eventually be tasked with deterring unacceptable internal uses of force by citizens (terrorism, guerrilla warfare) and states (state terror, repression, massacres).

(3) The more well developed the sense of community, the stronger the inclination to set general principles, universally applied (in the system), as the basis for general deterrence.

This can readily expand the perceived failures of general deterrence, the interventions to apply or uphold it, and fears about its credibility being at stake. With burdens rising, the objective becomes to maintain a capacity to use force to daunt almost any sustained violence.

(4) The greater the load, the more frequently general deterrence fails in individual instances and threats must be carried out.

The broader the definition of "attack," the more often it will be necessary *to practice deterrence via force* through intimidation, intervention, and fighting. This applies to immediate deterrence when general deterrence has failed, and general deterrence when using force now to discourage challenges in the future.

(5) The more general deterrence fails and crises arise that invite the use of force, the more that – at first – this expands the sphere of competence of the deterrence arrangements and – later on – the more observers and practitioners are likely to see deterrence as unreliable or ineffective, leading to recurring or mounting pressures to abandon the objectives it supports. There is a curvilinear relationship. When systemic general deterrence first fails, the emphasis is on shoring it up because the consequences of not doing so are now clear. But if it fails regularly, this eventually means a retreat to some other approach.

For instance, the more effort required to uphold deterrence the greater the strain on cohesion and effectiveness. This can exhaust support for sustaining general deterrence if there seem to be no limits on when and where deterrence is important, the burdens are rising, and success is uneven. This can eventually lead to cutting commitments or redefining interests and security in a narrower, non-collective fashion. There is tension between pressure to rely increasingly on deterrence and pressure to abandon it.

Taking these five points as a whole, to maintain effective general deterrence for a system it is vital *to break that chain* – to establish stable systemic security management that works but does not overreach and therefore does not exhaust participation and support. A theory of general deterrence must encompass the possible ways to do this. We know how actors do it – trying to curb further extensions of general deterrence (such as to intrastate conflicts), trying for rapid and decisive interventions to discourage future challenges and sustain domestic support, trying to avoid reliance on deterrence in favor of other methods for forestalling threats of attack – but we can't yet say much about which work well and when for collective actors.

General deterrence and the stability problem

Theoretical analysis of general deterrence must tackle the stability problem – ensuring that forces put in place to deter do not increase the likelihood of a military attack and war instead. This is a particularly intense version of the security dilemma. Exploring it in single-actor and mutual scenarios laid the basis for both deterrence and modern arms control. The problem was detected in envisioning crises, where it was generated by first-strike incentives plus some other aspects of crisis management. As an offshoot, it was described as extending to some arms races – to avoid unstable military postures in a future crisis agreements were sought to forgo destabilizing weapons and deployments. Hence instability could readily characterize general deterrence too. The SALT process, the nonproliferation treaty, the START agreement on eliminating land-based MIRVS, and other arms control agreements, plus unilateral steps to tighten command and control systems, were efforts to stabilize general deterrence.

Thus the preferred approach has been to try to anticipate stability-problem effects in crises and take steps to ease them before they arise. For instance, much attention was given after World War I to curbing capacities for rapid offensives to initiate a major war. However, the classic stability problem also applies to general deterrence. The most direct form this can take is inadvertent or accidental warfare – general deterrence military arrangements collapsing into war without deliberate decision, or even a crisis, because of an accident or other loss of control in weapons, delivery systems, or warning systems. Though there is no record of wars starting this way, the concern survives today in fears about residual alert and targeting arrangements for Russian and American nuclear weapons.

Other steps taken for general deterrence may subtly or openly undermine it (Lebow 1987a). The German high seas fleet prior to 1914 was to deter by being strong enough to cripple the British navy even in losing, but was seen by Britain as threatening the key to its empire and great-power status and thus as evidence of Germany's expansionist objectives and hostile intent. This increased tensions by pushing Britain into alliance with France and Russia; the resulting division of Europe proved unstable.

Lebow and Stein (1995) trace the same phenomenon in the run up to the missile crisis. To deter troublemaking by Castro, the US engaged in highly visible preparations for a possible invasion, while the CIA harassed through covert action. Washington was simultaneously bolstering (general) deterrence via a missile buildup and eventually indicated to Moscow that it now knew it had a huge strategic advantage – including a missile gap in its favor. These steps alarmed top Soviet officials, who thought the US was really planning an attack (on Cuba and potentially on the USSR), leading to the decision to send missiles to Cuba to close the strategic forces gap a bit and also deter an attack on the island (Garthoff 1998). In pressing for too great an advantage and too potent a threat, the US helped provoke the gravest crisis of the Cold War.[8]

The difficulty is readily found in deliberate systemic deterrence. NATO's enforcement of its wishes about Kosovo sought to uphold past deterrence threats and to maintain its credibility. But this involved skirting the Security Council, which angered Russia and China, and readily defeating Yugoslavia, which alarmed them. Their unwillingness to go along with American, British, and French desires weakened the utility of the Security Council's general deterrence.

China has a serious problem of this sort now. It does not want war, does not want to be attacked, does not want to be subject to containment or encircling alliances. In its foreign policy it stresses conciliation, cooperation, negotiation, and deterrence. But its actions in seeking the latter often outweigh the impact of the others. Belligerent statements on its territorial claims and acts like testing missiles near Taiwan, nuclear weapons expansion, and military-related steps in the Spratleys – have aroused suspicion plus US (and other) military reactions that might eventually put China's general deterrence in jeopardy.

The US has been practicing general deterrence in a politically provocative fashion, in ways I need not detail. Many governments are uneasy about military power that permits very inexpensive (for Americans) wars and the expanding research and development to make this power more effective (such as in ballistic missile defense – BMD). It is easy to see why American opponents feel this way, but allies are often uneasy too, fearing the US may use that power in ways that damage them, or conversely that a powerful US will soon regard its security as independent of system security management and do little to sustain it.

Beyond the stability problem lies concern about making general deterrence reliably effective. General deterrence is continuously pursued and meant to be consistently available. For instance, the US sustained its military presence abroad in the 1990s when the Cold War had disappeared, partly to reassure friends and others while regional security systems underwent great changes. That deterrence capability allowed governments to take their time in redesigning, and adapting to, regional security arrangements (Freedman 1998b). The British and French played

---

[8] The US buildup was stimulated in part by fears of falling behind which Khrushchev stimulated by lies about Soviet missiles and unwise threats – general deterrence in a destabilizing way (Lebow and Stein 1987, 1995).

a similar role in the 1920s. Hence, calling such deployments into question in the George W. Bush Administration made this general deterrence worrisome – its effectiveness became less certain. The war on terrorism helped ease those concerns considerably.

The effectiveness of general deterrence can be undermined in many other ways. Defects *due to its general design* can bring deadly interruptions. Let's ignore for the moment how general deterrence is undermined by lack of credibility. Apart from this, the most elaborately studied deterrence failure is probably the arms race, intrinsically threatening because it can:

> breed military breakthroughs that undermine stable deterrence;
> generate a fleeting military "edge" for one side which might exploit this "window of opportunity";
> incite fear and hostility that undermine deterrence stability; and
> promote excessive military influence in decision making.

This is not our most significant concern, however. Careful studies find no consistent relationship between arms racing and these results. Military breakthroughs often arise *outside* the military realm via scientific, industrial, or organizational triumphs. States often ignore windows of opportunity to attack. Societies have frequently carried on arms races with no mounting hostility; while arms racing can have nefarious effects, this is not automatic. And military leaders are often more hesitant to attack than civilians.

However, general deterrence effectiveness faces other challenges. It can readily be undermined when it is too easy to shift to immediate deterrence, to convert a peacetime posture into war, especially a peacetime posture suited for attack. This is how great-power military capabilities prior to 1914 look in hindsight. The great powers sought general deterrence but neglected the potential crisis effects of rapid mobilization plans. Today some analysts stress "offense dominance" – what makes deterrence weak is the superiority of offenses (or perceptions to this effect). I suspect that the impact of offense dominance is often mediated by the *speed* at which states can go from general deterrence to confrontations and attacks.

Since the 1960s nuclear weapons on missiles have needed almost no mobilization at all. With modern missiles as the backbone of strategic forces, curbing the ability to go to war too quickly is not a realistic option for major powers. But it is still an arms control target for others, as in the missile technology control regime. A strictly defensive posture ready at almost a moment's notice can enhance general deterrence stability, and limiting offensive capabilities to achieve stability is still an option for conventional forces – even for the United States getting ready for military attacks takes time, and others need still more. Europeans now live under agreements that sharply limit standing forces and weapons particularly useful for large-scale attack.

Inadvertent or deliberate systemic deterrence arrangements can have an inherent tendency to break down. For one thing, the international system can be *excessively dependent* on deterrence: when too much responsibility for preventing war rests on it and not enough on other conflict management or suppression arrangements. Symptoms include serious arms racing among some or all members, a high level of what Michael Howard calls "bellicism", intense rivalries among major actors in significant regions, little serious negotiating to resolve important issues, perceptions among leading actors that their counterparts are threatening and expansionist, and proliferation of nasty conflicts among smaller states. (As noted, offense-dominance analysts also see that as important – chances of war rise because leaders think they can win by attacking.) When these conditions are widespread, systemic general deterrence is under grave strain. This was the central problem with Cold War security from 1947 to 1972, an era of arms racing, robust belligerency, intense rivalries, and frequent fighting somewhere stimulated and sustained by the bipolar system.

This defect also characterized arrangements in Europe prior to World War I. In the end there was little general deterrence left in the balance of power on which everyone was relying; it could not handle even a modest conflict in the Balkans, much less the onrush of war planning that the conflict triggered.

In the 1930s the European and East Asian systems grew increasingly dependent on general deterrence but the arrangements were flawed. The US and Soviet Union made themselves unavailable for deterrence of Germany while Britain and France were unenthusiastic. In Asia the Soviet Union again opted out and Britain and France were pinned down in Europe. In each region general deterrence was in grave difficulty as early as 1936, with challengers sensing a great opportunity and planning to exploit it.

The Cold War global system displayed another sort of general deterrence instability. The general deterrence that grew out of interbloc rivalry – largely inadvertently at the start – provided the system with some constraint on intervention and a tendency for both sides to suppress or control trouble in sensitive areas. However, it is also possible to have general deterrence make lesser wars look safer and more feasible, the stability–instability paradox. In the Cold War alliances and other linkages for extended deterrence often gave superpower clients resources for trying to settle neighborhood or internal conflicts violently or refusing to settle or ease ones that might otherwise have been dropped. There were fears, which proved unfounded, that general (nuclear) deterrence made the world safe for major and minor conventional warfare even among the great powers. For years there was a similar worry about nuclear deterrence in South Asia – that it would allow vicious low-level warfare indefinitely, fears not eased by the tensions that rose in 2002.

Hegemonic stability analyses that stress preponderance for maintaining peace and security (such as Gilpin 1981; Organski and Kugler 1980), are theorizing about deliberate systemic general deterrence. Analysis of the destabilizing impact of declining great powers traces the implications of their relative weakness for general deterrence, as in Kennedy's study of the rise and fall of great powers. For these theorists, power predominance provides peace and security because it deters challenges and disruptions; as this general deterrence weakens, challenges and disruptions increase. If we regard such shifts as inevitable then general deterrence is always vulnerable in the long run.

What about the effectiveness in general deterrence at the system level when members have *deliberately installed it*? We readily appreciate why deterrence is common in a system where there is little sense of community. But we are unevenly social beings so even in established communities, at every level, community is imperfect and often needs deterrence to help prevent violent conflicts. In international politics deliberate systemic deterrence is rooted in the emergence of a sense of community and acceptance of responsibility for keeping it peaceful in a setting where this has been very uncommon. The versions noted earlier each involve a community, of sorts, acting to patrol a system. The deterrence is focused *inward* as opposed to externally.

In thinking about this kind of deterrence we don't need to use a serious conflict as a starting point. It does not fit various kinds of general deterrence, often used when conflict is far from serious in trying to keep it so. Systemic deterrence seldom involves a collective actor in an indefinite severe conflict (the UN–Iraq case is unusual) – the sorts of enduring rivalries common in dyadic relations are unlikely to dominate community-member relations. Finally, the stronger and more pervasive the sense of community the less necessary deterrence becomes. In more elaborate forms such as a pluralistic security community or the early stages of integration, general deterrence is only a residual resource if the community breaks down. Hence its effectiveness often has less to do with offsetting severe conflict than progress in community building to keep conflicts muted.

The three versions of systemic deterrence mentioned above (concert, collective hegemon, collective security) are of great interest today and in each deterrence can be hard to sustain. In a concert security is vulnerable primarily because cooperation and good relations among its members are potentially transient. A concert does not create a general deterrence that keeps great powers in line, deterrence emerges because they keep themselves in line. They may not do so indefinitely, something many analysts feel is inevitable. Many things might produce this and just operating general deterrence together can erode their cooperation. This was evident in both the Gulf War and the Kosovo operation, even though these affairs generated almost no casualties and only modest costs. And when the members do seriously fall out the system can easily revert to standard power balancing, just what they had hoped to avoid. If their cooperation remains limited general deterrence will be crippled; some conflicts among or inside other states normally handled by the concert will likely incite great-power friction so they are either ignored (the concert avoids further risking its cohesion) or become casualties of great-power strife and are not resolved. This was characteristic of the Security Council for years, and it may now be true of the Security Council again.

A concert may also practice a selfish general deterrence, attending carefully to great-power interests and paying little attention to threats where those interests are not engaged. It may even turn to collective exploitation. Chamberlain at Munich sought a security order based on cooperation of the Big Four by sacrificing the interests of Czechs and others in eastern Europe. In these circumstances lesser states achieve safety from each other only when the concert cares enough to provide it, in exchange for suffering rapacity when great powers choose to display it.

The collective hegemon, like NATO today, can also suffer from serious disagreements. Deterrence may then be paralyzed or severely constrained. Once this happens in particular cases general deterrence is in trouble, for it operates on a cohesion available only at the lowest

common denominator, which may preclude taking up some threats or making potent interventions. One offsetting development, evident in the West, is a single state taking over as the security manager – which the US has done and which has made nearly everyone uneasy. The other offsetting factor has to be the members' common interest in retaining an association for deterrence purposes, something bound to weaken if it is doing little good. This is what finally moved NATO to act in Bosnia and Kosovo. A similar concern about future cohesion is helping to drive current efforts for a European intervention capability.

Also possible is the reverse problem; effective intervention breeds resentment and challenges. Here, it seems nothing fails like success. This is one plausible long-term outcome of the Kosovo crisis. NATO cohesion (despite internal frictions) was not matched by support from Russia and China, which necessitated acting without Security Council sanction. The resulting resentment in Beijing could paralyze the Council for years. And the enlarged European doubts about American participation in future interventions could trouble transatlantic cooperation as well. Such unexpected effects are all in a day's work in complex systems (Jervis 1997).

In collective security the actors provide general deterrence for maintaining security via their overwhelming collective strength, like an international posse. This seeks to evade the traditional security dilemma – members are significantly armed without being threats to each other – and the stability problem – the forces that deter do not incite conflict and war. But this arrangement is vulnerable to member dissension and the perils of coping with a strong challenger or aggressive coalition. Dissension can readily paralyze action; all members are to contribute to any military endeavor but those opposed to the project will be highly reluctant. Confronting a strong challenger means costs that can drive states to defect.

Collective approaches to deterrence face unusually stressful decisions when trying to deal with serious *internal* violence. In a concert, collective hegemon, or collective security system, general deterrence rests on development of common norms about acceptable violence. The norm readily commanding approval is that states be safe from attack. But on internal conflicts, a norm legitimizing intervention puts states at risk of attack. It also clashes with the norm of sovereignty under which actors cannot treat any domestic use of force as unacceptable – after all, states are entitled to keep order. And it clashes with human rights concerns – after all, the oppressed are entitled to rebel. As a result, there is fear of setting uncomfortable precedents. So consensus is unlikely, and without it general deterrence is sometimes unavailable.

Internal conflicts are also difficult because sovereignty sets the external community more distant from the events. The community will normally not react strongly until unacceptable uses of force reach a serious sustained level, so general deterrence fails. The community seriously reacts only in either a crisis situation or worse. System-level general deterrence was too uncertain and began having an impact, if at all, well after serious violence had broken out in Yugoslavia, Somalia, Rwanda, and Cambodia, and it has had almost no impact in Chechnya. Compounding the difficulty is that it is hard to sort out the good guys and the villains. (In intervention for the general welfare it's nice to have an obvious criminal.) Both sides may well have been provocative, committed atrocities. Any government facing a violent internal challenge is automatically suspected of incompetence, deliberate mistreatment of a minority, grinding authoritarianism, or corruption. The opposition may project disturbing images through terrorist acts, frightening rhetoric, or a disturbing ethnic/religious/ideological zealotry.

General deterrence and the credibility problem

We can readily detect difficulties in sustaining credibility for general deterrence. Credibility means looking like you have the will and capabilities necessary to carry out your threats. This is seldom a problem where *national* defense is concerned; states and societies usually react violently if attacked. More difficult to convey is having suitable capabilities. Logically it is not necessary to be able to defeat an attacker, just make the response look unduly costly to him, but being militarily inferior readily translates into images of weakness, unwillingness to fight long and hard.

As discussed earlier, the concern with credibility has pertained mainly either to crisis or to upholding a commitment now so as to balk future challenges. The difficulty of ensuring one's credibility is why small states sometimes pursue a very tough, belligerent image – North Korea is a good example. Credibility with respect to power projection is very difficult to achieve consistently. Cold War America's initial fear was of failing to put forth a clear commitment – Secretary of State Dean Acheson's speech defining the US defense perimeter in Asia was the failure that shaped the proliferation of alliances under his successor

John Foster Dulles. It was revived when the US never explicitly told Saddam Hussein that seizing Kuwait would bring a military reaction, and it is why the US tries so hard now to ensure that its commitment to Taiwan is not taken lightly. However, the most influential concern has been that actions now do not suggest weakness someone later seeks to exploit – in particular when a commitment is not upheld.

We lack compelling evidence that commitments are interdependent in this way. Case studies and statistical analyses find little evidence that states assess each other's resolve on the basis of past actions vis-à-vis third parties, and only modest evidence that past actions vis-à-vis themselves shape images of others' credibility (Mercer 1996; Hopf 1994; Huth 1999). A deterrer's reputation certainly is important, it's just that (a) past actions don't always shape it, (b) there is no consistently reliable source of reputation, and (c) reputation is not always crucial or even important. This makes it hard to use analysis of the credibility problem to design an effective deterrence or explain reliably what happens when one tries to deter.[9] Nonetheless, explanations on how to achieve credibility had a huge impact during the Cold War. Since nuclear weapons cast doubt on whether states would carry out their threats, and readily using the weapons was not an acceptable response, analysts searched for substitute ways to achieve credibility. Treating commitments as interdependent was attractive for this (Jervis 1989a).

Identifying what makes for credibility in general deterrence is particularly difficult because often a failure is not followed by a reaction by the deterrer – making it hard to link current reputation to past reactions. Hence the analysis is nearly always of current deterrer action or inaction as responsible for the incidence of future challenges (success or failure in general deterrence is only implied). Huth (1999) indicates that alliances probably are useful for general deterrence, particularly if backed with strong evidence of commitment such as placing troops on the ally's territory, but this requires explaining why alliances are also not closely correlated with success in crisis deterrence.

Since the credibility problem is acute if commitments look hard to implement, it is not surprising that credibility below the nuclear level has been linked to actually using force. An example is the view that deterrence becomes most effective in extended rivalries because over time each side periodically carries out its threats. Unfortunately, things

[9] Huth (1999) summarizes many studies.

are not that simple. States would have to be constantly referring back to previous confrontations, and as they did we would expect to see a permanent decline in the intensity of the conflict – each renewal of fighting would clash with the thesis. But many extended rivalries don't fade in intensity over a collection of violent encounters. And if they did, the intensity can rise or fall for many reasons having little to do with credibility shifts. The best evidence would be that the challenger over time remains eager to attack but never does, presumably because deterrence credibility grows. But few extended rivalries display this pattern. Such rivals are inclined to think the opponent seeks to attack long after this intent has ebbed, crippling efforts to resolve the conflict.

Mercer's (1996) analysis is particularly relevant to extended rivalries and general deterrence. If rivals habitually think the worst of the opponent and believe it to be a credible threat, then in extended rivalries it is unnecessary to work hard at a tough reputation. If Mercer is correct credibility is most important, and most difficult to attain, not in extended rivalries but first-time encounters. This could pose problems for deterrence by a collective actor, like the Security Council, which seldom conducts enduring rivalries or violent disputes – most of its cases will be first-time encounters.

Two standard cognitive processes appear to be at work. States think they get constant attention and scrutiny, are the target of others' actions, much more than is usually the case. They think their messages are received more clearly and given more attention than they are, and often become convinced that what the rival is doing is aimed at them when it is not (Jervis 1976). This invites the belief that the opponent, and future opponents, will look carefully at the state's past behavior in assessing its credibility, which available evidence does not confirm.

The offsetting tendency is to think that "that was then, this is now." States and their leaders lean toward short-term thinking, giving too little attention to the large potential consequences of their plans (like the deterrer's threats) and neglecting to carefully assess relevant historical information. In Cold War crises involving nuclear threats, for instance:

> decision makers could rarely bring themselves to face fully either . . . the loss of political stakes if military stakes were not raised, or the results if threats failed to achieve their political purpose and military escalation occurred . . . the people at the top sometimes appeared to grit their teeth, close their eyes, and forge ahead.

And:

> Presidents and their principal advisers often appeared to make the threats without carefully thinking through whether they would be willing to initiate the use of nuclear weapons as implied by the signals or what the consequences would be if they did. They focussed more on the political imperative of blocking the adversary's advance than on the danger of war if the enemy refused to desist and the dispute intensified. (Betts 1987, pp. 9, 213)

Officials regularly neglect relevant historical evidence as to the feasibility of their plans. They treat current factors as a better guide, and look at past evidence rather selectively (Khong 1992; May and Neustadt 1986).

A neglected credibility problem of a different sort, particularly important in general deterrence, is arranging to be believed when offering benefits or concessions to supplement threats. A good example is the difficulty of making general deterrence more stable via bans on destabilizing weapons when the parties fear cheating. The commitments involved are often subjected to intense scrutiny and elaborate verification arrangements. In a severe conflict cooperative behavior is the least intrinsically credible.

On balance, credibility in general deterrence is a problem with no consistent solution. It is tough to construct a formidable reputation to which challengers defer and tough to get all challengers to desist from attacking even when you have one. The emphasis on credibility during the Cold War was harmful in many ways. Theory guided behavior by suggesting what rational opponents would do to assess credibility but opponents often disregarded the theory's expectations; analysts also consistently linked credibility to nonrational elements, and that did not work much better. Meanwhile, much that deterrers did to sustain their credibility was very harmful.

Since there is often no specific target and no precise attack in mind with general deterrence, it is difficult to decide what indicators a future challenger will use to evaluate the deterrer's posture. What results is guesswork dressed in theoretical garb – the challenger *might* look at the military balance, the defense budget, prior reactions to challenges, or myriad other measures (Betts 1987, pp. 208–209). It has been suggested that in moving into the Persian Gulf crisis Saddam was impressed by how passive the US had been about takeovers in Cyprus, Tibet, and Afghanistan! (Freedman and Karsh 1993, p. 59.) This seems improbable, but if true it was certainly not something the US could readily have anticipated. Ecuador's military challenge to Peru in the late 1970s has been traced to calculations that Peru was preoccupied with other domestic problems and interests so it would be willing to settle rather than fight (Mares 1996); how could Peru have known its seemingly unrelated concerns would incite a border struggle?

Two major dangers arise from this. Since almost anything might be used by opponents, virtually everything is treated as relevant: all commitments become interdependent, all bases must be maintained, every decision on new weapons is possibly signaling to opponents about whether you have the right stuff, every utterance of top officials must be vetted. This invites a kind of paranoia.

The other danger is deciding that, since little can be done, assessing one's own behavior with credibility in mind is a waste of time. While it is impossible to completely control how others think, one's statements and actions can have some impact. When Jimmy Carter announced he would withdraw US forces from South Korea, insisting this did not diminish the US commitment, one RoK response was to build its own defense industry (an economic millstone ever since), another was its program to develop nuclear weapons (which the US had to work hard to suppress).

Thinking about what makes for success

Deterrence is escalation control – the chief threat is conflict escalation, the chief challenge is preventing or limiting it. This includes escalation of political conflicts into outright clashes, of limited fighting into larger, more deadly warfare, and of the number of active participants. There is a broad belief that:

> the more intense a conflict the more likely it is to escalate;
> in wars there is a strong tendency toward escalation out of passions aroused or to avoid defeat;
> in an intense crisis there is grave danger of passion, misperception, or mistakes leading to the outbreak of fighting;
> in both wars and crises there is a tendency for others to be drawn in.

The burden on general deterrence is to prevent the deterioration of conflicts to the point where they become really difficult. Obviously, it is not the only tool available and not the only one that works, so it is often used with others. This makes it difficult to assess just what makes for general deterrence success since that is linked to contextual factors, the other resources used with it, and the dynamics of escalation. It is hard to detect the relative impact of threats and inducements, or sort out whether success depends on how general deterrence is conducted as opposed to how congenial the context is.

A good example is nuclear proliferation. General deterrence can be used to prevent proliferation by (1) broad threats to punish proliferators (sanctions, isolation, withdrawal of alliance protection, military actions); (2) security guarantees to potential proliferators or to those whom proliferators might target; (3) threats to maintain a safe, orderly, and stable international system. And there are policies like engagement, conflict resolution techniques, various inducements. They are all likely to be used in connection with *general* deterrence; which ones are best?

One way to probe causes of general deterrence failure is to classify general motivations that incite challenges. The most important might be dissatisfaction with the fundamental relationship or system of which general deterrence is a part and which it helps sustain, as when an actor finds the relevant system highly unsatisfactory in terms of its own unacceptable status, its repeated exploitation, the denial of its "rights" or "legitimate" goals. An example would be the German reaction to the Versailles arrangements. When the international system is deemed highly unsatisfactory by a large number of states, as in the 1930s, general deterrence will be unstable regardless of the power distribution in the system or the military capabilities of those managing it. This will be even more likely if there is profound dissatisfaction over *trends* in the dyadic relationship or the system, with expectations that things are not going well or will go well only for a short time. Japan's fear in 1940–1 that US rearmament would shortly cancel Japan's temporary military superiority and lead to war on very unfavorable terms drove plans for Pearl Harbor.

A second motivation for challenging general deterrence is deep dissatisfaction on one significant matter – a particular, deeply held grievance. This is the concern about the Taiwan issue today. Many aspects of the China–Taiwan relationship have gone well (economic links, flows of people) and China is very flexible about how it might develop in the future. The US–China relationship has numerous positive elements too. But Taiwan's resistance to being officially part of China and US insistence that China do nothing about that by force, rankles deeply in Beijing. This one grievance might unravel otherwise promising trends.

A third motivation is an actor's rampant ambition or greed, which might arise in connection with a new leader or new dominant faction, for instance. And a fourth is fear of the appetites and ambitions of another state or states. This motivation might expand as an after-effect of a confrontation, through frustration or fear about the capabilities and objectives the other side demonstrated.

I suspect this encompasses all the motivations behind collapses of general deterrence. But it offers little analytical payoff. Determining which motive is at play in a case is normally impossible for either actors or analysts to do with certainty. Often more than one motive is present, particularly among different officials or groups. Without knowing what the motives are a reliable judgment on how to respond – how to diagnose the relationship, the emphasis to place on deterrence, detecting when it is beginning to erode – can't readily be formed.

In addition, motive is not enough – there must be other factors at work. It is common now to stress the risk-taking proclivity of relevant decision makers – risk-taking impulses shape what becomes of actor dissatisfaction. This sounds good but is not much help in determining whether general deterrence is in trouble. The available evidence is almost always fragmentary, ambiguous, and based on too little experience with the opponent. And context is important in risk-taking; it shapes not only the perception of how risky things are but how costly it will be to take a gamble that fails. The same Khrushchev that took great risks in sending missiles to Cuba was quick to decide to pull them out (over strong objections from his generals, Castro, and others) when US responses drastically changed the situation.

Variation in risk-taking propensities is one basis for the view that a challenge is different if the challenger sees an opportunity to exploit – such as a flaw or weakness in deterrence – rather than being fundamentally dissatisfied. The latter is apt to be a major risk-taker, the former will readily retreat if the chance of success shrinks. Thus the key to doing deterrence is to figure out whether the challenger is deeply unsatisfied or just an opportunist. This is usually not possible; it is normally the heart of the internal debate the deterrer goes through. No government is unitary when it comes to motivation, and perhaps no individual decision maker is either; thus the evidence will be ambiguous. In addition, a willingness to bear costs and risks is related to the intensity of the conflict. But intensity is equally difficult to read.

Hence reliance on detecting motivations is bound to be deficient. "Determining the relative weight of need and opportunity as motivating factors of an adversary's strategic choices is extraordinarily difficult" (Lebow and Stein 1990a). No wonder policy makers sometimes use worst-case analysis or build in insurance against the worst by suspecting general deterrence is nearly always in trouble. But this may well be provocative and repressive (or look that way), when deterrence would not promote adverse reactions if it was kept more in reserve.

Looking beyond motivation and risk propensities, the following factors are usually believed to have an impact. One view is that the greater the deterrer's military advantage, the more success in forestalling challenges; as the balance between the parties approaches parity or moves to favor the challenger, success in general deterrence declines. The assumption is that challengers are moved by the likelihood of success. But this is often not correct. Having a clear military advantage is helpful, but many moves which culminate in military conflicts are initiated by the weaker party and not because of misperceiving the military balance. Close to 20 percent of wars are initiated by the weaker party. Attacks can occur because the attacker realizes that what matters is not overall military strength but the relative military power each party can bring to the matter at hand, which may be quite different. On the other hand, deterrence is often successfully pursued by the weaker party because all it needs is the capacity to do unacceptable damage, usually not military superiority. All this applies even more strongly in general deterrence, where there may well be no penalty initially for violating it and where military planning (for an attack) that does so can readily be put off or disavowed if developments look unpromising. "In general deterrence situations, the balance of military strength has weaker deterrent effects" (Huth 1999, p. 36). Indeed.

Other factors said to affect the success of deterrence are the relative strength or intensity of commitment or "balance of interests,"[10] or the distribution of willingness to take risks, including the willingness to gamble when all other alternatives seem unacceptable (Bueno de Mesquita 1989). This is clearly relevant but difficult to employ precisely. In dealing with Serbia over Kosovo, NATO assessed the balance of interests wrongly twice, overestimating the effects it could get from initiating bombing and then underestimating when the Serbs would quit. Often the best evidence is how the conflict turns out!

Another possible military determinant of success is being perceived to have a *capacity* to do unacceptable damage. This is always taken as a necessary, but not invariably sufficient, condition, which is particularly

---

[10] These are different but often used interchangeably. The idea is that the two sides differ in degree of insisting on their preferences. Citing "interests" is meant to make this more calculable, but the difference may simply be emotional.

true for general deterrence. Since violations are often not followed by serious punishment, general deterrence success *is not a product of threats in the usual way*. The threats are often just implicit in the deterrer's overall military capabilities, indirect in application, and delayed – sometimes indefinitely – in possible implementation. Thus the *standard way of designing, applying, and evaluating a deterrence threat often does not apply*. A deterrer's capacity to do unacceptable damage may do little to prevent initiation of a general deterrence failure. That capacity is not irrelevant but often its effect is broad and indirect, ambiguous. If the potential challenger is into doing "what if?" speculation, he has little on which to base a detailed cost–benefit analysis; there is as yet no finely honed concept for attacking, hence little basis for figuring out if it would be worth it. This leaves the deterrer with little to design general deterrence explicitly to convey. The only recourse is to look tough, competent, and determined – that is as easily grasped as looking able to do unacceptable damage.

If so, then bolstering general deterrence needs certain kinds of help. Perhaps another possible concomitant of success is a record and other evidence of consistently reacting to all sorts of challenges, military and otherwise, in a tough, competent, and determined way. Who knows what challengers may use to gauge will and credibility? But, as we have seen, the problems here are substantial. Rarely will a deterrer's record look straightforward to possible opponents. Pieces of evidence and the whole picture are always ambiguous. Will US missile defenses mean it will defend allies because it is better protected or that it can regard allies as neither necessary nor worth defending? In 1941 the US Navy wanted to strengthen deterrence by moving the Pacific Fleet to San Diego to put it in top shape; FDR thought Japan (and others) would see this instead as a conciliatory, trouble-avoiding posture, weakening deterrence.

Another difficulty is that there is often considerable delay in appreciating that a direct challenge is likely, with something important at stake. In the Falkland Islands case the British were slow to see the need to convey a strong general deterrence threat. In Korea in 1950 it was not until South Korea was attacked that the US appreciated how much it cared. *Context always matters*, real and perceptual. The attack came amidst deepening US concern about the overall East–West struggle and that shaped what Truman and others felt was required. In addition, the important political component involved when states choose to react strongly or not to a challenge cancels consistency. Given variable domestic support for reacting to a challenge, no reputation is secure. The US took the lead on

NATO's reaction in Kosovo, but afterward nearly everyone depreciated American general deterrence for future European conflicts.

All this strongly suggests that general deterrence is far more successful if backstopped by something more than military capabilities and reputation. Any number of contributions might be cited, but one long known to be important is that a potential challenger not see itself as having no option but to challenge and, if necessary, attack. Sadat's Egypt was in that position in 1973, as was Japan in 1941. The first case had general deterrence practiced in a politically inept fashion; Israel was unnecessarily rigid, hoping to extract maximum gains from negotiations. The second illustrates how unfavorable trends can leave few options besides attack. It also shows how, with some challengers, there is little room for providing political breathing space – the gap between the American and Japanese positions was hard to bridge by any conceivable compromise. The Kosovo crisis was another doleful illustration. NATO governments had seen the problem coming for years: a Serb leader's political base built on repressing a provincial ethnic group that would respond with an independence movement in a place dear to Serbian nationalists. General deterrence was practiced for years; warnings went to the Yugoslav government as early as 1991 but the leader could not, given his domestic political situation, afford to comply.

Since the obvious way to leave a challenger an out is to be conciliatory, we must distinguish the usual conception of appeasement from the better conduct of deterrence. It is usually possible to evade attack via appeasement, but governments often prefer deterrence. This makes it important to find ways to be conciliatory, open to compromise, without eroding deterrence, devising a deterrence posture that doesn't eliminate all options but attack (see George and Smoke 1974).[11] This can be difficult. Leaders and governments often undertake general deterrence with strongly held feelings that the opponent is irrational, immoral, or in other ways not worthy of conciliation – the other guy should give way. Those who would temper deterrence with more appealing alternatives are charged with appeasement. This is Senator Jessie Helms on Taiwan – the US should simply shore up deterrence; no conciliatory moves are acceptable.

Thus the Clinton Administration shift in the US general deterrence posture against China and North Korea to add a parallel policy of

---

[11] Even an approach seeing military predominance as the key to peace now emphasizes the need to ease the dissatisfaction of possible challengers. See Tammen et al. 2000.

engagement was uphill work. Some complained there was too little engagement. Others saw the US as an appeaser – in the deals with Pyongyang over its nuclear weapons program and ballistic missile testing, in putting trade with China ahead of human rights. The same range of views existed on general deterrence steps like selling arms to Taiwan and urging China not to use force, allowing expansion in the range of RoK ballistic missiles, refurbishing the US–Japan alliance. Some said these went much too far and were provocative, others considered them insufficient and, with calculated ambiguity about responding to threats to Taiwan, likely to incite an attack. And many in China and North Korea saw only the deterrence, with engagement just a cover or even a veiled attack deserving an angry response.

Freedman emphasizes that general deterrence involves establishing for a potential challenger that "it should not expect to be able to resolve its disputes with another state or group of states by military means," and that over time this can reduce the underlying antagonism (Freedman 1989, pp. 208–209). Thus it is best that potential challengers confront a *tolerable* status quo, tolerable now or in terms of the trends. This is more than trying to ensure that the possible challenger has an option that, for the time being, looks better than planning an attack. It means going beyond hoping the other side will eventually give up to encourage in the potential challenger a strong sense that its present situation is readily sustainable or that it can afford to wait. The difficulties and complexities of pulling this off are impressive. What can be done along these lines?

The initial requirement is to empathize, to see the other side's point of view and try to develop accommodations accordingly. This is hardly a new notion. Arnold Wolfers made the point well in his classic treatise on national security: "national security policy, . . . is the more rational the more it succeeds in taking the interests, including the security interests, of the other side into consideration." Once again, however, peering this effectively into other governments is no easier for designing conciliation than threats.

Thus governments are apt to feel that while it is necessary to approach general deterrence with a blend of threats and carrots the emphasis should be put on the threats, because threats are their insurance policy. This is also likely to be necessary to guard against domestic critics. Which is unfortunate. Theoretical speculations (Tammen et al. 2000, pp. 35–37) and empirical findings (Huth 1999) suggest that carrots be strongly, not tepidly, embraced. The central political judgment shaping a general deterrence policy is whether the opponent is set on conflict and maybe an attack, and if not what blend of conciliation and threat is necessary. In the Cold War the US soon came to assume that the Soviet bloc was constantly primed to attack. While many later shifted their view and promoted détente, this was always a hard sell politically and many never abandoned worst-possible-case analysis about Moscow. It was politically imperative to inculcate elements of that case in planning and policy, which produced endless difficulties because the best response to the worst possible case was a war-fighting posture.

When general deterrence fails there has been a *political* decision rooted in either the opponent's basic goals regardless of what the deterrer does – the motivation to challenge is very high – or in the nature of the deterrer–challenger political relationship which the challenger finds intolerable. Not that the challenger is determined from the start on war if necessary, but the chosen course is not rejected just because war is a good possibility. The challenger starts on a course of action and then developments make an attack either more or less likely. But support may build behind the challenger's demands to such an extent that retreat becomes politically impossible. Thus deterrence must be tried alongside strenuous efforts to keep the opponent from seeing the status quo as intolerable – not least because that makes it easier to decide whether the apparent is driven by need or opportunity. If your guard is clearly up the other side is probably not driven by opportunity, and if you are trying hard to conciliate and getting nowhere, then the perceived need driving the opponent must be substantial.

However, a deterrer often can do little *in a precise or neatly calculated fashion* to induce tolerance of things as they are. With the gap between evidence and reality that afflicts many political judgments, the deterrer's best efforts may still leave the challenger dissatisfied and prone to violence. Then there is serious difficulty when the parties' objectives are incompatible. This applies to more than political issues, as when the deterrer insists on keeping the challenger constantly vulnerable to defeat or destruction, always at the deterrer's mercy. This is what many in the US now want, such as through BMD, but Israel is the prime example. It is inherently unwise except for dealing with actors who will move toward attacking whenever there is a good chance, and even then general deterrence is pushing upstream. When frustration brings confrontation but immediate deterrence forestalls fighting, the frustration does not fade; it may even be heightened. If the deterrer has nothing better to offer it can only hope the challenger will gradually accept the status quo.

The difficulty in waiting for this is illustrated in the Israeli–Palestinian deterrence relationship.

The foremost difficulty in the US attempt to reinforce general deterrence with engagement in East Asia has been gaining sufficient credibility. The instinct is sound, but engagement there has rested on the US expectation that it (1) can make the status quo more bearable for North Korea and China, and (2) will culminate eventually in the end of both political systems! Contrast this with the engagement policy of South Korean President Kim, Dae Jung, who linked it to deterrence but was careful to state that the objective was not to eliminate the North and who strongly urged others to recognize and deal normally with the North, enhancing its chances for survival.

Even a tolerable present and rosy future may not do the trick. *The challenger's objectives are ultimately responsible for success or failure.* The deterrer can do only so much to shape the opponent's perceptions and actions. By 1938 Hitler had made remarkable progress on many of Germany's basic objectives – but not his. British and French efforts at appeasement and deterrence failed, but it is plausible that deterrence alone would have failed also.

One other relevant factor. The general deterrence of a single state or alliance is more likely to work when backed by systemic general deterrence, either by the deterrence inherent in the configuration of the system or the general deterrence arrangements built into it. During the Cold War a state thinking of attacking another often faced the possibility of having to confront a superpower and its allies as well – and occasionally of having to confront both superpowers (as Britain, France and Israel found in 1956). Today, those planning outright interstate aggression face the possibility of provoking a rerun of the Gulf War, of confronting a global or regional coalition. (This is only a possibility. Neighbors invaded the Congo in recent years without setting off such a reaction.)

Reverse linkage can be similarly effective. General deterrence as supplied by or inserted into the system is more feasible when it coincides with deterrence sought by great powers for their own purposes. If the UN wants to do something about aggression, on general principles, against Kuwait this is much more feasible if the US wants to as well out of concern about the credibility of its commitments in the region. In recent years UN deterrence (often compellance) of Iraq struggled when three Security Council members had interests to the contrary. Deterring nuclear proliferation for the Security Council was bolstered in northeast

Asia by US deterrence to preserve the RoK, Japan, and Taiwan, which strongly contributed to keeping them nonnuclear.

Often general deterrence fails due to a perceived disconnect between the general deterrence for the system and important states' interests. In 1991, Saddam refused to quit in part because he expected a divorce between Arab states and the rest of the UN coalition, particularly by posing the threat of or inflicting heavy casualties. Hitler expected the coalition against him to collapse once Poland was defeated, so its deterrence was undermined. Probably the stronger the challenger is in comparison with the deterrer, the more such perceptions are likely to flourish.

Therefore, success often lies in getting general deterrence at two levels working in tandem, not something governments always think about carefully. It can be done in a balance-of-power system but this is very tricky. The fluidity of alignments and perceptions, the complexity of the necessary calculations, and the specific distribution of power may, individually or in combination, leave a specific state on its own facing a potential challenger. It should be easier under a concert or collective security, but far from simple. The overall point would be that if general systemic deterrence is to be strengthened in the most "suitable" way, it should (1) link any additional deterrence capabilities clearly to the general welfare and not to the national interests of a dominant state or to some states' or coalition's distinctive conception of the general welfare, and therefore (2) it is best done through multilateralism.

Conclusion

General deterrence involves moving others by threats of harm, has the same overlap with compellance described earlier, and is burdened with both a credibility problem and stability problems. However, it is amorphous, so that theorizing rigorously about it is problematic. The United States is much taken with it. Officials and analysts constantly assert that American military power, particularly deployed abroad, is primarily responsible for peace and security in Europe, the Middle East, and the Far East. This gives general deterrence too much credit and neglects the impact of inducements to avoid conflict and war that have proliferated in the international system and to which the US also contributes. The US spends too much time attending to military contributions to international stability and the repair of domestic conflict situations and not enough on the other contributions it makes and can make.

Based on what we can say about general deterrence for a system, a dominant state seeking stable general deterrence is well advised to broaden participation by others in system security management, backstopping others' efforts when this is possible rather than pushing ahead as leader/organizer. In the long run the burdens of multilateralism are preferable to the misleading comforts of a rampant insistence on having things our way and doing things only as we see fit. The US should avoid pressing its views on many issues to avoid provoking challenges out of frustration at the sheer scale of American influence. It would do well to avoid overloading itself on military capabilities for the same reason. And it should continue to stress engagement as opposed to deterrence alone.

General deterrence is a disturbing phenomenon. In accounts of how governments fall into sharp confrontations and war there is recurring evidence that governments, elites, and leaders are often barely moved by general deterrence threats that they ought to take into account. Often they are driven by short-term thinking, not attuned to larger implications and potential consequences of what they are considering. They seem caught up in domestic political or ideological preoccupations (Lebow 1981; Lebow and Stein 1987; Chen 1994) or moved by wishful thinking or motivated bias. They are afflicted with serious misperceptions about the deterrer, or discount deterrence because they regard the deterrer and its efforts as illegitimate. They often start *by wanting to attack if necessary* to get their way and then keep looking for ways to design around the opponent's deterrence, which biases their assessments on what might work or when the odds of success have sufficiently improved.

This invites us to expect general deterrence to continue to be unreliable with some regularity – not always, or even usually, but frequently. It is, after all, a peculiar deterrence in that its initial failure often does not lead to punishment – challenges are therefore cheap, at least initially. This implies that the further from an immediate deterrence situation policy makers find themselves, the less value they should place on deterrence alone.

4 Testing, testing, one...two...three

> [T]he most important predictions of nuclear deterrence theory concern nuclear crises, and no one wants any more. This lack of evidence is one of the more important reasons for wanting to have a theory of nuclear deterrence,... But this lack of evidence also makes it difficult to evaluate nuclear deterrence theory empirically in the domain about which one cares most.   (Powell 1990, p. 184)

Deterrence theory developed in line with social *science*, when post-modernism was but a gleam in the academic eye. Hence it was subjected to three broad efforts at instilling positivist rigor: the assumption of rationality, quantitative empirical studies, and detailed case studies. The literature is more than ample, the results are uneven and satisfaction is underwhelming. The next several chapters are about what might be true about deterrence now and in the future, so this chapter summarizes findings from the past.

Some time ago two leading analysts offered guidelines for rigorous tests of deterrence theory (Huth and Russett 1990):

(1) Specify precisely what is to be explained.
(2) Present a theory or hypothesis that explains it, setting forth:

the assumptions used;
the concepts and terms used, carefully specified;
the factors used in the explanation and how they produce the explanation;
the conditions under which the explanation applies.

(3) Indicate how to know when the relevant elements are present – what indicators to use.

(4) Develop a representative sample or the entire population of cases of what is to be explained.

(5) Test the explanation by how well it fits the cases – exploring the links between what the explanation says are the important variables and instances of what is to be explained.

Considerable effort has gone into studying deterrence along these lines. It has turned out to be difficult. Each step has posed problems and generated complications. Understanding the difficulties is useful for evaluating the findings so we should start there.

Difficulties
Specifying what is to be explained

On what to explain we start with *prevention*. Deterrence is about preventing something. What springs to mind is war – preventing wars. But deterrence is also used to keep a war from getting worse, as well as to prevent confrontations in which war could readily break out from arising. That is four things to be prevented: serious consideration of an attack; nasty confrontations; attacks; and significant escalations of wars. A straightforward list.

We can skip over sorting deterrence from compellance. Suffice it to say that the overlap between them means that some things explained become more like occurrences (a North Korean weapons program that stops) than nonoccurrences. And our subject becomes more like "coercive diplomacy" (George, Hall and Simons 1971) or "strategic coercion" (Freedman 1998a).

The first problem is that interstate war is not common. By one count, of some 2,000 militarized international disputes (MIDs) since 1816 about 5 percent became wars (Bremer 1995). In 180 years covered by the Correlates of War project there were no wars under way in eighty-one of them, and usually no more than one in the other years, even as the number of states multiplied from thirty to almost 200. Among all the states ever in the system about 150 never experienced an international war, only eight had more than ten (Geller and Singer 1998, p. 1). Full-blown crises are more frequent but still abnormal. Extended rivalries are a small share of interstate relationships, and true arms races are rare. Plans to provoke a crisis or a war are more common but do not characterize most actor relationships most of the time. In the twentieth century ideologies and movements burgeoned that fostered conflicts, crises, and mayhem, yet while the lethality of interstate war grew its incidence did not. Deterrence theory was developed when wars seemed common or plausible – international politics appeared to be a state of war. But if wars seldom occur it is possible that they result from abnormal circumstances, with no set of regular "causes" and no common "solutions" either.

While we care about the incidence of crises and wars, deterrence is about their nonoccurrence. However, since their nonoccurrence is the norm it is not so useful for study because it could be due to many things other than deterrence. In fact, it must usually be due to other things. We want to explain a subset of the nonoccurrences – those "caused" by deterrence – and to specify in detail the link to deterrence.

Some analysts would expand this. One (Huth 1999) suggests deterrence is also used to avoid making concessions under threat. Others see deterrence as a success or failure depending on which side gained its policy objectives (Organski and Kugler 1980).[1] Each suggestion has appeal but only within careful limits. If deterrence is to prevent an actor from just seizing what it wants, surely it is also to avoid having to concede it under threat – the latter is an attack too. However, deterrence is not about keeping the challenger from getting what it wants; it is about *constraining the means* used. It is not a synonym for other policies to cope with nonmilitary challenges, nor always a recourse for offsetting failures of other policies. In addition, we must sort giving in to blackmail from other failures to sustain the status quo – otherwise we end up treating almost any pressure against the defender's position as an attack. What if deterrence forestalls an attack but the conflict convinces the defender to take the opponent seriously and make adjustments? What about concessions designed to make deterrence work better? If the deterrer had a weak position, expected a confrontation, and hoped that deterrence would limit its concessions, that would be a success if it worked, not a failure. (Many analysts see North Korea as belligerent precisely to limit its concessions.)

States are constantly pressured for concessions while giving in to open military threats is rare, so unless we confine ourselves to cases when concessions are obviously coerced we just multiply nonoccurrences to wade through to get to ones that matter. We are better off confining

---

[1] Or: "If states manage to elude war threatening the use of nuclear weapons but fail to (a) obtain policy objectives in that process, or (b) prevent the adversary/attacker from obtaining its policy goals, nuclear deterrence cannot be regarded as completely successful" (Harvey and James 1992).

deterrence, for study, to trying to prevent attacks, grave crises, or serious consideration of them, regardless of whether the challenger achieves its objectives some other way.

The point is that it is complicated to say just what is to be explained. Some suggest that deterrence be tested by including another nonoccurrence: when a nuclear power confronts a nonnuclear power and fails to gain its objectives (Organski and Kugler 1980). Alas, deterrence is not about extracting political gains from a military advantage; it's about threatening to prevent attacks. Achieving the former is not a necessary offshoot of the latter – there is neither a logical nor an empirical link between them.

There are other complications. Deterrence concerns attacks forestalled by threats of harm. It is not surprising that analysts (e.g. Russett) see deterrence as encompassing nonmilitary threats. This has some appeal. Sanctions, for example, are painful, regularly used to deter unwanted behavior, and work in the same way. Trying to influence via threats of some sort of harm is widespread. Unfortunately this applies to a vast range of interactions and is a huge portion of all the nonoccurrences in which we might be interested. Deterrence uses particular means to prevent a particular behavior – because that behavior and way of dealing with it are of unusual impact and interest due to their extraordinary consequences.

In works by Huth, Huth and Russett, and Lebow and Stein deterrence becomes avoidance of conflict escalation via threats *and* incentives. In a way this is useful; we want to know how incentives or related steps alter deterrence effectiveness. Actors also realize that carrots carry an implied threat (to cancel them) – beneficial interaction can breed exploitable dependence. But to make incentives integral to deterrence destroys its coherence as a concept – many, maybe most, attempts to influence involve incentives.

Offering a theory

When we turn to the explanatory tool, nearly everyone describes it as a rational decision theory. Rationality is indeed a starting assumption. But then:

> there are allowances for irrational elements in decision making; the explanation for credibility in mutual deterrence retreats somewhat from the assumption of rationality;

there is no consistent link between rationality and success; it is not clear if it matters to the theory whether decision makers are rational.

The highly rationalist version is one from which analysts and governments have frequently departed.

Also, no consistent conception of rationality is employed. At times analysts envision a vigorous rationality. Others cite a general purposiveness and an effort to think strategically, but with preferences unspecified other than, with nuclear deterrence, that survival dominates – usually! Others see the rationality involved as limited, then disagree as to how much is sufficient. Running through deterrence thinking is a tendency to design rational coping for an unevenly rational world. Perhaps deterrence rests on "sensible" decision making, where officials are suitably cautious due to a healthy appreciation of how irrational people and governments, including themselves, can be (Morgan 1983). The strategy mirrors the theory – built on assumptions of rationality, but with no great confidence in it, and an awareness that irrationality can sometimes be useful.

Other concepts and terms are not firmly established. Much turns on the roles of challenger and defender – their different perspectives supposedly shape their perceptions and actions – but often all the parties see themselves as defender. The distinction between deterrence and compellance breaks down in real situations. The conditions under which the theory applies are not specified with rigor and common agreement. For instance, there is no consensus on whether actors must be rational or how, if they aren't, this alters things. Speculations that deterrence is different when practiced with nuclear weapons are not derived in a consistent way from the theory. Is it that conventional forces don't threaten "enough" harm? Is it that officials' concerns about irrationality rise with the potential costs? Is it that nuclear weapons can overwhelm the limited rationality of officials, or are nuclear threats so fearsome even dim bulbs figure out what to do?

Operationalization

How do we know when the pertinent elements are present? We can start with immediate deterrence situations. The criteria usually used for detecting them include:

hostile states, at least one seriously thinking of striking militarily;

key officials of the target state(s) realize this;

there are threats to use force in response;

leaders of the challenger deciding to strike or not *primarily* because of the impact of those threats.

Thus if State B doesn't perceive an attack coming or does not threaten to prevent it, it is not practicing deterrence and we can't learn much from that case. If State A has no intention of attacking the case cannot tell us whether deterrence works or how.

This definition sounds more useful than it is. Often it is difficult to be sure a state was "seriously" thinking of attack. Leaders may be quite undecided even late in the day, for reasons unrelated to deterrence. And deciding when leaders went beyond noodling around and became serious is tricky. Is it when a detailed attack plan was prepared and appropriate forces were in place? When attacking became the dominant option? When officials merely headed toward a crisis thinking "we mean to succeed and will use force if necessary"? Another difficulty is that governments can be like gorillas in the forest – snarling, chest-beating, roaring, charging, all as a bluff. They look scary but don't need much deterring. There is the "attacker" who feels it is responding to a prior attack or grievous provocation, even one from long ago. This is important if, as analysts suggest, strength of motivation (balance of interests) and resulting behavior depend on what role the attacker feels it is playing.

Can we readily find deterrence situations? Apparently not. There is no consensus on relevant cases. An example is the India–Pakistan relationship in 1990. Washington felt that a war, possibly nuclear, was very likely and laid out in detail to those governments how devastating that would be. But they have denied they were close to a war or intended to attack. Analysts line up on both sides. In 2002, did either India or Pakistan ever really come close to deciding to attack, and thus was deterrence at work?

Can analysts themselves identify challenger and defender for purposes of their studies? Apparently not always. Observers disagree about particular cases (Lebow and Stein 1989, 1990a; Schroeder 1989). Sometimes those roles shift as the situation develops (Harvey 1997b). An actor often plays both, not just sequentially as a confrontation develops but because those roles are *simultaneously* present. When challenging, a state also wants to deter a military response or the escalation of any fighting. Therefore it is simultaneously a challenger and a deterrer – so the opponent may also be both.

As for key officials spotting a possible attack, often they don't. In numerous instances efforts to deter were not mounted, or mounted very late, because the necessity was not perceived. If they see a possible attack officials are supposed to issue clear deterrence threats. Sometimes they do but often, as in general deterrence, only an implicit threat is used. Or they mistakenly assume the threat is clear. Strengthening forces or the defense budget will not necessarily convey a warning. A very clear threat is unlikely in extended deterrence if the government is unsure how committed it is, which is common.

Finally, detecting success or failure depends on whether the *threat persuades*. This is very messy.[2] The challenger won't announce that it backed down because it was scared: instead, it never planned to attack, wanted to give negotiations more time, etc. This might be true. Perhaps other opportunities or responsibilities took precedence. Maybe many things discouraged an attack and the deterrence threat merely tipped the scales – do we then conclude deterrence was responsible?

If persuasion takes place (or not), that raises the matter of rationality. It is difficult to get consistency in operationalizing rationality. The key is preferences, then process. If preferences are supposedly *inherent* – in the circumstances, the role, the necessities of the international system – this can shape a conception of what is rational. There is some of this in deterrence situations, but usually there is a gap between what such a conception suggests and what actors do. The gap is often explained by citing the government's *real* preferences and amending the conception of rational accordingly. This allows treating nearly everyone as rational. Were Kim, Jong-Il and other North Korean leaders crazy in running their country on the rocks, placing the regime in grave danger, or did they see reforms as leading to their downfall and rationally preferred to hang on to power even if the country was wrecked?

The other option is to see people as rational because they use a suitable decision process (or a reasonable facsimile). But is someone irrational who doesn't do this and gets a good outcome? Is it rationality if the

---

[2] Because it is impossible to reliably identify one: "No analyst has yet succeeded, or ever will, in identifying the relevant universe of cases" (Lebow 1989).

choice among available options fits the problem well but is made by guessing, while failing or refusing to consider other options? Is it irrational to go through the process properly but not make the best decision? It's not easy to say.

Developing a sample or population

This has probably received the most attention. Difficulties in identifying relevant cases are well known. Deterrence seeks to create a nonoccurrence – reliably detecting one is tough. It calls for the use of counterfactuals, and one way to devise a counterfactual is by applying a good theoretical understanding of what causes things. But it is awkward to use counterfactuals to test the theory if the design of the counterfactual is a product or extension of the theory. To avoid this problem requires eliminating, instead, other possible reasons for the nonoccurrence, which is nearly impossible. There are any number of reasons for the absence of attacks and crises, and some may apply to any case. Thus considerable care is needed to detect a case – we often have to settle for a "plausible" or "probable" one.

Significant difficulties arise for testing due to assuming rationality. What counts for testing? If the theory predicts outcomes that are borne out in deterrence situations does this confirm the theory? Not if we think it is about how rational actors behave and we find evidence the actors weren't rational; if both rational and nonrational actors arrive at the same results this suggests that the predictions come from a flawed theory that may produce mistakes in other applications – it predicts but does not correctly explain. If we think the theory works because certain conditions make actors decide as if they are rational, then the theory is confirmed only if those conditions were present, increasing the number of things to be detected to confirm it – outcomes as predicted would not be enough.

What if, in many cases, the actors don't display impressive rationality and deterrence failed; is this evidence of a weak theory? Or not, because the theory applies only if they are rational and cannot be tested when they aren't? The latter position clashes with the view that the assumptions need not be empirically valid to produce a useful theory, that only the results matter, and that rationality is merely a useful assumption for theory building (see Zagare 2000).

Consider the difficulty in classifying a case. A threatens B with retaliation and B attacks anyway. We might conclude that:

(1) this is a deterrence failure, and counts against the theory;
(2) this is deterrence practiced incorrectly – it is a failure that counts in favor of the theory;
(3) the theory does not apply – one or both actors was insufficiently rational; the results have no bearing;
(4) the theory applies only when we fully understand the actor preferences, particularly the challenger's, and can figure out what was rational; only then can we decide whether the theory is supported or not.

The first treats any fighting in spite of a retaliatory threat as a failure, and may well treat a confrontation with no attack as a success. But states have confrontations that breed threats with no test of deterrence involved. If the challenger never intended to attack, deterrence has not worked.[3] If the "deterrer" realizes the challenger won't attack it may still threaten, to claim a (spurious) deterrence success – a leader can use that to look good. It is doubtful China intended to attack Taiwan in 1994 when its missile testing caused the US to send naval units there – it was a confrontation but not an immediate deterrence situation. So it was not a deterrence success but useful to the administration to call it one. And maybe it was successful general deterrence. Deterrence threats may also be issued when no attack looms just to reassure allies or others:

> Describing what is to be deterred and how it is to be deterred in terms that make more sense to friends, allies, and constituents than to adversaries makes perfect strategic sense, especially if their support may be vital [someday] – even if the net effect on the opponent may be to confuse more than clarify, to provoke rather than dissuade . . . eliciting a response from the declared target may not be the only, or even the most important, function of a deterrence strategy.
>
> (Freedman 1996, p. 15)

Option (2) above calls for careful judgment of whether deterrence was practiced effectively. That's hard (examples are cited later). But it is nothing compared to the complex judgments required in options (3) and (4). Assessing the participants' rationality is often impossible to do with confidence. To begin with, there is no consensus as to the rationality required for deterrence to work. Next, there are several possible ways to proceed. Maybe decision makers can act rational even if they aren't.

---

[3] Well before the missile crisis Castro incorrectly anticipated another American attack, and believed Soviet deterrence was effective, a serious mistake (Fursenko and Naftali 1997, pp. 52–70).

However, for analytical purposes this is useful only if we have a way of *specifying the rational choice independent of the actors*. Given suitable information we can then decide whether rationality applied in a case. Or maybe we can accurately grasp the real perspectives and preferences of the actors and accordingly reconstruct how they rationally behaved. Of these the first is more common because the second is almost impossible to do consistently. Rational choice usually takes actor preferences for granted, tracing them to some overriding situation or need, because social science is not very helpful on how preferences form and change. We can try to observe actor calculations but that is difficult, except perhaps in retrospect and then usually only long afterward. And there may have been hidden motivations or preferences. It can be difficult to get consensus among historians and observers in particular cases on participants' thinking, motives and preferences. A tendency to take unusual personal risks might be considered irrational unless the actor sought (as did Lord Nelson) to die acclaimed as a hero. Here are quotations (in Payne 1996) not easy to classify:

> Stalin to Mao in 1950: "If a war [with the US] is inevitable then let it be waged now" (Mansourov 1995, p. 101).
> Saddam: "You can come to Iraq with aircraft and missiles, but do not push to the point where we cease to care. And when we feel that you want to injure our pride and take away the Iraqis' chance of a high standard of living, then we will cease to care, and death will be the choice for us. Then we would not care if you fired 100 missiles for each missile we fired. Because without pride life would have no value" (Oberdorfer 1991, p. 39).
> The Japanese War Minister after the atomic bomb, calling for a last great battle: "Would it now be wondrous for this whole nation to be destroyed like a beautiful flower" (McCullough 1992, p. 459).
> General Galtieri on the Falklands War: "Though an English reaction was considered a possibility, we did not see it as a probability. Personally, I judged it scarcely possible and totally improbable ... Why should a country situated in the heart of Europe care so much for some islands located far away in the Atlantic Ocean ... which do not serve any national interest?" (Fallaci 1982, p. 4).

And it is easy to come up with plausible accounts of some puzzling behavior as rational, or find evidence of irrationality at work. "Each historical case is extremely complex, and it is often possible to construct plausible rational actor and psycho-dynamic accounts of the same events" (Tetlock 1987, p. 88).

We could just suggest preferences and see if the challenger's behavior fits them, or examine that behavior to infer what they must have been. Both are common enough but unsatisfactory. Behavior consistent with one set of hypothesized preferences may be consistent with another – if Iraq mobilizes forces along the border this could be a rational actor seeking bargaining leverage, or a rational actor planning to attack, or an irrational actor planning to attack, or...Guessing at the actor's preferences to see if its behavior fits is a problem since they could drive more than one behavior.

No wonder it is easier just to assert what a rational actor "ought" to be doing. And it seems like some conditions *should* drive state behavior or leaders' decisions – anarchy, the desire to do better or win, avoiding unnecessarily risky actions or ones with little chance of success. But what if we don't trust those judgments and want to uncover the real perspectives and preferences? We can let every analyst construct his or her version of what is rational for analyzing any particular case, but then we have analyses coexisting like parallel universes.

It is also difficult to cope with shifts in preferences. In a rational de-cision model preferences are usually fixed, but in deterrence situations they can shift. The theory focuses on threats that alter *cost* calculations, but they may shift *preferences* instead. They may help decision makers clarify their *conception of national interests* by providing data about the opponent's preferences and depth of commitment. Some interests seem vital until it looks necessary to fight for them.[4] This may affect defend-ers too. The US responded in South Korea in 1950 because the attack changed its view of Soviet intentions and in that context intervention was attractive (Roehrig 1995, pp. 114–115; Gaddis 1982). The Soviet in-vasion of Afghanistan brought an American reaction as if a commitment had been challenged, when none had been issued, because it shifted the President's view of Soviet intentions.

Hence the third option in the list; we get round these difficulties by focusing on procedural elements: assess real decision making against a model of rational decision making to see if the proper steps were fol-lowed. The trouble is that we normally treat rationality as an interplay

---

[4] On learning of this sort see Snyder and Diesing 1997; George and Smoke 1989; Freedman 1996.

of decision making and preferences, not simply procedures. Some people work out highly rational procedures for dealing with our imminent destruction in the second coming that is upon us.

Individual officials may act rationally but their interactions bring results a rational actor would avoid (Jervis 1989a). The bureaucratic politics model claims that organizations pursue their interests rationally but the national interest is often short changed. (Churchill once noted about building dreadnoughts in pre-1914 Britain that the debate was over whether to build four or six so the government compromised on eight.)

We conclude that to sort out cases for testing a theory based on rational decision making calls for analytical and empirical efforts unlikely to be fully satisfactory. Careful study of instances of deterrence at work will yield conflicting conclusions on how to classify cases, what they tell us, what the implications are. This is, in fact, what happens.

This discussion has pertained to operating on the assumption of rationality. The theory can't readily explain a failure of deterrence by citing actor irrationality either. Because it does not say deterrence won't work among irrational actors, we cannot say a failure *must* be due to any irrationality present. It is necessary to specify just what had this effect in a particular case. The theory has never been attentive to this problem; analysts have been content to note that at times irrationality is useful and let it go at that. But this makes it difficult to chuck irrelevant cases out of the population studied.

Listing cases properly also requires distinguishing a failure (or success) of deterrence from a failure to practice deterrence. Much is made of this: we want notions about deterrence tested only against cases where it was practiced. As a result all attacks are not cases of deterrence failure or of the failure of deterrence theory. This is correct, but only up to a point. Actually, a failure to practice deterrence can be, indirectly, a mark against the theory. Many surprise attacks occur between hostile actors that have had confrontations or wars before, so the victim should have been highly suspicious, should rationally have been on guard in these circumstances. Studies indicate that defender mistakes on this are due to preconceptions that discounted the possibility of attack. Thus some failures to practice deterrence suggest the absence of a mental acuity the theory assumes but governments have often failed to display.

Spotting a case is most difficult in detecting deterrence success. Here is what a success should look like. In the US–China quarrel over the Dachen Islands available materials indicate that Mao wanted to seize the islands, held off when US forces were in the area, then moved to seize them when the US–Taiwan mutual defense treaty did not mention it covered them and when US diplomatic overtures suggested the US commitment and will had declined (Chang and Di 1993). However, without such evidence nonoccurrence of an attack could be caused by many things, and since attacks are rare nonoccurrence is normal. The "challenger" may have wanted to threaten without attacking, so that threats in response had no impact. However, like detecting a deterrence failure, this is correct only up to a point. After all, general deterrence is often supposed to be present. But it is hard to be sure. The US asserts that its forces in the Far East deter destabilizing moves by its opponents and its friends, that general deterrence keeps the peace. This is counterfactual thinking because there is only limited evidence that there would be flame and ashes if US forces left – and much of it is assertions to this effect by officials who tell each other that what they think is true is true.

If it is difficult to detect successes in crises, it is even more so for general deterrence where success can leave few traces. Some argue, for instance, that deterrence does not apply to the Cold War, that neither side ever wanted to attack for reasons that had little to do with deterrence (Vasquez 1991). This is disturbing. Also, once a crisis erupts the chances for success are lower – the challenger's motivation is likely to be strong and crisis dynamics may push reluctant parties into a fight – so intermittent success in crisis situations might not tell us much about the utility of deterrence in general.

Another complication, particularly with general deterrence, is that there may be a success with no threat – the opponent reacted to a nonexistent threat. During the missile crisis American policy makers did not attack Cuba and the missiles in part for fear of a Soviet move against Berlin, but records of Soviet decision making and communications with Washington show no inclination to seize Berlin (Fursenko and Naftali 1997). Technically, this is a general deterrence success, but such cases are almost never catalogued this way. The threat was an offshoot of the *general* deterrence emanating from past Soviet actions not meant to produce deterrence but which eventually had that effect.

The difficulties don't end there. What about a case in which deterrence threats are issued but not taken seriously, seen as posturing or to express displeasure? North Korea has issued ferocious threats for years, usually dismissed not from doubts about its capabilities but as bluffs. Deterrence theory stresses the necessity for clarity in threats (at times) and for their being believable – usually in the sense of technique (how one threatens) or underlying capabilities (what one threatens with). But what if the opponent suspects a bluff and won't take the threats seriously? It's not a failure to practice deterrence, it's a failure to be seen as practicing it. Whose fault is that?

There is also a problem in picking out factors associated with successes and failures without evidence as to whether they are also present when deterrence is not involved. To look just at successes and failures risks serious selection bias (Downs 1994a; Harvey and James 1992). If cases selected are mostly or entirely attacks, because they are easiest to detect, the variation in outcomes is too limited to reliably determine the success rate of deterrence (Achen and Snidal 1989; Levy 1989a). For assessing rationality or analyzing other factors associated with success and failure it would be nice to have either all cases or confidence in the representativeness of a sample (Fischhoff 1987). In principle this can be achieved by successes and failures but it is difficult to find unambiguous successes (Lebow and Stein 1990a; Von Riekhoff 1987). The suggestion that this be fixed by drawing samples of dyads based on a "proxy" such as common borders and then computing the frequency of attack for various deterrence relationships among the hostile dyads (see Achen and Snidal 1989) is not helpful. The incidence of attack or not across a range of dyads can't confirm or disconfirm the theory unless the cases are free of the objections raised above and this procedure would not ensure that. And since the theory applies to both successes and failures the outcomes in a series of cases are not, in themselves, definitive.

Evidence on a grand scale

In assessments of whether and how deterrence works several kinds of evidence are often cited based not on detailed cases but broad features of the world deemed relevant. Bueno de Mesquita and Lalman (1992, p. 133) argue that the key to deterrence success is a high probability of retaliation. To show that deterrence works they note that in the latter half of the seventeenth century states moved to maintain standing armies drilled for war, making retaliation far more feasible and attractive. Wars in 1500–1650 were twice as frequent, and major power wars three times as frequent, as they were in 1650–1975 after those changes.

Similarly, Levy (1982) points out that in 480 years after the fifteenth century 75 percent of the great power wars occurred in the first half. Over time the severity of those wars rose, topped off by orgies of destruction in two world wars, followed by no great-power war since 1945. That suggests general deterrence at work and rationality, of sorts, responding to it. Mueller (1989) traces the end of great-power wars to the awful experience of World War II. Along the same lines all interstate wars have fallen off sharply. We have added many states, interstate wars were common in the decades after 1945, and modern weapons make it easier to push casualties over the threshold chosen to designate a war, yet the incidence of interstate wars has dropped to one or two a year recently. Maybe war's modern lethality and destructiveness are responsible. The potential costs of wars have been rising and their utility, in this sense, has been declining.

However, perhaps factors cited as applying to great powers are not responsible if the smaller states are doing almost as well at avoiding war. Or else we are burdened with parallel developments on war arising from different causes. It could also be, of course, that the decline of small wars (or, God help us, of great-power wars) is an anomaly and will soon end.

Certain theoretical perspectives explain the absence of great-power wars within a deterrence framework, often with little reference to nuclear weapons. Modelski's theory of the world system traces the great-power peace after 1945 to emergence of a global hegemonic state, as happened several times over the past 500 years (Modelski and Morgan 1985). Gilpin (1981) adds that with a hegemon there is no serious challenge, hence no great war, while its predominance is obvious, and when the hegemon fades a great war will occur again, nuclear weapons or not. Organski and Kugler (1980) find a state's predominance good for peace, while a period of transition when a dominant and an inferior state are about to trade positions is very likely to mean war – and nuclear weapons do not alter this. Charles Doran (1999) is also interested in power shifts and transitions, and explains the long peace since 1945 as due to no dangerous transition having yet taken place. The most telling response would be that the end of the Cold War was a huge system transition yet there was no war. This suggests that an end to bipolarity or the fear of a decline in relative strength and position are not sufficient conditions for war. With no war under either a rough superpower balance or the abrupt collapse of one side, nuclear deterrence looks more like the cause.

On the other hand there are complaints that the evidence shows no consistent link between power transitions, or power balances – toward equality or preponderance (discussed below). At least some game-theory analysis suggests that there should be no relationship between power transitions and outbreaks of war and that a rough equality between opponents is not an unusually dangerous situation more likely to result in war (Kim and Morrow 1992).

Other analysts cite war weariness, war wariness, and a tolerable status quo – nuclear deterrence helped but was not central. Really dissatisfied great powers – Germany and Japan – had to live within strictures imposed by the superpowers, while the others were basically status-quo orientated with no reason to war on each other. In particular, the superpowers were big winners in 1945 and had no direct territorial grievances with each other.

Of course, the alleged link between the rising cost of war and greatpower peace was and is crude. If rising lethality is responsible for war avoidance why was there ever a World War II? And after World War II why was there ever a major conventional war among *any* decently armed states? In many respects the Iran–Iraq war was a replay of World War I, down to the poison gas and primitive strategic bombing. Were they slow learners?

Maybe Cold War alliances made deterrence so effective after 1945. But compare this with data on alliances. They are often exercises in either deterrence or compellance, seeking to build up strength to deter an attack or compel a concession. But the formation of alliances is often followed by war. A review finds that: "Alliances that do not settle territorial disputes and consist solely of states that have been successful in the last war and major states have approximately an 80 percent probability of going to war" (Gibler and Vasquez 1998, p. 799). This clashes with the notion that deterrence works; various studies also find alliances negatively correlated with deterrence success. The usual explanation is that many alliances often emerge because there is a good chance of an attack – war is dead ahead. On the other hand, it is when an attack looms that we most want deterrence to work, so the fact that alliances don't help it in these situations is awkward for the theory.

Arms races end in wars a bit more than half the time (Downs and Rocke 1990), probably because, like alliances, they are often undertaken by states expecting a war. Also, while arms are accumulated for deterrence, sometimes the object is less benign. Still, deterrence is most needed if there is a good chance of an attack, so if arms races often have only a modest deterrence effect that challenges the theory.

Other sorts of evidence are cited about nuclear deterrence. It is argued that great-power behavior has shifted in the nuclear age. Since 1945 there have been no outright great-power wars – two borderline cases (US–China in Korea and Sino-Soviet border clashes in 1969) but

Table 4.1

Type of conflict	Wars	Interventions	Threats
Nuclear power vs nuclear power	0	2	4
Nuclear power vs nuclear power ally	0	6	7
Nuclear power vs nonnuclear power	2	13	8
Nonnuclear power vs nonnuclear power	17	31	10

Source: Bueno de Mesquita and Riker (1982).

no wars. And no wars among nuclear armed states – one borderline case (India–Pakistan border clashes in the 1990s) but no wars. Each nuclear power has been seriously at odds with at least one other nuclear power but with no wars.[5] Several times such a war seemed plausible but our nuclear war data base is still one. Martin van Crevald (1993) spots six crises involving nuclear threats in 1948–1958, then three in the next decade, and only two after 1969. He takes this as evidence that nuclear deterrence slowly took hold, and suggests that nuclear proliferation would therefore help quell dangerous quarrels elsewhere. Table 4.1, from Bueno de Mesquita and Riker (1982), makes the same point. Weede (1983) examined 300 conflict dyads from Cold War years and found that in the fifty-seven cases where US or Soviet nuclear deterrence applied there were no wars but where it didn't apply there had been twelve.

This evidence is suggestive. It was widely asserted at the dawn of the nuclear age that peace would not last long, yet we have no end in sight to a long period of great-power peace. Kenneth Waltz built an impressive theoretical edifice claiming that bipolarity and nuclear deterrence together had created an enormous stability, and other proponents of nuclear deterrence can readily be found. I laid out my view in chapter 1: nuclear weapons helped make the great powers far less willing to risk war. A nuclear war seemed too awful and conventional wars too likely to escalate. In particular, nuclear weapons *canceled the appeal of cheap-victory strategies*, the favorite great-power way to see war as worthwhile.

There is also a longstanding claim that nuclear weapons are not used because of a profound psychological reluctance to cross a threshold now over fifty years old. This has conflicting implications. The data on

[5] Israel and South Africa worried about possible conflicts with the Soviet Union (which took a hefty imagination).

conflicts between nuclear powers and nonnuclear powers are striking. T. V. Paul (1995) explored ten significant wars between such states where the nuclear power did not use those weapons even to stave off defeat. He believes that psychological or normative factors, a nuclear taboo, shaped their calculations. Thus nuclear weapons also offer scant political leverage since nuclear threats lack credibility. Geller studied almost 400 militarized disputes in 1946–76 and found that nuclear weapons did not prevent escalation. What does this tell us? It confirms that nuclear weapons scare the daylights out of governments, but can lead one to ask why nuclear deterrence *ever* works, except perhaps against a possible nuclear attack.

All this is far from conclusive. My argument is that nuclear deterrence just reinforced other factors and is given too much credit for the long peace. Ultimately, the question cannot be answered.

Rationality again

Since people see deterrence as based on standard conceptions of rationality, one way to test the theory has been to explore the application of that assumption.[6] This involves additional complications. We look at those first and then turn to the studies.

The complications start with designing a suitable test. Since the rational decision approach depicts the challenger as incorporating the retaliatory threat into a cost–benefit analysis, how do we follow this in real situations? Perfect information is never available about attacker perceptions and calculations, so one investigates in a roundabout fashion. Since perfect information is never available to the challenger, it does the best it can: it arrives at a "subjective expected utility of attacking" based on "subjective estimates of the expected costs of war, the probability of winning, and the estimated probability that the defender will retaliate" (Achen and Snidal 1989, p. 152). But subjective expected utility is extremely difficult to assess – perfect information not being available to analysts – so its rationality cannot be tested directly. (The deterrer normally also cannot be seen to have made the calculations.) Can it be tested indirectly?

A possibility is to derive hypotheses predicting the outcome of the confrontation, given various contingencies, and test them against the

---

[6] Informative discussions on rational choice approaches are Greene and Shapiro 1994; Halpern and Stern 1998; Simon 1985; Zey 1992; Farnham 1994; Achen and Snidal 1989; Jeffrey Friedman 1995a.

evidence. For instance, when defenders mount credible threats (in the eyes of challengers) this should boost chances of a deterrence success; where credibility is low the opposite should occur. By inferring that certain circumstances produce high deterrer credibility one can hypothesize that in these cases deterrence will usually work. In the literature such hypotheses cite the defender as possessing stronger military capabilities, or stronger local military capabilities, or having stronger interests at stake. The relevant evidence, in the presence or absence of these conditions, is the *outcome* – attack or no attack.

Is this a suitable test? Apparently not.[7] Cases in which the theory is not upheld can too readily be dismissed. When circumstances suggest the defender's threat was credible but an attack occurred maybe the attacker's "subjective utility of attacking" was not adequately captured by those circumstances. It is necessary to grasp the specific calculations behind the attack (Pearl Harbor is a favorite example). Perhaps the attacker was irrational. Then maybe the theory doesn't apply: "cases of psychopathological decision making are set aside as unsuitable for the rational actor approach" (Achen and Snidal 1989, p. 150). Here too, the outcome is insufficient. Perhaps the attacker's perception of the circumstances that supposedly made the deterrer's threat credible discounted that credibility. Again, the outcome would not be enough; one has to see how things looked to the attacker.

In view of deficiencies with looking at outcomes analysts have naturally wanted to look at *decision processes*. The indirect route is to ask how likely it is that decision makers are rational; the more direct route is to assess rationality in specific cases. Findings from the former often shape (corrupt?) the assessments made in the latter. The starting point is to look at human capacities for rationality. The findings are well known; here is a sample:[8]

(1) People are cognitive misers, employing preconceptions, heuristics, and other shortcuts to gather or process information and make decisions. They lack the time or capacity to make decisions rationally. Instead they satisfice, assessing alternatives until one seems good enough. Alternatively, they assess options

---

[7] Levy 1989a and Harvey and James 1992 review efforts to test deterrence theory this way.
[8] This discussion draws on Jervis 1976; Dawes 1998; Tetlock, McGwire and Mitchell 1991; Stern et al. 1989a; Levy 1992a, 1992b, 1996, 1999; Steinbruner 1974; Janis 1982; Mintz 1997; Vertzberger 1998; Stein and Welch 1997; Bendor and Hammond 1992; Allison and Zelikow 1999; Mintz and Geva 1997.

in terms of threshold suitability on one important value, then evaluate remaining options for suitability on a second value, and so on, concentrating on aspects of the problem they think important and shrinking searches for information and options accordingly. But they have trouble determining which aspects are important.[9]

(2) People with strong needs or facing strong pressures develop (motivated) misperceptions to see certain decisions as wise, correct, likely to work. They use defensive avoidance on unwanted information and views or pass them to others to handle or procrastinate with; they bolster – gathering further information to make their decisions look correct.

(3) People frequently don't update choices, in light of new information, on the likelihood of various outcomes. They become attached to their views and choice of means and resist negative evidence. They use selective attention and recall to avoid serious tests of their views; unknowingly bend information to fit existing beliefs; and subject negative information to much stronger tests for relevance, accuracy, and source reliability.

(4) People are overconfident about the accuracy and reliability of their views and judgments; they overestimate their ability to read subtle clues about reality.

(5) People display the fundamental attribution error – they are forced by circumstances to act as they do but others are acting out their natures or desires, particularly when doing unacceptable things.

(6) People are preoccupied with their own concerns and plans and interpret developments in terms of their current preoccupations; they overestimate their impact on others and the degree to which others are acting with them in mind.

(7) People err in metaphorical-allegorical reasoning, selecting metaphors or allegories unsystematically, often simplifying for ease of application. They focus on obvious similarities – the representativeness heuristic – ignoring important differences from the case at hand in detecting comparisons that fit or reinforce their views (their preconceptions drive the lessons derived).

---

[9] This is "bounded rationality." There is debate as to whether it is rational – doing one's best in the circumstances – or not because results fall short of what rationality should produce.

People are insensitive to the prior probability of the outcomes they draw on for lessons, to problems of sample size, and to the role of chance.

(8) People learn from the past mainly through politically or emotionally powerful events – the more vivid the better – especially from sensitive successes and failures.

(9) People have multiple goals and values, and thus multiple utility functions, making rational calculations of utility very difficult. They avoid value tradeoffs. They do not maintain a consistent sense of the relative importance of their values and goals.

(10) People treat losses as more important than gains of equal or greater value, going to greater lengths to make up losses, so their decisions differ depending on whether a problem is framed as a loss or gain. They quickly absorb new gains, so giving them up becomes a loss.

(11) People overestimate the probabilities of good things happening and underestimate the probabilities of unwanted outcomes.

(12) People are excessively impressed with specific examples, hard evidence, hard measures, unduly learning from direct experience or things most readily remembered.

(13) People can experience a decline in their decision making under high stress, becoming more black and white in their thinking; their cognitive complexity declines.

(14) People are influenced by social factors, morality, emotions, social structures, and concern about social harmony in making decisions – at the expense of utility maximization. They often adjust to others' decision strategies, even shifting their preferences. They are vulnerable to group pathologies when confronting tough decisions that carry serious consequences – leading to steps that increase detachment from reality.

(15) People fall into grooved thinking in organizations; they handle information, decisions and actions via standard operating procedures that are often outdated, inhibit learning, inhibit the ability of learning at one level to reach other levels.

(16) People adopt or agree to reflect the perspectives of their organizations. Information is manipulated to suit the organization's interests, and suppressed if harmful even if relevant for good decisions. Supporting those interests trumps accuracy, integrity, competence.

(17) People in different parts of organizations have different perspectives and conclusions so a collective decision takes bargaining and compromise; rational decisions and actions at one level often generate an irrational decision or action overall.

It would seem that people are not intrinsically very rational. Evidence suggests that this is often beneficial, that without these limitations and inclinations people find it harder to perceive and decide, and are more likely to be paralyzed by indecision. Thorough rationality could be unhealthy at times. Often great accomplishments come from being so attached to winning/achieving that great pain and costs are acceptable as long as success is achieved – a true calculation of costs and benefits is not done.

There are responses. Rationality oriented theorists argue that satisficing, incrementalism, decision heuristics, and other "departures" from rationality merely reflect the fact that decisions have cognitive costs – tradeoffs between the best decision and the need to decide and act is a rational way to proceed. Some analysts suggest that people may value spontaneity, forgoing cognitive effort in order to have it – though this comes perilously close to dissolving the concept of rationality. It has been suggested that since people know they can be irrational they sometimes restrict their freedom of choice so as to thwart temptations, which is rational (Elster 1979).

Another reaction is that decisions are part of a context, that seeing the context helps us appreciate a puzzling decision as rational after all. It is also possible to construe several findings on irrational behavior in rational decision terms since it reflects deeply rooted preferences that can be modeled. Then there are claims that people are rational. In a few studies of crises (Moaz 1981; Stein and Tanter 1980) the decision making is depicted this way, fitting the old notion that crises or other stresses tend to stimulate greater rationality. Decision makers may not look rational but they are, almost automatically, and even their own comments are not a good guide to this. Instead of claiming this, often the preferred response (sometimes labeled the concept of a "thin" rationality) is that the objective is not to describe the decision process but to construct a theory that accurately anticipates outcomes. (But how can a decision process that seems somewhat irrational nevertheless produce the expected decisions?)

Finally, it is not certain that defects in the rationality of individuals or groups apply consistently to governments. The pulling and hauling of intragovernmental and intrasocietal political processes, plus the vast experience and expertise in bureaucracies, may wash out the impact of departures from rationality. Perhaps people who rise to the top do so because of unusual capacities; they surmount stress and handle ambiguity and, through self-selection or political-administrative approval, are better adapted to making decisions in a rational fashion than most of us. Maybe over time bureaucratic SOPs reflect rationality reasonably well because of accumulated experience. Perhaps most decisions are made within serious constraints – international and domestic – that have a rationalizing impact, leaving motives to be of little consequence.

> [s]tatesmen do not usually act mainly because of motives, aims, and influences, even when they think they do... The statesman is acting within, and reacting to, a situation over which he has little or no control, playing a game in which fairly elemental rules and strategy largely dictate what he can and must do. The best practitioners of statecraft have always recognized that opportunities, capabilities, contingencies, and necessities take precedence over motives and intentions.
>
> (Schroeder 1972, pp. xiv–xv)

Maybe this is particularly true of deterrence situations, involving as they do matters of great importance with high stakes. Perhaps they evoke the best in decision making and constrain irrationality to an exceptional degree. The polluting effects of domestic politics may also be largely eliminated. So it is not enough to suggest ways decisions can be made that violate rational decision models. We must ask what patterns are found in cases of deterrence or related foreign policy decision making. Do governments behave rationally in deterrence matters or not?

According to many case studies and other available information they do not. Rational deterrence theory does poorly in describing behavior in many situations, including confrontations. Its partisans display uneven interest in description; sometimes they claim that proper descriptions would fit with the theory, sometimes that descriptions will fit the theory only in a limited way. Case studies of deterrence decision making constitute the leading alternative to rational decision approaches. Sometimes called a second variant of deterrence theory or strategy (Stein 1991), this is really a critique instead.

Are states vulnerable to the same deficiencies?

These studies find officials, and governments viewed as unitary actors, displaying the nonrational patterns summarized above. The defects appear in perception and learning, decision making, the implementation of choices, and assessments of how their decisions are working. Studies of organizations find that they regularly make decisions in ways that don't fit with a rational decision maker model. Jervis (1976) depicts foreign policy makers regularly displaying faulty cognitive patterns. He focused particularly on the coping mechanisms officials use to seek out information that confirms their views and resist information that does not, or how readily they take the state as a central referent of outsiders' actions. Officials often lack empathy, unable to see the world and themselves as their opponents do (Garthoff 1991).

Reiter (1996), studying alliances, finds decision makers and bureaucracies biased by past experiences, particularly high-impact events or prior successes and failures. Their tendency to be cognitive misers leads to clustering information in schemas, particularly analogies, and making heavy use of judgmental heuristics that provide short cuts to decisions but with loss of accuracy. Commonly utilized is a representativeness heuristic in which they use a superficial similarity to detect a helpful analogy, which often turns out to be irrelevant for later conclusions drawn by referring to it. (The Holocaust dominates Israeli thinking, the Korean War shaped decisions to escalate in Vietnam.) States learn best from their own experience, one reason why their leaders learn badly from history (May and Neustadt 1986).

Studies of crises long held that high stress readily distorts decision making. Holsti summarizes the findings: in crises officials are likely to lose cognitive complexity, to shrink the range of perceived alternatives, to feel unnecessarily limits on the time to decide. They are not at their best. Richardson's (1994) case studies of great-power crises find that even if governments conform to procedural rationality in decisions, misperceptions abound.

But there are strong criticisms of this view. Brecher and Wilkenfeld (1997), plus others, reach quite different conclusions! Decision makers typically approach a crisis by seeking much more information than otherwise and doing a more comprehensive analysis of alternatives. Analogies are used with caution. The mistakes made are avoidable, not driven by crisis itself (Herek, Janis and Huth 1987). As might be expected, these views have their critics (Welch 1989), who dispute the interpretations of the historical record and are in turn attacked by authors of the earlier studies (Herek, Janis and Huth 1990). The later studies of the missile crisis (discussed below) call the Herek et al. analysis into question.

Do states display the same deficiencies in deterrence situations?

On the whole the answer is yes – they do not consistently rise to exceptional decision making in serious crises, nor in broader interactions during conflicts like the Cold War. Wohlforth (1999) found evidence from the former communist bloc that

> appears to lend strong support to the contention that real decision makers do not think like deterrence theorists, and it surely will be used to buttress the case of scholars who are skeptical of rational choice approaches. So far as we are able to reconstruct the strategic preferences of Soviet leaders during tense Cold War crises or in key decisions concerning the arms race, the preferences appear utterly inexplicable in terms of influential models. Khrushchev's diplomacy is particularly paradoxical. Even if his missile deception had been successful, there is still no rational explanation . . . for his conviction that a nuclear stalemate somehow conferred a special bluffing advantage on him.
>
> (pp. 53–54)

Soviet deficiencies appeared in intelligence analysis, the intellectual caliber of the leaders, and inclinations toward snap decisions without careful cost–benefit analyses.

Gaddis (1997) agrees. Going over the new evidence he sees the Cold War in Asia initiated from excess emotion on both sides, including ideological euphoria in Moscow and Beijing. Mao in particular saw the US as much more hostile than it was, and acted on a strong desire to strike a heroic anti-US pose for China. After Sputnik, Khrushchev had wild mood swings, acted often on impulse, and was swayed by feelings of power the missiles conferred.

Lebovic (1990) found that decision makers dealing with Cold War deterrence displayed serious limitations. They were vague about goals and inconsistent in ranking them. Unmotivated bias appeared in how they dealt with the military balance or military capabilities; they overemphasized the concrete, using overly simple measures of the "balance" of power or how deterrence works. "Policymakers and policy analysts are enticed by what can more easily be measured, understood, and predicted" (p. 30). They gave excessive attention to measures best for selling policies politically. Policy analysts then treated the psychological impact of these simple, concrete measures as more important than careful analysis – it was not what was true but what people felt was true that mattered.

One critical study hits close to home. DeNardo (1995) used questionnaires to probe people's conceptions of deterrence and how it works and got puzzling results. He could explain the opinions of nonexperts if he assumed that standard sorts of heuristics shaped their views, heuristics as to what weapons are good or bad and whether security comes from "superiority" or "symmetry" in military capabilities. But he was surprised when *experts on security*, very familiar with deterrence thinking, assessed deterrence the same way: "strategic expertise appears to have little effect on the intuitive, ideologically laden conceptions of deterrence that already appear in novices with no formal training at all" (p. 227). Some experts were so attached to deterrence by symmetry they endorsed symmetry in destabilizing weapons. Ouch! Perhaps US strategy reflected the fluctuating strength of domestic factions holding competing intuitive conceptions, and not external events or deterrence logic.

Descriptions of how deterrence situations go have been largely the work of critics of deterrence theory (or tend to confirm their conclusions), and strongly suggest that cognitive and other deficiencies are widespread. Khong (1992) provides elaborate evidence from US involvement in Vietnam of policy makers dominated by analogies that often were inappropriate but widely used.

Zhang (1992) writes that the dangerous US–China confrontations in 1949–58 were afflicted by "culture-bound perceptions of and behavior by each country" which "confused important aspects of their strategic thinking" (p. 271). Neither properly understood the other's conception of its interests or its threat perception. Reviewing China's intervention in the Korean War, Jian Chen (1994, pp. 213, 216) writes of "two sides interacting with little understanding of each other's rationales." China "encountered an America that was not in a position to understand either the rationale or the mentality galvanizing Mao and the CCP leadership." The Americans were handicapped because China's actions reflected an "inner logic" and were not reactions to US policy. Whiting concluded years ago that Chinese deterrence in a series of cases reflected little learning over time – they made roughly the same mistakes trying to deter India in the late 1950s as they did with the US on Korea in 1950, and later in dealing with Vietnam. Steve Chan (1978) reached similar conclusions.

Perhaps the earliest case study of deterrence per se was Russett's (1967) examination of Pearl Harbor. It pointed out how a government could attack an obviously more powerful country if it was so disturbed about how things were going that war looked like the best of its bad options. Under these circumstances Russett saw Japan's decision as rational. However, it has also been treated as a case of deadly motivated biases that crafted a devastatingly incorrect choice.

Lebow and Stein provide the most extensive case study analysis on deterrence situations (Lebow 1981; Lebow and Stein 1994, 1995). They believe a challenge usually emerges due to important pressures the challenger faces, perhaps from the international, particularly strategic, situation, but often domestically. Political threats to the regime can provoke a strong, even desperate, motivation. Sometimes deterrence measures exacerbate this: the challenger must offset the political criticism at home (or among allies) which the deterrer's moves promote. It searches for ways to ease the pressures, rebuff critics, and shore up the government's political situation, and comes on one that involves a risky challenge – it "finds" an opportunity. In adopting it, the challenger is preoccupied with how it will solve *its own problems*; little attention is paid to the likely consequences and how others, particularly the defender, will respond. Motivated biases are at work, and the challenger tends to ignore or rationalize important tradeoffs.

Once the challenger is committed, there are powerful psychological pressures to conclude that the chosen option will work. If information indicates it won't succeed, the defender will fight, the costs will be too high, the challenger engages in wishful thinking (the deterrer will acquiesce), defensive avoidance, or a biased assessment of the information. Meanwhile the defender assumes the challenger is reacting largely to information from outside, misunderstands and underestimates the challenger's motivation, and therefore overestimates how likely deterrence is to work.

In the crisis the actors face political and cultural barriers to empathy, plus cognitive shortcomings – various heuristics that distort perception and judgment. As a result there are common failings in deterrence/ compellance situations:

> no internally consistent set of objectives, ordered in terms of importance;
> the availability heuristic produces reliance on readily available, familiar conceptions;
> the representativeness heuristic exaggerates similarities with past events;
> egocentric bias incites misinterpretions of the other's behavior;
> overconfidence flourishes on whether officials know what they are doing and what will work;

the proportionality bias leads to misjudging the opponent's intentions from the effort it makes;

the fundamental attribution error has each ascribing unwanted behavior by the other to its intent or disposition (and not the fix it is in);

each sees the other as more centrally run, coherent, and calculating than it is – when something happens it is for a reason.

> These departures from rational norms lead to the misperception of intentions, commitment, resolve, or values, and to major errors in the cost–benefit, calculations required by deterrence. These kinds of errors and biases occur with sufficient magnitude and severity in cases of deterrence failure to challenge the assumption of rationality so central to theories of deterrence. (Lebow and Stein 1987, p. 166)

The ultimate Lebow–Stein investigation (1994) is of the Cuban missile crisis and superpower involvement in the October 1973 War. They find that Khrushchev felt a strong need to send the missiles out of fear the US would soon attack Cuba, resentment at US missiles in Turkey, domestic pressures, and concern for the strategic balance. The US had shored up its general deterrence unwisely – using a huge missile buildup and military planning of a possible invasion of Cuba. This led to a rising missile gap plus Soviet (and Cuban) fears of an attack. (The missile buildup had been provoked, in turn, by Khrushchev's efforts to exploit Sputnik and Western fears of a missile gap: boasting about missiles he did not have, putting pressure on Berlin. These were equally unwise moves.) The US did not appreciate how threatening its actions looked. In responding, Khrushchev displayed inconsistent preferences, leading to tradeoffs he never faced up to – he selected an option that gravely threatened his other important values. Once committed he engaged in wishful thinking: the missiles could remain secret (the chance of exposure was objectively quite high), the US would acquiesce (contrary to all its recent statements). He did not consult closely with specialists on the US in Moscow or the Washington embassy. All this reflected his emotional, compulsive nature. "Khrushchev's behavior bore little relationship to the expectation of rational decision making that lies at the core of deterrence theory and strategy" (p. 93).

Meanwhile, Kennedy and others were overly preoccupied with looking suitably committed. Hence they assumed their clear threats, to deter any sending of missiles to Cuba, would not be challenged. It did not occur to anyone that if Khrushchev did not question Kennedy's resolve he could still be motivated to challenge that commitment. Concern for resolve continued to drive US policy during the crisis and almost led to harsher steps than necessary. The immense stress affected the participants, but it eventually got each leader to better appreciate the other's motivations and become more flexible so as to resolve the problem.

In 1973, the American, Soviet and Israeli governments ignored mounting evidence of the intense pressures Sadat faced, his growing desperation over his domestic political situation. All three were pursuing policies comfortable with the status quo; the difficult task of moving toward peace was bypassed. Each pursued unilateral interests even after the fighting broke out and this led to missing early opportunities to stop it. Kissinger, for example, was preoccupied with the American image for resolve which meant showing no early willingness to compromise. There were motivated and cognitive biases at work.

> Leaders on both sides badly underestimated the risks of the strategies they chose. The explanation lies partly in well-documented psychological processes people use when they confront painful choices. Leaders denied the adverse consequences of their choices. They persuaded themselves that there was no contradiction between their pursuit of competitive advantage and crisis prevention. At times, Nixon and Kissinger also convinced themselves that there was no alternative to the strategy they preferred. (Lebow and Stein 1994, p. 223)

The US then staged a confrontation and employed deterrence unnecessarily, taking risks without justification including a dangerous naval interaction in the eastern Mediterranean in which nuclear armed ships on hair trigger alert were tracking each other.

Other recent studies of the missile crisis, and tapes Kennedy made of important White House meetings, support this (Fursenko and Naftali 1997; Blight 1992; Blight and Welch 1998). US leaders had an inadequate grasp of Khrushchev's motives. They worried greatly about how actions that would kill even a few Russians could provoke escalation. The Russians, meanwhile, worried about Castro, who had no qualms about starting a nuclear war and pressed for actions that would have made war more likely. The initial instructions to Soviet forces in Cuba were to use their tactical nuclear weapons to resist an American invasion with no prior approval! Eventually it dawned on Moscow that this was terribly dangerous and the instructions were withdrawn. The Americans, meanwhile, did not know about those weapons until well into the crisis, yet after they were spotted invasion plans went forward.

Blight and Welch (1998) focus on the misuse of information. Castro's intelligence people believed, correctly, that the US was not planning to invade but Castro dismissed this – he expected an attack and therefore sought the missiles and other Soviet assistance. During the crisis they feared Cuba would become a great-power pawn but this assessment could not be sent to Castro because he disagreed so strongly. Khrushchev ignored significant value tradeoffs in sending the missiles, perhaps due to a strong desire to avoid losing Cuba, as prospect theory suggests. Fischer (1998) concludes that the leaders were more prone to motivated biases than their intelligence people. Blight and Welch summarize:

> We have studied ... with a profound sense of wonderment that the world managed to escape disaster in 1962, because of the depth and extent of the mistakes and misunderstandings on all sides, and because of the bloomin', buzzin' confusion both within and between all three countries.
> (p. 13)

Each crisis offered numerous signs that accidents happen, that subordinates or allies could provoke a loss of control. Soviet generals shot down the U-2 without permission, the head of SAC went to DEFCON II in the clear and without permission, the US Navy resisted taking direction from civilians in running the blockade; the Soviet government initially left using nuclear weapons at the local commanders' discretion; British air forces were put on a higher alert than authorized; the hair-trigger naval situation in the Mediterranean in 1973 was extremely dangerous; the US leapt into that confrontation unnecessarily; etc.

Lebow and Stein conclude that a strict deterrence approach results in:

> insensitivity to need-driven challenges, and thus improper responses to them;
>
> an exaggeration of threats by seeing others motivated by disposition, not circumstances;
>
> the proportionality bias – the opponent risked a lot so must have big gains in mind;
>
> fear that if deterrence fails, bolstering one's image is even more important;
>
> fatigue and stress producing defensive avoidance, procrastination, bolstering and a tendency toward overly rigid public commitments;
>
> all of which present serious problems in retaining control.

Thus studies find that standard errors in perception and judgment afflict decision makers, errors responsible at times for the emergence of a crisis, for incorrect or inadequate application of deterrence, for incorrect or inadequate responses to deterrence threats, for failures of deterrence, and for inadequate responses to them. Decision makers often fail to calculate relevant military balances, carefully assess how the opponent sees the situation and ascertain its preferences, try to determine how committed it is (Stein 1991). Studies of strategic surprise find that governments often fail to see an attack coming even from a longtime enemy, don't press deterrence strongly enough – often out of fear of being provocative – and believe mistakenly that the alternative strategy they are using – conciliation, negotiations, scrupulous neutrality – will work despite mounting evidence to the contrary (Knorr and Morgan 1983). Governments are often driven to taking irrational actions to sustain credibility (Morgan 1985; Hopf 1994; Mercer 1996), despite evidence that this is unnecessary.

Top decision makers rarely understand the military preparations made to deal with crises, resulting in force postures unsuitable for deterrence situations (destabilizing, or not fitting the situation). Analysts have found numerous instances in which careful control from the top was violated by the organizations responsible for nuclear weapons, such as by unauthorized alerts in deterrence situations, and which would have been responsible for carrying out orders for a nuclear war (Sagan 1994). Organizations with deterrence responsibilities are dominated by SOPs. The Soviet deployment of missiles in Cuba followed organizational routines that made them easier for the US to spot. For years SAC planes had a switch to set so that if a B-52 crew was killed the nuclear weapons would be automatically released when the plane went below 20,000 feet, hardly suitable for fighting a controlled war to avoid escalation (Sagan 1994, pp. 131–133). Organizational arrangements can break down and organizations then hide deficiencies, adopt their own versions of crisis response, and have objectives that may clash with leaders' goals in crises (Sagan 1994; Bracken 1999). Out of domestic and other considerations governments often purchase and deploy weapons and forces in ways harmful to effective deterrence.

In terms of what seems to work and how things go in crises there are a variety of studies. In the missile crisis and in 1973 leaders saw themselves as defenders having the most at stake, entitled to not back down. The crises were settled not because of the credibility of the threats issued, but because they drove home to leaders the particular interests at stake and the strength of the motivations involved. Policymakers had to retreat from strictly deterrence thinking to understand the other side better.

Yair Evron (1994) surveys Israel's experience with deterrence and concludes that it was unsuccessful until the mid-1970s in trying to prevent terrorism, that it failed in 1967 when Egypt went beyond an Israeli threshold (by reoccupying the Sinai) in trying to deter Israel from attacking Syria and then escalated its objectives in the euphoria of the moment, and that deterrence might have worked in 1973 if Israel had better appreciated the political situation in key Arab countries. Deterrence failed even though Israel was militarily superior, its resolve was clear, and it communicated threats clearly. The failures arose out of Arab domestic political pressures and the impact of crisis on Arab decision making. Israel's nuclear weapons had little relevance right up through the Gulf War.

Shai Feldman (1994a) stresses that Israeli deterrence has rested not on defense or countervalue retaliation but on the threat to win the next war (though this seems incorrect for its attempts to deal with terrorism). In the Gulf War, however, threatening Iraq did not work since Saddam *wanted* Israel's retaliation to widen the war, capitalizing on Israeli resolve. Feldman thinks deterrence did work in confining Iraq's attacks to conventional weapons.

Richard Betts' (1987) study of American nuclear threats in Cold War crises finds that decision makers consistently felt strong internal political pressures to challenge and threaten, but did not carefully calculate the possible costs and whether they were rationally worth it. Instead "the people at the top sometimes appeared to grit their teeth, close their eyes, and forge ahead." In the Cuban missile crisis:

> In terms of risk-minimizing standards for decisionmaking on war and peace, the reality appears frightening: U.S. leaders felt required to take what they saw as a high risk of nuclear war without examining how it would be undertaken or waged to advantage and without confidence that the consequences could be "acceptable." (p. 118)

Trachtenberg (1985) agrees with Lebow and Stein that in the crisis the specific strategic nuclear balance made little difference. American and Soviet leaders simply knew the other side could inflict disastrous consequences, and were moved greatly by fear of escalation.

In terms of how deterrence works, the most striking things about the missile crisis are the following. First, nuclear deterrence did not work in a strictly existential fashion. True, it did instill great fear and caution in the end, fear of nuclear war even in Washington despite vast American superiority in nuclear weapons – the Russians had "enough" and that was what mattered. There were grave fears on both sides about killing even a few Russians or Americans – fear that a provocation could readily set off an irrational escalatory spiral. But Soviet deterrence did not prevent the blockade, and the Americans were prepared to invade Cuba even though some of the missiles were ready to fire and despite the risk of a Soviet riposte against Turkey or a new Berlin crisis. Willingness to attack extended to the nearly half of the Executive Committee of the President (ExCom) that preferred an air strike to the blockade, to Senator Fulbright, and former President Eisenhower. The Joint Chiefs were more eager to attack Cuba than ExCom members, much more so than the President. It is amazing that the Russians prepared to defend the island with tactical nuclear weapons – the armed forces were more eager on this score than Presidium members. And Soviet military officers in Cuba were quite willing to attack US overflights. Finally, Castro seems to have been prepared to accept war as an outcome. That so many of those involved were ready to enter into a probable nuclear war clashes with the notion of existential nuclear deterrence.

Even great deterrence/compellance successes are suspect. Hybel (1993) describes the US decisions initiating the Gulf War as bordering on groupthink. Top officials for months overrode rising uneasiness among others about Saddam; thus they were badly surprised when he attacked Kuwait. Then Bush and presidential Assistant for National Security Brent Scowcroft agreed to force Iraq out without consultation with experts or careful consideration of others' views (as Truman and Acheson did in deciding to enter the Korean War). They did so on the basis of the Munich and Vietnam analogies. (Hybel finds schema and attribution theory best at capturing this decision process.) Others opposed war, wanting further use of sanctions instead, but were "unwilling to put their political prestige on the line by advocating a policy they knew the president did not favor." Meetings were run after preliminary indications from Scowcroft (speaking for Bush) or Bush on how the situation should be defined and assessed, sharply curbing discussion.

An evaluation

What shall we make of this? The case study evidence is widely cited in attacks on deterrence theory and deterrence policies. It certainly can't be neglected. Much of the work is detailed. Many of the findings reinforce each other. Can decision makers learn to avoid mistakes of the sort described and do better? Sometimes they do, and there are suggestions about how they can, but success in overcoming cognitive biases, heuristics, etc. is very uneven (Fischhoff 1991) and officials often learn badly from history. Yet analysts have not abandoned deterrence theory and governments have not abandoned deterrence.

One difficulty in findings of decision-maker irrationality is that detecting the irrational requires a clear conception of the rational: a model of rational behavior; clear indications how that would apply to a particular actor in a particular situation; and clear evidence that the actor did not fit the model. But this means using an independent basis for judging rationality or detecting the preferences and perceptions of the actor, and both are hard to do. This makes it difficult to know how often irrational behavior exists; perhaps the case studies have a severe selection bias. If rational decision making usually applies it might still be the proper basis for theory. Here the difficulty in testing deterrence theory via its failures is disturbing since failures seem easier to detect.

There are other deficiencies in the application of cognitive models. Lebow and Stein (1987) once elaborated them effectively. There are both cognitive and motivational factors at work, but they aren't closely and systematically linked in these models. There are numerous cognitive biases or heuristics at work but it is not specified as to just when each applies or how they relate to each other and, when they diverge, which one dominates. It's not clear whether they vary in relevance depending on the circumstances and if so in what fashion. It's not clear whether lab findings apply consistently or only occasionally to the behavior of governments, particularly of experts or experienced officials.

The case study literature has not been well designed to generate an alternate theory of deterrence. The findings critical of deterrence theory "neither individually nor collectively … lead to law-like generalizations, even highly contingent ones" (Stein and Welch 1997, p. 62). Nevertheless they offer suggestive conclusions:[10]

(1) Deterrence is most appropriate when the challenger is motivated primarily by prospective gains and not fear of losses, has freedom to exercise restraint, is not misled by gross misperceptions, and is clearly vulnerable to the deterrer's threat. It is most vulnerable when the challenger acts out of vulnerability at home

---

[10] Sources: Stein and Welch 1997; Lebow and Stein 1990a, 1994.

or adverse military trends internationally because deterrence can readily cancel prospects of gain but does nothing to fulfill a real challenger need. Deterrence is best when the challenger is just after a gain, probing instead of already decided, has limited intensity, and worries about the domestic costs if things don't go well. (In principle, this could be accommodated in a rational decision approach since the preferences could be modeled – though generating the required information for analysis or strategy would be onerous.)

(2) The strength of the challenger's sense of injury, desperation, or other motivation is very important in determining deterrence success or failure – no absolute level of retaliatory threat guarantees success. (This can fit within some rational approaches.)

(3) Thus strong commitment by the deterrer, and a reputation for resolve, can be important if absent but are no guarantee of success if present. (This can also fit in rational decision approaches.)

(4) Deterrence is more likely to work when tried early, before the challenger is strongly committed to challenge or attack. (This fits poorly with a rationality assumption – it implies that deciding to attack creates psychological and political barriers to contrary evidence this is wrong.)

(5) Overall military superiority is not vital for deterrence success, at least not in crises involving nuclear powers. (Easily included in a rational theory since deterrence rests on a capacity to inflict unacceptable damage.)

(6) Deterrence is more likely to work when accompanied by rewards or reassurances, particularly if the challenge is need driven; an opportunity-driven challenger may treat rewards as weakness to be exploited. (A version of manipulating the challenger's cost–benefit calculations.)

(7) Deterrence is more likely to fail if both parties feel aggrieved, see themselves as defenders – especially of important national interests. (A poor fit with a rational decision model, since the perceptions may reflect biases, but not impossible – a balance in terms of unacceptable damage should work no matter what role the parties feel they are playing; seeing oneself as "defender" merely raises the threatened level of damage required.)

(8) Deterrence threats raise a diffuse fear – leaders don't carefully assess possible war scenarios. Thus deterrence can be relatively

robust when both parties are known to be afraid of a war, even with military imbalance.[11]

(9)   Deterrence is more likely to work when the challenger is not seeking to redress losses. (This fits uneasily within rational deterrence.)

The generalizations do not amount to an alternate theory. In many cases they could be encompassed within an emphasis on rationality in the existing theory. That's not saying much since the existing theory reflects the defects many critics cite about rational choice theories in general. It is also difficult to test since it is so fluid – what is rational keeps changing, or the assumption of rationality is not meant to apply to real actors.[12]

We have been examining studies, mostly attacks, on the theory that disparage the assumption of rational actors. As suggested in chapter 1, this is not fully satisfactory. It trashes the assumption of rationality as accurate with respect to decision makers. Depending on whether that assumption is for theoretical purposes only or is taken as a reasonable approximation of reality, the attack severely damages deterrence theory. But there is a flaw in that deterrence, in concept and in theory, does not need rationality. Rationality was assumed to initiate theory building but has often been abandoned as a way to explain how deterrence works. Policy makers seem to stop short of assuming rationality, even doubt their own at times. Thus the attack does not destroy the concept of deterrence or the strategy. It does, however, make things nasty for those who think rationality is common in decision making – this seems increasingly untenable. It challenges the notion that this is a good basis on which to build a theory. As noted in chapter 2, proponents of this view should explain why the assumption is suitable for constructing a theory about reality, particularly as the theory is to be used in foreign policy. How do we explain that the rationality of actors is important for

---

[11] On the most dangerous great-power confrontation after the missile crisis, Karl (1995) concluded that nuclear deterrence was robust, that the Chinese eventually gave way due to Soviet threats, and that "the nuclear dimension the Soviets then introduced . . . rested primarily on exploiting the fear of the unknown . . ." (p. 47).

[12] "Attempts to modify equilibrium analysis in rational choice theories have been largely comic: if we find people are ignorant, then ignorance is optimally rational given the costs of information; if we find that people are impulsive and passionate, then passion and impulse are optimally rational, given the costs of deliberation; if we find that people act out of habit, then habits are optimal decision strategies, given the costs of thought, and so on" (Murphy 1995, p. 172).

figuring out how they will behave, and then that whether they are rational is irrelevant to how they behave? Finally, the attack questions the enterprise of constructing a relatively simple but very powerful theory based on rationality – that seems unlikely to turn out well.

Doing it by the numbers

Deterrence has also been studied by aggregating data from many instances, as opposed to intensive analysis of specific cases. This is a tricky undertaking. Identifying and classifying cases is complex and sometimes controversial. Undaunted, numerous analysts have tried to statistically profile deterrence situations.[13]

Jack Levy (1989a) drew on his data on great-power wars to explore several questions related to deterrence. He suggests that the expected utility of a war, shaped by the strength of the motivation to start it, is of greater influence than the military balance, and thus deterrence failures are best traced to an imbalance of resolve, not power. While measuring this is difficult, Levy finds that in sixty-five of seventy-six wars since 1815 (86 percent), the challenger had a positive or zero expected utility in fighting. He believes that nuclear deterrence works (by confronting states with terrific potential damage) and therefore a nuclear war can probably occur only if a state sees that as unavoidable and, particularly, thinks it will suffer less by attacking first.

Betts (1987) studied twelve US crises during the Cold War. He finds that American decision makers were not clear-headed or consistent. They did no careful analyses of what a nuclear war might mean, yet offered threats that risked nuclear war. They seemed to draw comfort at times from US nuclear superiority but did not lean heavily on this in resolving crises; they continued to feel vulnerable to unacceptable damage. Strength of motivation had much to do with determining outcomes, and he notes that if advantage in the balance of motivation normally goes to the defender it is very awkward that governments often feel like defenders no matter what outside observers think. He notes how, by the late 1970s, the American concern was less with the nuclear balance than with how it was *perceived* – whether it would convey an *image* of weakness.

---

[13] A few studies not mentioned here are summarized in Levy 1989a; Harvey and James 1992; and particularly Harvey 1997a.

Lebow (1987a) explored a series of wars and crises since 1898. In most, the conditions usually cited as making for deterrence success seemed present but deterrence failed anyway. He concluded that the major factor was not the military balance or the capacity of the deterrer to do serious harm, nor the credibility and clarity of its threats. It was the degree to which the challenger felt driven to attack, and cognitive biases that made it convincing that the challenge would be successful – the deterrer would back down or lose.

Much empirical analysis of deterrence has been conducted by Bruce Russett and Paul Huth. Russett (1963) initiated this with seventeen crises of extended deterrence, six identified as successes and eleven as failures (an attack occurred). The major finding traced success to the deterrer having a credible commitment as demonstrated by its elaborate ties with the friend or ally it was trying to protect in the form of significant trade links and arms sales. In short, for credibility it was necessary to go beyond a formal commitment. But the study made no provision for states just threatening an attack as a bluff to see what they could get (since they had no intention of attacking a "success" is spurious), or for a deterrence threat being credible but not painful enough so that a deterrence failure confirms the theory (see Fink 1965).

In 1984 Huth and Russett examined fifty-four cases (in the twentieth century) of extended immediate deterrence situations, looking to see whether an attack occurred, or the challenger gained its political goals, or occupied the target state's territory for some period. It assumed that actors operated on the basis of an expected-utility model. They found deterrence successful in thirty-one cases, or 57 percent. Testing a wide variety of hypotheses from the literature or a logical analysis, they developed a model incorporating various factors that matched 78 percent of the outcomes. The local military balance was important (challengers apparently are looking for a cheap victory or a fait accompli), but not the larger strategic balance between challenger and deterrer. They could find no impact of nuclear weapons, nor of a formal alliance – neither made deterrence more likely to be successful. But they reaffirmed Russett's earlier finding that substantial economic ties and political ties (in the form of arms sales) between deterrer and client makes deterrence much more effective. And the deterrer is more likely to fight not only when these ties exist but when the protégé's military strength (which could be lost by not defending it) is substantial. Dismissing claims about the interdependence of commitments and the importance of reputation, they found the defender's past behavior in crises did not matter in achieving a success.

This study provoked several complaints. One was that they had made the same mistake as Russett's earlier study in assuming that a failure is evidence of lack of credibility and in using measures of credibility that might not be warranted (Harvey and James 1992). Lebow and Stein (1990a) charged that if the cases were correctly classified only nine of the fifty-four were legitimate examples of extended immediate deterrence – that thirty-seven were not, four were examples of compellance, and four were hard to classify.

Russett (1987) had offered a preliminary defense in assessing findings on fifty-eight cases of extended immediate deterrence. He said again that the primary military factor was the local conventional balance, that the overall strategic balance or the deterrer's nuclear weapons were not important. He agreed with Lebow and Stein that challenges often arise from domestic political pressures, which affects the likelihood of deterrence success, but added that the cases displayed few irrational leaders. He linked successful deterrence to the proper use of rewards or reassurance as well, though "To understand and act upon the incentives facing one's adversary, and to achieve the proper balance between threat and reassurance, is extraordinarily difficult, especially for the national decision maker in time of crisis" (p. 103).

Huth reacted to the Lebow and Stein criticisms in a book on those same fifty-eight cases from 1885 to 1984 (Huth 1988; see also Huth and Russett 1988). There were, in his classification, twenty-four failures and thirty-four successes. To explain the outcomes he devised a model; the key factors were the balance of military forces, the value of the client to the deterrer as reflected by the usual measures, the defender's over-all bargaining strategy, and the defender's past behavior in confrontations, and he found he could predict 84 percent of the outcomes.[14] He concluded, again, that the local conventional military balance was important but not the larger balance.[15] Deterrence failed in only 17 percent of the cases when the defender and protégé had equal or better military forces on hand than the challenger, supporting once again the conclusion that a challenger normally looks for a quick victory or fait

---

[14] For a game-theory analysis using an expected utility model that closely overlaps this finding see Wu 1990.
[15] A later study explicitly testing power structure hypothesis against deterrence theory hypotheses on why great-power conflicts escalate found the former explained none of the escalation that took place (Huth, Gelpi and Bennett 1993).

accompli.[16] He found, as before, that nuclear weapons played no role against nonnuclear states. However, it appeared that strong economic and political-military ties between defender and client *did not* increase the chances of a deterrence success (instead, the challenger used crisis bargaining to assess the deterrer's commitment). He also concluded, contrary to the earlier finding, that the defender's past behavior did matter: if in a preceding crisis he had backed down success was less likely; if he had been very intransigent success was also less likely. (Huth believed the attacker learned from the intransigence that only an attack, not a threat, would work on that defender so it challenged again only when fully prepared to attack.) Perhaps the most important finding was that if the deterrer adopted firm but fair bargaining, and a tit-for-tat strategy, in responding to the other side's steps success was much more likely – 93 percent of the time, in fact, strongly supporting a blend of deterrence with conciliation, rewards, or reassurance.[17] Huth concluded that deterrence worked and that a model derived (more or less) from the theory could explain most of the outcomes. In an additional response to Lebow and Stein he added that while challengers may be moved by domestic pressures they are also often probing to see what they can get and not rigidly and irrationally committed to an attack. Thus properly conducted deterrence (firm not rigid) is quite capable of working, particularly if the deterrer is sensitive to how a challenger will worry that abandoning its challenge will damage its reputation.[18]

Lebow and Stein were not impressed (1990a). By their count, though sixteen of the original cases had been dropped only one of the thirteen new cases was a true deterrence situation and only ten of the total were definitely cases of deterrence, while three others that should have been included were not. They held that in most instances the challenger's intent to attack had not been clearly established. They found cases mislabeled in earlier studies by George and Smoke (1974), Organski and Kugler (1980), and Kugler (1984) – complaints that were justified. George

---

[16] This drew on Mearsheimer's (1983) analysis of the three strategies attackers use.

[17] In a tit-for-tat strategy a player starts with a cooperative step and never defects first from cooperation, but if the opponent defects the player responds in kind and then imitates the other side's moves, matching cooperation or escalating and deescalating on the same scale as the opponent. Being consistently tough or consistently conciliatory leads to lower payoffs (Axelrod 1984).

[18] This fits the Lebow–Stein description of the missile crisis in which Khrushchev's retreat was facilitated by JFK's concern that he needed to save a little face and the secret trade of the missiles in Turkey.

and Smoke, for example, had treated political challenges – just stirring the pot – as the equivalent of a general deterrence failure, and had several "failures" where no deterrence threat was issued. Lebow and Stein also correctly criticized the Organski–Kugler desire to assess deterrence by looking at whether the "challenger" achieved its goals.

Lebow and Stein soon received similar criticism. Orme (1992) challenged their case classifications and their basic explanation for deterrence failures. Orme's theme is that deterrence is often badly conducted and this accounts for most failures. He detected a correlation between when the overall military balance seemed to favor the Soviet Union and when it pressed for gains against a seemingly irresolute American leadership. Reputation mattered and the US did not always maintain its reputation sufficiently. Earlier (Orme 1987) he had charged that the cases in Lebow's book were improperly classified. "In each case, this reexamination has shown that there were in fact weaknesses in the commitment, credibility, or capability of the defender sufficient to tempt an aggressive, perhaps risk-prone, but not necessarily irrational opponent" (p. 121). He concluded that when defenders restrained themselves to avoid provocation "the effects seem to have been uniformly disastrous" (p. 122). Later (Orme 1998) he explained the attack on South Korea in 1950 as due to a US failure to be either clear or creatively ambiguous about its commitment. Then China was similarly inadequate: it did not state clearly what it would defend and hid its preparations to intervene so as to achieve a surprise attack – the surprise worked but it was necessary because China did not properly discourage UN forces in the first place. Orme noted that US attempts to reassure China as UN forces moved north failed dismally.

Huth and Russett replied that Lebow and Stein wanted to include at least one case where there was no outright military threat, that they had misinterpreted several cases, and that compellance cases were omitted because the focus was on deterrence. There were more cases of deterrence success and fewer of compellance success than Lebow and Stein reported. They also argued that Lebow and Stein were incorrectly looking for certainty about challenger intentions – often the challenger thinks to attack but remains uncertain or is willing to change plans depending on how the confrontation goes; the Lebow and Stein approach thus neglects genuine cases of deterrence success. Lebow and Stein had stressed the need to document challenger intent and other aspects of the cases, but Huth and Russett claimed that documents are often misleading, that decision makers themselves may be cloudy about their motives and intentions, and that judgments of historians and other experts are also of dubious value. The best that can be done is to see whether at least some elites/leaders pressed for an attack on the basis of military movements, statements, and other evidence.

Huth and Russett (1993; Russett 1994) eventually turned to the tricky topic of general deterrence in comparing rational decision theories with a cognitive processes approach. Their focus was a modern-day variant of the argument that governments sometimes try to shore up domestic support by a war abroad. Jack Levy (1989c) had reported that the evidence was inconclusive; many cases seemed to show officials doing this but they had been inadequately selected and analyzed. Huth and Russett explored fourteen extended rivalries since World War II (ones of twenty or more years) over serious territorial conflicts and looked just at direct deterrence efforts and excluded extended deterrence by outsiders. They offered three competing perspectives for comparison. In one, rational decision makers compute the costs and benefits of initiating a challenge. In the second they also consider domestic threats to their power and whether a foreign challenge would help ward off domestic rivals, while seeing if the defender is in a similar situation and might seize on the external threat to look tough and win points at home. In the third, decision makers facing a political threat at home become more willing to gamble abroad, especially if the military balance is uncertain or because they are driven to wishful thinking.

They find elements of all three models seem to fit, so general deterrence failures are complex. The military balance had some effect on whether a challenger initiated a dispute, particularly if it was shifting or the parties had been boosting their military spending. So did the challenger spotting considerable intraelite political conflict in the deterrer; chances of a challenge then rose unless that internal conflict became a mass phenomenon, for then the challenger was likely to hold off. With severe internal turmoil the chances rose considerably that a government would ignore an unfavorable military balance and issue a challenge, as the cognitive process model suggested.

Uri Bar-Joseph (1998) has studied Israel's deterrence experience. He examined a lengthy list of cases of general and immediate deterrence. Where the goal was to prevent some new challenge in a preexisting low-intensity conflict (what he called "current" deterrence) there were seven failures and only four successes. Since Israel was always clearly superior militarily, the military balance must have had little to do with the variation. What was important instead was *Arab motivation*, strong dissatisfaction with the status quo and the fact that the Arabs involved often had few assets to lose from Israeli retaliation. There were twenty-four cases of Israel drawing "red lines" to identify Arab actions that would be grounds for war, making commitments crystal clear. But in nineteen deterrence failed to some degree anyway. In addition to strong motivation he finds cognitive pathologies at work in Arab leaders and some conflict escalation on their part due to the stress and euphoria of crisis, with Israeli military pressure sometimes aggravating the situation.

In "strategic" deterrence, where Israel sought to quell threats to its existence, there were just two failures in fifty years – the March 1969 war of attrition and the October 1973 war. Despite Israeli military superiority, Arab motivation again caused those failures, along with excessively rigid Israeli behavior. Finally, "cumulative" deterrence (his term for general deterrence) to convince the Arabs that attacks would never work was unsuccessful for years because Israel was unwilling to compromise. It began to be more effective after the Israeli victory in the 1967 war and was pretty secure by the mid-1980s. On balance, then, deterrence not accompanied by sufficient reassurances, rewards, and concessions was unreliable as long as this kept the Arabs deeply dissatisfied.

The recurring themes in these studies are the importance of challenger motivation and the uneven relevance of the military balance in deterrence success. There is a long tradition of seeing deterrence work in stabilizing an international system because of military *superiority*, most strongly championed for nuclear and nonnuclear deterrence by Organski and Kugler (Kugler and Organski 1989; Tammen et al. 2000). There is an equally long tradition of seeing a power *balance* as best, not military superiority. The two traditions survive because there is no sound empirical evidence that power distribution really makes a difference to the likelihood of war. (See Zagare and Kilgour 2000; Wagner 1994; Powell 1999, p. 109, summarizes the many available statistical studies.) Bueno de Mesquita (1989) argues that whether deterrence works depends on the interplay between either balance or preponderance and (a) the expected utility of war for the challenger; (b) the challenger's risk acceptance; and (c) the intensity of each side's feelings. For example, where both parties expect a war to pay off handsomely a rough equality of military power is a recipe for war, but where neither sees much benefit a rough equality will readily sustain the peace.

Levy (1989a) suggested a curvilinear relationship is at work: equal military power is destabilizing, a moderate advantage in power for the defender is stabilizing, and a very high inequality favoring the defender can provoke challenges out of fear of hegemony. However, in broad analyses of numerous cases there is a real selection bias problem. Since the cases are normally ones with a threat of attack perhaps the challenger is unusually confident of winning, or feels stronger. That would miss cases where the military balance caused the other party to decide not to challenge. If an attack occurs the same problem arises – maybe those cases are ones where challengers already thought they had a military advantage so the failures of deterrence tell us very little.

Does deterrence work? Certainly not all the time. But is it a good bet to work? Since the point of this chapter is to suggest that we aren't sure it is fitting to finish up this review of empirical studies with a clash in views. Susan Sample (1998) explored the data for 1816 to 1993 on the escalation of disputes into wars. She finds that a typical dispute had an 8 percent chance of escalating. But if both parties took to arming (an arms race), that rose to 21 percent. Or if one or both were carrying a heavy defense burden (and about to run out of resources for further arms racing), or the dispute was over territory, then the chance of war rose to 20 percent. If all these things were present then it was 59 percent, and if the parties had rough military equality after a rapid buildup and a power transition it was 69 percent. Naturally enough, she concludes that deterrence is not very effective. With nuclear deterrence things are more complicated. The probability of disputes among nuclear powers escalating to a war fell off after 1945 to almost nil. However, this was not because they were terribly cautious – as was noted in chapter 1, she stresses that they were not inherently cautious, unwilling to challenge each other and use nuclear threats. She thinks war did not occur because the nuclear powers evolved rules and norms to keep their disputes from going too far. Geller (1990) had earlier found that nuclear deterrence does indeed work among nuclear powers but that it had, as Huth and Russett found, little effect in nuclear powers' disputes with nonnuclear powers.

Frank Harvey (1997a, 1997b) looked at twenty-eight crises involving the superpowers in 1948–88 and found that nuclear weapons had, in fact, made them behave exceedingly carefully, which he felt fit very well with what deterrence theory leads us to expect. However, he suggested that just a few nuclear weapons won't have a sufficiently sobering impact, so he suggested that nuclear proliferation was not a good idea. He also examined the Bosnia case, using the innovative technique of breaking it into the individual encounters between Serbia and NATO so as to provide fourteen instances (not just one) of a deterrence or compellance attempt. He found that if an event had the defender or "coercer" follow-ing all the prescriptions of deterrence/compellance theory then success usually followed. Thus deterrence theory was useful. But deterrence, pushing all the right buttons, *did not dictate the outcome* 30–40 percent of the time.

Analysts therefore keep coming back to the idea that the perceptions of actors are very important. This focus on what the actors perceived is part of what has been emphasized in game-theory based analyses. One way to evaluate deterrence is to see if the theory is rigorous, logically consistent, and then develop models on that basis to derive conclusions about it (to compare with empirical findings). This usually involves game theory. We can bring this review of the testing of deterrence theory to a close with some of the findings.[19]

Many of these analyses assume that crises and wars arise because of uncertainty about the distribution of power and how a war will go. Rational decision makers should settle a conflict short of war if the out-come is not in doubt – when the deterrer is more powerful there is no challenge; when the challenger is superior there is no resistance to the challenge. We reviewed a variation of this in chapter 2; it is also well known as the basis of Geoffrey Blainey's (1973) view that war results when the parties disagree on their relative power and ends when fight-ing makes them agree. What makes for crises and wars is uncertainty and the lack of transparency. Often cited as important is "private infor-mation" the parties have about their own and the other side's power and resolve that generates the conflicting estimates. This is important because governments have strong incentives to hide, or lie about, that information – seeking leverage, hiding weaknesses or lack of resolve and thus strengthening their hand in bargaining, etc. (Fearon 1995; Wagner 1994).

Without transparency each side sends signals which are then used to help estimate resolve, detect misperceptions, etc. However, each side may have good reason to distort or manipulate the signals – to bluff, for example, to display more resolve than it has. Hence, it is important to find ways to send highly credible signals. Normally this means sending signals that are quite costly or irreversible, for then one's commitment and the resolve backing it would have to be taken seriously. Fearon (1994) finds that costly signalling (or not) fits the evidence on success

---

[19] For other game theory studies of deterrence see, for example, Nalebuff 1991; Sorokin 1994; Langlois 1991.

and failure in deterrence better than explanations that cite the balance of interests (and resolve) or the balance of power (capabilities), which would explain why deterrence success is unevenly correlated with military balances of any sort and not consistent with the balance of resolve. Fearon emphasizes that putting out credible signals is most effective in reinforcing general deterrence; such steps in a crisis, on the other hand, can sometimes look very provocative because they escalate the situation.

Other game theorists, however, find that deterrence failure is usually due to an imbalance of resolve favoring the challenger (Zagare and Kilgour 2000). This leads them to also favor the power imbalance view – uncertainty and divergent views on how things will go is much lower when the parties have very different capabilities. But Wagner (1994) argues that even when the parties agree on what would be a possible resolution of their conflict based on their relative power they may still be unable to avoid a war. If the possible deal would further enhance the dominant state's power it is not self-enforcing: that state can use the additional power to eventually demand more and may well do so and, fearing this, the weaker party will then refuse the deal. Also, if the dominant state gains more power from the deal other states will also be adversely affected – it will more readily make demands on them – and they may interfere to prevent the agreement.

Powell (1999) also disparages the impact of the power distribution. His models of bargaining suggest that the probability of war is highest when there is a significant gap not between the parties but between the distribution of power and the distribution of benefits in a conflict relationship. With little gap, the dominant state has no reason to challenge the status quo – it is getting as much as it can. Obliquely, this confirms the vital role in deterrence cases of the challenger's level of satisfaction with the status quo. He also finds that power transitions, fast or slow, do not erode deterrence and make war significantly more likely.

Powell's earlier models (1990) indicate that each party's uncertainty about the other's resolve, and effort to manipulate the other's view, can lead to escalation even by relatively irresolute parties, producing situations in which the most resolute party does not prevail. This is rational actor modeling of Schelling's conception of deterrence as a competition in risk taking or resolve. In game-theory modeling, seeing resolve as very important for the outcome of confrontations leads to describing the parties as "hard" or "soft," to indicate whether or not they are likely to be impressed by threats and to compromise (Zagare and Kilgour 1993b, 2000). A related distinction is between "risk-acceptant" and "risk-averse" actors, the former being more resolute. Often these distinctions are linked to interests: the parties are hardest or most risk acceptant when they have vital interests at stake. Others see them as character traits or preferences; analysis starts once actor preferences along these lines are specified.

Finally, some game theory analyses find the massive retaliation capabilities of the Cold War era useless or bad for deterrence (Zagare and Kilgour 2000; Powell 1990). One argument is that when unacceptable damage can be imposed, increasing the threatened damage has no additional effect. Another is that smaller flexible nuclear forces are inherently more credible – it is more plausible that they could be used and this makes threats of escalation more believable, which is Powell's approach to resolving the classic credibility problem in nuclear deterrence.

To summarize the major conclusions in the quantitative studies and game theory analyses about deterrence situations:

(1) The overall strategic balance is often insignificant, the local conventional balance is more salient.

The rational-decision explanation is that attackers seek quick, cheap victories and not a long costly conflict. Why this is not irrational is not explained, and other explanations can fit. After all, why expect the militarily superior state to suffer a fait accompli by quitting when it could eventually reverse the situation? Expecting the US would not respond was disastrously inappropriate in Korea in 1950. Maybe challengers ignore the larger strategic balance because of wishful thinking or ignorance. Another possible explanation (Lebovic 1990) is that decision makers are focused on the excessively concrete. A local military balance is concrete but good decision making calls for considering the larger strategic situation.

(2) Nuclear weapons and the nuclear balance are important in discouraging rash and rigid actions, but not in helping decide who "ought" to win a confrontation (Zagare and Kilgour 1993b). They don't help nuclear powers in conflicts with nonnuclear powers.

This can be seen as a triumph of rationality, or as an illustration of nonrational elements (taboos, image considerations, morality) voiding cost–benefit calculations that ought to apply.

(3) Mixing deterrence and conciliation is best – be tough but not bullying, rigid, or unsympathetic; be conciliatory without being

soft. This is because, as discussed below, the strength of the challenger's motivation is crucial – weakening it by concessions and conciliation can make chances of success much higher. However, if the challenger is motivated by hopes of gain only, conciliation may only provoke further threats. Hence it is important to also guard against being exploited.

This easily fits a cognitive processes approach – threats might evoke dangerous emotional reactions unless handled properly with some conciliation.

(4)   The strength of the challenger's motivation is very important for whether a challenge emerges and how far it goes – the balance of resolve is important. Deterring a highly dissatisfied challenger is very difficult. This conclusion appears in game theory analyses (Stein 1990; Zagare and Kilgour 2000; Powell 1990) as well as quantitative studies – challenger satisfaction with the status quo is very important for the chances of deterrence success (Zagare and Kilgour 1993a, 2000). For example: "the problem with the United States' strategy of putting pressure on North Vietnam was not that the threats were not believed, but rather that the North preferred to take the punishment rather than stop supporting the war in the South" (Jervis 1976, p. 79).

This need not reflect rational decision making – strength of motivation may derive from nonrational elements and can be an index of irrationality.

(5)   Decision makers are basically rational. They try to avoid falling into preemptive spirals,[20] they assess the expected utility of war, etc. But there are psychological factors at work as well.

(6)   The best strategy is tit-for-tat as part of being firm but fair. By mimicking the opponent it is possible to promote cooperation that maximizes payoffs for both sides.

(7)   Challengers are often motivated by internal pressures and are not simply opportunists.

This is a cornerstone of the cognitive processes approach.

The tit-for-tat strategy is very widely touted, so we should note some criticisms of it, as well as some mixed evidence. Downs notes that in

---

[20] Reiter (1995) examined all sixty-seven wars since 1816 and found only three were preemptive in origin – World War I, the Chinese intervention in Korea, and the 1967 Middle East War. He thinks leaders have strong inhibitions against preemptive war, and avoid crises that might spiral into preemptive attacks.

modeling tit-for-tat a 1 percent chance of misperception means states that start out cooperating end up in an arms race 75 percent of the time, and he believes actors easily fall victim to misperception of responses to their actions (Downs and Rocke, 1990). Lebow and Stein suggest that whether a response is reciprocal depends on perceptions, particularly of the motives behind it. Reciprocity works better when the parties have shared values. A tit-for-tat strategy is also up against the human tendency to see others' actions as caused by their dispositions. Finally, conciliatory steps are most potent when offered by the stronger party (as in the success of GRIT). Tetlock (1987) contends that in some international conflicts (and, I suspect, many internal ones) the parties don't want to cooperate (Jonas Savimbi in Angola for years) so neither tit-for-tat nor GRIT will work.

Finally, being conciliatory is often not popular – it may take a government insulated from criticism or unusually able to take the risk to pursue it. Consider dealing with North Korea. After years of isolation and deterrence the US and RoK started combining deterrence with engagement. The US made progress via a clear two-track policy: offering cooperation in response to cooperative steps and planning harsh responses if the North chose conflict, which is almost tit-for-tat. But the RoK eventually achieved a partial breakthrough by applying GRIT – consistently offering concessions no matter how badly the North responded. However, criticism of being "soft" was fierce in both countries and the conflict was not promptly resolved due to either strategy.

Conclusion

Surprising things emerge from all this. First, the conclusions offered overlap considerably! They agree that challenger motivation is the most important factor in deterrence success or failure, especially if "motivation" covers both the desire to challenge and a willingness to take risks. *The deterrer doesn't control the situation unless that motivation is low enough to permit it.* Deterrence theory is about controlling conflict via suitable threats, but even when the deterrer does the right things the challenger may still attack. When the defender alone has nuclear weapons the challenger may still attack. These approaches differ over what causes the challenger to behave this way. Is it irrational or can it have a rational determination to attack when the prospect is unacceptable damage? Even here there is overlap. Huth and Russett and some game theorists agree that cognitive factors play a role and cognitive process analysts accept the view that actors often regard the status quo as more unaccept-able than prospective punishment. So the question is less about what drives the strong motivation than about how to describe where it comes from.

The three types of testing produce the finding that deterrence is best mixed with something positive. In a general theory of influence deterrence threats would be treated as useful but sometimes provoca-tive, useful primarily in conjunction with carrots and for protect-ing carrot-givers from exploitation, while rewards would be seen as helpful but sometimes provocative or ineffective and often politically unpopular.

Third, the various kinds of studies agree about the importance of the challenger's rejection of the status quo and that this can be provoked by domestic considerations, the challenger's strategic situation, or percep-tions of adverse trends. Fourth, they mostly view military superiority as not the key – the overall military balance is often relatively unimpor-tant for the outcome. Various studies cite the local military balance as important, which may show either rational or nonrational processes at work.

Fifth, except for Organski–Kugler, these studies agree that nuclear weapons are not irrelevant but not dominant; they promote a broad re-straint in interactions among nuclear powers but this may take some learning to fully apply. This is not a popular view. In chapter 7 we ex-amine widespread assertions that nuclear weapons are very important. Many people, certain leaders, and various analysts reject contentions that they are not (and show little concern for the evidence one way or the other).

As I tried to indicate all along, the conclusions reached by each of the various approaches can usually fit the others. Why, then, have they often been so emphatic in critiquing each other? The *prescriptive* im-plications seem to be the main factor. From the cognitive process per-spective, deterrence must be used with great care because perspectives and motives are distorted, communication and understanding are in-adequate, and grave mistakes readily occur – the limitations of human beings are dangerous and practicing deterrence can incite or reinforce them. For rational decision analysts deterrence is often an important constraint on dangerous actors in a dangerous world; deterrence works because actors typically think strategically and can be influenced accord-ingly. However, many of them would ultimately agree with Zagare and Kilgour when they write that "deterrence is, at best, a tenuous and fragile relationship: conflict is almost always possible. At worst, deterrence is a patently unstable relationship: at times, conflict may be inevitable" (2000, p. 291). After all, attacks are launched not only by the party that is weaker but sometimes by one that is exceedingly weaker (Arquilla and Davis 1994; Wolf 1991).

Disagreements often arise over how to classify cases and thus on how often deterrence is successful or fails. When Lebow and Stein (1990a) looked at the studies by George and Smoke, Huth and Russett, Organski and Kugler, only twelve cases were coded the same way by all the studies. A recent assessment of case lists for seven major studies finds an overlap of less than 60 percent on the coding decisions, particularly on successes and failures (Harvey 1997a, 1997b; see also Harvey and James 1992). Since history lends itself to various interpretations, this seems unavoidable.

> The... evidence in the case summaries compiled by Huth and Russett to support their coding decisions was as persuasive as Lebow and Stein's. The reason, of course, is that both are right; each side focused on different periods (and exchanges) throughout the crises.
>
> (Harvey 1997b, p. 12)

Game theorists are attacked on various grounds. As we know, one is that they assume rationality. What does it mean to assume rationality when the world often seems decidedly less so? Most game-theory modeling builds in imperfect information, uncertainty, and misperception – but not irrationality. Is this is a wrong-headed oversimplification or a uniquely effective strategic simplification? As Powell (1990) admits, deterrence is complicated and in comparison game-theory models seem simple and artificial. And much they refer to, and model, is inherently difficult to measure. These difficulties were discussed earlier.

Another criticism of game theorists is that most of their conclusions are trivial. Stephen Walt (2000) is not the first to make this charge, but he goes furthest. Findings he cites as very simple or not original include (a) war is most likely when the challenger is superior to the defender; (b) war is unlikely when the conflicting parties highly value the status quo; (c) deterrence is strong when both sides have an existential fear of escalation.

The best answer to the charge is either to cite lots of profound findings or argue that modeling to reach simple or well-known conclusions builds a way of thinking that will soon result in profound findings. It is unfair to say that rational choice studies offer no new insights and are never stimulating, and it is certainly useful to have conclusions reached by one method upheld by another. But there are no overwhelmingly profound new findings yet.

Neither purveyors of rational deterrence nor their critics provide a reassuring theory for guiding policy. As a result, debates about deterrence strategy never get resolved.

> Given the absence of a powerful and convincing theory that might unify the participants in the nuclear debate, strong held worldviews have tended to play an especially influential role, producing doctrinaire positions – what some have called *nuclear theologies*.
>
> (Tarr 1991, p. 16)

It is bad when theory ends in theology.

Clearly, the best way to confront deterrence theory is with an alternative theory. But critics of rational deterrence theory have not supplied one; in fact, they have rarely tried to. There is no consistent theory along the lines of : "I threaten you and as a result you are scared (outraged, indifferent, frantic)...and as a result you..." Instead, they have tried to develop accurate descriptions of deterrence situations: what preferences, perceptions and judgments are like, how actors define their choices and evaluate them, and why outcomes are too often contrary to what deterrence was to achieve. They have accumulated generalizations but not into an alternative explanation as to how threats produce decisions not to attack. They have cared greatly about reducing reliance on deterrence as a strategy.

Some critics have felt that pressing conflicts all the way to war, and conducting conflicts by threats, is primitive behavior, tapping nonrational or irrational elements in leaders, governments, and societies. It may be useful to construct a rational model of this or that aspect but to focus on the supposedly rational elements and advise policy makers accordingly ignores or dismisses other crucial features. The proponents of the theory show insufficient respect for the limitations of deterrence and too little interest in alternatives.

Other critics (with no detailed empirical analysis of deterrence) have felt that war is appropriate for dealing with certain opponents because they are probably not deterrable, and in any event deterrence is so unreliable against those opponents that fighting and winning is the only suitable choice. (The first group of critics finds this perspective even worse.) These critics have also not worked hard to devise an alternative theory. They stress that deterrence comes from being able to win a war, but mainly seem to worry about being able to win because deterrence will never be fully reliable.

In prescribing, the first group calls on policy makers to emphasize the possible fallibility of the opponent *and* their own limitations. Hence deterrence should be used with reassurance (Stein 1991) or with conflict resolution efforts (George and Smoke 1974), should be practiced with a healthy respect for misperceptions (Stern et al. 1989a; Jervis 1984), so planning for rationally conducted crises or limited wars is foolish (Steinbruner 1983; Ball 1984). The response that wanting better decision making only makes rational decision analysis all the more relevant (Downs 1989) misses the thrust of their view that little can be done to correct human, organizational, and governmental limitations.

During the Cold War the second group prescribed military superiority and a war-winning capability, often with preemptive capabilities if necessary to survive and win, and they still do. This was Kahn's view in the 1950s, one rationale for flexible response in the 1960s, the heart of much criticism of MAD in the 1970s and 1980s, and the basis for support of missile defenses. The closest this gets to a coherent theory is the contention that challenger motivation is crucial and that, due to irrationality or intense determination, there are challengers against whom deterrence won't work. But why will other governments settle for being at the mercy of the US, the West, or other powerful countries and not therefore do things that force the powerful to rely on deterrence again? They will at least try to get to where they can do unacceptable damage so they themselves can rely on deterrence.

The other objection has been not just that deterrence won't work well enough but that it often cuts the ground from under other tools – efforts to be conciliatory will convey weakness that will be exploited. The weak spot in this argument is evidence in the 1990s that deterrence postures need not bar substantial, even remarkable, shifts toward cooperation. Still, it cannot be just dismissed; it may be applicable mainly in crises, when threats interfere with the use or impact of conciliation.

To be truly effective the critics needed either an appealing alternative theory or a compelling explanation as to why deterrence is not necessary and what could be used instead. Neither has ever been put forward. Deterrence continues to be necessary (there are Saddams out there) and possibly unavoidable (see chapter 7), so governments need a theory that produces a strategy. It doesn't help much to tell a man that the boat he is using to get to shore is leaky, hard to steer, and too small; not offering another means he will use the one he's got. We can readily dump theories flatly contradicted by the evidence; we seldom dump theories when we really need them and the evidence is ambiguous. Criticisms of a well-established theory need links to a competing theory that has fewer defects and better explains what needs explaining.[21] This has not happened in the study of deterrence. Without alternative theories even the critics work within a rational decision paradigm.

Why is there no alternative theory? It would have to be based on limited rational, or nonrational, behavior and we have no compelling overall theory of either bounded rationality (DeNardo 1995, p. 5) or cognitive processes as a whole (Stein 1991). The trouble with bounded rationality is that it knows no bounds; all sorts of constraints can apply and all sorts of decision errors can thus occur. Without a link between types of irrationality or limitations on rationality and the varying outcomes of deterrence situations there can be no theory built on elements of irrationality. What we have are cases that look like they might fit with a particular explanation selected from the many explanations available.

It is easy to appreciate periodic assertions that we need a theory of *influence* – that an isolated theory of deterrence will always be deficient.[22] However, explaining influence by other means poses the same intrinsic difficulties, for theory and testing, as deterrence. Also, gentler ways of dealing with severe conflicts are often discarded precisely because they are conflicts: the more intense the conflict and the need for not relying only on deterrence, the less open to this the contestants may be.

What might an alternative theory look like? We can finish up with a few examples. The most difficult problem in sidestepping assumptions of rationality is that decision makers display bounded rationality or outright irrationality but not in universal or consistent ways. A theory might someday build on patterns of nonrationality, suggesting that deterrence works only when it fits with the impact of standard cognitive processes on the challenger's perceptions, judgments, and decision making, with estimates of when and how often that is likely. To derive a strategy would call for the manipulation of a challenger to be pursued in the same way that advertisers exploit standard cognitive processes,

---

[21] Lakatos 1978, p. 32: "A scientific theory is *falsified* if and only if another theory T′ has been proposed with the following characteristics: (1) T′ has excess empirical content over T: that is, it predicts *novel* facts, that is facts improbable in the light of or even forbidden by T: (2) T′ explains the previous success of T, that is, all the unrefuted content of T is included (within the limits of observable error) in the content of T′; and (3) some of the excess content of T′ is corroborated."

[22] Singer said this in the 1960s, as did George and Smoke in the 1970s, followed by Lebow and Stein, Russett, and Tetlock in the 1980s and 1990s.

or magicians, or the police in interrogations. Simon's (1985) satisficing is one pattern. The best candidate these days is prospect theory because it identifies patterns of cognitive errors and lends itself to specifying what conditions make which errors more likely, as with framing. The problem here would be to get a grip on the roots of framing decisions.

An alternative basis might be the poliheuristic theory (Mintz and Geva 1997), where officials select from among their options by first using one crucial dimension along which the decision must be made and discarding options if they don't reach a critical threshold of satisfaction on that dimension. The most probable dimension is that an option be minimally acceptable *politically*. Surviving options are then evaluated in the same way on other dimensions considered (more or less) serially. Hence it is not only the threshold on each dimension that is important, but the order in which they are considered because that affects how far an option survives. It is a simplifying and satisficing decision process. Applying it to the missile crisis, for example, political criteria were paramount. Kennedy immediately eliminated leaving the missiles in place, Khrushchev engaged in very risky bargaining to extract some gains, each because the political fallout would otherwise be intolerable.

Another kind of theory would identify types of governments and political systems on which deterrence is least likely to work, refining the notion that the key variable is challenger motivation. If most regimes will not attack an opponent which has done the required things to make deterrence effective, regimes sufficiently committed to attack may often have distinctive characteristics. The preliminary cut at such a theory I offered years ago (Morgan 1983) is an example. "Normal" governments are very uneasy in crises due to the uncertainties involved. They worry about their limitations, about how gains and losses, especially the total consequences, can be misestimated, etc. That leads them to try to avoid very large, potentially very consequential, leaps into the unknown. For deterrence to work, they don't have to calculate the specific consequences of a potential war, just know they will be large and are uncertain. They refuse to leap into the unknown and settle for a less risky, less consequential step instead – they are "sensible." But some governments are likely to be abnormal in this respect – less concerned about big risks or more confident they know what they are getting into and will do fine. For instance, governments created by revolutions or other major domestic political upheavals could be more apt to behave this way.

No one has really developed this notion, but it shows up. Walt (1996) thinks revolutions have an impact along these lines in stimulating crises and driving conflicts toward war. James Blight (1992) finds that leaders plunged into the missile crisis and then became deeply fearful of setting off events that would get out of control and have enormous consequences. They feared war by inadvertence. Stress and fear improved their decision making but they feared its limitations. A standard approach to deterrence now is to stress risk propensity – deterrence is most likely to fail when two risk-acceptant actors face each other or a risk-acceptant actor faces one who is risk neutral. Examples often cited are Hitler, or Khomeni, or "rogue states" – with leaders who came to power in unusual ways (Saddam Hussein) or are not sensible (Kim, Jong Il) There is also the Mansfield–Snyder (1995) analysis of the different propensity for war of "democratizing" and "well-institutionalized"democracies. In the former the political spectrum expands to include too many irreconcilable elements, so competitive efforts to mobilize support resort to nationalist, ideological, or ethnic/religious, appeals. Eventually, leaders logroll on policies like overseas expansion, pursue legitimacy via triumphs abroad, are prone to overcommitment and avoiding tradeoffs. Such a nonsensible government can be unusually difficult to deter.

5   Collective actor deterrence

We turn now to a topic seldom addressed in analyses of deterrence. Few analysts who examine collective actor peacekeeping and peace enforcement endeavors employ a deterrence perspective. Until recently those endeavors were typically confined to interventions with which the conflicting parties concurred and the coercive measures were limited to sanctions. Now we have a global system and several regional systems where forceful security management by collective actors is prominent and promises to grow in importance, management with a deterrence component. It seems worthwhile to begin exploring the features of deterrence when used by collective actors.

Collective actors

A collective actor is a cluster of states established and designed to decide and act for the general welfare. The term is awkward since alliances are – in a sense – collective actors and I do not mean to discuss alliances here. My target is actors constructed and charged to act for the general welfare, the collective good, as opposed to pursuing member interests only. The topic is the use of deterrence by such actors in attempting to maintain peace and security for an international system (regional or larger). This can include the use of force when deterrence fails and threats must be implemented. There is now a notable level of this multilateralism, including threats to induce acceptable behavior and force to compel it.

The contemporary epitome at the global level is the UN Security Council, an institutionalized great-power concert charged with maintaining peace and security. In any concert serious disagreement among the great powers cripples effective action and an understanding of this was institutionalized in the great-power veto. The only wrinkle is the requirement of a majority vote of the entire Security Council involving its additional members. The great powers cannot act on their own, at least not in a UN-authorized fashion, when the others disagree with them. On the other hand, nothing gets done without the great powers' approval, or at least acquiescence, so if something gets done they usually do it.

A second example is the new NATO. The old NATO was an alliance to protect its members, hopefully by deterring attacks. It had no commitment to uphold peace and security elsewhere, no matter how much this might enhance member security. Unofficially, NATO was strongly interested in the security of nonmembers like Sweden and Yugoslavia, so it might have tried to defend them. NATO is still an alliance but much more. It has declared itself entitled to project military power to maintain peace and security anywhere in Europe, which is what it has done in Bosnia, Kosovo, and Macedonia. Initially, it said this would be under UN authorization, but in Kosovo it had that authorization only indirectly and demonstrated it was prepared to act on its own.

A third example is a great-power concert which assumes responsibility for managing peace and security. The Concert of Europe adopted this role after the Napoleonic Wars. Concerts can be officially established or more informal. A concert was roughly what Britain sought in the 1938 Munich settlement – the four great powers would settle outstanding issues and ensure future order on the continent. An example is the – often tacit – cooperation among the US, China, Russia, and Japan that gravely crippled North Korea and halted its existing nuclear weapons program. (The North eventually started another.) The members put enormous pressure on Pyongyang – withholding support, curbing trade, ending alliance ties, making military threats. Like any concert the members had to defer to each other's wishes and concerns. The Chinese had to accept contributing to North Korea's isolation and demeaning a fellow communist government, deferring to American insistence that the problems posed by the North could not be ignored. The Russians, in voiding their alliance commitment to the North, suspended their influence there. The US, in turn, bowed to Chinese and Japanese reluctance to have force used and turned instead to conciliation and negotiation, easing the North's security concerns and promising more normal relations.

Finally, a collective security system converts the members into a collective actor for, among other things, deterring any breach of the peace among them – an exercise in collective actor deterrence. This is now relevant again, long after the demise of the League of Nations, because it is where NATO is headed. As NATO continues adding members and deepening its cooperation with nonmembers, Europeans will end up in a security association that exists mainly so the members are safe among themselves.

Collective actors concerned with security are widely involved in general deterrence and occasionally in immediate deterrence; this is normally one of their primary objectives, along with handling the consequences when deterrence fails. Collective actor deterrence is meant to be a considerable improvement over deterrence by individual states or alliances. It is to be in the general interest. It is also to be more effective by confronting a challenger with the collective power of the group. Furthermore, it is meant to avoid the security dilemma inherent in deterrence by individual states and alliances, where actions taken for self-protection can make others insecure – the collective protection mutes the threat from each member's might.

I must emphasize that this concerns liberal-democratic collective actors, formed on the basis of liberal-democratic principles. These are the only relevant ones today: for the most part they hold open discussions, operate with majority voting or consensus building, have fundamentally liberalist goals and principles and eschew classic imperial objectives of aggrandizement and exploitation. We can envision other sorts of collective actors seeking order and security from a different political orientation but there are none in operation now. While their behavior and that of liberal-democratic collective actors should have a good deal in common, there are significant differences.

In the collective actors of significance now even minor states can participate in deterrence. This helps explain their support of system-building or system-maintenance endeavors resting on (in part) deterrence – the NATO Partnership for Peace (Euro-Atlantic Partnership Council) being a good example. Smaller states want to participate because they have specific interests at stake or a broad interest in effective security management. But they also are eager to have some say and this helps offset free-rider and other collective goods problems – states want a seat at the table and will pay to get it. This applies to large states too, of course. Germany and Japan sent money for the Gulf War but they found they had no influence on the operations – correcting this was a major motivation for Germany's effort to secure the legal and military ability to send forces to Bosnia, then Kosovo. The NATO Partnership for Peace worked far better than expected because it offered a way for nonmembers to join the emerging security management system in their region.

EU members are building their own military intervention capability to have more influence over the decision making.

Deterrence by collective actors

We should speculate about the dynamics of collective actor deterrence. Its importance will almost certainly grow. We need to think about what this may mean, and have only limited experience to draw from. We can't learn much from the Cold War with its inoperative Security Council and regional actors dominated by superpower ideological/political interests. It is too new to analyze with confidence; there have been a number of surprises, so we should try some speculative propositions. Finally, the context is shifting and context is important for deterrence; chances for its success are altered by the nature of the system and the conflicts which stimulate deterrence efforts. Confidence that we fully understand how the global and regional systems operate today and will in the future would be misplaced – better to speculate about collective actor deterrence via hypotheses for future study. The suggestions below come with tentative explanations; undoubtedly they will turn out to be incorrect or need revision, but this is a start. In developing them I drew on the following assumptions. Collective actors:

> will be moved by liberalist perspectives in deterring or upholding deterrence threats;
> will be uneasy about transgressing sovereignty – in those cases the justification required will be higher;
> will be quite cost conscious;
> will vary widely in cost and risk acceptance, on particular cases and particular means;
> will operate within substantial two-level game pressures, facing coalition-building and coalition-maintenance burdens internationally and at home.

We begin with *general deterrence*, since it is especially important to collective actors.

General deterrence

General deterrence is a broad image of being ready to respond forcefully so *potential* challengers decide it is not worth the effort even to consider an attack. When successful, this keeps serious confrontations, where war is a distinct possibility, from emerging. Collective actors have a special interest in it. When established to manage peace and security, and uphold it by force when necessary, a collective actor is the crux of a general deterrence arrangement – it is meant to mount threats that forestall misbehavior. The paramount objective is never to have to use force.

Broadly speaking, it has these specific functions. First, the collective actor seeks to prevent the use of force by states or other actors for their own narrow purposes, so effectively that using force is not a serious policy option. Second, it therefore promotes dealing with problems in other ways. Third, on this basis, it is to greatly enhance how secure states (and citizens) feel. These are not abstract objectives. The collective actor normally facilitates peaceful dispute resolution via conducting negotiations, stimulating agreements, peacekeeping, peacebuilding and related efforts, all of which are easier with general deterrence as a backdrop. States like security but not at the price of being run from above – they don't want to be told what to agree to but can appreciate help in working out agreements. Collective actors don't get to tell states what to do very often – they rarely dictate terms to resolve a conflict – and must try instead to effectively facilitate. When things work right, general deterrence is a deep background condition, partly visible but never forgotten.

General deterrence by a collective actor derives its legitimacy from being collective in orientation and its effectiveness from the coalition's immense weight. The intent is to transform much that is standard behavior in international politics. Thus our initial comment (*Proposition 1*) is that for a collective actor, getting general deterrence to flourish is of greater importance than for most national actors. The collective actor strongly wants to avoid physically coercing states and domestic actors into abjuring force; so instead it wants to convince them that there is no point in thinking about force. For many states or movements in serious conflicts and seeking to deter, this is more a wish than a realistic goal.

This makes credibility of great importance, not because the collective actor fears attack on itself but because credibility is vital for performance of its central function. Credibility is also important because a collective actor can have a significant legitimacy problem; given the strong attachment to sovereignty, it must establish that it is the most reliable route to security and conflict resolution. There are competing routes available (sheltering under a major power, the use of alliances, seeking hegemony) that favor some states over others, and a collective actor must forestall their use as best it can. It's not just that without sufficient credibility the efforts to sustain peace will fail, but that the *method* of sustaining peace the collective actor embodies could be discarded. For instance, the Security Council is readily discarded when great-power equanimity disappears, in favor of other ways of managing regional and global security.

Credibility is difficult to achieve. For various reasons (discussed later) collective actors find credibility difficult to sustain in both immediate and general deterrence. One problem is that collective actor general deterrence *is almost always extended deterrence*, long considered very difficult to practice, with greater intrinsic credibility problems. But this is exacerbated when there is no deterring actor *in the normal sense of the term*. The collective actor is a creature of its members. It has no territory, no forces of its own, no elaborate government (in making crucial decisions), no sovereignty. It practices extended deterrence in an unusually abstract fashion. The interests it defends may well be more abstract as well – the deterrer is not defending *its own* territories, forces, citizens, and wealth from potential attack; normally it has none of those things itself. It conducts deterrence in and through its members, who may be unenthusiastic about this, particularly when they are at some remove from the specific conflict.

As a second broad comment then (*Proposition 2*), we should expect that the more highly institutionalized the collective actor, the more it can pursue deterrence in its own right, the less its *intrinsic* credibility problem. By institutionalized I have in mind the things associated with NATO – well-established officials, a common command structure, elaborate forces assigned in advance to the organization, well developed planning and training processes. It may have plenty of ways its threats seem insufficiently believable but it should have a heftier deterrence profile than, at the other extreme, a group of states that meets periodically to consider security issues and decides what to try to do about them, possibly including deterrence.

The viability of collective actor deterrence – its ability to underpin a broad security framework for a system – has always been controversial. Collective management is meant to replace national and private coercion. That won't happen unless, at a minimum, states and other actors have confidence in it, and for that it must have a suitable capability to coerce. But unless states see it as highly viable and beneficial they won't supply the necessary forces. This is a disturbing circularity: coercion capability is vital for management but viable management is what ultimately generates that capability. However, it may be more spiral than circular, the key being to get the spiral started. Once it is started, this helps explain how the collective goods problem can be overcome. As "club goods" theory (Downs and Iida 1994) suggests, when a non-universal group sees collective management as important (because it works) members are moved to help in order to have a say in the decisions, increasing the likelihood it will work again. This gives us a third suggestion (*Proposition 3*): the viability of collective actor deterrence depends on the viability of collective security management (and vice-versa).

Immediate deterrence

We now turn to propositions on *immediate* deterrence. Recall that deterrence threats can be based primarily on either defense or retaliation. Remember as well that retaliation can be designed to be selective in its damage or quite nonselective, even random.

The fourth suggestion (*Proposition 4*) is that collective actors will not soon get forces of their own suitable for deterrence and compellance, especially to meet all plausible contingencies. That will be seen as too large and costly a step. That a collective actor will be assigned its own nuclear weapons, as has been suggested, seems quite implausible too. Instead, deterrence will be provided by some or all members by collaborating. This has several implications. The collective actor will be dependent on selected members to do any fighting that is required or to supply other crucial military services. Its deterrence will rest on their military capabilities and perceived willingness to use them. Hence the *relevant* collective actor, for purposes of deterrence and which a challenger must confront, will be much smaller than the membership roll.

It will be necessary to distinguish broad political decisions on violations of peace and security from decisions about when and how to threaten the use of force and, if necessary, use it. The key states for taking military action will dominate, have a veto over, the latter decisions, and this will give them disproportionate, though lesser, influence over the political decisions.

The fifth comment (*Proposition 5*) is that collective actor deterrence will normally be based on threats to *defend*, not retaliate. A corollary is that it will not rest on threats of using weapons of mass destruction. Collective actors will be unable to offer threats of a nuclear response to forestall a nonnuclear attack or to reverse a grievous case of aggression. Some suggest that this should not always be so. For instance, analysts have long proposed that nuclear nonproliferation be bolstered by guarantees from nuclear-armed great powers to nonnuclear armed states of protection in any confrontation with a nuclear-armed state, including retaliation in kind for a nuclear attack. This would offer every state the benefits of nuclear deterrence and backing by great-power allies. The great powers have not undertaken this obligation, though they have promised to assist any nonnuclear power attacked by a nuclear-armed state.

Deterrence by threat of broad retaliation will rarely, if ever, be viable for collective actors. (The closest they are likely to come is threats of sanctions, a well-established practice.) A major objective in establishing collective actors has been to diminish reliance by states on deterrence based on WMD by providing a potent alternative. This makes it most unlikely that a collective actor will be able to openly, or even indirectly, promise pure retaliation – certainly not via WMD and probably not by conventional forces. A policy of retaliation only – especially indiscriminate harm – will not get wide support from the members. Programmed indiscriminate destruction in Cold War deterrence incited widespread revulsion, which will spring up as well if proposed for a collective actor.

The ultimate reason for this is that in representing the general welfare a collective actor must regard even the target actor *as one of its clients*, which it serves in upholding peace and security (this is usually done by distinguishing an offensive regime from its citizens). Hence members will be much more comfortable applying only the force necessary, which will in turn be reflected in any deterrence threats.[1]

Of course, we must distinguish between deterrence threats *issued* and *implemented*. Retaliation might be less selective than promised, particularly if the challenger resorted to WMD or wildly indiscriminate attacks. It is also possible that individual members who were the target of such attacks might retaliate viciously. The proposition says only that a collective actor will not be able to base deterrence threats on nonselective and highly destructive retaliation. It will have difficulty threatening even unintended escalation – escalation might happen but threatening it would scare the members as much as the challenger! Of course, mission creep is possible as provocations provoke escalation, but escalation is more likely to be debated, calculated, and openly threatened (probably repeatedly). And officers are likely to have strict instructions to refer back to HQ, or higher, even to respond equally to escalation.

---

[1] Might a collective actor *ever* deter by threatening highly destructive retaliation? Yes, if it was nonliberalist. An Axis great-power concert would have readily threatened massive, indiscriminate punishments.

It follows that collective actors must base deterrence on promising an effective defense – "don't attack or we will defeat you." This has important implications. One is related to the "existential deterrence" supposedly attached to nuclear weapons (and other WMD). Watman and Wilkening (1995) suggest that for the importance of credibility in deterrence there is a tradeoff between scale of punishment promised and reliability of delivery. When the potential punishment is vast even limited credibility is enough; when it is modest, certainty that the threat will be carried out is needed. If so, collective actors must compensate for lacking threats of massive punishment by consistency in delivering on their coercive threats; otherwise, the threats will be of limited effectiveness, frequently challenged.

This is not clear cut, however, in light of chapter 4. There we saw that the link between credibility of a current commitment and past behavior on prior commitments is often tenuous. More important is the balance of available military power (or the ability to issue credible signals). If so, success in collective actor deterrence by the promise of defense is particularly dependent on a demonstrated ability, in past cases, to mobilize the military power needed combined with clear signs this can be done again.

Next, nuclear deterrence has had adherents because of the unattractive consequences of defending if deterrence failed; a large conventional war might rival the damage anticipated from a nuclear war. During the Cold War European governments wanted to avoid both. Moreover, they did not like what preparing to defend would have meant in military spending and related burdens, skewed investment, and forgone social expenditures. This will burden members of collective actors too. The larger the opponent and the more fierce and protracted the anticipated fighting, the more unhappy they will be with possibly having to defend and thus with threatening to defend.

Another concern will be that deterrence via threats to defend can be indeterminate in costs, duration, etc. (Officially, the UN is still deterring another attack in Korea!) This is not deterrence a collective actor can easily supply. Of the Korean War participants, the US still provides extended deterrence but what other government, especially a democracy, could have kept significant combat units there on high alert all this time?

This suggests the sixth comment (*Proposition 6*). Deterrence via collective actor defense is best attempted by promising overwhelming force in a highly offensive fashion used to settle the issue decisively, but such an approach by a collective actor is *highly improbable* unless the opponent is quite weak. It is possible to deter by promising to defend sufficiently to drag matters out and draw the attacker into a frustrating conflict, but this is not normally a plausible option. Maintaining the cohesion for an indefinite effort on a large scale is at best difficult; maintaining it for repeated engagements because none of them settles the issue will be extremely so. The collective actor should instead threaten to be "overwhelming" militarily, not in destructiveness but in comprehensiveness and sufficiency. Presumably it should be promising other significant costs as well (diplomatic isolation, economic embargo, seizure of attacker assets). The defense to be mounted should look impossible to beat, with vigorous offensive action to follow if necessary. It would be highly desirable to promise not only to defend so as to maintain or restore the status quo but to then bring about the removal or ouster of the offending government and responsible leaders.

All this is highly improbable. The problem lies not in mounting overwhelming force to win quickly and decisively, but in the self-limiting of objectives. Promising to smash the challenger's forces or cripple its ability to defend itself makes good sense not only as a threat but as the way to fight if the threat doesn't work. But threatening to obliterate the enemy or occupy the entire country and oust its leaders will clash with the desire to avoid indiscriminate damage and with the additional desire to avoid more substantial fighting and greater costs. So it will be adopted as policy only when it becomes unavoidable. Instead, there will be pressure to go for a quick restoration of the status quo or delivering a limited military response followed by a negotiated settlement. It will be said that to threaten the existence of the regime will incite it to fight to the bitter end. Thus promising a huge military effort to settle the matter for good would only make it harder to forge consensus among the members initially and then maintain it.

More is involved than concerns about costs. In collective actor deterrence members have a vested interest in limiting its scope and frequency. They don't want it used often, and frequently enforced, because many will worry that it might someday be directed at them, or at someone else when in their view it seems unwarranted. This should be a concern of almost any state below the rank of a great power (in the relevant system) which has a severe conflict with another state and can envision someday having to fight and be condemned for it. All members must also worry that keeping collective actor deterrence healthy will allow it to take on a life of its own, becoming a primary objective that overrides other policies they prefer in specific cases. States must also suspect that this will spill over into "related" activities that expand the costs and the interference with national autonomy. Examples: the aftermath of halting aggression by an unrepentant state A brings continued sanctions against A and limits on its involvement in normal political relations, limits which hurt those who want or need to deal with A; action against B because of its hidden nuclear weapons program leads, in the name of proliferation control, to much broader restrictions on what any member can do.

An important offsetting factor is that when a collective actor threatens and then begins to use force, power gravitates to those most willing and able to bear the burdens. Inside any collective actor is a smaller group that dominates the decision making and any action taken. This shift in influence is not fully beneficial or acceptable to most states. It can increase the chances that something will be done but shrink their ability to determine what that "something" is. But it enhances the likelihood of coherent decisions and forceful threats, as well as their being upheld. Multilateralism is often made effective by a core "minilateralism" – a small group that acts and lets the others just tag along. This leaves far fewer members needed to get threats and actions mounted for the sake of deterrence. However, this offsetting factor will not be enough in most cases to provide for threats of decisive military action.

The next comment (*Proposition 7*) is that collective actor deterrence *will consistently not be mounted effectively in a timely fashion*. This is despite a growing literature urging the use of preventive diplomacy (Zartman 1989) and the use of force for preventive intervention to suppress near-violent conflicts (Lund 1996). There will be a significant lag between the "attack" and the response. Collective actor deterrence will lag behind developments, be too little too late, at least at the start. This is very significant for the chances of preventing attacks and serious fighting. To prevent a breach of the peace via threats, it is important to deliver them as early as possible in the developing crisis. It is vital to affect the challenger's thinking while it is still in a formative stage, before it has hardened into convictions, decisions, and policies. Once a conclusion is reached that an attack can succeed and preparations are under way, receptivity to contrary information declines. When the plans and preparations are far advanced, to get the challenger to stop is even more difficult. In many ways an attack starts with plans being adopted and preparations put in train; when that is far along it takes virtually a very strong threat to get it halted, if threats will work at all.

An additional factor is that it is common in designing attacks to seek either a quick, complete victory or a more modest gain to settle down to consolidate and defend.[2] This would confront the collective actor with a fait accompli costly and difficult to reverse. It makes for less time in which to attempt deterrence, and when it fails the collective actor is in a difficult situation – deterrence now applies in reverse. The collective actor is now practicing compellance and is subject to the attacker's deterrence. This means partly ceding the psychological and political advantage of being on the defensive, of upholding the status quo.[3]

Deterrence, of course, is threats of *hypothetical* military responses. Once it fails, the possibility of having to act looms; additional threats can be issued but the odds are rising that they will have to be carried out – the challenger ignored the earlier threats and has demonstrated a willingness to fight. Deterrence is cheap compared to upholding it, and with that in mind the members' cohesion may slip. This is what the opponent is counting on, mounting a deterrence effort promising that the costs will be very high (see, for example, Lepgold 1998).

Thus usually mounting deterrence threats only late in the game, when an attack is a good possibility, has potentially serious consequences. Nevertheless, collective actors will be consistently afflicted by this. Compared with national actors, the collective actor has an additional level of political consensus to establish. Some members will want no action taken or no action as potentially costly as fighting, or will want more evidence that such a drastic step is really required, or will fear that getting confrontational may exacerbate the situation. Often this opposition can be surmounted only when the attack occurs.

In addition, the reason for being of collective actors for peace and security is to ensure that peaceful means of resolving disputes have been exhausted before forcible steps are taken. States do not construct collective actors so their military forces can be off fighting in faraway places. They want collective actor deterrence to work precisely so they won't have to fight. They are naturally inclined to hope that collective pressure and diplomatic intervention will work and reluctant to begin issuing deterrence threats and institute suitable military preparations. Some members will press for additional overtures and call for avoiding threats and threatening buildups that might poison the atmosphere and

---

[2] An illustrative analysis along these lines is Mearsheimer (1983).
[3] As noted in chapter 2, prospect theory says people absorb recent gains into what is "theirs," for which they are more willing to fight than to make new gains.

kill chances that the overtures can be successful. The same applies to action after an attack – some members will *still* want to try political and diplomatic measures. Even after a military response is prepared the collective actor will usually continue trying not to use it, pressing negotiations of various kinds instead.

Finally, a state can often respond quickly by threats and related military steps because it has long anticipated a conflict with that particular opponent, perhaps in that theater and in that way. This comes from being preoccupied with only a few other states as threats, usually in the neighborhood, typically over well-known issues. Thus a state is likely to have suitably prepared forces and contingency plans. A collective actor is unlikely to have this capability available for many of the contingencies it has to face. The military forces have to be mobilized by members on a case-by-case basis, and may be unsuited for the specific mission. Though it was a success, the Kosovo case fell somewhere in between. NATO had seen it coming and had thought about it for quite a long time, and individual members had done the same. However, NATO then selected a way of implementing its threats that, at first, seemed unsuitable to dealing with the problem.

Therefore, it is highly likely that the military action the collective actor hoped to forestall will take place, or be about to take place, before heavyweight deterrence threats are mounted. The attack will come before the collective actor has put military forces in position to fight. The collective actor relies on deterrence via threats of defense with little sign any effective defense is ready. The threat must work despite being largely abstract, hardly a recipe for consistent success.

Anticipating that collective actor will be too little too late leads to still another comment (*Proposition 8*), which is that collective actor deterrence is at least relatively free of the standard stability problem and does not readily create a security dilemma. The collective actor's tardiness in reacting means there is less likelihood of interacting military displays or buildups provoking a war. The nature of the stability problem is different – what is most likely to provoke the use of force is the lack of suitable collective actor military preparations or a visible reluctance to fight, with the opponent likely to be confident that in the end the collective actor won't really do anything.

However, once the collective actor has mobilized forces and sent them into action the danger of instability grows – fears emerge that the forces will go too far or be used for other purposes, which is plausible given instances of mission creep. The best example may be how the defeat of

North Korean forces led to escalation of the objective which sent UN forces surging to the Yalu and provoked a very nervous China.

Next, collective actors cannot threaten massive destruction so their most impressive threat would be to inflict a rapid, decisive defeat at low cost. But how often will they generate the capabilities or consensus to drive home such a threat? Their most realistic and potent threat is probably one of limited but significant military action followed by determined efforts to politically eliminate the offending regime. But this may well be insufficiently daunting to the challenger, particularly as it would be politically difficult to sustain for a lengthy period.

So, then, what does deter? It is probably the combination of a threat of some damaging military action, the possibility of adopting a nasty political objective (ousting the regime), and the legitimacy and moral weight behind the collective actor's coercion. In short, what deters in part is the nature of the actor. It is important enough that it should be cherished and sustained.

Nevertheless, this leads me to suggest (*Proposition 9*) that collective actor deterrence will consistently confront larger credibility problems than national actor deterrence. This is implied by several of the earlier comments. To begin with, the collective actor has the usual credibility problem: threats are cheap, implementing them usually is not, so it is always questionable whether they will be carried out. Challengers are tempted to think that the threatened response can be deterred.

This is exacerbated by the difficulties in constructing a consensus among the members, for the reasons cited. When they disagree about characterizing the situation and what to do about it, this conveys the image of a coalition that is weak and half-hearted about military action, that will not hold together especially if the costs jump or the matter drags on. Having a similar impact are any signs that members are seeking to free ride, voting for action but not planning to seriously participate. The same will be true if members are reluctant to cede a slice of autonomy to shape a cohesive military force or operation, for instance by resisting service under someone else's command; or if casualties are politically unacceptable back home; or if members seem uneasy about precedents that may be set. These things make it easier for a challenger to find the evidence it wants to find that if it acts firmly, and says forcefully it will fight, and drags out the whole matter through negotiations and minor concessions, it will deter, wear down, or fragment the coalition.

We must also recall that the main burdens will fall on only some members, those that are the most powerful, most suitably armed or located, or the most able to project power. Everything therefore turns on the credibility of these members; if they have a credibility problem the organization does too. When the challenger tries to discourage the organization, it can concentrate on discouraging some or all of those particular members and ignore the rest. (In Somalia the UN effort died away when the US was "persuaded" to pull out.) Certain members, therefore, have a veto, whether instutitionalized or not, which can add to the credibility problem.

Collective actors also have problems in delivering credible threats due to the availability of information. They are normally highly transparent. The information age can now greatly complicate the collective actor credibility problem. The failed attempt to get Iraq to withdraw from Kuwait illustrates this. The US and others sent strong, clear messages to Iraq – official statements, unofficial communications, Security Council votes, then a huge military buildup. Iraqi leaders understood that war was possible but they were willing to take the risk. They also had a strong political and psychological motivation for refusing to believe that war was coming. But clearly it was also easier to believe a war would not occur because of the enormous information available. Iraq easily learned that the American public was reluctant to go to war, that many members of Congress were opposed, that there was opposition at the highest levels of the armed forces (i.e. General Powell). Iraq could readily see expressions of pessimism about a war – that casualties would be heavy, long-term effects in the Arab world would be pernicious, etc. It was easy to discern how reluctant other governments (France, the Soviet Union) were through the alternative strategies they pursued. In short, *the scale and depth of available information heightened ambiguity as to what would happen*. This made it easier for Saddam to conclude that the allies would not choose war, that the coalition would not hold together, that modest casualties would unravel it. Plenty of information sustained Iraqi preconceptions, prejudices, and wishful thinking.

This problem seems inherent in the explosion of information and modern communications. It poses a particular burden for collective actors who have minimal control over information about their internal disagreements and doubts plus members who take competing and conflicting steps (statements, actions) which convey an ambiguous picture and who are reluctant to go to war. There are also the members who disapprove or support the challenger – they can be potent sources of inside information (e.g. the Soviet Union for the Serbs). Those who utilize deterrence in service to global peace and security through collective actors must accept the fact that while they can deliver threats more clearly than ever, the same is true of messages contradicting those threats. For the same reason it is harder for a collective actor to deter by bluffing. The target state will know almost as much about how uneven support is for carrying out threats as those who issue them, just through media coverage, discussions among the members, votes in the meetings, and the like.

Finally, collective actors will have a serious credibility problem because they exist to promote nonuse of force and the peaceful resolution of disputes, and to shield members from having to use force through effective deterrence/compellance. Along with this they have a very limited history in practicing deterrence compared with states, and no extensive track record. A challenger can count on the use of force being treated as a last resort. This weakens credibility, since who can tell how long it may take for all, or enough of, the members to decide that reasonable avenues other than threats and a fight have been exhausted?

The next point (*Proposition 10*) is that there is a continuum of situations along which it becomes progressively more difficult for a collective actor to effectively pursue deterrence. Deterrence (and compellance as well) will be easier for a collective actor to conduct:

> when it confronts blatant interstate aggression, than
> when it confronts ambiguous interstate aggression, than
> when it confronts a blatant threat of an interstate military clash, than
> when it confronts an ambiguous threat of an interstate military clash, than
> when it confronts intrastate violence and/or threats, than
> when it confronts terrorist violence and/or threats.

The further along the continuum the challenge falls the harder it will be to make a strong, effective deterrence threat or a military response if deterrence fails.

The reasoning is straightforward. Dealing with interstate violence is the prime purpose of collective actor management of peace and security, but building the necessary support is never easy. The more ambiguous the threat the greater the difficulty. It may be unclear whether the attack is really likely unless something is done, or who caused the conflict to get to this point, or whether what looms is aggression. Consider, for instance, the difficulties for a collective actor if China moved toward a military confrontation with Taiwan or initiated military action.

Applying deterrence to prevent or halt internal warfare, today's most pervasive security problem, is important and complicated. To begin with, it should be inherently more difficult for a collective actor to intervene in a domestic situation. The precedents are more disturbing to members, and the desire to avoid violating sovereignty unless absolutely necessary will make consensus harder to come by. This broadening of the concept of an "attack" on peace and security will be so sticky that states will proceed more on a case-by-case basis than by settling on some fundamental values and agreeing on what they mean in practice. There is always fear, as well, that domestic disputants may be unusually dangerous – the conflict is intractable, resistance to intervention could be nasty, etc. Since it is difficult from outside to accurately assess the intensity and complexity of such a domestic dispute, uneasiness is reinforced; it is not clear just what the members are getting into. Observers readily overestimate (and underestimate) the intractability of these conflicts, the degree to which the parties are hurting and willing to stop fighting, the degree to which there will be outright resistance.

It is hard to intervene without taking sides, or appearing to. Often one party's behavior primarily provokes the concern that evokes deterrence and any eventual intervention. Even without that, the intervention normally benefits the parties unevenly, conveying an image of partiality. It is hard to avoid pressing for an outcome one side opposes more than the other – hence the interest in waiting until Zartman's "hurtful stalemate" applies, until the parties have come to see the struggle as more intolerable than each other. It is less attractive to intervene in domestic quarrels out of concern about the length of time that it will probably take (to get a settlement and to closely monitor it for the necessary time); and the amount and cost of the peacebuilding that may be required.

We must also not ignore another consideration (*Proposition 11*): the great powers are relatively immune to collective actor efforts at deterrence. For a collective actor that aspires to comprehensive membership, tackling a great-power member will very likely split and destroy that community – in those circumstances collective action becomes more like an alliance endeavor, one side against another. Most likely, the members will choose not to do this. A collective actor facing unacceptable behavior from an external great power (NATO dealing with Russia on Chechnya) will attract little support for tackling such a potentially vast endeavor. This is the single greatest flaw of collective actor deterrence and no significant remedy is in view.

Collective actor advantages

To this point we have been discussing the difficulties facing collective actors. Now we do the reverse and explore the difficulties collective actors can make for challengers. In general (*Proposition 12*), collective actor deterrence poses serious and complex problems for a challenger that make success more plausible than it might otherwise seem. The challenger wants to forestall that deterrence or negate it. One recourse is the challenger's own deterrence, but trying to target an entire coalition is difficult, sometimes impossible. This is particularly true in deterring by threats of retaliation – any attempted retaliation is likely to be selective or partial in effect. Unless this drives the other members to cancel military action it will be unproductive. A challenger is better off trying to attempt deterrence by threatening a potent defense instead, or trying to split the coalition by threatening retaliation against crucial members (militarily) and hoping this does not reinforce the coalition's determination.

Failing to solve this problem puts the challenger in a morale-straining situation – it suffers serious harm but cannot inflict all that much in return. The coalition will likely start with sanctions, for which there are normally few useful punitive responses available. Then the coalition may apply force on a large scale and from (in part) a considerable distance, things the challenger cannot readily match. It is difficult to accept such a situation indefinitely, with no way to end the damage other than to concede defeat. It is hard to hit back at "everyone."

Another problem for the challenger is how to keep its threats from heightening the coalition's unity because the members are apt to view those threats as compounding its misbehavior, confirming that it is reckless and dangerous, further justifying a harsh response. In such cases there is usually a perceived moral superiority in numbers – members feel right is on their side partly because so many governments are working together. This suggests that the collective actor is likely enjoy greater legitimacy with third parties, particularly in upholding or seeking to restore the status quo. The typical challenger response, that the collective actor is just the mouthpiece of a particular state or cabal, tries to challenge this aspect of its legitimacy.

The challenger will, of course, worry about the costs of carrying out its threats and have other credibility problems. A militarily superior collective actor, when mobilized, will likely feel that the opponent won't fight or won't fight hard, will just go through the motions. This is reinforced because the challenger knows that putting up a nasty retaliation or a very vigorous defense could lead the collective actor to escalate its objectives, maybe to elimination of the offending government.

Finally, the challenger will know that the collective actor is naturally concerned about its reputation, about its own credibility. Thus the members can have a strong incentive to hang tough regardless of the matter at hand. They have a stake in effective security management and thus in maintaining the collective actor's credibility even when this is painful (or appears likely to be so); indeed, a painful case may incite special concern about not backing down for fear of its effects on future credibility and effectiveness.

Further implications

Are there other implications of these propositions? We can start with the difficulty of getting collective actors to take problems seriously enough soon enough so as to issue deterrence threats when they have a better chance of working, the burden of Proposition 7 (page 182). This can be eased considerably if the information identifying the threat and defining its nature looks very sound. Since members themselves usually provide the information (as do the parties to the dispute) and are the main judges of its significance, it is better if perception of a threat comes from several of them independently, especially ones with no specific stakes in the situation. This is a strong argument for effective national intelligence capabilities or other substantial information gathering and analytic resources in many places, not just Washington. It would be even better if the collective actor had an independent capability for monitoring peace and security as well, but this is very unlikely any time soon. It is nice if the information comes from an independent or semi-independent international organization established to detect threats – the OSCE, for instance, or the IAEA on nuclear proliferation. This suggests that such agencies also need a dedicated, effective information-gathering capability, maybe even an intelligence capability. Less valuable is threat perception by just a few national sources or only one, particularly via sources or methods not readily confirmed or checked. However, this often happens and the difficulties are acute if that government has a strong interest in the situation, e.g. charges of mistreatment of minorities from a country with ethnically related people. Some steps toward multiple surveillance and monitoring resources are occurring through globalization of the world's media but the development of commercial monitoring, from satellites on down, will probably have the greatest impact in the end.

This does not invalidate Proposition 7. Abundant and compelling information helps stimulate the collective actor to consider deterrence seriously, but is not necessarily enough. Collective actors will still be slow to mount deterrence threats. It helps if the members (or the entire community) are already clearly and consistently on record as completely opposed to the reported violation of peace and security. That short-circuits an important step in getting to the use of threats – deciding whether to care much about what is going on. Still, it doesn't always work. Taking a stand against something is often done vaguely, and even opposition to aggression doesn't guarantee a consensus in a particular instance as to what constitutes it. Consensus is more likely when the "aggression" comes after a lengthy series of events long seen by members and others as provocative, as instigating military reactions.

While a decentralized system for generating information about prospective threats is helpful, a consensus for doing something is more easily developed when the decision process is concentrated, when others can cluster around a powerful member or core group. This is partly because the powerful members usually shoulder most of the burdens; for others, the decision is to authorize actions they won't have to carry out. It can be easy to get broad support for threats of military action when the key members for carrying them out agree, and next to impossible if they don't. This comes with a price. With a dominant member or group around which others rally for threatening or carrying threats out, the challenger's task in deterring is simplified: concentrate on deterring that leader or group. Discourage it from acting and there will be no collective military response.

With regard to credibility, Proposition 8 (page 184) suggests that the collective actor has special difficulties. What about reputation and credibility – does a collective actor gain or lose credibility in future cases by its actions in the case at hand? It seems clear that it should when involved in repeated encounters on a particular matter with a specific opponent – we can assume that the recurring interaction breeds (on both sides) images based on experience, and that they are somewhat manipulable by each side's behavior (see Harvey 1997a). This classic lore about deterrence in crises and enduring rivalries is upheld, within limits, by empirical studies and there seems no reason it cannot apply to collective actors.

But what about its actions over multiple deterrence situations with different challengers? Are its commitments interdependent so that behavior on one can dictate credibility on others? Mercer's (1996) analysis is that serious continuing opponents readily take each other's threats seriously. Even when the opponent is conciliatory and cooperative it is seen as being so only because forced by circumstances – no reputation is generated for being "nice" or a pushover when threats lead to good behavior. But does this readily apply to a collective actor? First, can the Security Council, by being tough on someone, readily build a reputation for credibility with that government in the future? And would that reputation persist if it wobbled on its threats in a later confrontation with that actor (or even ducked a confrontation)? After all, a collective actor is not a "personality" like a national government. Or is it? It seems possible that it can be when embroiled in a longstanding conflict, but this is unlikely to happen very often. (Though Frank Harvey's work shows how a conflict consists of numerous deterrence situations and thus the parties might build reputations on credibility fairly quickly.)

And how readily does the collective actor's behavior in one situation shape its credibility with quite different opponents later on? It is often claimed that this is the same as for national governments; the Security Council or NATO must build a reputation for acting decisively or its deterrence will often fail. But this is open to the objection raised in chapters 2 and 4 – we lack solid evidence that actors carefully review information about the past behavior of a new opponent (or even an old opponent) to assess the credibility of its current threats. Challengers may be less "rational" than this. Substate actors may not think in these terms at all.

What we can say is that the argument that future challengers will be affected by past behavior *will always be made* by proponents of deterrence – and *will always have some appeal*. It will contribute to building a consensus for issuing threats and, if necessary, upholding them, not because of what future challengers will think but because of what members fear they will think. And if the collective actor behaves as if it matters, that probably strengthens its credibility.

Preliminary evidence

The propositions were not devised by canvassing experience in the post-Cold War era. We have too little to go on and too few detailed studies of what there is. However, it may be useful to survey relevant aspects of prominent cases.

Proposition 1: For general deterrence, collective actors need credibility more than national actors do.

To wean states from relying on their own military capabilities requires, in part, instilling confidence that another effective capability for managing peace and security exists. This has had great influence in shaping European security since the Cold War. The fundamental argument for making NATO the basis for managing peace and security has been that NATO has a highly visible capability and that its leading member has ample military capabilities for either deterrence or intervention and a history of carrying out both, which is not true of either the UN or western Europe. The fear was that, without a NATO seen as effective, European governments, starting with Germany, would renationalize their security policies. This is not evidence, but it is not irrelevant. Governments acted to forestall an alternative approach, power balancing, which they thought likely to emerge.

These governments were also very interested when NATO added a new function. Projecting power to protect nonmembers, including minorities within those nonmembers, was something on which NATO had no reputation. Much of the commentary prior to NATO's Bosnia intervention emphasized this and suggested that the results might be so unsatisfactory as to undermine the organization. Also relevant is the common view that governments primarily pursue their own interests, narrowly conceived, in international organizations. Some analysts contend that collective actors change members' preferences, and that their continued viability and effectiveness can become very important to the members, but the first view is widespread. And from that perspective a collective actor inherently lacks credibility in threatening violent intervention. Analyses prior to the intervention held that NATO would not act because most members had few interests at stake in the Balkans.

There was also widespread disgust with the UN in its Bosnia peacekeeping effort because it consistently refused to take military action to defend the peacekeepers or uphold their efforts to prevent fighting. Supposedly this timidity led directly to the eventual seizure of peacekeepers by Bosnian Serbs as hostages to prevent any military retaliation and ensured that a great deal of further fighting took place. Much of the justification for turning to NATO was that the UN lacked credibility. It seems that the influence of the realist tradition makes the burden of gaining sufficient credibility for collective actor general deterrence quite substantial, even when the actor works to display its interest and its plans to back up threats with action.

Proposition 2: The more institutionalized the collective actor the less intrinsically serious the credibility problem.

This certainly seemed true in Europe. The usual contention was that only NATO had sufficient credibility to cope with Bosnia – the UN had no command structure, no planning staff, no combat elements used to working with one another, no established logistics – despite NATO having no history of anything like the intervention. The closest it had come was the Gulf War, but that was not run through NATO, just assisted by NATO experience. Mistrust of the UN had risen out of the Somalia disaster, where there were no arrangements to quickly help UN units in trouble, and from the lack of a strong decision-making center on UN peacekeeping in Bosnia – everything had to be referred back to the Security Council.

Proposition 3: The viability of collective actor deterrence depends on the viability of collective actor security management.

It is much too early to assess the future viability of collective actor security management in the eyes of governments or other actors. But we can see what happens when it is called into question. In mounting the War on Terrorism the Bush Administration ignored collective actors for anything but rounding up support – they were seen as likely to get in the way of an effective response to terrorism. The administration charged ahead and plugged others into its plans in Afghanistan as needed. Then it mounted threats toward other governments on its own initiative.

Proposition 4: Collective actors will not get their own forces soon.

This is debatable. In the 1990s, for the first time in decades, there were serious discussions about giving the UN forces for peacekeeping or preventive interventions where time would be of the essence. Nothing came of this, governments showed no interest. However, the EU is currently establishing its own intervention force for a Bosnia-like effort lasting up to year. If fully established as an independent force, this would partially negate the proposition. However, descriptions of it stress that it will consist of national military units *assigned* for *possible* use in interventions, that the arrangement will resemble NATO where forces come together under a single command for an operation when necessary. Does the proposition fail if a collective actor has national forces it can call on *automatically*, with a unified command reporting to the collective actor's executive, and with governments serving as powerful advisors? That arrangement may exist in the EU eventually, but maybe only when the EU is a semi-sovereign actor.

Proposition 5: A collective actor will rely on threats of defense, not (or not just) retaliation.

This fits the cases to date, if we confine the discussion to *military* responses. There is no instance in which a collective actor threatened to kill and destroy solely for retaliatory purposes. Collective actors have worked hard at careful targeting – in Bosnia, Kosovo, Serbia, Iraq, and Sierra Leone. The media consistently played up stories of collateral killing and damage but that was because when precision-guided weapons were imprecise it was news.

However, the same restraint has not applied to sanctions. Collective actor sanctions do not aim at *deliberate* fatalities, but they have imposed privation on the elderly, children, the sick, etc. and they typically hurt the general population far more than the elite (Mueller and Mueller 2000). Despite the impact of the regime in a case like Iraq complaints about the civilian deaths or privation from sanctions energized efforts to have them more precisely targeted or abandoned.

The NATO bombing in Serbia also had broad debilitating effects on the society and some of this was intentional to put pressure on the government – to coerce the government at least partly by hurting the society. Thus late in the war NATO knocked out roughly 70 percent of Serbia's electric power generation by dropping graphite threads. This is close to punitive retaliation. It does not contradict the proposition because NATO asserted that the prime objective was always to weaken the regime militarily prior to occupying Kosovo, and the regime quit when the possibility of occupation was growing as its military strength, from KLA attacks combined with NATO air power, was shrinking. But future cases should be closely scrutinized on this.

In the same way we note the mixed threats to Iraq. French President François Mitterrand said deliberately that nuclear weapons were out of the question, but US Secretary of State James Baker deliberately sought to give the impression that their use was a possibility if Iraq used WMD, and the US deployed ships known to carry nuclear weapons in the region during the war. While they would have been used solely against Iraqi forces, this would have been close to punitive retaliation.

Efforts at a controlled response are apt to have additional nasty results, and collective actors may build on this if they become frustrated in an intervention. The implication would be that in such cases there will be unintended consequences – eroding the impact of complaints about it and putting more pressure on governments facing collective actor deterrence in the future. The other possibility, however, is that collective actor deterrence enforcement will someday have harshly indiscriminate effects that end up magnifying the limits suggested by Proposition 5.

It also seems that a point in an earlier chapter and developed further in the next one applies here. There is now a race between the effect of modern military technology in facilitating collective actor interventions by promising a relatively painless outcome in casualties (on each side), which can strengthen deterrence credibility, and the way that this development is driving down the threshold of acceptable costs and casualties, which can erode support for interventions and therefore the credibility of threatening them.

Proposition 6: Collective actors should plan to use overwhelming force to win quickly and decisively, and to settle the issue decisively, but won't do so.

This has been unevenly but often reflected in cases. Collective actors *deployed* overwhelming capabilities to reverse aggression (in Kuwait) or to deter attacks on occupying units (Bosnia, Kosovo, Haiti). The liberation of Kuwait was the use of overwhelming force to minimize allied casualties. But overwhelming force was not used to decisively *settle* things. No effort was made to occupy Iraq and oust the regime – it was hoped that elements in Iraq would take care of this. There was a desire to avoid additional casualties, fear of civilian harm and military slaughter, and concern about Arab reactions. There was no deliberate effort to seize the Bosnian Serb leaders, including those indicted for war crimes. Less than overwhelming force was used to deal with the Somali warlords. As for the Kosovo case, NATO did not massively attack Serbia at the outset as the air force commander wanted – then limited attacks were used to minimize allied casualties, air attacks were canceled on cloudy days, Serbia and Kosovo were not invaded (Lambeth 2001). It has been typical to limit the force used or go for limited political aims. (The latter was the case, eventually, in the Korean War.)

Pressures to win quickly lest the coalition fray were certainly evident. In the Gulf War the forces assembled could not sit there indefinitely; there was such concern about heavy casualties prior to the fighting – and thus such opposition to initiating it – that political support probably would have been fragile had the fighting dragged on. NATO played a risky game in Kosovo. Having counted on victory after a short bombing effort, in a replay of its Bosnia experience, it settled for applying force in a controlled fashion and that lumbered on for some time; it became clear that political support was eroding and that NATO feared it would not sustain doing more (Priest 1999d). Europeans found it alarming that building up invasion forces seemed best for a quick victory but the US held back for domestic political reasons and to soothe internal NATO tensions (Erlanger 1999; Williams 2000).

Proposition 7: Collective actor deterrence will not be mounted in a timely fashion, nor will it be upheld immediately on being challenged.

Judging by the complaints, this has been much in evidence. (On Europe see Spezio 1995.) It was true leading up to the Korean War and the Gulf War. Both the UN and NATO were faulted intensely in the Bosnia case for not threatening the combatants early on – particularly the Bosnian Serbs – to try to prevent fighting and human rights abuses, and then for issuing threats not backed up when ignored. The members didn't agree on the need for or use of deterrence, then could not quickly agree on building up appropriate military forces, nor on using those forces, until much fighting occurred and atrocities multiplied. Only where serious casualties were no concern, as in peacekeeping, the weapons blockade, or overflights, was action possible in a timely way. The traumatic effect of delay in Bosnia played a major role in shaping NATO determination to intervene early in Kosovo, and warnings to Serbia about Kosovo had been issued as early as 1990. Yet the Milosevic government conducted a campaign to suppress the guerrillas built on terror and indiscriminate destruction, and prepared a massive enlargement of that effort, before NATO was fully ready to act.

As for Kuwait, the UN had to engage in compellance because it mounted no deterrence prior to the invasion. The necessity was not appreciated until Saddam's plans were very far along, and it would have been impossible to build consensus behind a military buildup to forestall an attack – prior to the invasion neither Kuwait nor Saudi Arabia would have permitted foreign deployments on their soil. Efforts to get a peaceful Iraqi pullback continued up to the moment the war began.

Proposition 8: Collective actor deterrence does not generate the standard stability problem.

There is no evidence yet that a collective actor precipitated someone's military action in a crisis because it took steps that provoked the target into striking first. It is likely that Milosevic planned to repress Kosovar guerrillas and clear out their supporters before NATO could act, much as North Korea planned its attack in 1950. In both cases the aim was to forestall a decision to intervene rather than to preempt the intervention. The closest a collective actor has come to a standard stability problem was the jockeying to seize land just before NATO intervened, but this doesn't quite fit – often there is last-minute fighting before a cease fire to gain bargaining leverage in the ensuing negotiations. More problematic is the Chinese intervention in the Korean War; the UN offensive to the Yalu was very provocative. However, it was a continuation of fighting in progress and not deterrence – a deterrence effort did not provoke an attack. But the intervention did.

Proposition 9: Collective actors face graver credibility problems than state actors.

This is difficult to explore with available evidence. In addition, it is hard to know how particular cases would have gone if a single state had been involved. (The US military buildup did not shift Taliban policies.) However, it seem likely that a state actor marshalling as much military power as NATO in the Bosnian and Kosovo cases, or as the UN did along the borders of Kuwait, would have less trouble being taken seriously. There are alternative explanations to the lack of credibility: perhaps in the first two cases Milosevic knew he would be attacked but needed that to make his retreat politically tolerable at home, while in the Persian Gulf the unexpected impact of new technology on the military balance was crucial because Iraq expected to put up a much better fight to gain important negotiating leverage. Thus we can't be certain. But it seems that in each case the challenger hoped to avoid or ride out an attack based on evidence that the coalition was not unanimous, with members who were reluctant to use force and would call for an early halt to give negotiations a chance. On Kosovo, Italy and Greece openly opposed the bombing, Germany resisted the idea of an invasion, and there were real strains over how the bombing was conducted.

In addition, the collective actors consistently treated force as a last resort, used deterrence only when other efforts at a peaceful resolution had failed, and used it mainly to bring the other side to negotiate or retreat so there was no hurry to use force. All this can readily be interpreted, and was at the time, as evidence of weak cohesion and other qualities bearing on credibility.

There is the contrary example of Haiti, however. There, the first US effort to send forces was called off at signs of just the slightest resistance.

The US had a significant credibility problem – at least as great as any collective actor in our cases. Virtually all efforts at extended deterrence face credibility problems and this is probably a good part of collective actor difficulties on this score, not just the nature of the actor.

Proposition 10: The further along a continuum from outright interstate aggression to terrorism, the harder deterrence is to operate for a collective actor.

This assumes that consensus for deterrence is weaker when the challenge is less clear cut, the guilty party is harder to ascertain, and upholding the threats will intrude significantly on sovereignty. The most notable collective actor responses to aggression are Korea and the Gulf War; in both a huge response was quickly organized with participation by many nations. Since there were no clear deterrence threats beforehand, the evidence in support of the proposition is indirect. And there are cases of blatant aggression where nothing was done: Vietnam's invasion of Cambodia, China's attack on Vietnam, Iraq's attack on Iran. Since they occurred during the Cold War perhaps they don't apply – maybe something else barred formation of the necessary consensus.

But we readily see the impact of ambiguity. The clash between Armenia and Azerbaidzhan was hard to sort out in terms of blame. The same was true of the Ethiopia–Somalia war, or the constant fighting in the 1990s between India and Pakistan. A truly messy conflict, simultaneously intrastate and interstate, first ousted the Mobutu government in the Congo and then threatened the Kabila government. In these instances no serious attempt was made to build a coalition for deterrence; collective actors settled for putting political pressure on the parties to stop fighting.

Most severe *internal* disputes have generated no systematic attempt at collective actor deterrence followed by intervention when necessary. The exceptions in the 1990s were Bosnia and Kosovo, Sierra Leone, Rwanda (far too late), and East Timor. Contrast these with the lack of threats or intervention in Angola, Algeria, the Sudan, Afghanistan, Colombia, etc. Such conflicts cannot normally be stopped, with any follow-on success, without in effect putting the nation in receivership, taking over its governmental functions and attempting to rebuild from the ground up. This is certainly beneficial for the citizens and carries none of the risks of a permanent colonial relationship like a government's intervention could. It is certainly cheaper than letting conflicts produce floods of refugees, illegal activities to finance the fighting, border area sanctuaries, transborder terrorism, threats to foreign investors, and the like. Thus reluctance to intervene must be due, beyond the short-term considerations that loom large in any political system, primarily to uneasiness about the precedents, particularly when sovereignty is now assaulted from so many directions.

Though not often put this way, extensive intervention in internal conflicts can also strain the sovereignty of countries that supply most of the forces (when fighting is anticipated) and financing. If precedents pile up that make threats of intervention and then military action a routine feature of international life, a curbing of autonomy results – leading governments are supposed to undertake them when required and not just when the national interest is involved or they feel their participation is suitable. In the East Timor case, for instance, Australians and other observers complained mightily about the US decision to not join the military intervention as a shock to its allies, that Australia would have to reconsider how reliable its ally really was. The US had taken the lead elsewhere so why not in this case?

Such concerns helped shape Bush Administration efforts in its first months to shrink American foreign involvements and assert a more unilateralist stance. There was a barrage of complaints that the US had lost control over its foreign policy through being assigned, and accepting, responsibility for too many problems in too many places. Of course, the administration soon found that shrinking military involvements and ducking obligations to help manage security in the Middle East was easier said than done.

Proposition 11: great powers are immune to collective actor deterrence.

Thus far there is no evidence to the contrary. We can imagine possible cases, involving NATO for example, but there is nothing on the horizon that is likely to produce even a serious attempt at collective actor deterrence against a great power, much less a successful one.

Proposition 12: a collective actor poses severe problems for any challenger seeking to deter it.

In Bosnia and Kosovo, against whom was Serbia to offer a military riposte? The neighbors that allowed use of their air space or the bases from which the bombing came? Those doing the bombing, who were almost entirely out of range? How was Serbia to do enough harm to erode the coalition? It was stuck trying to put up a stout defense against overwhelming forces able to attack from all sides. Iraq faced the same problem. It tried to stir up something by attacking Israel, surely a desperate move, and resorted to the spiteful torching of Kuwait's oil wells. In both Serbia and Iraq, morale crumbled. The government did not emerge from either war with strong support for putting up a good fight, but faced recrimination for having promoted such a hopeless situation.

Conclusion

This discussion has been speculative. We are in the early stages of a significant new development in the management of peace and security, envisioned early in the last century but receiving serious implementation again only now. There is no guarantee it will be successful. The Security Council may not be useful for some time, given the strains over the Kosovo case. But this might be offset by an increase in regional efforts elsewhere to imitate NATO, not necessarily in design but in the resort to collective decisions and action.

It is reasonable to expect the following. Multilateral security management seems here to stay. If the great powers avoid serious conflicts it should be possible to mount collective responses to outbreaks of violence through global institutions. Otherwise regional security management, already growing, will become even more important. The number of interstate wars has declined and the incidence of intrastate wars has been stable for the past decade, so security management is not beyond our resources. As many analysts suggest, war may have a declining legitimacy, making it easier to get instances of deliberate violence condemned, contained and repressed.

However, the burden of collective actor management will be eased by restricting the cases in which intervention is undertaken, starting with a reduced load on the US, particularly in the wake of the War on Terrorism. Security management and the deterrence on which it rests will therefore be intermittent, inconsistent, somewhat tenuous. Troubles in various places will be less guaranteed to get the attention they deserve and deterrence via threats of intervention will be less widely employed or less effective than many would like.

The cornerstone of any security management system is its provision for what is to be done when all else fails. The answer in all major organized societies and in international affairs is the use of force for either damage control or outright suppression of the violent. Collective actors have a long history of using force for damage control, primarily in peacekeeping, but no experience in depth with suppression of violators.

And the suppression starts with attempts at deterrence, both for the case at hand and in hopes of preventing cases from emerging in the future.

Deterrence by collective actors is the same basic operation as deterrence by other actors, and much of the theory built up to explain its dynamics, its strengths and weaknesses, should apply. But it does have distinctive wrinkles and we should be thinking about how to take these into account, guiding the accumulation of evidence and analysis so as to better understand its uses in the future.

6 The revolution in military affairs and deterrence

In earlier drafts of this chapter, I spent a good deal of time defending the idea that a revolution in military affairs was in progress and explaining many of its main features. Events have moved faster than I have. The RMA is now much more familiar and, on the whole, much less debatable. However, little attention has as yet been given to its potential impact on deterrence, a subject quite relevant to topics in prior chapters but left undiscussed until now. Deterrence will probably be deeply affected by these important military and related changes. How?

Revolutions in military affairs

It is not certain that a revolution in military affairs is occurring or will soon. Historians have "found" such revolutions in the past but argue about just what belongs on the list.[1] While analysts may still disagree sharply about whether another one is in the offing recent events reinforce the view that it is. The "revolution" is widely accepted in the American armed forces, is being vigorously pursued elsewhere, and is now a major element in weapons and military-related procurements. *I think the revolution is unavoidable.* It will change many aspects of the use of force and greatly affect deterrence. However, the discussion that follows is often speculative, because the specific course that technological change and military applications of it will take is not known.

First, we must sort out what constitutes a revolution in military affairs. There are several possibilities. Normally these revolutions involve a major shift in military technology that greatly alters weapons and their

---

[1] The term was used by Parker (1988) concerning the rise of the West after 1500. The ensuing debate among historians is covered in Rogers (1995).

effects. The result must be so significant as to adjust the impact of war in general, or dominate the course or outcome of specific wars. The simplest conception, therefore, is that *the technological shift constitutes the revolution.*[2] This could involve a change in the basic nature of key weapons or delivery systems, as with gunpowder or ballistic missiles. It might sharply alter the effectiveness of existing weapons, outmoding or negating some and bringing great improvements in others so as to fundamentally alter warfare. Nuclear weapons added little, at first, to destruction available from existing weapons but could deliver it far more swiftly and efficiently; eventually they vastly enlarged it.

Such changes can have great impact. A perennial concern in the last century was whether technological shifts altered the relative effectiveness of offenses and defenses. Changes prior to 1914 favored defenses, contrary to expectations and plans all across Europe. The result in World War I was battles, casualties, and consumption of national outputs far beyond anything ever before seen or considered possible, lasting far longer than expected, as the strength of defenses imposed a stalemate and forced a war of attrition. Nuclear weapons later favored offenses because so few could destroy a nation and no defense could ward off every nuclear weapon fired at it; eventually even great powers could not guarantee their survival unilaterally – the best they could do was practice deterrence.

As the examples suggest, a shift in military technology can fundamentally alter war and its uses by substantially changing the nature and scale of fighting capabilities. Nuclear weapons altered great-power behavior – those governments became able to do vastly more damage in a war than ever before and to inflict it almost instantly. On the other hand, this made them very reluctant to fight anything other than a limited war with anyone else and particularly reluctant to fight even the smallest war with each other. This reluctance applied not only in confrontations with another nuclear power or its ally or associate, but in wars against non-nuclear opponents who had no powerful allies. The *realistic military capabilities* of nuclear armed states *declined* because of their nuclear weapons. The United States felt it could not use nuclear weapons in Korea and could not afford to attack Chinese territory after China became the primary enemy. It felt it could not use nuclear weapons against North Vietnam, bring itself to invade the North, or use its air power

---

[2] Sullivan (1996) stresses technological shifts in detecting at least eight prior revolutions plus many other military technical upheavals. O'Hanlon (2000) also focuses on technological shifts.

indiscriminately. The Soviet Union could not use nuclear weapons in Afghanistan nor openly attack rebel sanctuaries in a US associate next door. The nuclear revolution confined the realistic functions of nuclear weapons to deterrence and use of superpower conventional forces was also somewhat contained.[3]

Thus a technological change, in itself, *may* be a revolution in military affairs. Nuclear weapons qualify because this breakthrough (a nuclear fission chain reaction) was virtually born as a weapon, was used as a weapon almost at once, and changed great-power warfare soon after. But normally a technological shift has to be accompanied by the recognition that new possibilities have opened up plus additional changes to realize them. To get from the first planes to strategic bombing involved much more than changing technology.

A second conception is that a revolution in military affairs occurs when a major shift in military-related technology is combined with *new social and organizational arrangements* to produce a great change in warfare (Krepinevich 1994; Latham 1999). It is the *combination* that produces the revolutionary transformation. In fact the technical changes might be incremental yet, when combined with other shifts, bring on a revolutionary change. This is part of the basis for claiming that the revolution is:

> when new technologies (internal combustion engines) are incorporated into a militarily significant number of systems (main battle tanks) which are then combined with innovative operational concepts (Blitzkrieg tactics) and new organizational adaptation (Panzer tactics) to produce quantum improvements in military effectiveness.
>
> (IISS 1995–6, p. 29)[4]

Another illustration would be the radical shift in warfare inaugurated by Prussia in the 1860s. Prussian weapons were not, in themselves,

---

[3] The general expectation is that a government would not use nuclear weapons inside its territory because of the environmental after-effects – the territory would not be inhabitable and the fallout would affect other areas of the national territory (as well as neighboring states). The same effects don't have to arise for chemical or biological weapons (there are environmental effects, but for many of these weapons they can be more transitory), so Saddam used chemical weapons against the Kurds on his own territory – with lasting genetic effects on the Kurds about which, as with the casualties in Chechnya for the Russians, he didn't care.

Of course, there's always a first time. Some NATO allies had plans to use nuclear weapons on their territories against invading Soviet bloc forces in Europe. And Saddam might use a nuclear weapon, if he had one, against invading US forces.

[4] The IISS found three such revolutions in the twentieth century – mechanized warfare, nuclear weapons and ballistic missiles, and automated troop control.

revolutionary. But they were devastating when linked to a general staff, shifts in military organization, and transformed planning/management of national transportation (especially railroads). As a result Prussia overwhelmed other great powers in a series of brief wars by moving and coordinating very large forces in a novel way. This reintroduced great-power wars into Europe after a long absence and greatly changed the military plans of many states in ensuing decades.

I prefer a third conception of what constitutes a revolution in military affairs, in which existing or new technology plus new social and organizational arrangements are joined by *a new strategic approach* to exploiting the other changes (see Murray 1997; Freedman 1998c; Cooper 1997). Blitzkrieg warfare as displayed in World War II and later in the Middle East is an illustration. The technology was not new; German and Israeli weapons were not always superior. New social and organizational arrangements – training men for this style of fighting, granting initiative and flexibility to units within broad guidelines on objectives, the use of close air support – helped make a big difference. Behind all this was a novel strategy, a new conception of *how* to win: victory not by physically overwhelming forces and seizing territory until the enemy surrendered but by slicing through and bypassing those forces to disrupt their rear areas, cut them off from support systems, isolate and disorient them. This would spread panic and disarray in command and communications, promote debilitating retreats, and instill psychological paralysis, the collapse – not physical defeat – of enemy forces and a *political* collapse of organized resistance. By avoiding costly efforts to annihilate enemy forces it was a cheap-victory strategy.

Speculation about the RMA is spurred by the technological changes of the information age and, as a result, initially reflected the first conception. Some analysts emphasized the second. They felt the technology would force militarily significant changes in how societies, organizations, and armed forces are organized to fully exploit the possibilities. Thus far we have only preliminary speculation that fits the third conception. Steps toward new strategic thinking began in the late 1970s under the aegis of Marshal Ogarkov in the Soviet Union and in the development of the AirLand Battle approach for American and NATO forces. (On technology then see Office of Technology Assessment 1987). Ogarkov predicted a revolution based on emerging technologies and argued strenuously that Soviet armed forces must be reoriented or they would be outclassed (IISS 1995–6). But the costs were daunting and he was eventually dismissed for being too insistent. By the 1980s a major

American debate had emerged over whether high technology weapons would radically change warfare (Commission on Integrated Long Term Strategy 1988). Efforts to think strategically went forward, particularly as an extension of the AirLand Battle conception and in planning for a shrinking army after the Cold War. The RMA concept was most closely associated with Admiral William A. Owens, former JCS Vice-Chairman, who pressed for joint programs to develop a comprehensive approach (Owens and Offley 2001). In 1996 US JCS Chairman Shalikashvili ordered development of a new "doctrine", resulting in "Joint Vision 2010." However, it was widely dismissed as strategically routine, as having changed little in the Pentagon (Hillen 2000; O'Hanlon 2000).

Several points deserve emphasis. *A military revolution need not take place quickly.* What is revolutionary is its impact, not necessarily the rate at which it takes hold. There is a tendency to think of these revolutions as overnight shifts, but this need not be so. Some analysts believe the RMA will take fifty years to develop, that we have seen only the first phase.

The revolution is *not necessarily a surprise*, particularly since it may take years. Strategic analysts often anticipate the changes – the problem comes mainly in adapting to them – which will often not surprise experts since they flow from broader scientific and technical progress. The atomic bomb rested on spectacular developments in physics achieved decades earlier, and the idea of a bomb occurred to scientists in various countries well before one was built. Many who helped develop it therefore assumed, correctly, that Russians or others could rapidly duplicate it because the basic knowledge was widespread. A breakthrough may be important, even hard to duplicate, without being much of a surprise.

Next, the revolution *need not benefit only one or a few governments*, putting all others at a severe disadvantage. For some reason this is hard for people to accept. The alternative view often dominates American discussions – the RMA will provide a "commanding lead" or "unmatched capability." This is possible. However, a military revolution can diffuse so rapidly that many states transform their approach to warfare almost simultaneously; the initiator's advantage is fleeting at best (Krepinevich 1994). The radical transformation World War I represented did not benefit either side – it meant the absence of decisive superiority and a stalemate.

Using these three conceptions we can now review elements of the RMA. We will look briefly at technological changes and related social and organizational adjustments, before contemplating strategic possibilities inherent in these changes that have implications for deterrence.[5] What follows is a sample of changes frequently discussed and the available analyses.

Technological changes

The RMA is at the confluence of three streams of technological change.[6] The first is in surveillance – detecting, observing and tracking. For some time our ability to find things has been outrunning our ability to hide them. Improvements have come at all levels from outer space to the individual soldier. The second stream is the most familiar – the transformation in information processing, delivery, and presentation; displaying information in a timely, easily understood form so it is easy to plug into decisions and their implementation – such as meshing it with the user's location and readiness. Part of this is the amazing expansion of computer speed and capacity plus an equally amazing reduction in size and weight. The third stream is a rising capacity to hit what can be seen whenever necessary – much more accurate weapons. Together, these changes have important implications for military activity.

Surveillance and detection technology continues to improve steadily, as does the technology for rapidly absorbing and distributing the resulting information, and there will be great progress in both areas in the coming decades. (A good example of this is unmanned surveillance aircraft.) It will be increasingly easy to spot weapons developments, training programs, and military buildups earlier and with more precision. Transparency of military capabilities, weapons developments, and battlefields will steadily expand. In the past weapons

---

[5] A sample of relevant literature: IISS 1995–6; Bevin 1995; Millburn 1991; Brown 1992; Utgoff 1993b; Butterworth 1992; Buzan and Herring 1999, pp. 33–100; Carus 1994; Garwin 1994; Krepinevich 1994; O'Hanlon 2000; Arguilla and Ronfeldt 1996, 1997; Johnson and Libicki 1996; Rogers 1995; Freedman 1998c; Lambeth 1997; Khalilzad and White 1999. O'Hanlon has an extensive bibliography. On prospective technological developments: Markoff 1998, 1999; Lambeth 1996; *Defense Intelligence Journal* 1999; IISS 1998a, 1998b; Richter 1999a; Gaillard 2000; General Accounting Office 1999; and Noonan and Hillen 2002.

[6] This discussion stresses changes in conventional forces or technology, the thrust thus far of the RMA. But there are technological changes at the strategic level too: earth-penetrating nuclear warheads; more accurate delivery vehicles; enhanced sensor systems and C^3I (command-control-communication-intelligence) capabilities; stealthy hypersonic boost-glide vehicles; etc. (Garrity and Maaranen 1992). Many analysts believe that BMD will be feasible, perhaps with the Chemical Oxygen Iodine Laser (COIL) (Vartabedian 1995; Adams 1997; Cambone 1996).

development often took place in a military-oriented sector or government arsenals, with high secrecy and few spin-offs to the civilian society. Since the reverse is now common weapons development is inherently more transparent; systems under development can be predicted via extrapolation from civilian efforts. With improving surveillance, fiascos like the failure to perceive how far Iraq's nuclear weapons program had developed will be easier to avoid. On the other hand it will still be difficult to detect development of weapons for interfering with electronics and communications systems, to destroy data banks and foul computers.

In training, improvements in simulation allow ever more elaborate and realistic exercises, benefitting training in general and the design of specific missions by constructing realistic depictions of what will be encountered (Naylor 2000). There are complications, of course. As with any training, simulations are fine as long as they fit the situation and counterproductive when they don't. And with the rate of change it will be difficult and expensive to keep simulations up to date. Advanced countries enjoy an advantage here and will benefit as such training spreads in the private sector. Simulation also helps develop and refine weapons – combat is a costly way to uncover deficiencies. It may someday be feasible to produce weapons tailored to the specific forces to be confronted, much as commercial manufacturing produces goods tailored to individual customer needs. This has already been applied in the US Strategic Integrated Operating Plan for nuclear war which now almost automatically adjusts to inputs of different or new targets, enemies, and plans.

The information and communications revolution gives information a more central role so it is breeding new weapons that destroy, disrupt, or corrupt information flows – lasers to attack satellites, new ways of damaging information channels, computer viruses. There is revived concern about possible use of high-altitude nuclear explosions to disrupt communications or burn out circuits and information/communication systems through electromagnetic pulse (EMP), an effect that can now also be generated in a conventional and controlled fashion. Concern about "cyber-security" is burgeoning. (See, just from RAND: Molander, Riddle, and Wilson 1996; Hundley et al. 1996; Molander and Wilson 1998; Ware 1998; and Arquilla and Ronfeldt 1996, 1997).

The digitalizing of battlefield forces is incredible. Gulf War commanders could transmit 2,400 bits of information per second; the US Global Broadcast System installed since then handles 23 million bits per second – an hour-long transmission in 1991 took less than a second by 1999 (Gansler 1999). The communications revolution is shrinking the occasions when military forces are out of reach of updated information or instructions, or are unable to continuously report back, and even small units can now deliver vast information to higher levels, often automatically. In turn, real-time images, computer interpreted and enhanced, drawing on even distant sources, give units a perspective once available only to headquarters and give commanders a bird's eye view of any sector.

The major change in information available to commanders was demonstrated in a preliminary way during the Gulf War (Lambeth 1996) and is expanding continuously, drawing on data from many sources to display overviews of the entire theater, the battlefield, any portion, or the battle as it has developed over time. This is combined with elaborate information about terrain, weather, other factors. Coming is the automatic monitoring of people and units – sensors beneath the skin or within equipment and clothing – monitoring their condition (assess wounds, determine level of stress), available resources (ammunition, weapons), and unit fighting capability. There is more accurate assessment of damage to opponents. The flood of information now available for units in the field is processed by light but powerful computers for soldiers, tank crews, aircraft crews, ships. (The US Air Force reportedly has new computer batteries of malleable plastic, infinitely rechargeable, good even at extreme temperatures.) As was evident recently in Afghanistan, units and individuals now determine their exact location, then use range finders to exactly locate targets for weapons platforms elsewhere ready to fire almost at once. Surveillance has vastly upgraded the accuracy and detail of maps, which units can obtain electronically. Units increasingly draw on real-time surveillance or data banks for information about terrain, enemy units, the weather. Small units employ this approach to defeat much larger forces (Adams 1997).

Commanders and personnel in the field draw on increasingly accurate weapons that steer themselves to targets with microprocessors using target location information plus advanced recognition systems to better distinguish friend from foe (Windle 1997). Sensor and surveillance systems support virtually automatic, very accurate responses to attacks (O'Hanlon 2000) – like countering artillery fire. (In the Gulf they discouraged Iraqis from firing their weapons; they discouraged Iraqis and Serbs from turning on antiaircraft radars.) The accuracy of fire-and-forget weapons is steadily improving, as are precision guided munitions

(PGMs).[7] And in Afghanistan, inexpensive kits attached to dumb bombs turned even them into PGMs so that over half the bombs used were high precision weapons (Schmitt 2002; Schmitt and Dao 2001).

Use of self-operating equipment is rising: mines that explode only when encountered by the enemy (or may be remotely turned on or off depending on who is in the area); robotic and other automated weapons to detect and attack vehicles; unmanned aircraft (widely used in Afghanistan, including for close air support),[8] unmanned aerial decoys to protect aircraft (used in the Kosovo bombing). Unmanned systems will soon cover many dangerous tasks, handle routine chores, and do automatic diagnosis and standard repairs of some equipment and facilities.[9] Eventually "smart material" in equipment will sense its environment and adjust/repair itself as necessary – like plane wings that alter shape depending on the runways, or sensors that automatically detect and guide repairs of cracks in structures, or automatically offset the impact of a sonar wave (to create a stealthy sub).

Weapons get steadily more destructive because they are more penetrating, carry varying charges for particular targets, and accurately hit the most vulnerable part of a target (Revkin 2001; Oliveri 1996). Advanced planes incorporate stealth technology and stealth is coming to submarines, surface ships, tanks, drones, helicopters, cruise missiles, satellites. Systems to jam or disrupt opposing surveillance and weapons are improving. The battlefield is getting much more lethal for those without access to advanced technology. Target spotting is getting steadily better; increasingly, anything seen can be hit – with fewer weapons and less collateral damage.

There are multiple military implications. Large weapons and surveillance platforms may soon be too detectable, too slow, and too vulnerable. Radical redesign and stealth can help but probably not enough. (Advanced tank designs now call for plastic, more speed, lower profiles, equipment to jam or distort detection systems, antiair and antihelicopter missiles, detachable parts, etc.) Large platforms may be less necessary if small units deliver the requisite damage or information. With smaller, more potent, and more accurate weapons, fewer will be needed. Small

---

[7] PGMs come in smart bombs, antiship missiles, torpedoes, mines, and artillery shells. Steering can be by light (TV picture), heat, radar, laser beam, sound, or electronic emissions.
[8] Drone aircraft are expected to play a huge role in the future, being used steadily more for combat missions as well. See Mitchell 2002; Pae 2002; and regular issues of *Defense News.*
[9] *Defense News,* September 14–20 1998, has several articles on UAVs.

yet lethal, flexible, and mobile units will be preferred, easing logistics and power projection.

Facing comparably equipped forces, rapid maneuver and the ability to evade or disable detection systems will be critical. This will require sophisticated personnel with unprecedented training. Combined arms operations will be vital, drawing on surveillance and firepower from all the services. It will be vital to deny such capabilities to the opponent, so much will go into blinding or destroying satellites, disrupting information flows and information processing, and disabling sensors. Electronic countermeasures will grow in importance, including devices that distort (as opposed to jamming or evading) sensors. Steps to limit vulnerability will get priority.

Forces for peacekeeping or other noncombat missions will also be affected. Refined sensors can make them less vulnerable to hit-and-run attacks. Robotic equipment can perform tasks where snipers are a threat. Soldiers or small units will be able to call on precise artillery or air support. There will be more nonlethal weapons, especially for use in peacekeeping to minimize destruction and casualties. Examples of actual or prospective technologies include:[10]

> for incapacitating people – flash blinding grenades, shells, and mines, disorienting ultrasound waves, sticky substances or electronic nets that paralyze;
> for incapacitating equipment – microbes that turn fuels to jelly, high-powered microwaves that create electromagnetic pulse (EMP) effects, chemical sprays that make rubber or metals brittle; ceramic shards fired into the air to damage plane engines; carbon fibers dropped to short-out power plants; lubricants that destroy traction and foams that maximize adhesion on surfaces.

New social and organizational elements

In civilian sectors and activities these big changes have come from combining new technology in innovative ways with new social and organizational arrangements. This will apply to the armed forces as well. The services must be comfortable with the information age at all levels. Training helps, but it is valuable to have a society where new technology is ubiquitous, full of people who design, build, maintain, and use

[10] See IISS 1995–6, pp. 40–48; Alexander 1999; Garwin 1999; Morehouse 1996; Wiener 1995.

advanced systems. Innovations with important military applications now arise primarily in the civilian sector – abilities and skills vital for the armed forces will too. Judging from the evidence to date, the information revolution will continue to undermine hierarchies, promoting lateral networks as the primary form of purposive social organization. This will spread in military organizations. With immense information processing to serve the central command, and individual units tapping pools of available information, an effective military operation will be driven by a vast efficient conversation.

Micromanagement will be a terrible temptation, raising the danger of information overload, magnification of the effects of headquarters misperceptions, and insufficient flexibility. The tendency for civilians to oversee every detail of politically delicate operations has been growing for years: in the missile crisis, in Lyndon Johnson's control of targeting over North Vietnam, in the Iran hostage rescue attempt, and (at its worst) in the US intervention in Lebanon. (Marines patrolling near Beirut airport needed approval from Washington to put ammunition in their weapons.) In Afghanistan, the rules of engagement called for a large number of types of targets to be off limits without direct approval from either Washington or the Central Command headquarters in Florida (Arkin 2002a).

New strategy

It is easy to see how to use the new technology to do the usual things better. It is more difficult to get from there to meaningful shifts in strategy. The Gulf War prefigured things to come with regard to new technology and organizational arrangements. It established that sophisticated weapons systems can withstand combat conditions and work effectively (which many had disputed). It showcased the massive use of information by leaders and forces at all levels. Space systems provided complete battlefield monitoring with a modest delay (it took 12–13 hours to get the data to the field). The Global Positioning System was used by artillery, precision guided munitions (PGMs), map designers, planes, and soldiers. Weapons delivered death and destruction at a distance with precision, and demonstrated how collateral damage could be contained. The sorties required to destroy standard targets were way down, and laser guidance on penetrating warheads put even hardened shelters at risk. Also illustrated were the ways sophisticated but older systems can readily be outclassed by the latest ones. Over 40 percent of

Iraqi aircraft shot down were hit from beyond visual range. Iraqi tanks were often hit by tanks not within their range or view (Keaney and Cohen 1993).

But the Gulf War offered no new strategy (IISS 1995–6; Keaney and Cohen 1993). The purpose was classic: defeat and oust enemy forces so as to seize territory. UN forces used a standard approach: control the air, pound the enemy to fix him in place, then maneuver around him. As in the past, bombing disrupted the civilian sector (attacks on the power grid), threatened headquarters, disrupted communications, and interdicted logistics. And it also provided an immense amount of close air support for ground forces that seized territory – Iraqi forces took a terrible beating from the air. Target sets were roughly the same as in World War II. The strategy turned on defeating the enemy's forces in the field. Most of the strategic, technological, and organizational arrangements reflected longstanding plans for war in central Europe.

The wars over Kosovo and in Afghanistan are more instructive about the directions in which strategy will go. The war with Serbia showcased the precision air power side of the RMA and possibly a new approach to strategy. Led by the US, NATO imposed a precision-guided air campaign. However, the alliance did not use a shattering opening attack, aiming to collapse the enemy war effort, which is what the advocates of a classic strategic bombing approach called for – it did not completely disrupt Serbia's infrastructure, communications, etc. It just did enough damage to make life hard, demonstrated periodically that it could make life a lot worse, and inflicted damage while remaining out of reach. The strategy was to avoid casualties on both sides but put great pressure on Serbia physically and psychologically. And it worked. Air power enthusiasts were both pleased (air power had won a war by itself) and underwhelmed (air power was not used in the "right" way).

The most interesting feature of the war was how it disturbed the Serb leadership – damage was done but Serbia could inflict none of its own, the damage could readily increase at little cost to the alliance, and thus Serbs could not control what happened to them. Many analysts have disparaged this as simply an alliance (and particularly its leader) so concerned about casualties, so uneasy about using ground forces, and so politically reluctant about the war that it really had no strategy and, at some risk of failure, simply applied bombing in hopes Yugoslavia would quit rather than moving to decisively defeat it. But this may actually (however inadvertently) have been a new strategic approach: do heavy but precise damage from a great distance, out of reach so the enemy suffers and faces prospects of more without inflicting serious punishment of his own. This cuts casualties and losses of equipment and makes things look hopeless to the enemy (the government and its forces look futile) while stripping him of any bargaining leverage from inflicting punishment.

In Afghanistan, by contrast, the war showcased an alternative component of the RMA – small forces linked to modern surveillance and communications able to call on vast and precise firepower from far away to outmaneuver and defeat significantly larger forces. Even more than in Iraq the air power supported ground forces. In that sense it was what many of the champions of the RMA had always envisioned, except that the enemy was so primitive that it was not a serious opponent. Both the Northern Alliance and the special operations forces were light and mobile, the US precision air power made it lethal to stand and fight and lethal to try to move about.

Other strategies are equally plausible against the sort of opponent that makes them appealing. One would be to try to pin down the enemy throughout a theater in contrast to isolating one area for a breakthrough (IISS 1995–6). It will also be possible to attack massively over a much broader area, looking to flatten or shock the opponent's entire system. Or the attack could be a precise strategic strike to destroy the opponent's forces or its ability to use them. "Sophisticated forms of information warfare and long-range precision weaponry even raise the prospect of inflicting strategic damage on a country's national assets without using weapons of mass destruction" (IISS 1995–6, p. 32).[11] The latter fits better with the contemporary desire, at least among Western governments, to cripple rather than destroy so as to minimize casualties on both sides.

There is already movement away from using large forces to find and fix the enemy. For now, until the opponent is forced into the open his forces can remain hard to destroy. In Kosovo, Serb forces hid very successfully, as did some enemy forces in Afghanistan. In each case ground forces were needed to draw them out, and in Afghanistan those forces supplied the exact location of the enemy to guide the remote attacks.

A central objective will be to cripple any modern enemy's ability to conduct modern military operations – blinding surveillance, destroying communications, damaging information processing, and of course

---

[11] Taken seriously in Beijing and Moscow since the Kosovo case (Hoffman 1999b).

this can be useful against lesser opponents. This was employed in the Gulf War via the initial stealth fighter attacks, cruise missiles, showers of carbon fiber strands, and – in some accounts – a computer virus to cripple Iraq in the first days of the war (Adams 1997). Stealth fighters were able to attack without the US first achieving air superiority in a conventional fashion – with 2 percent of the sorties it eventually destroyed 40 percent of the strategic targets hit (Keaney and Cohen 1993, pp. 223–230).

The Pentagon worries about enemies eventually giving the US a dose of its own medicine. Of particular concern is defending against electronic warfare – hackers launch hundreds of thousands of attacks each year on the Department of Defense from the US and around the world, the most elaborate having come from Moscow in the Moonlight Maze case in 1998 (Drogan 1999a, 1999b). Since the defense establishment has over two million computers and over 100,000 networks, completely barring penetration is impossible. The Chinese have been especially vigorous in pursuing the study of "cyberwar" (Baocun and Mulvenson 2000). American concern was heightened by the Y2K problem and some devastating viruses, with special concern for vulnerable civilian sectors like banks, the power grid, communications, or air traffic management (Graham 1998b; Wald 1998; Pomfret 1999; Black 1999).

It is not clear this is a new strategy. It strongly resembles a classic strategy for strategic bombing – disrupt the underpinnings of a war effort so battlefield resistance collapses. The targets were economic, logistical, and morale, now they are detection and information systems – but the principle is the same. On the other hand, strategic bombing sought to exploit a new vulnerability that emerged when military forces became dependent on a supporting economy and society. War by exploiting the vulnerabilities of the information age may be just as new. Maybe at a fundamental level there are no new departures in strategy, but that at levels we most care about these sorts of changes are indeed revolutionary.

Strategy will usually focus as well on attacking especially sensitive elements in the opponent's military, economic, social, and political systems to disable or cripple as opposed to indiscriminate destruction. This will very likely include attacking the headquarters of elites, personal quarters of rulers, and military centers to make the war most costly to those in a position to stop it. This was attempted in Iraq and again in Serbia. Civilian casualties were quite limited in the bombing of Serbia and Kosovo (Lambeth 2001) and in Afghanistan.

A revolution?

Why is this a revolution? The best answer is that it should greatly affect the way force can be used. Force has usually been a blunt instrument. Precise battle management has been just an ideal. Commanders have seen their forces inflict indiscriminate damage or take inappropriate steps that brought excessive casualties. Clausewitz's "fog of war" generated by one's own actions, the other side's resistance and concealment (or deception), communication overloads, and the psychological/perceptual impact of stress has been unavoidable.

In civil–military relations, the armed forces always press for autonomy, especially in operations and the details on equipping, training and deploying forces. One consequence is slippage between broad operations plans and their implementation. States seldom order atrocities, but they occur, and rarely order deaths by friendly fire but they take place. Specified targets are not hit, but others things meant to be avoided are hit. Armed forces sometimes ignore orders they find professionally or politically unacceptable, or exceed orders and confront their governments with a fait accompli, or honestly misinterpret orders.

Force has also been blunt because of the nature of military resources. It was normally difficult to hit a target precisely. Improvements in accuracy had uneven results so a standard solution was saturation – a hail of arrows, a rain of artillery, a carpet of bombs. Some weapons have been inherently imprecise. Mines attacked anyone; artillery destroyed whatever was there; strategic bombing leveled whole areas. Technological progress greatly improved precision in some weapons but often enlarged the indiscriminate nature of warfare. This was particularly true of strategic bombing. Then early ballistic missiles were so inaccurate only the hydrogen bomb made them practical. Strategic nuclear weapons are so indiscriminately destructive that, as Michael Howard once said, "they are not the sorts of things with which one instinctively jumps to the defense of one's friends." Nuclear deterrence ultimately rested on indiscriminate retaliation threats, with entire populations and societies held hostage.

Indiscriminate effects have made it difficult to keep war moral. If the goal was to use only the force necessary, to avoid indiscriminate damage, and to hit only military and military-related targets, military instruments didn't fit very well, making restraint one of the first casualties. Most nuclear war plans promised to ignore all principles of restraint.

The revolution in military affairs and deterrence

How will all this affect deterrence? To imagine the impact of the RMA on deterrence we can start with the problem of knowing when to use it. The crucial initial step in bringing deterrence directly to bear is grasping the fact that it is necessary. As the Gulf War demonstrated, this is often difficult. In many instances states have failed to perceive signs an attack was coming until it was too late. They are often victimized by strategic surprise attacks or shocking diplomatic/political developments that presage an attack (e.g. the Molotov–Ribbentrop Pact in 1939). The Gulf War grew out of just such a surprise; Saddam's intentions were misjudged and no serious effort at deterrence was mounted because no one realized it was necessary.

Much of the problem lies with the information available. Terrorists, states seeking WMD, and governments planning attacks seldom advertise their exact intentions, using secrecy and deception. Efforts to develop a nuclear weapons capability have either succeeded in evading detection until it was too late to halt them (Israel, India, South Africa, Pakistan) or came much closer than the outside world realized (Iraq). (Some would put North Korea on the list.) With further vast increases in surveillance and flows of information, it will be steadily more difficult to hide significant activities. Worries about conventional strategic surprise attack may be eased because surveillance is making it almost impossible to achieve and sustain the necessary secrecy. While these improvements do not eliminate the difficulty of accurately ascertaining actor *intentions*, progress has been made. It gets more difficult to hide one's intentions as the amount of information detected about one's preparations rises. Serious plans for attack leave tracks, and improved surveillance means more of them will be picked up. Also, practice makes perfect. Much has been made of failures in detection that occurred in past cases of nuclear proliferation but these occurred when information-gathering efforts were less intense, less sophisticated, and less well equipped. The failures provided much information about how to do better. The Iraq case, for example, demonstrated that it is wrong to discount outmoded routes to nuclear weapons. Iraq also supplied an extraordinary opportunity to detect the limitations of existing technical capabilities for grasping the dimensions of a proliferation project and its progress. This is priceless for enhancing future monitoring.

Offsetting these improvements are contrary factors. If emerging forms of warfare can do much with small units or electronic and stealth resources, then the tracks left by the preparations may be greatly reduced. If weapons of pinpoint accuracy can be fired from far away and make use of surveillance that is always operating, then detecting the preparations to fire them is bound to be much more difficult. And the more devastating and disruptive the initial attack in its effects on command systems, communications, facilities, depots, weapons, and the like – because of extreme accuracy – the more vulnerable states and other actors will feel.

With respect to collective actor deterrence, a major problem is that information and analytical resources remain decentralized among actors and unevenly coordinated. Some sensitive information is not shared for fear of compromising the ability to gather it in the future. It is also unevenly distributed; some states can track the emergence of serious threats far better than others. Some information is withheld, even from close allies, for fear of leaks or political complications or vulnerability to spying. (The three parties to the WEU satellite intelligence capability at Torrejon in Spain set up elaborate arrangements to permit each to keep most of what it gathered from that common resource hidden from the other two!)

Next, studies find that the crucial factor in successful surprise attacks is usually defender misperceptions, arising from incorrect conceptual frameworks, despite the presence of information that points to the truth. Recent cases conform to this. Misperception afflicted Kuwait, Saudi Arabia, and the United States before Iraq seized Kuwait. The US and Britain had moved toward normal relations with Iraq during and after the Iran–Iraq War. When Iraq set about building nuclear and other WMD and prepared to attack friends of the West in its neighborhood, the evidence was discounted by the highest US officials, who thought they had a deal with Iraq. Kuwait and Saudi Arabia, meanwhile, treated Iraq's behavior as its usual negotiation by threat.

The same factor was at work when the situation in Yugoslavia deteriorated. European governments and Washington were not just reluctant to threaten intervention when it might have prevented genocidal excesses, they found it hard to believe such things could still happen in Europe even as the evidence mounted. For years they did not clearly see either when Milosevic would fight or how.

Thus having lots more information will not solve the problem of knowing when a vigorous deterrence effort is called for; governments will remain vulnerable to misperceptions on this. It will also remain vital to avoid assuming the worst and acting accordingly. This often operated during the Cold War and was very dangerous; the superpowers, encouraged by domestic political pressures, bureaucratic politics, ideological fervor, and competitive anxieties, often overestimated threats. To detect serious threats in good time, yet avoid manipulation by fears that the sky is falling, will require combining enhanced surveillance with more sophisticated analysis.

Once a possible attack has been detected, how else will deterrence be affected? In particular, how will it be affected by opportunities to conduct far more precise military activities? The starting point on this is that the RMA reflects the desire for a cheap-victory strategy common in international politics for over a century.[12] The US leads in pursuing the RMA not just to retain a technological edge but from a desire to make war far less costly. This makes it easier to deal with opponents, including those with weapons of mass destruction, and thus retain American deterrence credibility (IISS 1995–6, pp. 40–48). One way a cheap victory can be achieved is through strategic surprise – Iraq suffered the final defeat in part via a strategic surprise attack. While this was not the *result* of the RMA, it is easy to see how the RMA enhances the vulnerability to this of those who lag behind technologically.

The impact of the RMA on deterrence credibility is difficult to assess. The straightforward view is that a state which exploits the RMA while others do not will boost the credibility of its threats through its enhanced willingness and ability to use force – the RMA will ease the burdens of using force. If it is possible to dispel much of the "fog of war," minimize collateral damage, impose harm safely (for oneself) from a distance, suffer few casualties, and even inflict few casualties, then willingness to use force should rise.

The easier force is to use, the more readily states, or the Security Council, can choose to practice deterrence. This is particularly true for modern liberal democracies. Thus if the RMA does not readily spread, it should make deterrence a much more appealing option for advanced states. This will encourage the US, other great powers, and the UN (when it can draw on RMA-related capabilities of members) to intervene in outbreaks of violence or dangerous situations in ways that go well beyond peacekeeping. Thus the RMA will encourage continued regional and global security management via deterrence.

---

[12] I trace cheap-victory strategies to a recurring technical/political problem in modern war; see A. J. Bacevich (1995) on linking them instead to an effort by officers to retain an honored, useful role.

If casualties and collateral damage can be limited this will ease the moral burdens of using force and it will be easier to gain international political support for threats of intervention. International support and a reduced fear of casualties will ease domestic political problems in mounting interventions. Again, this will apply to countries equipped to exploit the RMA, including the modern liberal democracies and particularly the US. The credibility of their deterrence will likely rise, as will the credibility of deterrence by collective actors they dominate. This will apply to deterring proliferation as well – a more precise military instrument would be very useful against governments seeking WMD (Pilat 1994).

However, the straightforward view may be incorrect. The RMA has created an unprecedented race between the rising ability of Western nations to minimize destruction and casualties and declining Western acceptance of almost any. The latter sets the crucial political threshold for military activities on behalf of order and security as an international public good (this threshold is much higher now for direct attacks on the nation). In effect, *the easier it is to conduct fighting the harder it is becoming to keep fighting politically acceptable.* Fear of this happening in the US is one rationale for the new European drive for a separate military intervention capability. This is a wholly unanticipated development (especially the sharply declining tolerance for unnecessary enemy losses) with potentially immense implications. Obviously, it could significantly handicap deterrence by eroding the credibility of collective actor threats.

There is another category of potentially diverse effects. The RMA will make power projection for the most powerful states easier and less costly. Since costs rise and power falls off at a distance, military intervention far away – always a difficult option politically and psychologically – will become easier to contemplate and conduct. This will increase the utility of extended deterrence and its credibility.

This is true in another way. In the modern era, advanced states have had a significant military edge but it was seriously limited when they:

> had to project power over a long distance;
> had to confront opponents in very rough terrain;
> had to penetrate deeply to root out the enemy (as with guerrillas);
> lacked hard information on enemy location.

In these circumstances, in places like Vietnam and Afghanistan, their firepower and other advantages were often far from decisive. This enlarged the credibility problem in places like Chechnya. The RMA will make overcoming these difficulties easier. Imagine an intervention readily projecting damage deep into the target society via long-range weapons, with few casualties, using detailed information from global resources, through forces more flexible and effective in rough terrain than the locals – which was sometimes the case in Afghanistan.

States which fear being subjected to this will pursue ways to deter it. Some are already inclined to rely on WMD, seeking to trump the current revolution through diffusion of the last one. The RMA might end up stimulating proliferation of WMD, not a pleasant prospect, though critics of rogue states argue that they are seeking or have obtained WMD irrespective of any RMA. This helps explain the intensified US-led campaign against WMD proliferation in recent years and the heavy emphasis on extending the RMA into effective ballistic missile defense. The advanced countries say they want to diminish the role of nuclear deterrence but critics like India assert that the goal is really to lock in the advantages nuclear powers enjoy. The truth is more complicated. While major states fear instability stemming from proliferation, they also worry that proliferation will make various states impervious to deterrence for general peace and security such as by the Security Council, that states like Iran, Iraq, Libya, and North Korea have sought WMD to be able to defy UN, Western, or American deterrent threats with impunity. What the US is trying to protect is not just its advantages as a nuclear power, which are small, but those associated with the RMA, which are huge. One of those advantages is that the RMA has the potential to make global security management easier.

However, the RMA will also confront less advanced states with a serious dilemma if they try to offset it via WMD. Responding to a highly discriminating use of force with nuclear or other WMD will invite escalation, particularly of their opponent's objectives. This is what Iraq faced; using chemical or biological weapons might easily have incited the coalition to persist until the regime was ousted. It will always be difficult to introduce WMD after fighting starts – the gap between what is being done and what those weapons would do in response will seem glaring – something the US confronted as early as the Korean War. The improved surveillance associated with the RMA will also make it more difficult for these countries to secretly prepare to use WMD or to find suitable military targets if the opponent attacks entirely from the air, from afar, etc. The RMA will probably strip less advanced countries of many options by producing effective missile defenses, disruptions of command and communications systems, etc. In short, the counter-deterrence threats of these countries will be difficult to make effective and thus credible.

The RMA could pose another problem. The chief strategic use of WMD now in a war would be to impose heavy casualties in hopes of convincing the United States or others to stop. But if the RMA makes small units, calling in attacks from long distance, highly combat effective, there may be no major military concentrations to attack. "Rogue states" have been seeking even rudimentary ballistic missiles of more than tactical range to achieve some retaliatory capability to offset deficiencies they now face in practicing deterrence by defense.

This suggests that deterrence as Western countries, particularly the US, want to use it will be considerably enhanced. A supporting development is that the RMA, in connection with the Gulf War, the Balkan interventions, and Afghanistan, is pressing Western nations to make their military forces significantly more compatible with US forces primarily with future interventions in mind – European, Japanese and other forces are being redesigned accordingly. This development will quite likely have lasting consequences for the future development of international politics.

However, less comfortable possibilities deserve attention. Deterrence will work differently than during the Cold War, work much more like it has in traditional international politics (as discussed in chapter 5 and further explored in chapter 7). It will normally threaten not vast damage but unacceptable damage in controlled amounts. Motivating opponents via threats of a precise loss is far more complex. The RMA will encourage deterrers to think they can use force discretely to convey precise messages that compel specific responses; while sometimes done successfully this is very difficult. The American experience in Vietnam was that using limited strikes on the North, to inflict unacceptable (though limited) damage and convey messages (deterrence via demonstration), was not successful. The damage was acceptable and the messages were not received.

Moreover, the force employed will be limited enough to be "usable," but that will often make it more "bearable" for the challenger. As a result, states facing, say, American deterrence threats will be more likely than America would like to imitate Iraq and take their chances with a war, expecting to recover readily if it occurs. If so, deterrence will more often involve not just threats but force and will be less likely to work quickly, requiring repeated applications of force in repeated confrontations instead. This will make deterrence expensive, difficult, and hard to sustain over a long period, markedly *eroding its effectiveness against opponents determined to outlast it*. Iraq took the gamble that the UN coalition would not attack and suffered greatly, yet the regime remains in power, has rebuilt some of its forces, has probably sustained its capacity to build WMD, has plenty of grievances to pursue if it gets the chance, and thus remains a serious threat.

It may also be a problem to communicate threats when military capabilities are being altered by the RMA, although this is undoubtedly diminishing. Widely used measures of military power are becoming steadily less relevant and thus more misleading. Prior to the Gulf War, few suspected how completely ill matched the two sides were – making it easier for Iraq to miscalculate. And there were plenty of skeptics as the US and its friends prepared to act in Afghanistan, people constantly citing the Russians' experience without seriously considering whether it would apply. Standard ways of estimating military power have needed revision and more miscalculations by challengers might result (Watman and Wilkening 1995). However, the string of American military successes has done much to reduce this possibility.

Offense versus defense

There are several potential consequences of even greater significance. The first concerns the relative advantages of attacking and defending.[13] We need to consider the following possibility. The Gulf War and Kosovo interventions demonstrated how the RMA enhances offensive weapons and strategies; the US has been able to nullify the defensive capabilities of several states. In Afghanistan, the RMA was applied even to dealing with irregular forces and with very good results. However, in the long run an extreme improvement in target detection and in the ability to destroy what is detected should *favor the defense*. This is important because deterrence flourished after World War II as the only feasible response to offense dominance. It was created, theorized, and rationalized as the solution to an unavoidable mutual (and universal) vulnerability to destruction. While deterrence can certainly be achieved via an impressive defense, normally such a defense seems particularly valuable because it

---

[13] I have never been comfortable with much of the debate about the role of the offense–defense balance, particularly the treatment of retaliatory weapons as defensive. I avoid reviewing the debate here; those interested can find a good summary and relevant citations in Lynn-Jones 2001.

obviates the *necessity* to rely on deterrence. With a good defense hopefully you are safe even if deterrence fails and the enemy does his worst; with deterrence by retaliation you are safe only if he *chooses* not to do his worst. Hence shifting to a defense-dominant world could have major implications.

Why should the RMA favor the defense? A common view is that to conventionally attack a prepared defense successfully requires either achieving a major surprise or having significant military superiority at the point of attack; otherwise well-prepared defenses come off best. This inherent superiority of the defense means that offensive weapons must be too speedy to be reliably detected and hit (in missiles, planes, tanks), too difficult to find (low-flying planes and missiles, submarines, stealth weapons), too overwhelmingly destructive (nuclear weapons – if a few get through, so are you), too numerous (the nuclear triad or floods of planes), or too self-protective (tank armor, radar-jamming planes). Combining the ability to spot and track objects, effectively process and transfer information about them, and hit whatever is tracked should eventually nullify all those advantages. It is already increasingly dangerous to fly over a serious air defense, to fly over battlefields with light planes and helicopters, to move around in armored vehicles, to take major surface combatants close to enemy ships or a hostile shore. For some time offenses have become steadily more dependent on negating, rather than being inherently superior to, defenses.

I can not think of an advanced technology now or in prospect – even stealth – which, when fully developed, would consistently make it more attractive to be on offense than defense. Stealth comes closest because it allows early attacks to degrade defenses, allows the offense more options, and conveys the advantage of surprise. But stealth would surely be very useful for defenses too. In addition, spotting things is getting steadily easier – why expect stealth to be permanently successful, any more than mobility, hardening, and speed have been? Unless the offense-minded strike a deal with the Klingons, stealth will likely become steadily less stealthy.[14]

A surge in the relative strength of defenses would have a major impact on deterrence. To see how, we need to imagine what a truly defense dominant international system would be like. Let's start by assuming that states embroiled in conflict are evenly matched with the most advanced

[14] There is much research into systems that defeat stealth, like low-frequency radar, and not just in the US (Lariokhin 1999; Fulghum 1999). This will apply to misdirection too (decoys, issuing misleading signals) – surveillance will become more discriminating.

forces available, RMA-derived capabilities that find, track, then hit better than today. This would mean much more effective defenses which could, in principle, enhance for these states the feasibility of forestalling attacks by threat of defense, displacing the utility of deterrence by threat of retaliation. *That would be as significant as the shift ushered in by the nuclear revolution.* Preoccupation with deterrence in the Cold War came from the need to offset the inadequacy of defenses by taking advantage of it, exploiting the other side's weakness on defense through threats of a devastating retaliation. Conflicting states in a defense-dominant world could pursue security via offsetting defensive systems instead. This would make the stability problem much easier to contain since there is little threat of attack. It would make nuclear weapons linked to existing (and already increasingly vulnerable) delivery systems designed for rapid delivery, like missiles and bombers, outmoded.

In a defense-dominated world actors would mainly fear either technological shifts that outmoded defenses (at least temporarily), or secret penetrations that compromised or undermined a defense. Broad efforts to alter the status quo by force would be discouraged. Strategies for attacks would probably emphasize making war by probing defenses to make quick gains and then turning to the advantages of the defense to hold on to them (updating Japan's strategy in 1941–42). This has long been considered a very plausible way in which deterrence at the conventional level can fail (George and Smoke 1974; Mearsheimer 1983); now its appeal would be enhanced.

However, the main appeal of defense dominance would be in reducing the attractions and likelihood of war in general. If defense dominance sharply reduced vulnerability to attacks this would also go far toward easing the security dilemma – their main forces would not as readily arouse insecurity in others. If they could afford the best defenses available, states also could achieve a high degree of security from attack without having to cede some sovereignty to a strong collective actor in exchange for protection. If this was a pleasing prospect they could pursue arms control on principles the reverse of those instilled in the Cold War. The ultimate in strategic arms control would not be preserving deterrence from the development of defenses, but preserving defenses from development of new offensive systems.

Perhaps highly advanced defenses will be relatively cheaper (something not true now) and a larger percentage of states could therefore avail themselves of roughly the same level of protection. If so, the RMA would flatten the international hierarchy that has long rested on an ability to generate offensive power for winning wars or wreaking dev-astation in retaliation. (Hierarchies based on other capabilities would rise in salience.) This could be very beneficial since much ambition, in-security, rivalry, and conflict have flowed from the uneven distribution of offensive military capabilities.

Talking strictly about interstate conflicts, a defense-dominated system would have much less need of collective actor deterrence, which would be less attractive and therefore less credible anyway other than when the collective actor was primed to defend the target state (which could not defend itself) from the outset and therefore enjoyed the advantages of fighting on the defensive. If the collective actor had to respond to an already successful attack by a defensively powerful state this would not look very appealing.

This sort of speculation envisions a defense-dominated world decades in the future, if ever, with the relevant capabilities fairly widely dis-tributed. This is most unlikely. Realistically the world will have all the complexities of falling short of complete defense dominance. For in-stance, the initial phases of the RMA have fostered a huge inequality in distribution of the resulting capabilities. The US has benefitted enor-mously, its allies less so, others very little. As a result, the RMA has eroded the deterrence of many states vis-à-vis the US and its allies – the utility of deterrence for them has declined sharply. Analysts in places like China have been appalled at the implications if their governments ever come to blows with the West.

What we will almost certainly see is the following:

(1) States with great superiority vis-à-vis actual or potential serious opponents due to the RMA.
(2) Sets of very hostile states gradually moving toward defense-dominant deterrence relationships.
(3) Hostile states largely unaffected by the RMA with nuclear and conventional forces of a traditional sort as one basis of security.
(4) States with no hostile relationship, and none in prospect.

Deterrence, and its contribution to the maintenance of peace and se-curity, will have to be analyzed accordingly. For instance, deterrence relationships will be altered by the speed and degree with which the RMA spreads. There is already concern that the RMA will allow certain states, the US in particular, to launch strategic attacks with nonnuclear weapons, providing new and very appealing first-strike capabilities. Like ballistic missile defenses that finally become technically proficient, this would be yet another way in which the RMA undermined, for various governments, the utility of resting deterrence on traditional retaliatory threats. Thus for states caught up in very hostile relationships, the transition to a much larger role for defenses will be highly disturbing, even destabilizing, in many instances.

The implications of defense dominance will most likely have to be faced first in regard to ballistic missile defense. The most telling complaint about BMD efforts has been that the technology isn't up to the job, but this will be less and less true. Improving BMD technology will make it steadily less feasible in the future to sustain security on the basis of mutual vulnerability to missiles and bombers. The political and other complications stemming from this promise to be immense. One response to an inability to keep up with this will be to emphasize WMD in hopes that even a small penetration of defenses with those weapons could do enough damage that deterrence would hold. A parallel to this has already appeared in Russia. The collapse of Russia's conventional forces led it to rely more heavily on nuclear deterrence and a first-use posture because it feared confronting a state or alliance able to attack successfully at the conventional level.

The United States initiated the nuclear age and then tried to exploit it for security purposes unilaterally. It sought to curb proliferation of nuclear weapons and to maintain both a preemptive posture and strategy and elaborate continental defenses against the second nuclear power to emerge. While analysts soon grasped the inherent interdependence of security under those circumstances and suggested that cooperative management of deterrence was a necessity, the two governments were slow to get the point, and in some ways they never did get it. As a result, the cooperative management of nuclear deterrence was intermittent and it showed: deterrence was often potentially unstable, competition in the introduction of new offensive capabilities was dangerous and expensive, the size of nuclear arsenals was ridiculous, and their military efforts constantly hampered their efforts to leaven their political disputes with détente. They were not as successful at barring nuclear proliferation, horizontal or vertical, as they should have been, and the aftereffects are ugly. In the nuclear age the good old days were not good.

The best lesson we could draw from this for the future would be that a new RMA, starting with ballistic missile defense, *should be approached cooperatively, not unilaterally*. The RMA is bound to be very disturbing when it spreads unevenly, increasing states' military vulnerability in various ways. That is only exacerbated if states must scramble for themselves in

...acting to the RMA. Unless we think that living on the edge of a nuclear cliff is safe, that nuclear deterrence is the ultimate in civilized living, we should be looking to exploit the possibilities the RMA offers to move toward defense dominance and the outmoding of nuclear weapons and nuclear deterrence. For instance, we should be seeking ways to use improving defenses to shelter states seeking to eliminate nuclear weapons by guarding against breakouts from nuclear arms reduction agreements. We should also be looking to strengthen the ability of collective actors to promote peace and security for weaker states by exploiting the offense dominance that the early stage of the RMA has greatly enhanced for using conventional forces in humanitarian, peacekeeping, and peace imposition missions. Effective collective actors might help reduce incentives for some of those weaker states to reach for WMD. We should be doing this by curbing propensities of powerful states to act militarily outside of collective actors.

Thus far this lesson has not been learned. With regard to the latest RMA the United States is driving forward just as unilaterally as it did with the last one. It is operating as if security can be unilaterally, not interdependently, achieved and that the former is better anyway. It is also operating as if, whether security can be obtained that way or not, it doesn't hurt to try. This makes other states more insecure and the United States is irked by their responses. The US has been on the right track only in seeking to reduce strategic nuclear arsenals, but this is more than offset by its reluctance to seek a realistic chance of abandoning nuclear weapons in cooperation with others, by its headlong pursuit of conventional military superiority, and by its growing disinclination to deal with threats through true multilateral decision making (it prefers to have others jump on its bandwagon). To many, this converts its missile defense program and unilateralist interventions into steps to clear away the last obstacles to rampant domination.

The US pioneered in promoting advanced multilateral relationships to build a new approach to international relations among its friends, and led the way in developing multilateral management of nuclear deterrence, including cooperation with opponents to keep the international system stable. Failure to do the same in the context of, and in exploiting the potential of, the RMA would neglect an unparalleled opportunity to make security in this century a great improvement over the last one.

Failure to do so will open up quite a different possibility. It is safe to assume that defense dominance will be some time in coming. If it does, at least among the most advanced states, there is a final, potentially very disturbing, possibility. The RMA promises to sharply alter the fundamental basis of deterrence among the great powers. During the Cold War deterrence rested on weapons so destructive that war could have been catastrophic. Even a strictly conventional great-power war could have been unacceptably destructive. In this sense, war among great powers became obsolete – it could not be conducted to achieve anything worth it (or the risk of it) and this helped bring about its disappearance. Recently, interstate wars of other sorts have become scarce, often arising only among the fragments of former states as they contest boundaries. A plausible explanation for this war shortage is that conventional warfare below the great-power level is also too costly and destructive, particularly if viable options exist for achieving the gains sought by war in the past.

This was not what many analysts expected. For years there was speculation that nuclear deterrence would make the world safe for big conventional wars and pitiless little ones which would therefore proliferate. Fortunately, that was untrue (in the end). However, eventually the RMA might do what nuclear deterrence did not and make the use of force more tolerable. There would still be the risk of escalation to nuclear weapons but this might be controlled, as it is now, by nuclear deterrence among states able to at least partly offset ballistic missile defenses in some fashion. And nuclear weapons might then remain obsolete for any other purpose. History is littered with weapons that still worked but became obsolete, disappearing because others outmoded them. (There is nothing wrong with a Mauser rifle for killing someone, it is just inefficient.)

If so, the RMA might permit a great power to impose a significant defeat even on another great power with nothing like the destruction of World War II or a nuclear war. Or great powers might fight high-tech versions of limited wars, seeking or settling for limited gains and suffering in limited ways, in keeping with their much reduced tolerance for casualties. This could broaden the perceived utility of military forces and war, one reason many officers (particularly after they retire!) support the reduction or elimination of nuclear weapons. They undercut the meaning of being ready to fight for the nation; moving away from them would refurbish the profession's purpose. Thus the RMA, accompanied by the decline or elimination of nuclear weapons, *could end up making the world safe for great-power and other conventional wars again.* If great-power rivalries revived as well, international politics would become more dangerous, though less lethal than feared during the Cold War.

Of course, the major nations have recently been pushing nuclear deterrence into the background, not to make war viable again but because they see little likelihood that war among them will be a serious problem in the foreseeable future. Cutting nuclear weapons is a way to continue reinforcing that prospect. If they are correct, then new technologies that removed the aura of Armageddon would not necessarily promote a resurgence of great-power warfare. If they are wrong, we could get a recapitulation of the end of the nineteenth century if great states decide that war among themselves is again feasible. In that earlier era, they counted on keeping such a war short and victorious. Great states in the future might envision a great-power war readily contained and then find, once again, that it was far too costly in the end. The same could be true for warfare among lesser states; inhibitions on interstate warfare in general might be diminished. This is an equally unwelcome prospect. It would mean that the RMA had retrograde effects on international politics.

Such an argument has been made for years, especially recently, by critics of nuclear disarmament who believe nuclear deterrence has generated the great-power "long peace," and by the champions of nuclear proliferation. I do not endorse that criticism for several reasons. As noted in chapter 1, evidence for such a pervasive effect of nuclear deterrence is weak. And chapter 4 suggests that the key variable in deterrence success is not the manipulation of challenger motivation by deterrence but the intensity of the motivation to challenge. However, the belief in deterrence is widespread and deep-seated and a decline in nuclear deterrence along with the spread of techniques for less destructive conventional wars could revive the prospects of war and warriors.

The critics

We cannot conclude without considering critics of the RMA, and offering possible responses to their objections.[15] There are at least four broad potential flaws in the idea of an RMA. One is that shifts in technology, the thinking about them, and the changes that result will turn out to be, as is normal, just incremental adjustments and not revolutionary. True revolutions are rare; lots more are predicted than actually show up. If so, then:

[15] Critics include Shapiro 1999; O'Hanlon 2000.

> Americans must also be disabused of the notion...that technology
> is sanitizing war or paving the way for an era when technologically
> advanced countries...will employ the military instrument bloodlessly.
> With rare exceptions, the effective use of force will almost invariably
> carry with it a substantial risk of American casualties.
>
> (Bacevich 1995, p. 62)

The US has a long history of searching for technological ways to win wars.[16] Skeptics suggest the RMA is another American pipe dream.[17]

To illustrate how slowly fundamental changes occur remember that ballistic missiles, like nuclear weapons, were invented in World War II. Long-range bombers are even older. Jet aircraft flew in World War II and became common in the 1950s. Tanks date back to World War I. Modern artillery is decades old. Poison gas appeared widely in World War I. Cruise missiles stem from World War II. Automatic rifles were widely used in World War II and machine guns go back to the American Civil War. Incremental improvements in these weapons produced today's armed forces, extensions of technological changes that occurred years ago. The same might be true of RMA technology. Many recent steps are also incremental advances on existing technology; others may be fundamental but will need years of refinement to make a major difference (O'Hanlon 2000).

A second critique says that the major changes apply to a style of warfare going out of date (Bacevich 1995). Interstate wars are declining; internal wars are proliferating and they are the wars for which the RMA is least significant – outright battles are uncommon, the battlefield is hard to find, there are no large weapons systems to seek and destroy,

---

[16] Thus: "Above all, the US military remains wedded to technology as the primary means to win war. This is the American Way of War and nothing short of a catastrophic defeat is going to change the basic nature of US military culture" (Sullivan 1996, p. 141). Or "...American culture...loves the latest technology, believes it enjoys a long lead in exploiting that technology, and yearns to find, clean, discriminate, (American) casualty-minimal modes of war. Cyberwar is particularly appealing to a mind-set that seeks to avoid war's brutal realities, instead finding ways to play at war in cyberspace" (Gray 1998).

[17] In 1971 General Westmorland said: "On the battlefield of the future, enemy forces will be located and targeted almost instantaneously through the use of data banks, computer assisted intelligence evaluation, and automated fire control. With the first round kill probabilities approaching certainty, and with surveillance devices that can continuously track the enemy, the need for large forces to fix the opposition physically will be less important...no more than 10 years should separate us from the automated battlefield" (Dickson 1971, p. 169). This was cited in Rapoport 1995, pp. 130–131, to illustrate our worship of technology.

the terrain is rugged, the enemy immersed in the population, maybe in sprawling cities (van Creveld 1989; Metz and Kievit).

The third possible flaw is that countermeasures will vitiate the supposed revolution. The Iraqis used rapid deployment, high mobility, camouflage, decoys, and set ups with no prelaunch electromagnetic emissions to frustrate attempts to destroy Scud missiles (Keaney and Cohen 1993, p. 86). They quickly replaced downed bridges with temporary ones. When the Iraqi air defense system was attacked by cruise missiles in 1996 it was rebuilt in roughly two weeks. The limits of modern reconnaissance were displayed when the West learned how little it knew about Iraqi nuclear weapons programs. The effectiveness of UN forces in the war was less than it seemed, the RMA had less impact than traditional military factors including enemy incompetence (see for example, Biddle 1996).

And there can be more to victory than discrete destruction or damage from a distance – opponents can take a lot to defeat. As noted above, there are moves afoot to cancel stealth, develop countermeasures to cyberwar, etc. Some analysts think it a law that countermeasures always offset any major technological development. Thus analysts critiquing the Kosovo operation argued that NATO forces failed to find Serbian forces in the province, conducted the air war high above Serbian antiaircraft defenses rather than challenging them directly, and didn't actually force the Serbs to quit so NATO was lucky to get the eventual outcome. They complained about how political criteria barred the proper strategy.[18] Hence the RMA was less impressive, less effective, than advertised. Steps to offset its effects were quite successful in some areas.

A fourth possibility is that the RMA will readily diffuse – deterrence against a country like the US can be sought by turning those capabilities against it. At present this does not seem promising because of the cost involved, or because diffusion will take time.[19] Still, there is a possibility the RMA will, in the long run, *benefit other states more than the advanced ones*. The technology is being driven by the private sector, and manufacturing capabilities for advanced technologies are being widely dispersed. Fiber optics, ever better computers and software, satellite imagery, worldwide communications, and other elements of the RMA are dual-use and already widely available. Many governments will soon obtain stealth technology, precision guidance, cruise missiles,

---

[18] See, for example, IISS 1999a; Myers 1999; Richter 1999b. The NATO response is NATO 1999.

[19] Estimated costs of the full RMA run well above $100 billion.

sophisticated mines and torpedoes, advanced SAMs and air-to-air missiles, high resolution satellite imagery, and high quality communications and computers (IISS 1995–6). Global Positioning System signals can be used to obtain accuracy of delivery (Bevin 1995).[20] The data for precise map making is now available from commercial satellites with a resolution of a meter or less, so many more states can do elaborate reconnaissance.[21] Many countries have satellites for domestic use (over 900 are now in orbit), providing access to the technology and some understanding of how to evade it. The use of computer viruses is hardly confined to advanced countries.[22]

As has been evident for years, advanced countries sell military hardware to almost anyone. This will continue, particularly if the technology involved is commercially available. (In 2000, Japan tried to limit exports of Sony's PlayStation2 video game because it could process high quality images quickly, just what advanced missile guidance systems need; see Senate Armed Services Committee 2000. Since the Gulf War laser range finders, thermal imaging systems, drones, precision guided munitions, and night vision equipment have proliferated. Many RMA components are cheap and getting cheaper. The Chinese and others are seeking to be able to attack satellites (Richter 1998).

It may also be easier for less advanced countries to exploit technological change. With its wide-ranging concerns, the US pursues the entire range of new developments; others will focus on only capabilities for their limited needs (IISS 1995–6). They will exploit elements of RMA information processing and communications highly vulnerable to disruption. In this way advanced societies become more vulnerable to a strategic surprise attack or some RMA version of blitzkrieg. Imagine how an effective antisatellite capability could disrupt RMA-based forces.

As for the RMA building semi-permanent military superiority, great changes in military capabilities are rapidly imitated – the stakes are too great for it to be otherwise. Sometimes the first to go through a

---

[20] GPS satellites initially emitted two sets of signals; one for anyone and good enough for steering cruise missiles without extreme accuracy; the other for American forces (for accuracy within 10 meters). Now the latter is broadly available too.
[21] On commercial satellites see Otsuka 2000; Baker, O'Connell, and Williamson 2000; Broad 2000; Wright 1999; and IISS 1996.
[22] Ballistic missiles illustrate how technology spreads. By 1990 sixteen states possessed ballistic missiles and twelve manufactured them (Nolan 1991). In 2002 thirty-five non-NATO countries may have had them, and eighteen could use them with WMD (*Economist* 1997).

revolution have the hardest time; imitation is easier and cheaper than innovation. Those who come later avoid the initial mistakes; those who go first grapple with the initial effects and settle down, while those who come later take the changes further. Thus going first can be a fleeting advantage as imitators do better than imitate.

Finally, a true revolution not only outmodes old weapons, doctrines, and strategies, it may outmode an old inferiority, making it easier to close a gap in capabilities. Britain's introduction of the dreadnought turned a huge British lead over Germany in warships into a lead of one in the only ships that now mattered for naval superiority. Nuclear weapons turned the backward Soviet Union into a superpower.

Possible responses

While a detailed answer would take us far from the focus of this book, some response is in order. While changes instigated by the emerging technologies may yet be incremental for military forces, they have not been so in other sectors – why should the military be unique? The on-rushing technology seems certain to push us off the plateau of the past century into weapons based on new principles. We should also recall that a revolution need not take place overnight; what matters is the scale of the changes. When incremental improvements produce massive changes in the use and conduct of war, a revolution has still taken place. Many analysts are mesmerized by the notion that a revolution makes for huge advantages for a particular state – if the RMA will readily diffuse there is no revolution. However, a revolution can take place across many states, with no lengthy or decisive advantage for one.

As for where the RMA is applicable, it will definitely have major effects in subconventional warfare. Afghanistan demonstrated how new technologies can be very effective in irregular warfare. Technologies that can spot weapons on a person at some distance (Grey and Haynes 1997), small and highly mobile sensors, and nonlethal weapons will have multiple uses particularly in urban warfare, internal conflicts, and interventions for peacekeeping (Hall 1998; IISS 1999b). The same applies to precision strikes for dealing with guerrillas.

As for the Kosovo case, the criticism offers a good description of what happened but a dismal grasp of what it meant. The limitations on the force used reflected proper concern for the political objectives and the need to sustain allied and US public support. It would have been disaster to have NATO fragment or lose public support not only for the war but future endeavors. In view of how strongly various states felt about the war, to have attacked Serbia massively would have provoked much stronger reactions. Next, the damage done to Serbian forces was light because the Serbs realized their forces *could not be safely used*. Such forces are virtually irrelevant militarily. Collapsing the enemy's will to fight is outstanding – the less killing and destruction needed the better. At the end Serbia faced the prospect of an invasion that would compel its forces to come out and be killed with little chance to fight – lost to no purpose. There is often a correlation between national willingness to endure suffering in a war and ability to inflict some in return. The RMA ensured that Serbia felt the full effect of that.

As for the RMA diffusing, I expect a considerable diffusion *eventually*, one basis for the discussion about a defense-dominated system. However, for years the RMA will not be readily imitated, and being out in front will not be hard to sustain. A common mistake in the US is to conclude that either one dominates new technological developments or inferiority results. However, being atop a military revolution is only vital for coping with a serious rival. If you enjoy a great military edge overall it is unlikely that being matched in some aspect of the revolution will cancel it. Much of the fear of others adopting asymmetrical warfare is overblown.

In addition, we are accustomed to military history as a series of plateaus. Technology, craft, and capabilities reach a plateau and then progress comes in refinement. After a jump to a new plateau the process starts over. But the RMA, and the larger changes it embodies, will outmode this pattern. Any future plateau may exist only briefly. Changes will be more continuous and of greater magnitude. Success will lie not in going through a revolution first but in *being able to embrace a continuing revolution*, being sufficiently flexible and adaptable to absorb the changes to come. Such a society will be admirably placed to exploit not only its own revolution but one initiated elsewhere.

The United States is well into the RMA and has considerable military advantages as a result. However, it is preeminently equipped for coping with continuous change – life is closer to a continuous revolution there, in more sectors, than anywhere else and expectation of large-scale continuous change is widespread. It is wrong to expect permanent advantages for the US because it is out ahead. But others will not readily gain if the foremost American advantage is the ability to adapt faster. Catching the US at the current plateau will mean little if progress now requires leaping from one plateau to another.

Of course, if it is difficult to use the RMA to catch up, more states may be interested in WMD. This will be especially true of those that expect to be targets of deterrence for global or regional security management. And probably not just them. The RMA has alarmed the Chinese and helped foster their renewed reliance on nuclear weapons. Indians who justify nuclear weapons sometimes cite the need to offset radical improvements in Western conventional forces they cannot hope to match.

Conclusion

There are disturbing possibilities that might offset the generally favorable impact the RMA could have. There might be increased incentives for WMD proliferation. There might be less to the RMA than meets the eye, particularly for the most developed states. Or the developed states themselves, several decades hence, might renew the great game of international politics on traditional terms. The great powers have already demonstrated a strong commitment to change the nature of international politics. This must be nourished. We may have to count on that, far more than deterrence, to keep our future world safe.

7 Deterrence in the post-Cold War world

This chapter offers an overview of how the nature and functions of deterrence in international politics have begun to change, applying themes of preceding chapters to contemporary concerns. To more clearly identify what has changed and what has not, I briefly review deterrence during the Cold War, then try to characterize the international system today with deterrence in mind. Then the discussion moves to the heart of the subject. One theme is that deterrence is now of sharply diminished relevance in relations among developed countries, and of continuing or rising relevance in other places. The other recurring theme is that deterrence theory will be poorly applicable to the most likely contingencies not only due to difficulties with the theory, explored in chapter 2, but because central concepts can't be operationalized in a satisfactory way by policy makers in the situations they will confront. This applies to concepts of rationality, credibility, stability, unacceptable damage – nearly every facet of deterrence. As a result, a consistently effective deterrence strategy is impossible. It is not that deterrence can't or won't work if used, but trying to guide its use by an overall strategy will not work well.

Deterrence in the Cold War era

As indicated in chapter 1, deterrence during the Cold War existed simultaneously in three forms. The first was as an old, well-known *tactic* in managing a relationship, just a variant of using your elbows. Deterrence/compellance is as old as international politics, natural for confronting competitors in a dangerous environment. However, during the Cold War deterrence evolved beyond this. Nuclear weapons forced the superpowers (and others) to turn deterrence into an elaborate national security *strategy*. Without the Cold War it would probably have remained an "occasional stratagem" (Freedman 1996, p. 1). As a strategy it offered an elaborate guide for bringing military power to bear on central national security objectives. It became the dominant strategy, the one on which great powers bet their lives.

In addition, superpower (and bloc) nuclear deterrence gradually generated an interdependent security management for the international system, a *global security management* regime. Derived from steps taken by individual states for their own security, deterrence-related policies came to shape and sometimes contain conflict at lower levels in the system. This was often on display, from particular conflicts to controlling proliferation. Hence for the Cold War we can "view deterrence not merely as a war avoidance concept but rather as a world order concept, akin perhaps to the Concert of Europe" (Kaldor 1991, p. 321). Or that a "common deterrence...served as a functional equivalent to a monopoly of violence at the global level" and thus amounted to "a rudimentary functional equivalent of the monopoly of violence of the state" as an order-maintaining capability (Van Benthem van den Bergh 1996, pp. 27, 31).

Appreciation of all three is important for understanding deterrence today. Superpower deterrence was shaped by the intensity of the Cold War; it seemed to be the primary element preventing another great war. General deterrence appeared pervasive, often a step away from turning into a crisis. This heavy reliance on deterrence, the essence of a "Cold War," drove unprecedented peacetime defense spending and military capabilities.

Deterrence also was shaped by nuclear weapons. In the shadow of the vast arsenals, preventing a major war was the paramount national security objective and the focus of superpower efforts to manage global or regional security. This *simplified* certain aspects of deterrence and served as the basis for deterrence theory, deterrence postures, and specific policies.

It is important to revisit points made earlier, to be clear about what nuclear weapons and the Cold War did and did not do. There is a tendency to see them as having made it simple to define interests and threats, to distinguish challenger from defender, to define "unacceptable damage," to detect problems in credibility and stability, to establish what constituted deterrence success, and to shape the strategy. Not so. The Cold War provided a clear focus for policy but, as Vietnam demonstrated or as Kennedy found in the missile crisis, there were serious complications. The exact nature of the threat was perennially in dispute domestically and between the US and its allies (and for years between the Soviet Union and China). The US got the primary "challenger" wrong in both Korea and Vietnam, thinking it was really the Soviet Union, China, and the Soviet bloc. Defining American interests turned out to be quite difficult in the Berlin and Taiwan Straits crises, and in relations with China. What nuclear weapons simplified was destructive capacity. Defining unacceptable damage for the opponent was in constant dispute at other than the most extreme level, while the problems of credibility and stability were never resolved to general satisfaction. Even treating nuclear deterrence as a success came to be seen by some as problematic.

Nuclear weapons made it simple to threaten unacceptable damage, and that made it plausible that deterrence might work consistently. Because only a modest number of weapons could do overwhelming damage and nuclear arsenals (even in Britain, France, and China) were greater than needed, there was no choice but to rest deterrence on retaliation capabilities rather than defenses. This was very uncomfortable, leading to unsuccessful searches for ways to escape the resulting vulnerability, from a first-strike capacity to effective defenses (Jervis 1989a). The great powers remained dependent on deterrence, which ultimately rested on the threat of a terribly punitive retaliation, and many others depended on the great powers' deterrence too.

Turning deterrence into a regime for global security management was forced by the combined effect of Cold War rivalry and nuclear weapons. With much of the world an arena for the East–West dispute, superpower rivalry carried much further than it otherwise would have. The Soviets held the so-called global "correlation of forces" ultimately responsible for deterring the imperialists. The American view, first fully enunciated in the famous 1950 government study NSC-68, was that in a psychological and political sense a loss anywhere was a loss everywhere. Defining what happened in many areas as directly bearing on their security, and frequently undertaking interventions, the superpowers broadened the impact of their conflict on everyone else.

Superpower nuclear deterrence contained other built-in pressures toward enlarging global security management. When relying solely on it eventually seemed too dangerous, deterrence was extended into maintaining large conventional forces and preventing any conventional war in East–West relations. While not fully successful, this at least kept a lid on some wars that involved a great power and eliminated such wars in a highly sensitive area like Europe. Deterrence stability also required containing direct superpower confrontations in various trouble spots.

Finally, deterrence dragged the two parties at times into trying to limit others' conventional warfare or internal conflicts. The motivation was fear of escalation. East–West deterrence became global security management when, out of concern for stability, it made "local" conflicts of concern at the highest level. In security management mutual deterrence was a bilateral and sometimes multilateral endeavor, involving cooperation among friends and enemies alike.

There was, therefore, more than a little tension between the imperatives of Cold War competition and the necessities of deterrence. The former incited military interventions, the accumulation of client states and allies, taking sides in local conflicts in ways that exacerbated them, huge arms transfers, and other steps that often made global and regional security more tentative. Offsetting this, acting as a governor on the Cold War engine, was restraint out of the preoccupation with deterrence stability. Thus the Middle East became a very dangerous place and the superpowers played a large role in making it so, yet their forces were never drawn into fighting there and wars in the region were limited at their insistence.

However, there were also tensions within the mutual deterrence atop the system. The military equivalent to political concern about a loss anywhere being a loss everywhere was preoccupation with credibility. Deterrence stability required credible threats, but nuclear deterrence made credibility suspect. Fear of escalation made even threats below the strategic level suspect. Concern to convey strength and will led to insistence on the interdependence of commitments that played such an important role in American foreign policy.

Though it had many important traditional elements, *this was not a traditional international system*. It has often been described as a bipolar, balance-of-power operation in classic international politics, with nuclear deterrence as the latest version of the balance-of-power process (Kugler 1993), but this is incorrect. In a balance-of-power system war is normal, deterrence is used to discourage a variety of harmful actions, not just war, and war often used as a form of deterrence. Under Cold War deterrence the goal was to prevent major war completely, and the separate capacities for destruction did not have to be distributed in any "equal" or "balanced" sense once they reached a sufficient level (though the superpowers' forces eventually became symmetrical). With it, war among great powers was no longer normal and acceptable. This was not a standard balance-of-power system but a deterrence-dominated system. As the East–West conflict was expected to continue indefinitely,

Cold War deterrence was operated accordingly. Reinforcing this was the widespread belief that even without the Cold War nuclear weapons would make deterrence permanent. It would have to keep us safe from nuclear weapons forever. Even disarmament would not eliminate their shadow, because we could never unlearn how to make them.

The post-Cold War era

Now we turn to relevant characteristics of the contemporary international system. Deterrence is shaped by the systemic context in which it operates; in particular by conflicts. The scale and intensity of the conflicts determine its salience, functions, utility, and mode of operation. For instance, if great-power relations today remain markedly different from the past, deterrence will be different as well.

We start with the great powers: the US, Russia, Britain, France, China, Germany, and Japan. The most striking feature of the system is that currently there is no serious conflict among these states, no intense conflict involving even any two of them. This holds even if we include the best candidates for future great-power status – India, Brazil, Nigeria, and the European Union. The most serious friction, between the US and China, is a far cry from the Cold War or the conflicts that animated the great powers leading up to the two world wars, though it is certainly of concern (see below). Neither China nor the US behaves as if war is highly likely in the foreseeable future, steadily bearing down on them, probably because they actually agree about the proper final disposition of Taiwan – the only plausible spark for a war.

This critical shift in the context is directly pertinent to deterrence. Analysts disagree about why great-power relations are now mostly benign, whether this can last and for how long. If serious conflicts emerge again, then deterrence will be in vogue – if not, at least for a lengthy period, then deterrence will operate offstage, held in reserve, and will not be the cornerstone of security management for the system.

How long can great-power relations remain congenial? We have numerous descriptions and explanations for the world today and they are far from compatible on this. Various analysts, governments, and officials believe this relative affability cannot last. Usually they cite anarchy as driving feelings of insecurity in states which inevitably incite a struggle for power, noting that a real peace among the great powers is rare in the history of international politics. Paramount here is John Mearsheimer's recent work (2001) which predicts that the European and East Asian

242

regional systems will become highly competitive and conflictual again, with China's drive for regional hegemony challenging a central US foreign policy, making warfare very plausible. That conflict up to and including war will result is due to two (quite familiar) sources. One is that a state is really safe only if it dominates its system – great powers all want to be hegemons and struggle accordingly (the Mearsheimer view). The other is that states' aspirations to exercise a dominant role in world affairs rise with their power, so their "interests" expand, they have much more to worry about, and their security concerns grow (Zakaria 1998). In short, insecurity drives states' vicious grabs for power or power breeds aspirations to run things that incite insecurity. This leaves no conceivable route to a peaceful international politics – anything that looks peaceful is a dangerous illusion.

The reference to dangerous illusions is needed to make such an analysis viable because the great powers are in no hurry to resume international politics as usual and seem eager to avoid a heavy reliance on deterrence again to keep safe. For instance, in Europe the consensus recipe for security is to have former Soviet bloc states and Soviet republics join the West – join NATO, the European Union, the World Bank, the G-8, etc. – becoming liberal democracies, developed societies, market economies. Doesn't sound much like traditional international politics. Why is this so? After the conclusion of the world wars any such behavior could readily have been explained by exhaustion, but that does not apply here. Another description of international relations today would stress American hegemony as the explanation. Great power conflicts are in abeyance because American hegemony forestalls them. As standard analyses of hegemony have it, hegemony produces bandwagoning and order – it is when a hegemon is in decline that conflicts, especially among great powers, rise and challengers to the hegemon appear. There is plenty of evidence to cite in support of this view, from data on American power to signs of American leadership and influence – in particular, there is the great continuity in American security responsibilities and the instruments for maintaining them (military forces, forward deployments, alliances, bases, etc.).

Perhaps the best explanation, because it can incorporate the preceding one, has to do with modern democracies and economic systems. Under the conception of the democratic peace, democracies have a marked ability to avoid war with each other. As long as this continues to hold, especially if they continue to spend almost no time worrying about or preparing for even the *possibility* for going to war with each other, their international politics represents a sharp departure from standard international politics. Among democracies there is only a limited connection between anarchy and insecurity, not much in the way of a security dilemma, little necessity to practice deterrence. Security concerns do not sharply constrain cooperation; there is no need for power balancing apart from the competition for power, status, and interests that is integral to politics at any level. Under the democratic peace, it takes a paradigm shift to understand international politics.

Democracies have been closely associated with market economies, which have typically been reliable generators of wealth, power, and other forms of national progress. Mature market economies and their consequences, like mature democracy, also tend to drive states out of traditional international politics (for complicated, widely debated, reasons). Also, democracy and market-based economic activity clearly feed on each other, making it likely that both are responsible for the democratic peace.

This suggests that the history of international politics since the late eighteenth century will eventually come to be understood as, more than anything else, the slow unfolding of effects of the democratic revolution – of the development and spreading of democratic political systems with capitalist economies. This is how we would explain the decline of empires, the steady rise over time in the proportion of great powers and other very advanced states that are democracies, or the fact that the highest and most integrative levels of international cooperation exist among these states. American hegemony then becomes the lead or facilitating element of a much larger phenomenon – it is this phenomenon that is truly hegemonic.

From this perspective the current rather benign relationships among the great powers constitute a test of a profound working hypothesis: that serious (war-threatening) great-power conflicts now normally arise due to simultaneous sharp differences in (1) great-power domestic political and economic systems and (2) great-power ideological orientations. This is a test not designed by social scientist observers but because that working hypothesis is the fundamental principle shaping the great powers' current pursuit of peace and security. Their recipe for a stable and peaceful international system has become reconciliation across old ideological divides, movement toward parallel political and economic systems, further development of an open global economy, continued expansion of international information flows, and ever more extensive interdependence. This has been moving the great powers toward universal membership in the institutions for cooperation in the management of international affairs established by the Western democracies among themselves during the Cold War. All of these states are likely to end up as liberal democracies, market economies, and developed societies. This is the pursuit of security via the proliferation of homogeneity (see Clark 2001, particularly pp. 167–192).

The future of deterrence will be determined, initially, by whether this conception passes the test. To assess the future of deterrence we must monitor evidence on the success or failure of the conception; that is where the future of great-power security relations will be shaped. Previously those states, and outside observers, endlessly monitored relative military capabilities, particularly those on which deterrence was believed to depend. Domestic developments worth tracking were those bearing on, or with important implications for, relative military strength. Also monitored were international alignments and associations, particularly alliances. Some people still concentrate on these things.

Today, indicators worth monitoring pertain to the stability and democratic development of great-power political systems, plus their prosperity and openness to flows of technology, trade, and investments. The critical alignment information is how well associating Russia with the EU and the G-8 is going, the degree of Russia–NATO compatibility and cooperation on European security management, the progress on blending China into the WTO and other multilateral endeavors, and great-power solidarity on issues like nuclear proliferation or management via the Security Council. Unless and until the experiment clearly fails, tracking the strategic balance and tracing conventional force dispositions will be far less rewarding analytically than in the past.

Right now the odds look pretty good, better than 50–50, that these states will not return to stark and bitter rivalries. They are becoming more like each other, removing the spur and fervor to fight injected by past ideological and ethnocultural differences. They are mostly liberal democracies.[1] Interdependence, and a greater density in their interactions, is rising.[2] All understand and accept the logic of the nuclear age, under which great-power wars are likely to culminate in disaster. Most of what they sought in the past through conflict and war – national development, economic progress, domestic political legitimacy

---

[1] "Well-institutionalized democracies that reliably place ultimate authority in the hands of the average voter virtually never fight wars against each other" (Mansfield and Snyder 1995, p. 21).

[2] On the importance of this see Buzan, Jones, and Little 1993.

and stability, national security – is now readily available without it. Legitimacy for the domestic system no longer rests, as it sometimes did, on making war. Finally, growing transparency via the communications revolution is easing (though certainly not eliminating) the impact of suspicion, ignorance, and misperception which helped bring about war in the past.

For assessing the specific role of deterrence today several other features of the world are also of particular interest. Noteworthy is that outright interstate wars have declined. Violent conflicts that are technically between states are now usually between parts of a former state that has partially (the Congo) or fully (Yugoslavia) dissolved, a continuation of an internal conflict, not one between established nation states. To date we have no confirmed explanation for this, probably because it is new and may not be permanent. Many expected that the end of the Cold War would mean more instability in regional systems as superpower links to clients declined and superpower interventions to suppress fighting dropped, leading to more fighting between states. Conflicts suppressed or contained during the Cold War would grow; insecurity would mount; arms competitions would flourish; incentives for acquiring WMD would rise. This may yet occur but thus far has not (see Wallensteen 2002).

In stark contrast the number and intensity of internal wars remains disturbing, though it has been roughly steady in recent years (Wallensteen 2002).[3] For many states the meaningful threats arise from within more than from outside, and internal fighting typically reflects some citizens' view that the state is the biggest threat to their security (Buzan 1991b; Job 1992; Booth 1991). It is unlikely that internal conflicts will subside. Ethnic and religious tensions, arising from the need for a viable collective identity, have promoted demands for autonomy or independence, on the one hand, and struggles over control of governments on the other. Since we see serious, though nonviolent, manifestations of the same pressures in developed, long established states – Canada, Belgium, Britain – it is hard to see how this phenomenon will fade.

There is something profound at work. The state is a bundle of functions, political activities, and symbolic representation. When important state functions are ceded to markets, information-age communications, and other competing authorities, the other elements associated with

---

[3] Brecher and Wilkenfeld (1997) object to the term "long peace" because during the Cold War small wars and internal conflicts killed over 20 million people, creating vast insecurity (some estimates are as high as 30 million).

the state rise in significance. Its everyday functional activities are an important glue in otherwise fractious societies; weaken the glue and fractiousness increases. In reaction, we see more salience in politics and symbolic representation given to ethnic and religious identity as an alternative glue, but issues having to do with such identities are inherently divisive as well.

For this chapter the central questions are: What happens to deterrence now? What role does deterrence play at the global and lower levels of international politics? How applicable is our theory of deterrence? How reliable will deterrence, direct and extended, be? We divide the discussion into four categories:

> Deterrence among great powers.
> Deterrence in the global management of security.
> Deterrence among states other than great powers.
> Deterrence in intrastate conflicts.

Deterrence among great powers

The most important development is that nuclear deterrence has been pushed into the shade. The operating consensus is that nuclear deterrence must recede further via a continuing deemphasis on its role in security relations among great powers. This involves, in the first instance, not living on the edge of immediate deterrence – the great powers have not brandished nuclear weapons and threats for some time, their nuclear arsenals are well in reserve as a general deterrent instead, nuclear deterrence is far less salient. In the West this is clear. As Freedman notes: "From dominating Western strategic thinking, it now appears confined to the margins" (Freedman 1996; see also Freedman 1997). The same is true in Russia, which has joined in implementing important reductions in strategic forces. While Russia relies more heavily on nuclear weapons now, in the abstract, because of the decay of its conventional forces, the parallel decay in its strategic forces reflects a shift toward minimum deterrence and the fact that it sees a nuclear attack as very unlikely because it has no great-power relationship where deterrence is consistently necessary. Hence it puts up with a very deficient early warning system, highly vulnerable strategic weapons, and as few as 200 on alert.[4]

---

[4] Blair, Feiveson and von Hippel (1997) say there are perhaps 200 invulnerable Russian strategic nuclear weapons in comparison with over 2,000 for the US, even though Russian analysts see no alternative to nuclear deterrence as an ultimate resource since the conventional forces are so weak (see, e.g., Grigoryev 1999; Hoffman 1999c).

A significant exception is China. It is the only great power with a growing nuclear capability, the only one where profound uneasiness about security has heightened concern about nuclear and conventional deterrence. It is still pursuing nuclear deterrence out of serious concerns about its own security. But China has sharply deemphasized nuclear deterrence in relations with Russia and approaches only a general deterrence in relations with the US. It is enlarging and upgrading its strategic nuclear forces at a measured, not frantic, pace. Its military planning is now focused on local conflicts in which nuclear deterrence would be irrelevant, and on coping with modern RMA-shaped forces. Even while refining its strategic weapons it has abandoned nuclear testing.

China is the most uncomfortable with the new conception of how to conduct great-power relations mentioned above, often seeming to display a preference for traditional international politics. Some think this is because China feels too weak – too weak to be safe or too weak to achieve the regional hegemony it wants. In fact, China feels threatened mainly because it is least like the other great powers in terms of its political, economic and social systems, and the least comfortable with ever greater information flows and other aspects of the liberal great powers' international order. In its reactions China illustrates the gap between the new conception of international politics and the old. China is cultivating military strength, territorial grievances, and spheres-of-influence notions. Like a classic great power, though it now faces no direct military threat it is preoccupied with adjusting its relative military strength and detecting potential enemies in a realist fashion. It finds multipolarity comforting (constantly asserting this is coming as if wishing could make it so); the American preeminence is *in principle* disturbing and threatening. This affects its neighbors, many of whom give more attention to their own military forces these days than they would if China seemed less traditional. And the crisis over the 1995 Taiwan elections provoked a standard US demonstration of power to signal commitment and practice deterrence (as if this was 1912).

The US–China relationship is where China's incompatibility with the global system is manifested. That relationship is not a cold war, so that expectations of war or estimates of the possibility of war are not as high as a cold war would imply. But each side now takes the possibility of war quite seriously. This has affected China's arms purchases (seeking weapons to deter the US) and its military deployments (shifting away from the north, toward the east and south). Repeated Chinese statements that China is ready for war with the US over the Taiwan issue have sharply affected American military deployments (an increased naval presence in the Pacific), American relations with states from Russia to India, and American military planning for a possible war.

The most disturbing features of the dispute are (1) that the only plausible spark for a war is the Taiwan issue, despite the fact that both countries agree on the most desirable outcome; (2) Chinese insistence that they will not be deterred on the Taiwan question and expect to deter the US (not the most plausible analysis of how the US will react); (3) the current Chinese position of regarding Taiwan's independence as a grave threat to the survival of the regime and China itself when going to war with Taiwan, and certainly with the US, would clearly put both at a much graver risk – from having to back down, or suffering a humiliating conventional defeat, or initiating a nuclear war; (4) the current Chinese reliance on a malignant realist perspective, so that the view of the US as a grave threat has little to do with US actions and US treatment of China. Hence at least half of the American concern stems from the fact that these attitudes do not seem *rational or sensible*. The result is reactions that would otherwise seem provocative and unnecessary. Washington has been rife with depictions of China in the worst light.

This is an overreaction. First, if the Taiwan issue disappeared the whole notion of a serious China threat would be a very hard sell. Second, this is because China is not a traditional great power. It has worked hard in recent decades to improve relations with neighbors, open up to the global economy, and join important arms control agreements. For years it has settled for a minimal nuclear deterrence posture and eschewed power projection capabilities on any large scale. It now practices a form of "engagement" with Taiwan. It seeks a stable international environment, not normal international politics, so it can go on emphasizing national development. This leads it to join the US in various cooperative endeavors and a burgeoning economic relationship, and to do no outright anti-US alliance building. Other states take cues from this. Under traditional perspectives they should treat China as a threat and contain it. Instead they pursue engagement too. The rationale is that moving China toward Western economic, social, and political systems and into management of international politics will lay the basis for an indefinite peaceful relationship – the new conception at work. A flood of contacts and information is expected to subtly erode China's distinctiveness, resulting in a continuing decline in the salience of deterrence.

China today offers the central test of the idea of pushing deterrence into the background by avoiding serious conflicts. That would be a fundamental transformation of international politics in East Asia and important globally. Some analysts have expected such a test via Russia, and it could happen if Russia returns to authoritarianism and the pursuit of imperial dominance. This has not yet occurred, at least partly because of the way the Cold War ended: the Russians did not just quit; they moved to embrace fundamental elements of the West. Russia has so far accepted the idea that serious conflicts are not inevitable and thus deterrence can be relegated to the periphery of security affairs. Behaving as if it faces no significant threats, it has let its military strength deteriorate for years and now pursues adjunct membership in NATO. It envisions cutting its strategic arsenal to 1,500 nuclear weapons in a deal with the US for parallel reductions.

Nuclear weapons are also less salient in extended deterrence. The US does not use nuclear weapons to protect Europe like it did and NATO has shifted from an early-use doctrine to use only as a very last resort. The US sees no likelihood it would use nuclear weapons in another war in Korea. The Russians have let Soviet extended deterrence commitments lapse and no other great power is into extended deterrence through nuclear weapons.

The American government is, as befits a transitional era, fraught with ambiguity about these matters. It seeks to deemphasize strategic deterrence via missile defense and big cuts in strategic arsenals, but plans no elimination of nuclear weapons and foresees a mix of deterrence and defense well into the future. It wants to cut nuclear weapons greatly but keep lots in storage, to demote reliance on nuclear deterrence yet find more ways to plausibly use nuclear weapons to better deter. The target is similarly unclear. Russia is now a friend, a close associate of NATO – one justification for abandoning the ABM Treaty is that relying on MAD is passé since conflict with Russia no longer exists – so that nuclear weapons are (as in US relations with Britain or France) not central to the political relationship. As for China, a suspicious administration falls well short of confrontation or containment. As was true in the 1996 confrontation, both governments are intent on reinforcing *general* deterrence yet pursuing cooperation on some matters, greater interaction (especially economically), and considerable consultation. We can't say the relationship is mostly about deterrence, for all the rhetoric in each capital that the other is somehow the great threat of today and tomorrow. As a whole this does not amount to a strategy or even a coherent policy for the US – it has no intellectual cohesion. The world's only superpower totally outclasses everyone militarily, particularly its enemies in conventional forces, and professes to be so seriously threatened by some of the world's poorer societies that it needs to be able to fall back on nuclear weapons.

Finally, the administration is devoutly unilateralist and skeptical of nontraditionalist ways of managing international security affairs only to find how unnerving this is for its friends and allies who see the new conception of great-power relations as very important for keeping life with the US tolerable. Accepting long-term constraints on American power through cooperative engagement, rather than avoiding them via unilateralist impulses and selective withdrawal, is almost certain to return to driving the American pursuit of security and order (Ikenberry 2001). It is what Americans do best and know best – building better international relations with its friends and then expanding the members of the club.

It might seem that the great powers have settled for general deterrence via nuclear weapons, but this does not capture what has happened. Those with nuclear weapons still have some on a nearly hair-trigger alert and poised for an immediate deterrence situation. Yet the general deterrence they live with in their relations is mostly in very deep background. That we can marginalize nuclear deterrence this much, shrink political conflicts among nuclear powers so significantly, and continue deploying reciprocal hostage-taking capabilities without poisoning great-power political relations, is an amazing political adaptation. It testifies to the importance of politics, of specific political relations, in comparison with "structural" factors.

Some analysts dispute this. After all, nuclear arsenals are still large, the nuclear powers are not likely to disband them any time soon, and the great powers still insist that nuclear deterrence is essential for security. This is a failure to distinguish nuclear weapons from nuclear deterrence. It is clear that nuclear deterrence is not at the forefront of their relations and that it would be terribly difficult for them to use nuclear weapons at all, even under extreme provocation (see below).

We return to the point that deterrence is highly context dependent. Nuclear deterrence emerged to cope with a fierce political conflict. End the conflict and associated threat perception, and deterrence hardly seems vital, has much less riding on it. The current security focus for these states is not deterring war but management of great-power relations so war-threatening conflicts do not arise. With success in that, deterrence (other than of the most general sort) is unnecessary. Added in most great powers is a strong sense that emphasizing deterrence, particularly nuclear deterrence, could erode their cooperative relations: setting aside the Cold War required setting aside Cold War attitudes, and in turn this meant distancing interstate relations from the Cold War's threats.

Nuclear deterrence is also less salient because of widespread distaste for it and much of the East–West conventional-forces deterrence as well, a distaste that had been around for years. Critics had insisted that nuclear arsenals were irrational, that East–West military postures were grotesque. Sophisticated analyses asserted that nuclear deterrence was unreliable, which accorded with many popular views, and that it may have had little to do with the "long peace." Alienation from deterrence, widespread in Europe and the Third World, appeared in the US in the 1980s in such varied forms as the Nuclear Freeze Movement, the SDI program, calls for a nuclear no-first use policy, and the campaign for big cuts in START. When the alienation was voiced by Gorbachev and his associates too it helped unravel the Cold War (Bobbitt 1988, pp. 118–120). It was not just nuclear weapons or the scale of nuclear and conventional deployments that was so uncomfortable, but the way they were constantly primed for use. It is here that the greatest changes since 1990 have been instituted. The presence of constant reciprocal deterrence threats has come to be widely perceived as an insurance policy and last resort, a necessary evil but not an unavoidable fact of life or barrier to close relations.

Leaders began taking these concerns and criticisms to heart some years ago. For instance, a severe crisis is a bad environment for sorting out one's specific interests and educating oneself and the opponent about serious misperceptions. The most severe critics of deterrence are those who believe that crisis distorts information flows, induces rigid thinking, skews perceptions, limits the attention given to alternative perspectives and emotionally twists images of the opponent and his concerns. The Cuban missile crisis provided direct, disturbing evidence of this, which may be why such a crisis never occurred again – the great powers did their deterring without such confrontations.

Now they have gone further. The results are all around of converting deterrence from primary resource to backup capability for only the most improbable occurrences. (A partial exception is China.) The US nuclear stockpile peaked in 1967 (at 32,500) was down to 22,500 by 1989 and to 10,000 by 1996–2000 (Thee 1991; Panofsky 1999; Norris and Arkin 2000). Huge numbers of WMD (in intermediate and shorter range forms) have been destroyed, thousands more have been removed from active service and stockpiled, many more will get the same treatment. American, Russian, and French nuclear weapons at sea are gone from all but submarines and there are no nuclear weapons in several great powers' ground forces. Under START over 15,000 strategic nuclear weapons and delivery systems have been or are scheduled to be eliminated, reducing US and Russian arsenals to less than 20 percent of what they were. British and French nuclear forces have been reduced significantly. The French cut deployed nuclear weapons by 15 percent after 1991, more since, ended nuclear testing in 1996, eliminated nuclear bombs, eliminated the Pluton missile and canceled development of the Hades missile, and reduced the SLBM fleet by one sub (Delpech 1998). Britain cut its stockpile to under 200 strategic nuclear weapons, and has eliminated nuclear bombs (Willmer 1998). Many weapons have been taken off alert and the US airborne command posts operate at much lower tempo (Larson and Rattray 1996). The US has ended production of new weapons and fissile material. There is now a comprehensive nuclear test ban (which the US adheres to without ratification), and the nonproliferation treaty has been renewed. The US and Russia have reduced targeting with strategic weapons on high alert. NATO has cut its nuclear forces by over 90 percent, with US nuclear bombs stationed there down to 150–200. This is a rejection of the view (Intriligator and Britto 1984) that large arsenals are stabilizing and deep cuts are dangerous and irrational. It makes sense if, in fact, most of the weapons were never needed (they were overkill), and are not now, to do unacceptable damage.

There is an agreement to ban chemical and biological warfare and destroy stockpiles which will eliminate the bulk of those weapons in the world. At the conventional level roughly 100,000 items of military equipment have been moved out of central Europe and many (over 40,000) destroyed, many states are significantly below the force levels to which they are entitled under CFE agreements, US forces have been cut by one-third, Russian and Chinese forces even further, and these forces are deployed far less provocatively than in the past. The military confrontation in central Europe and along the Sino-Russian border is gone. Unilateral and cooperative arms control endeavors are widespread. In all these ways the great powers indicate that they are not counting on, have not arranged forces for, a rapid and vicious riposte to an attack (they are not practicing something close to immediate deterrence) because they don't foresee any attack and do not expect this to change.

Proposals for complete elimination of nuclear weapons are now more widespread and get a more serious hearing. There are even calls for unilateral nuclear disarmament on grounds that the US has the necessary capabilities for defeating opponents with conventional forces (Nitze 1999).[5] However, without certainty that good relations can last (and with the argument that nuclear weapons as insurance allow more risk taking on cooperation) there is no plan to abandon nuclear deterrence. The great powers have deemphasized nuclear deterrence without delegitimizing it. They worry, of course: about Russia, about NATO intentions (in Russia), about the future behavior of China, and (in China) about American intentions. It is wrong to think this means nothing has changed; in fact, the entire basis of great-power relations has shifted. Since this is very rare, it is hardly surprising that the great powers retained some insurance (Slocombe 1992), but that does not make the change insignificant.

However, no security evaluation is complete without a worst-case analysis. If traditional international politics returns with a vengeance, what happens to deterrence? The following seems most plausible. First, new conflicts would not return all the elements of the Cold War. Particularly at first, Cold War decision making in the West operated on pervasive ignorance and misperception in dealing with the Soviet Union, the Soviet bloc, and China. The difficulties in getting reliable estimates about bloc defense spending, economic growth, GNP, political stability, normal decision processes, the strength of political leaders and factions, and almost every other important matter were huge. One reason the West relied heavily on deterrence was the scale of its ignorance. It is fair to say that ignorance and misperception on the other side were also quite high, without as good an excuse. Ideologically and politically driven misperceptions, on both sides, were particularly powerful.

Great powers are now far better equipped to gather information than before and learned much from the Cold War about how to better use it. The Cold War was a fine, if gigantic, case study on misperception. Much has been learned that would be very useful next time, and any hostile relationships would be better managed than before.

---

[5] Studies calling for very substantial cuts in, or elimination of, nuclear weapons include: Karp, 1992; Rotblat 1998; Rotblat, Steinberger and Udgaonker 1993; Bundy et al.; CSIS Nuclear Strategic Study Group; Stimson Center 1995,1997; International Network of Engineers and Scientists Against Proliferation; Canberra Commission 1996; National Academy of Sciences; Turner 1997; Schell 2000; *The Morality of Nuclear Deterrence: An Evaluation by Pax Christi Bishops in the US*; *The Report of the Tokyo Forum for Nuclear Non-proliferation and Disarmament* (1998). The full citations for these and related studies are very usefully compiled in Sauer 1998.

Second, the return of severe conflict would take place among states well versed in Cold War deterrence. They would not need the lengthy apprenticeship the US and USSR stumbled through and should be less prone to serious missteps. They are highly familiar with each other, which was not true of the American and Soviet governments in the first decades of the Cold War. As a result resistance to a buildup of vast arsenals would be more pronounced. The defects in Cold War C^3I systems and nuclear war postures are better understood.

Finally, rivals would be immersed in vast information flows and have far greater capacities to monitor each other plus expanded routes for direct communication. This is no guarantee of avoiding serious misperceptions and miscalculations, but the stumbling about in the dark that took place in 1950 would be less likely. The Korean War occurred when North Korea, China, and the Soviet Union miscalculated the American reaction while the US "knew" the invasion was a Soviet decision. China very openly tried to deter US/UN forces from going to the Yalu and the US simply refused to get the message. The West proceeded to rearm mightily because it "knew" the Soviet military threat everywhere was immediate, producing the massive forces-in-place in central Europe for the rest of the Cold War. None of these governments knew what they were doing and the immediate and eventual costs were immense.

Thus nuclear deterrence among the great powers is (a) not about to disappear completely and (b) not likely to be important. The chances of a catastrophic failure are quite low but this has more to do with political relations among the great powers than nuclear deterrence. It would be nice if they were discarding nuclear weapons at a more rapid rate since nuclear deterrence is not very relevant, but without a national consensus in each that this is feasible and desirable it is politically unlikely (unless someday a neat little nuclear war finally scares the daylights out of everyone). The best we can hope for is that we slowly *outgrow* nuclear weapons, that they sit quietly tucked away nearly out of mind until it is possible for enough of us to be certain that life without them is quite plausible.

Deterrence in the global management of security

We are also experimenting in a determined fashion with further developing – apart from great-power relations – some sort of global and regional governance, however crude, on peace and security. Interesting literature on this is emerging but it seems much too soon to approach the subject without even referring to deterrence (as in Hewson and Sinclair

1999, for example). Deterrence was central in the Cold War not just to superpower and East–West relationships but for security management at lower levels, and it remains important for dealing with regional and local threats between and inside states. In this regard global security management contains two distinctive components. There is much interest in multilateralism for managing peace and security not only for conflict resolution or peacebuilding but for making deterrence threats, authorizing the use of force, and shaping how forces are mobilized and used. Two superpowers and blocs running much of the world's peace and security has given way to often involving more states in making the decisions and carrying them out in the UN and regional organizations. The range of potential actions is unchanged, from peacekeeping to large interventions and heavy fighting, but while the Cold War confined multilateral organizations to limited forms of security management they now operate across the entire range of options.

The other component is unilateral security management. Used in various neighborhoods by local great powers, only the United States now has the power-projection capabilities for it on a global scale. Early in the Cold War three, possibly four, states had them, then two, now one. This makes the United States, for some time to come, central for multilateral security management. Added are unilateral American security responsibilities – the US retains its alliances, keeps significant forces abroad or at sea, actively deters North Korea and Iraq, and sees itself (and is seen by others) as the key to security in Europe, the Middle East, and the Far East. Forward presence is deemed crucial for credibility because, while no state or group thinks it can defeat the US outright, some think it won't always fight (O'Hanlon 1992, pp. 19–20, 87–90). Forward presence and the alliances are also seen as repressing nuclear proliferation (Reed and Wheeler 1993).

Thus global security management rests in part on deterrence, but via a unique blend of one state's capabilities and a multilateralist framework within which those capabilities are often situated, with significant participation by other states at times. It is a hybrid of collective security efforts and hegemonic stability (O'Hanlon 1992, p. 13). The blend is tenuous – the multilateral portion is now under considerable strain because of the Bush Administration's near mania about unilateral security approaches.

Each component raises important questions about the future of deterrence. One is: how significant will this management be? It is unclear how far multilateral management will be carried. Several forms will continue to be periodically on display. One is a concert. If great-power agreement continues, it will often operate inside the concert at the heart of the Security Council, especially if Germany and Japan are added. A concert can readily operate outside the Council too in selected regions on particular matters. Another alternative is a not-fully-institutionalized collective security, where everyone opposes any state that engages in outright aggression – President Bush's "new world order" as displayed in the war against Iraq with its many participating states. In either alternative, vigorous security management will periodically need deterrence and/or compellance. This will mean more Gulf Wars and Bosnia interventions, with deterrence not only by threats but by military action.

This is what to anticipate. Multilateral security management is an idea whose time has come. There is a strong consensus on the need for it. The UN vigorously took it up until the Cold War intervened, and started where it left off once the Cold War stopped. Broad security management is one legacy of the Cold War, which instigated much thinking about security in global terms. It is also a spin-off from the distaste for nuclear deterrence, which makes curbing WMD proliferation a strong motivation. There will also be more security management efforts at the *regional* level, involving NATO, the OAS, and ad hoc concerts, perhaps especially when the Security Council is inhibited. With great-power conflicts muted or set aside, it is in regional systems that the most significant conflicts can be found today: on Taiwan, the division of Korea, Kashmir, the West Bank, etc. The global system is no longer dominated by deterrence but this is far less true in regional systems. In some collective actor deterrence is highly relevant, in others (Middle East, South Asia) there is little system management beyond the crude deterrence threats of the members in ugly balances of power.

Intervention to prevent or end violence will be supported by emerging international norms. The decline in interstate wars suggests that their expense and danger, compared with other options, is being supplemented by spreading appreciation that many objectives no longer require war.[6] This is shrinking war's legitimacy other than for self-defense or to uphold general peace and security, making it easier to get instances of deliberate violence condemned and collective responses mounted.

However, deterrence to uphold security management by great powers or a larger collective will be fraught with difficulties, some noted

[6] This decline can't be traced to nuclear deterrence. Buzan and Herring (1999) cite the rising fear and cost of war, increased interdependence, the spread of democracy, and a growing sensitivity to casualties.

257

below and others discussed in chapter 5. The burdens will have to be eased by limiting instances of intervention. Concerts may form to confront serious threats, but the great powers will not always see specific threats as worth their attention. The UN may often choose not to intervene, in part because of the crucial role of a reluctant US. Thus, security management – and the deterrence on which it rests – will be *intermittent, inconsistent, tenuous*. True, the competitive great-power meddling that makes matters worse, provides resources for fighting, complicates political settlements, and ups the risks escalation is now less likely. In that sense security is enhanced. But troubles in many places will not get suitable attention and deterrence via threats of intervention will be less used or effective than many governments and observers would like.

As for unilateral American security management, several things are clear. The US is not about to abandon the military capabilities needed. There is no domestic pressure to cut defense spending and the War on Terrorism will go on increasing the defense budget for some time. However, unilateral (and often multilateral) security management lacks deep public support when the problem seems remote, appears intractable so US action will likely produce no lasting benefits, and promises to be burdensome.[7] "Put simply, in most cases of discretionary intervention, if the price is dead Americans or dead civilians in the target country, America is likely to consider that price too high" (Kanter and Brooks 1994, p. 26). Resistance to using US forces abroad remains strong (Bacevich 1995). Kosovo offered a clear example of initial US hesitance. Eventually the US reluctance to risk casualties provoked widespread conclusions that the US is tired of such activities.

Thus it is unclear how extensive US contributions to global security management will be. Perhaps it is only a matter of time until the US confronts a serious conflict, faces strong pressure to do something, has the usual limited support at home for acting, acts anyway, and the results are bad – costs and casualties but no satisfactory results. That will restrict future interventions. The Clinton and first Bush administrations successfully intervened in Panama, Iraq, Haiti, Bosnia, and Kosovo while

---

[7] Tolerance of damage and casualties – the threshold of unacceptable damage – has declined in the West. IISS 1995–6 (pp. 48–57) notes that the British commander in Desert Storm liked the end-run strategy precisely to avoid casualties. At one point daylight raids on Baghdad were halted because two F-16s had been lost, and A-10 attacks on the Republican Guard halted after two were lost; "no target is worth an airplane" became the rule (Keaney and Cohen 1993, p. 248). Some believe that while the American public dislikes casualties it won't demand withdrawals and thus declining tolerance for casualties is overdrawn. I disagree.

narrowly avoiding real damage in Somalia, but each was a gamble. Someday the gamble will not pay off, and current Bush Administration rhetoric indicates it may be less often taken.

Other states are worried, some about dependence on an uncertain, sometimes wrong-headed, American deterrence. This has incited steps toward an autonomous intervention capability, based on the EU and using NATO assets, to act when the US will not (at least in Europe). European (and other) states now seek more flexible and mobile forces that can generate a larger role, and voice, in interventions. That will, in turn, probably end major American participation in future Bosnias or Kosovos – Americans are unlikely to intervene when others will do it. While China worries about US interventions, others – more accurately – fear a US retreat from its engagements, maybe upsetting regional security arrangements.

It is significant that objections to American management stop short of organized or systematic resistance. France objects but has been unable to gain support for an independent European capability to act outside the continent – there is little support for broadening European security horizons like this and for the costs – and even France does not seek an end to the American military presence in Europe and American participation in operations like Bosnia. China officially supports the withdrawal of American forces from East Asia,[8] but as of this writing even North Korea disagrees.[9] No one seems to be competing for the American role. Russian power projection forces decay; the EU is just beginning to construct a common foreign/security policy and shows no signs of wanting global responsibilities; Japan only gingerly participates in peacekeeping; China is focused on neighborhood contingencies.[10] There are complaints about what the US does or does not do, but not as challenges to American management in principle. Indeed, the US is frequently criticized for not doing more.

Within deterrence for security management, the role of alliances is shifting. US extended deterrence remains but the context has changed.

---

[8] Many analysts claim that China would not like a withdrawal that led to Japanese nuclear weapons and power projection capabilities.

[9] The North sometimes hints that US forces should remain in Korea to prevent a regional power vacuum.

[10] Why no challenger? Probably because of the costs and lack of political support for this role in other democracies. Possibly because no other actor really has global interests, which would be why the costs are unacceptable. Maybe because the US enjoys legitimacy and the confidence of others as global security manager, but that may be a function of the other explanations.

During the Cold War extended deterrence brought unprecedented peacetime intimacy between the US and its allies. That is declining as the perceived likelihood of war shrinks. Alliances that once contributed to global security management now operate in separate spheres with only regional or local significance, mainly as reassurance of American engagement and the basis for an American military presence.

However, the US has led the way in adjusting NATO to be a vehicle for regional security, not just collective defense, and is nudging it toward becoming a true collective security arrangement. As conditions permit it will want the same in its other alliances. If they become important for collective responses to outbreaks of violence, then some intimacy will be retained – there will be meaningful operations to plan, train for, and conduct. Without such functions, the alliances will likely atrophy into agreements on paper to cooperate in case of attack. Thus in the Far East the US has bilateral alliances and security associations but will continue pressing for a collective approach. It insists the alliances are a good base on which to build, which means giving them new responsibilities and a new orientation, and rejects the view that they stand in the way of a collective approach to regional security. This partly shaped the American view of refurbishing the alliance with Japan. Although American officials regularly talk about how the US is vital in regional security, a unilateral approach is not preferred. This is why the second Bush Administration's unilateralism was, from the start, combined with cutting American responsibilities abroad. That has failed and unless it can be revived the American inclination to want something done to manage security will again stimulate more recourse to multilateralism.

How feasible is deterrence now? Chapter 5 indicated that deterrence by a concert or a collective actor has many of the strengths and weaknesses of deterrence by a state but to different degrees. The problem of detecting when to use deterrence and deciding when to use force is the same, with the decision additionally complicated by having to build an international consensus. The process starts with issuing threats, moves to nonmilitary punishment – economic pressures, diplomatic isolation – and only then contemplates military action. Normally, a major state takes the lead and a consensus forms around it. If threats don't work, typically some members resist carrying them out. Unhappiness at the prospective costs increases with the target's military strength and the scale of the proposed operation. Differences arise as well because participants know the casualties will not be equally shared. These qualms parallel the ones in any nation that practices deterrence.

It is no surprise, then, that multilateral deterrence can have a serious credibility problem, leading to familiar concerns about maintaining a reputation for upholding commitments that can sometimes become the main justification for taking action. As with a national deterrence effort, credibility concerns may sometimes lead to unwise and unsustainable involvements, multilateralist versions of Vietnam. Predictably, critics will assert that the ill-chosen intervention will damage the group's ability to act in the future.

The credibility problem can be eased if more responsibility for security management is turned over to regional organizations or groups – letting states most directly concerned, and thus most likely to do something, be responsible. In fact, this consideration may promote use of regional security management, with action authorized, i.e. legitimized, by the UN and then conducted relatively autonomously, as happened in Bosnia and East Timor.

Beyond these difficulties, however, lie others. For a collective actor it will be extremely difficult to mount a massively destructive response to misbehavior and thus next to impossible to threaten this, as explained in chapter 5. Deterrence will rest on threats of limited but effective responses. Exceptions might come if the challenger appeared ready to use WMD, but even then mounting such a threat in response will be far from automatic. And military responses will have to be limited and controlled. There will be great reluctance to authorize even conventional actions like indiscriminate bombing or collaterally destructive ground-fighting. This reflects the ethos of collective actors pursuing the general interest. It fits current great-power efforts to push weapons of mass destruction into the background. It is shaped in part by today's immense information flows about what war is really like.

The same will apply to the US in using deterrence for global security management. Threats of a massive response will be known to be extremely difficult to carry out. Controlled responses will be the rule if threats do not work. The possible exception is responding to the use of WMD, but even then this may be quite limited. Claims that the US must maintain a capability to respond in kind, or worse, to the use of WMD by states like Iraq or North Korea, that this is crucial for deterrence (Bailey 1995; Betts 1998), underestimate how difficult it will be to actually do so. We went through all this during the Cold War.

Recognition of this has promoted American efforts to develop more precise nuclear weapons – "micronukes," "mininukes," and "tinynukes," (with yields of 10, 100, and 1,000 kilotons).[11] The idea is to make these weapons more acceptable to use, hence more credible to brandish (Dowler and Howard 1995). Republicans have championed research on them in recent years, and the Russians have been thinking along the same lines (Hoffman 1999c). But this will not solve the problem. Decision makers treat WMD with great reserve, which is good.

Hence "it is extremely unlikely that the United States would do to Iraq or Iran what it threatened and promised its allies it would do to the USSR with nuclear weapons in the event of an attack" (Ullman 1995, p. 97). Years ago American officials dropped plans to use nuclear weapons against North Korea even after a North Korean nuclear attack on the South (and US nuclear weapons were withdrawn from South Korea). The political and psychological barriers seemed too formidable, especially since those weapons were not necessary for an effective military response. In the Gulf War, the US threatened terrible consequences if Iraq turned to WMD but not that it would respond in kind, while France explicitly announced that using nuclear weapons was out of the question. The US and Russia are committed to having no chemical and biological weapons stockpiles, eliminating any in-kind response to others' use of those weapons.

Does this make effective deterrence more difficult? Yes and no. One view is that deterrence was once simpler (Watman and Wilkening 1995) because the US could assume that:

> the Soviets fully appreciated the effects of modern war and modern weapons,
> the Kremlin valued the survival of its population and economy,
> the Soviet leadership was largely satisfied with the status quo;
> hence the big risk was of inadvertent war;
> hence the fear of escalation made even extended deterrence modestly credible;
> hence enormous arsenals compensated for uncertainty about what it would take to deter.

Things are supposedly more complicated now because a big loss is harder for leaders to accept than being deterred from a big gain,

[11] This is one use of the terms. Others define mininukes as 5 kilotons or less, etc. (see Goldstein 2000).

especially if the status quo is very unappealing, and many opponents will face big losses if they don't go through with challenges to the status quo. Facing such strong incentives to attack, the US can best deter by having forces that can be rapidly mobilized to deny the opponent a quick victory/fait accompli. In addition, most regional adversaries, especially nondemocratic ones, value regime preservation above all and deterrence threats can exploit this.

Unfortunately (see chapter 2) things were not so simple back then. A popular argument was that Soviet leaders did not care about great losses as the price of victory. In calculating how to deter the Russians the US ended up redesigning the SIOP to target the ruling elite since regime preservation was supposedly all they cared about.[12] The basis of flexible response was that the Soviets might risk war because an American nuclear response to an attack in Europe would be irrational, and thus readiness to fight conventionally was vital for deterrence. Throughout the Cold War American officials and analysts expressed concern that Soviet leaders facing a serious loss or relative decline vis-à-vis the West might attack out of desperation.

If massive responses are improbable deterrence does indeed become more complicated, but in other ways that also make it less likely to work. Nuclear weapons easily displayed a capacity for unacceptable damage and provided incentives for superpower global security management. That incentive remains (in nonproliferation efforts, for example) but it is less vital now in great-power relations and thus less likely to be applied consistently. Whatever might take its place will be difficult to link consistently to the interests and concerns of specific governments like Cold War deterrence. Instead, deterrence is once again, to a much greater extent, the *tactical* foreign policy tool it was earlier. The difficulties and complications involved are substantial as deterrence is unevenly effective, and thus very troublesome, when used this way. The Cold War and nuclear weapons gave deterrence an undeserved good name. In prior periods the mixed utility of deterrence was much clearer in that it was often not very effective, sometimes counterproductive. That will be true now.

For instance, what kind of threat will most effectively deter now? To find out what a regime values most can be a daunting task. Detecting

---

[12] This grew out of requests by Assistant for National Security Zbigniew Brzezinski in the Carter Administration; by 1982 the SIOP had over 5,000 leadership/elite targets, plus roughly 2,500 nuclear forces, 1,500 economic/industrial, and 25,000 other military targets (Ball and Toth 1990).

its exact goals and preferences calls for sophisticated political analysis, something governments regularly botch.[13] NATO had no sense of how Milosevic would actually react to the initial bombing over the Kosovo problem (prior experience was a poor guide), and soon found itself scrambling to conduct a much longer campaign than expected and by means ill suited to quell Serbian attacks on Kosovars. If massive responses (even with conventional forces) are virtually beyond the pale then threats and their implementation must be quite controlled and measured, ideally tailored to damage things of value without large casualties or gratuitous destruction. The goal might be to punish leaders or the dominant elite, or damage economic targets, or cripple military capabilities. But outside of some obvious targets the information requirements are onerous because this calls for detailed knowledge not only about the opponent's condition and its assets but about which assets *it most values at that time*, plus knowledge about where they are.

The best recent example is the bombing of Serbia. There is already a large literature on how badly it was conducted, i.e. Serbia was really not defeated – it just quit, NATO was far too modest in the initial attacks (they should have been shocking and crippling), too slow in preparing to invade Kosovo. This is silly. The war was a textbook example of collective actor deterrence at work, and a resounding success. As suggested in chapter 5, the collective actor only slowly got to the point of seriously threatening and had a considerable credibility problem when it did. Then it sought not to *defeat* Serbia but to compel Serbia to quit *short of being defeated*. It was very successful in this; it just took longer, with much more bombing, than anticipated.[14] However, we can hardly say that NATO knew what it was doing. It fought as it did so as to avoid massive damage and casualties in Serbia, allied casualties, and political disruptions in its fragile coalition – all of which will be typical of collective actor deterrence efforts.

The war also took time due to the difficulty in figuring out just what would move the Serbian regime. Postmortems make clear that NATO did not know just what to bomb for best effect, that the allies and their commanders frequently disagreed about targets, and that it is still unclear why Milosevic quit – whether the bombing was responsible or not.

---

[13] For an attempt to show how this might be done better see Payne 2001.

[14] It was inadvertently more successful than thought. Critics cite clear evidence that bombing did much less damage to Serbian military forces than believed; Serbia was better equipped to resist an invasion of Kosovo than NATO thought (IISS 1999a; Graham and Priest 1999). If it nonetheless quit, making it quit cheaply was an even greater success.

(For example, Priest 1999b–e; Harden 1999; Gellman 1999; IISS 1999a; *House of Commons Defence – Fourteenth Report* 1999–2000).

As noted earlier deterrence can set off emotional fireworks, can provoke a highly dangerous response, can readily stiffen resistance by upping the opponent's threshold of acceptable harm. That is why various findings suggest blending it with reassurance or other cooperative steps. Thus:

> Deterrence makes sense only in certain situations, and identifying those situations requires an analysis of the adversary's motives and power. If this political analysis is done by assumption or, worse still, by a simplified stereotype, then the application of the strategy may be misplaced. The real task is political analysis and interpretation, not the rational formulation of deterrence in economic or game-theoretic form. (Hermann 1997, p. 96)

But how likely is such knowledge to be consistently available? Sometimes it is missing among adversaries who have been fighting for years.[15]

It will also be difficult to know what will deter even if it is reasonably well known what would constitute unacceptable damage. *Unacceptable damage may not be enough to deter.* It is important to distinguish "unacceptable" from "unbearable" damage. In deterrence theory emphasis is on making attacker costs "unacceptable." But if suffering these costs cannot, by their nature, be exactly predicted – it is possible they may not be incurred – the relevant attacker calculation is whether, if the worst occurs, it will be at least "bearable" for the leader, the regime or the nation. The more bearable it looks, the more acceptable the gamble, and thus the harder it is to deter.[16] This is even more the case because decision

---

[15] As one former high official asks: "where is the lower threshold of credibility for deterrence? What constitutes the lowest rung of the nuclear escalatory ladder? Is deterrence logic credible in case of nuclear threats or attacks only, or does it apply as well in cases of chemical or biological threats or attacks? What of a response to conventional aggression on a large scale, or what during the Cold War was referred to as the tactics of 'salami slicing' – limited operations designed to steadily undermine the strategic position of an adversary? We have had experience with these questions lately, but still have not developed satisfactory answers" (Cambone 1996, p. 106). There are no reliable answers now – and there never were.

[16] Prior to the nuclear age "the nature of the then prevailing military technology did not suggest that the cost of losing would be either disproportionate to the stakes for which the military gamble was being played, or wholly catastrophic to the historic destiny of their nations. In the event, the costs of losing, though substantial, were bearable . . ." (Buzan and Herring 1999, p. 274). This is overdrawn since great powers began worrying about what their wars could do as early as 1815, but the general point is sound: nuclear weapons made obliteration the "worst" that could happen, overwhelming detailed calculations about risks and gains.

makers strongly motivated to attack, as we saw in chapter 4, often do not do much calculating of potential costs or discount information about what they could be – they make the gamble look more acceptable in this way too.

This distinction is also useful for tracing the implications of the decline in nuclear deterrence in global security management for deterrence of countries like Iraq. Deterrence for dealing with Iraqs and North Koreas will be far more episodic, only occasionally rising to the clear danger in a grave crisis. But it will culminate much more often in being practiced *via force* and not just to avoid the use of force, which means it must rest on conventional war-fighting capabilities. And the objectives will be broader than war avoidance. For instance, the US threatened military action if North Korea kept developing nuclear weapons, deterring not to prevent an attack but to forestall another unwanted action. This requires promising something costly and harmful, but not total destruction. The harmful consequences threatened will be unacceptable but bearable – they can be survived, recovered from, tolerated. That is what makes the force "usable" if deterrence doesn't work initially. This is the deterrence Israel has long practiced: deterrence via threats, then via inflicting punishment. It is what the US used against Iraq after the Gulf War. In such cases, in other words, deterrence is more likely to fail repeatedly and require the use of force serially.[17]

This helped instill an Israeli view that once deterrence fails only decisive victory, imposing severe costs, can restore it (Inbar and Sandler 1995). Otherwise repeated military actions will be necessary. The implications are not comforting. A search for decisive victories could be bad for deterrence in practice because it would conflict with the desire to avoid massive destruction. This is where the revolution in military affairs now plays an important role. It has allowed the US and US-led coalitions to evade the dilemma – to respond in a nasty way that avoids massive destruction. In comparison, the use of economic sanctions is often much less discrete, having scattershot results comparable to siege warfare.

In US deterrence of Iraq after the Gulf War, the force employed was "usable" and, in some sense, "bearable" by Iraq and it had to be repeated

---

[17] "Where the cost of deterrence failing is not immediate, ruinous, or overwhelming, there is a greater chance for miscalculation, self-delusion, and simply stupid behavior. This is why purely conventional deterrence can fail and frequently has" (Reed and Wheeler 1993, p. 35).

regularly. This has been Israel's experience.[18] In such circumstances it is difficult to carefully calibrate "unbearable damage" and then effectively threaten or inflict it. The punishment must fit the specific society, government, and leaders involved (see Watman and Wilkening 1995, pp. 27–55). Tailoring deterrence in this way is usually much too complicated and often unacceptable. No wonder it was difficult to deter Iraq. Some feel the trouble was that the coalition promised to damage Iraq's economy and society, which Saddam never cared about. That was entirely "bearable"; he was always willing to sacrifice his citizens to his ambitions. The way to deter Iraq was to have promised to kill him or remove him from power – the only things he really cared about (Byman, Pollack and Waxman 1998). For well-known reasons this was a promise impossible to make. And extended military pressure – damaging anti-aircraft sites and enlarging the no-fly zone – was similarly unproductive. It was unacceptable but "bearable."

The result can be quite disturbing. For antagonists caught up in serial deterrence unwritten rules often come to apply so that both attack and response are limited, making them "bearable." The parties settle for recurring vicious low-level strikes and raids. Like a bad marriage, they learn to do mean things in a relationship in which deterrence rests on each regularly hurting the other. This is how the Israeli–Palestinian conflict evolved and has long characterized the India–Pakistan relationship. Deterrence is employed all the time but frustration over the results is substantial. Threats do not prevent attacks and violence, just keep them within limits. Needless to say, this can be difficult to sustain indefinitely for a democratic government or an actor like the Security Council.

The distinction between "unacceptable" and "unbearable" punishment helps explain why deterring terrorism is so difficult. It is like deterring crime. The roots of the attacks go deep, often have profound emotional sources, and the behavior that results is apt to be woven into self-identity aspects of character and personality as opposed to being consciously crafted for a specific purpose. What is unbearable to the terrorist is the situation he wants to change and his not trying to do anything about it, and thus he is willing to risk, and endure, many unacceptable consequences. It is possible that he could be deterred if we were willing to threaten the grossest of consequences. Why don't we promise to

---

[18] Sadat is an example of a leader willing to risk war because the potentially unacceptable results would still be bearable.

kill the entire extended family of Osama bin Laden and everyone else around them, and to raze Mecca and Medina and other Islamic holy places; why not deal with guerrillas in Afghanistan by threatening to kill every living soul within an area infested with them? This is, after all, precisely the sort of threats on which Cold War deterrence ultimately rested – we promised to wipe out whole populations and civilizations. It is obvious why we don't offer those threats – we can't. We promise unacceptable but not unbearable costs instead (killing people willing to die for their cause).

Concerns about credibility are profound under these circumstances because the relationship is truly, in Schelling's formulation, a competition in inflicting and bearing pain; each is reluctant to show it has reached its limit. This is why deterrence can be difficult to use successfully in internal wars. Each side uses violence to deter but must retain its reputation for not being cowed if it is to remain a viable actor, so a cycle of violence results. It is almost as difficult in cases like Iraq and is certainly so for North Korea. Trying to build credibility for dealing is beset by the same difficulty – steps to demonstrate deterrence should be tailored to the opponent. "[I]f . . . the challenger uses bounded rationality and only operates within a limited menu of critical variables when assessing the world, it is crucial that the defender know what these variables are before designing a policy to teach this challenger the right set of lessons" (Hopf 1994, p. 242).

But successfully tailoring deterrence is much easier said than done. "As a general rule, the US and NATO grasp of the political and strategic cultures of likely wrongdoers . . . will be so inadequate as to render much, if not all, of the theory of deterrence simply irrelevant. One will not know whom to deter, when, over what, or by which threats" (Gray 1996, p. 46). Thus in Vietnam, according to Maxwell Taylor, "we knew very little about the Hanoi leaders other than Ho Chi Minh and General Giap and virtually nothing about their collective intentions" (Gray 1996, p. 46).

Unlike Cold War deterrence, intense hostility of long standing between deterrer and challenger cannot always be assumed for purposes of analysis – their conflict may be far more episodic in nature. This makes it much more complicated politically to define interests for which deterrence is a proper recourse; they are fluid, context-dependent, related to the means that might have to be used, etc. (Freedman 1996). It is impossible to assume the opponent intends to attack if it gets the chance. Perhaps a state will see global or regional security management as a threat in itself, to be attacked wherever possible, but this seems implausible. More likely the challenger will have specific objectives and attack if it spots a suitable opportunity, viewing the Security Council, a regional collective actor, or the US as an obstacle to that limited goal.

Another complication (noted in chapter 1) is that when deterrence is practiced by applying force, the goal is not only to avoid attack. The conflict becomes a series of engagements by force and it becomes steadily more difficult to determine who is deterring and attacking. Defining an attack becomes harder and deterrence is fuzzy. Anticipating the response of the other side is more difficult.[19] When the United States punished Iraq for threatening the Kurds was this deterrence or compellance? Did *Iraq* view this as deterrence or an attack? Calculating whether deterrence will produce the desired effect is therefore more difficult. The ambiguities in explaining how and when deterrence works are also magnified. It is harder to be sure deterrence will work, that it won't exacerbate the conflict indefinitely. Deterrence does not become more successful just because the violence involved is more "acceptable."

Deterrence and rogue states

There are other grounds for concern about deterrence for global security management. Much attention goes to two topics. First is the fear that in US (or UN or other collective actor) conflicts with smaller states, deterrence will work in the "wrong" way. It won't work consistently for upholding global security, but *for states resisting outside interference it will work too effectively.* Deterrence will be of declining use against dangerous states, while they will find it easier to deter military action against them, especially with WMD. "Military interventions against states that possess even a small number of nuclear weapons will be vanishingly rare" and possession of nuclear weapons guarantees a state's territorial integrity (Weber 1992, p. 208; Beckman et al. 2000, p. 196). There are repeated suggestions that in the Gulf crisis it would have been even more difficult to deter Iraq, and far easier for Iraq to deter the UN, if Iraq had nuclear weapons. Martel and Pendley (1994), for example, assert that then there would have been no Gulf War, and that "Even a casual observer of international politics understands that states which possess nuclear

---

[19] This probably caused NATO to incorrectly anticipate the initial Milosevic reactions to the Kosovo bombing. Bombing Bosnian Serb positions had more impact because Serbia proper was not at stake; attacking Serbia over Kosovo threatened dismemberment of the state and was bound to be seen as an attack, not deterrence.

weapons gain considerable political and military leverage over their adversaries" (p. 87). Surely this is more complicated than Martel and Pendley imagine – they see nuclear weapons conveying considerable leverage and then discuss the Gulf War as necessitated by the lack of US and other nuclear powers' leverage on Iraq!

The concern about nuclear proliferation and deterrence involves a two-step argument. First, that proliferation will spread. There is a range of views about proliferation and its effects (Davis and Frankel 1993, for example), which also apply to other WMD. Some think it will flourish (Davis and Frankel 1993; Martel and Pendley 1994), particularly since even a simple WMD capability will do (Zimmerman 1994); others see states turning away from it (Reiss 1995). Frankel argues it will occur as multipolarity erodes any superpower commitment to protect clients with serious security threats. Other analysts trace the impetus for proliferation to the ambitions of national elites, rationalized by arguments that security threats require a nuclear deterrent. For Goldstein (1993) it is a straightforward result of the inadequacy of the conventional forces states can afford to purchase – nuclear weapons are a cheap alternative.

Second, it is asserted that states will use WMD deterrence to forestall interventions by either a collective actor or the United States. The most alarming analysis says the US must plan for regional nuclear wars (designing weapons, facilities, and deployments accordingly), build a ballistic missile defense, and be better prepared to rapidly deploy nuclear weapons to meet regional contingencies (Millot 1995).

Wilkening and Watman (1995) detail possible implications of nuclear proliferation for American deterrence. A rational opponent will know that nuclear weapons do not erase its military inferiority yet it must try to deter intervention, or limit the objectives of the intervention, by threatening a nuclear response. This will turn confrontations into contests of risk-taking where credibility and fear of the ultimate consequences are crucial. The opponent will bring a tenacity born of having core interests and big stakes involved. US credibility may be bolstered by having strong interests and well established commitments, but often this will not be the case and it must compensate by the leverage that lies in military superiority: "the approach taken here emphasizes asymmetric US military advantages to compensate for what frequently may be the opponent's perception of a weak US commitment or resolve" (Wilkening and Watman 1995, p. 22). For effective deterrence the US must use escalation dominance, based on the credible threat of a nuclear response to any nuclear attack on the US or its forces.[20] To this it must add its conventional superiority, active and passive defenses against nuclear attacks, and counterforce capabilities (conventional, which are ideal, and nuclear to cover all contingencies). As for deterring other WMD, since the US will not be able to respond in kind nuclear deterrence could be used and thus a nuclear no-first-use pledge would be unwise. In sum, actors are rational, credibility rests primarily on interests and the scale of the harmful consequences an actor might inflict – adjusted by bargaining tactics (à la Schelling) and the legitimacy of the means to be used, and deterrence rests on leaving the opponent no advantage from nuclear weapons because of US war-fighting superiority, especially in damage limitation.

This analysis needs augmentation. Deterrence is not strictly a rational process and the theory cannot explain credibility purely in terms of a nuclear balance. If we understand this, we can see that the spread of WMD, while complicating matters, might actually improve the possibilities for effective deterrence of the new nuclear powers. Though this is not widely appreciated, a state that is not a great power but has WMD should be easier for the US to deter than one without them!

Nuclear weapons simplify some things. To have them and face threats from the US or the Security Council is, in important ways, to be in the deterrence that operated during the Cold War. In these circumstances, an Iraq will fear that using its most fearsome weapon against, say, the US means the regime's destruction, escalating the conflict from one in which the weapons used, and a war, are bearable to one in which they are not. *This is true even if the US or UN response is entirely conventional.* When a forceful response is controlled, not utterly devastating, the attacker's concern must be whether the other side is limiting its objective. To disregard deterrence by a much superior opponent risks provoking a furious determination to destroy the offending regime. The use of WMD could readily have that effect – use of nuclear weapons, for example, would breach important political and psychological barriers, invite universal condemnation, and provoke a thorough effort to stamp out the regime. Barbarous actions of a nonnuclear sort can also have this effect. The resulting fierce determination can drive a controlled response to destroy the regime.

---

[20] Similarly, Utgoff writes that "the United States should retain ready nuclear forces in reserve that regional challengers should see as substantially more capable than their own weapons" (Utgoff 1993a, p. 274).

Even if Iraq fights solely with conventional weapons this becomes infinitely more dangerous if it has nuclear weapons; the other side will be strongly tempted to strike them, or the conflict may escalate to the nuclear level under the pressures of war. In either case the Iraqi regime faces the possibility it will be totally destroyed. Hence, what was intended to be a modest conventional war might easily become unbearable. As in the Cold War, nuclear weapons on both sides make *any* war more dangerous and an Iraq with nuclear weapons will normally behave far more cautiously than one without. Hence one view of the North Korean nuclear program was that possessing nuclear weapons would not improve the North's strategic situation, just make it more likely that in any war the North, regime and state, would disappear even if the response was not nuclear. Thus deterrence should be no more difficult than before, and it would not be necessary to attack the North if it refused to abandon nuclear weapons because they would not make it any more difficult to deter than it was already, and would not increase its capacity to deter the US.

It can be argued that Iraq will have more at stake, the survival of the regime, and therefore will more readily risk a nuclear war, winning the competition in risk taking (Powell 2002). But for a rational government trying to stave off its possible disappearance by threatening to do something that would *guarantee* its disappearance has to be unacceptable, and thus lacking in credibility, so its rational opponent will not back down.

However, real deterrence by a great-power concert, or the US or UN, against states like Iraq will always have questionable credibility because of the costs, casualties, and other difficulties in using force. If Iraq has nuclear weapons, or other WMD, that credibility problem will be worse; deterrers will be more hesitant. Why? Because while it is irrational for Iraq to use its ultimate weapons governments cannot guarantee to be completely rational and in control. Thus a state can threaten nuclear retaliation and be believed enough to make deterrence work. An Iraq (or a North Korea) with nuclear weapons will be more difficult to confront because even though it would be a terrible mistake for Iraq to use those weapons no one can be certain it would not do so.

However, *this applies to Iraq as well*. If Iraq has nuclear weapons and receives threats from states with nuclear weapons, like the United States, it is much more difficult for Iraq to decide to do whatever it wants anyway. It, too, must live with the possibility that a war could escalate with its complete destruction almost certain. Therefore, *the spread of nuclear weapons* (or other WMD) *does not dictate how confrontations will go, who wins and who loses*. A situation like this, where both parties possess nuclear weapons, is not, however, the equivalent of Cold War deterrence. One party has survival at stake while the other does not, not just because of the nuclear superiority one side possesses but because it also possesses conventional forces to end the other regime even if it employs WMD. Thus a regime like Iraq's lacks a good scenario for survival by escalating. If it is rational, as Wilkening and Watman assume, it can be deterred without threatening a nuclear response – it is the clear conventional military superiority that really matters.[21] Closer to the truth, then, is the contention that "The role of nuclear weapons in . . . regional confrontations is likely to be much the same as in the Cold War: an inducement to caution in and before crises, and a deterrent of last resort against nuclear powers, credible only if it is associated with strong conventional forces in the region under threat" (May and Speed 1994, p. 19). All I would add is (1) that the conventional forces dictate the outcome, not last-resort nuclear weapons, because they make it possible to threaten destruction of the regime via useable, "legitimate" means while offering the chance that the opponent's losses will remain "bearable" if he does not escalate; and (2), the best threat would be not only just to use conventional forces but to stop short of the ultimate punishment of the regime.

Does this explanation fit the real world? It is too soon to say. But in the Gulf War Iraq was willing to take a seemingly moderate risk in invading Kuwait and we understand why – it was hard to believe the US and others would intervene. Then it accepted the much higher risks of staying in Kuwait – counting on prospective costs to erode the unity of the coalition and cancel its attack, despite plentiful evidence that the coalition was sound and would attack. Iraq seems to have believed that being thrown out would be bearable. It had WMD but, despite its threats, the coalition was not deterred and it chose not to use them. Most analysts believe this was because the United States promised a massive, i.e. nuclear, response.[22] This misses what was central to the outcome.

---

[21] Brito and Intriligator (1998) report that Colin Powell drafted a warning to Saddam on the eve of the Gulf War stating that: "Only conventional weapons will be used in strict accordance with the Geneva Convention and commonly accepted rules of warfare. If you, however, use chemical or biological weapons in violation of treaty obligations we will destroy your merchant fleet, your railroad infrastructure, your port facilities, your highway system, your oil facilities, your airline infrastructure" and will consider destroying the Tigris and Euphrates dams (p. 9). Exactly right!

[22] Freedman and Karsh (1993) says the 1,000 or so available US nuclear weapons probably deterred Iraq.

The US certainly did promise something terrible, to end the regime, but not necessarily via nuclear weapons – and was quite capable, alone or via the UN coalition, of achieving this. Iraq was deterred because there was no plausible scenario for success if it escalated the weapons used.

Iraq did directly attack a nuclear power (Israel) and thus risk destruction – it was not deterred from that. This was a grave risk since Israel might have responded with nuclear weapons, and it illustrates how deterrence can be just as risky as in the Cold War. Israel made no nuclear response because this was unnecessary and illegitimate, and no conventional response because a suitable one was already in place.

If we assume rationality and want to apply deterrence on that basis then the proliferation of nuclear weapons or other weapons of mass destruction does not make those states less deterrable and does not enhance their ability to deter the US or a concert or the Security Council. This leads to the obvious question: what if the opponent is not rational?

Earlier analysis helps us better understand the use of deterrence in situations of possible irrationality. There is much concern about the utility of deterrence in dealing with allegedly irrational states (for instance P. Williams 1992), and this is largely the rationale for the US BMD effort. This arises particularly when the presumed opponent has WMD but lurks in anticipating confrontations with nonnuclear opponents too. It is not new. Britain worried about trying to deter an irrational (German) government in the 1930s (Overy 1992). Analysis of the problem of deterring "crazy states" appeared years ago (Dror 1971). What about the utility of deterrence in these circumstances? Can the United States, or other actors, readily deter states with "irrational" leaders or moved by irrational forces?[23]

This is the wrong way to state the problem. Rationality is not a prerequisite for deterrence to work. It can work against irrational as well as rational leaders (it depends on the way they are irrational – or rational). A parallel fear is a deterrence failure because the opponent has values or perspectives alien to us – he is not irrational but *might as well be* in terms of our understanding how to effectively threaten. When deterrence does not work and the target behaves oddly, it is impossible to

---

[23] After the Gulf War some stories concluded that deterrence could daunt even a possibly irrational opponent, referring to Iraq's nonuse of chemical weapons after US and Israeli threats and sometimes citing Israel's earlier bombing of Damascus after Syrian missile attacks – which then stopped. (See Ignatius 1992 and Fitchett 1995, for example.) I suspect these reflected government studies on deterring irrational states.

know whether this is a case of irrationality or of the attacker rationally applying alien values and objectives.[24] If we can't know whether the opponent is rational, and if rationality is not required, then it is wrong to depict the problem as facing irrationality. Asking whether a state is irrational poses a question that can't be answered, so there is no point in asking it.

What matters is the relative balance between, for example, Iraq's willingness to accept painful and risky consequences and the willingness of, for example, the United States to impose them. It is this balance that is unfavorable when deterrence fails, not that the other side is irrational. We have to ask how likely it is that rogue states, or fanatical fundamentalists, or highly egotistical leaders, will readily accept more punishment, and thus threats of punishment, than the US or a collective actor is willing to inflict. There is no way to decide this in advance, or to supply precise guidance on the utility of deterrence in such cases. What we can say is that there is no consistent link – logical or empirical – between being "odd" and a willingness to bear high costs. Even past behavior of the target is not always a good guide.

Apart from fear that deterrence won't work, analysts have suggestions for increasing its success. Most are along the lines of trying not to provoke unnecessarily, providing the clearest possible signals (to break through misperceptions), and tailoring the threats *so that they fit the specific fears of the regime* such as threatening to destroy the ruling elite. This is well illustrated in Garfinkle's (1995) analysis of deterring Iraq in 1990–91. He stresses that rationality is culture- and context-dependent. Saddam did not back down not because he was irrational but because in Arab cultures it is better to fight and lose than be dishonored. Honor requires equality of stature – even in defeat it is important to inflict harm, impose some pain, show a capacity for harm (such as setting the oil-well fires). Thus to deter we must assess the adversary's "strategic culture" – how it defines a bluff, treats lying, pursues honor, relates to violence, etc. Maybe, maybe not. Even if this is so, this calls for the cleverest empathy, and is unlikely to be successfully employed other than by chance.[25] After several decades of the Cold War Americans were still strongly debating just what kinds of threats would specifically deter the Soviet

---

[24] Hence, in such cases, "the standards of rationality are clearly more complex than before" (Reed and Wheeler 1993, p. 35).

[25] It's not impossible. In deciding to use the atomic bomb American officials felt that in the Japanese system and culture it would take an enormous shock to allow leaders in favor of surrender to prevail over military opposition. That is roughly what happened.

leaders. Fitting deterrence precisely to the target is difficult to do and makes deterrence much more complicated.

Success in deterrence will also depend on how painful and costly it is for the deterrer to deliver the punishment, which in turn depends on such things as how advancing technology alters the costs and the threshold of acceptable costs (for both sides), one topic of chapter 6. Circumstances alter the judgments involved. The costs for the UN coalition to defeat Iraq and throw it out of Kuwait were minimal; in Somalia, much lower costs turned out to be much too high. Threat credibility and effectiveness also depend on the perceived *legitimacy of the means*, and here conventional forces are far more suitable.

As a summary we can say:

(1) Nuclear (or other WMD) proliferation is not irrelevant to deterrence of rogue states or others – such weapons inevitably induce caution and this afflicts the challenger and the deterrer, but

(2) they do not significantly improve the challenger's ability to deter a superior opponent on the conventional level, and

(3) the best way to deter their use is not by threatening a massive WMD response (that just invites further risks they will be used irrationally or in a loss of control) but by being able to threaten destruction of the leaders and regime with conventional forces – and threatening somewhat less than that if the opponent does not resort to WMD.

(4) Asking whether the opponent is rational is of little help. The deterrer should offer not only the risk of destruction of the regime if it escalates but also a defeat, apart from this, that is more bearable.

(5) Where the threat is less than destruction of the regime, it is possibly bearable so deterrence is less likely to work consistently and may have to be sustained by fighting, perhaps repeatedly.

Deterrence among states other than great powers

On deterrence among states that are not great powers, we must consider relations among states without WMD and those with. On the former, I just reiterate what was said earlier. Deterrence was for centuries a tactic, very difficult to use with consistent success. The nuclear age made deterrence more central and seemingly more reliable, more elaborate in our theoretical understanding and, in some ways, more simple in practice. With the current deemphasis on nuclear deterrence at the top of the international system, states without nuclear weapons live in a world that – when it comes to deterrence – is like past international politics. Thus we can expect deterrence to have very uneven results. When states feel they can no longer count on outside assistance – from great-power allies, the UN or an actor like NATO – and move to provide deterrence themselves, they will have limited success. For making the international system safer for all its members, proliferating conventional military capabilities is a very bad alternative. The ongoing proliferation of conventional weapons, especially in areas like East and South Asia, should arouse grave misgivings. Hopefully, those seeking the arms will not have excessive confidence in deterrence, be highly skeptical and regard it as a last resort. Unfortunately, it is hard to be this optimistic.

The better solution is rising availability of a *collective deterrence* for these states, through the Security Council or regional organizations. This is less provocative than deterrence by individual states and should look much more daunting when it is credible. It can better manage the classic security dilemma, as Europe has shown in recent years by national forces for defense and participation in collective peace efforts that don't disturb the neighbors. Putting primary control for these forces under both the EU and NATO will be even better for this.

More often discussed is concern that many less powerful states will, sooner or later, develop or obtain WMD and practice deterrence accordingly, with disastrous results.[26] This is not a universal view. Some people argue that nuclear deterrence worked well during the Cold War, that virtually any government, even the dumbest or the most irresponsible, will be deterred. By extension, deterrence with nuclear weapons (or other WMD) will be equally stabilizing elsewhere. Martel and Pendley (1994) agree, and call for efforts to prevent only "harmful" proliferation.

Most analysts and governments reject this view. It is said that Cold War nuclear deterrence emerged gradually, so armed forces, leaders, and analysts eventually grasped the complexities involved, but new nuclear powers will lack that sophistication (Beckman et al. 2000). For instance, they may have only first-strike capabilities, and under these circumstances reciprocal fears of surprise attack can be destabilizing in the extreme and make war virtually inevitable in confrontations. These states may well be unable to ensure that their WMD are never used

---

[26] "[O]ne of the most important developments during the 1990s will be what might be termed the regionalization of nuclear deterrence..." (P. Williams 1992, p. 95).

without proper authorization. The great powers learned only slowly how elaborate the precautions had to be to ensure effective command and control or prevent accidents, theft, overreactions to warning-system failures, and the like. And there is the fear, outlined in the preceding section, that some of the small or recent nuclear powers will be irrational in some fashion.

Which view is correct? From the history of nuclear deterrence the answer seems obvious: proliferation is likely to have disastrous consequences somewhere. It will not work well enough, cannot be counted on to work well enough, during and after extensive proliferation. As DeNardo (1995) has pointed out, the logic of deterrence is not inherently attractive – it does not easily sink in. Expectations that it will readily be understood are suspect. It is not reassuring that India and Pakistan lack clear nuclear postures or strategies and that India's nuclear program was shaped by technocrats with little influence by the armed forces, the cabinet, or the civil service (see Chellaney 1994). Nor is it comforting when an Indian general asserts that both nations will settle for delayed retaliation postures without explaining why – and that Western fears this won't happen are patronizing and racist. He adds that if the US and others keep nuclear weapons to deal with regional threats, then nuclear discrimination remains and "There is no alternative to nuclear weapons and ballistic missiles if you are to live in security and with honor" (Sundarji 1996, p. 193). That is about what we would expect.

Recall the difficulties the superpowers and others had during the Cold War in keeping deterrence stable. The record is scary. The superpowers sought first-strike capabilities, and flirted with or implemented launch-on-warning postures. There were numerous accidents with nuclear weapons (maybe over 100; Sagan 1993). The superpowers made serious mistakes in perception, judgment, and decision in the Cuban missile crisis and other confrontations. In three of the first five nuclear powers the political systems eventually collapsed, throwing command and control systems into question. South Africa abandoned nuclear weapons not long before its system collapsed. Things are no better now. There are fears about the durability of the Pakistan regime and nation. China specialists wonder about the survival of that political system under the onerous pressures of rapid modernization. In Russia the Strategic Rocket Forces can't meet their electric bills so sometimes the power is shut off, while controls for strategic forces malfunction and shift to combat mode for no obvious reason. On seven occasions in 1996 alone, operations were disrupted by thieves trying to steal cables for the copper. Many Soviet-era radars no longer operate and the nuclear suitcases for top officials are in disrepair (Blair, Feiveson and von Hippel 1997). This history generates little confidence in the uplifting effects of proliferation on deterrence. More likely is a disastrous collapse of deterrence or a horrendous accident someday.

It is also hard to believe that states lacking the resources of great powers will not be deficient. All complex systems are vulnerable to breakdowns, and it helps to have resources for redundant controls, backup systems, and damage control. States like India and Pakistan will not have enough resources available and the risk is accordingly greater. That this won't apply to military forces and deterrence is improbable.

Therefore, the great powers are well advised to be pursuing nuclear nonproliferation and the complete elimination of chemical and biological weapons. The great majority of nations who agreed to extend the NPT are to be commended; opponents of banning nuclear testing and further reducing the importance of nuclear weapons are wrong. Reducing their salience deserves the best efforts of mankind. However, nuclear proliferation has taken place, although more slowly than expected (chemical weapons proliferation is far more extensive), and if disaster can be avoided will the new nuclear powers thereby gain security? It seems likely that they will. There is no reason why nuclear deterrence should work any differently among these states than among the superpowers. As noted in chapter 2, in the Cold War nuclear weapons did make a difference, did reduce recklessness, contributed a degree of caution. The same should be true among the new nuclear powers.

Unfortunately, the lessons of the Cold War all apply – *it is important to get them right* in analyzing proliferation. The lessons are not just that deterrence worked but that (a) much of the war avoidance that resulted was achieved, and could have been achieved, without nuclear weapons and (b) nuclear deterrence was insufficiently stable and reliable – too often we lived close to the edge of the cliff. The recent decline in interstate warfare suggests that war avoidance can readily take place without the assistance of nuclear deterrence and its risks.

Deterrence in intrastate conflicts

This discussion fits under the subheading of deterrence for global (or regional) security management but separate treatment of it is worthwhile. Discovering things worth fighting about mainly occurs domestically now. The way a deterrence situation normally arises in *international politics* on a domestic conflict is when an outside actor seeks to prevent or halt it. (It is the rare internal conflict that has no involvement by outsiders.) The outside actor has various options, one of which is deterrence. This starts with a threat to intervene militarily. If this fails and has to be carried out then deterrence shifts to the use of force. What can we say about deterrence now in such situations?

Many elements of the prior discussion in this book apply here. The outside actor won't threaten a massively destructive intervention. Intervention will have legitimacy in the international community only if it is limited, thus the threat of it must be limited. Neglecting this, the Russian interventions in the two Chechnya wars were widely seen as illegitimate, even when the intervention was "inside" Russia itself. The difficulty will come first in ascertaining that deterrence is necessary; it will usually be practiced late in trying to prevent or end violence. The added urgency helps build support for intervention but heightens fear that the forces involved will be in danger. There will be a significant credibility problem as well. Fears of casualties and other costs will lead to elaborate efforts to find a way of terminating the conflict without intervention. Treating hard fighting as a last resort will encourage the parties to think it won't be used. Credibility will be most easily attached to an intervention that reflects a profound interest specific to the state or states concerned (Turkey in Cyprus, Russia in the "near abroad") or to the regional system (the Kosovo case).

Once preparations are made to intervene a different problem may arise. The combatants want to stop fighting but want foreign intervention to be what brings that about, so they go on fighting! Threats don't work, only intervention does. The parties expect intervention to freeze their military positions so they scramble for the best position and bargaining leverage either after the intervention or in case it fails and the fighting continues – the nearer intervention is the harder the participants may fight, making it all the harder to intervene. This is one reason interventions often are too long delayed and go better than expected. Delay is reinforced as all the fighting makes it looks like intervention will not make a significant difference in the long run because the conflict seems intractable.

To go beyond threats and do harm to halt intrastate fighting blends deterrence with compellance. A threat of massive force can be conveyed by sending heavily armed units when the parties are lightly armed – as in Bosnia and Kosovo. But massive violence cannot be openly threatened or deliberately used in a humanitarian intervention, so deterrence threats and actions must be tailored to the target, and this is even harder to do precisely in intrastate conflicts. It is difficult to grasp precisely the combatants' values and priorities – their struggle is immersed in a history outsiders only partially know. Their preferences are home grown; thus it is difficult to decide whether they are rational, rational based on unfamiliar perceptions and preferences, or irrational.

Thus it is hard to identify unacceptable damage for them; the target decision maker may see whatever is threatened as "bearable" and be willing to risk it. She may well believe she can control the damage after an initial intervention – the deterrer will persist only so long as she misbehaves.

Another problem is that in such interventions deterrence is based on a very broad conception of "attack." Threats look most credible when issued by a country with ethnic/religious compatriots in one or both parties or with nationals threatened by the fighting. Otherwise, an "attack" is abstract – a "threat to international peace and security," whatever that is. This is especially so when the fighting has crossed no international boundary or *directly* harmed another state.

Once military intervention begins, the deterrer is within range and can be attacked directly. (Obviously, air attacks may leave interveners rather safe while sending ground troops will not.) Thus the motivation for military action can swiftly change. We are familiar with this in mission creep: an intervention to protect aid workers in Somalia leads to casualties which leads to a decision to impose a broader order which brings more casualties which generates a decision to militarily disarm the factions, etc.

Another difficulty is that there may not be an identifiable decision maker to deter, or too many. If Polywogs and Pinwheels are killing each other again after years of strife, the violence may have little direction or control, leaving few real targets for deterrence unless violence is threatened/used almost indiscriminately. Intervention then involves imposing order via curfews, disarming all sides, etc., which are time consuming, take many personnel, draw them into activities difficult to end soon and offer endless opportunities for inflaming the population.

These problems don't mean deterrence is impossible but do show how messy it can be, how theory captures little of what may be involved, and how its complexities aren't readily sorted out in any neat strategy. We can avoid undue pessimism (after all, interventions often succeed) by noting that there are offsetting factors at work. As indicated in chapter 5, collective actors, and states acting on their behalf, often have things going for them that enhance deterrence. Their size and collective power, for example, or resources to effectively combine rewards with deterrence. Their interventions threaten less destruction and death than each party expects from the other (sometimes correctly) if it loses. They can sometimes enter when, in Zartman's (1989) terms, a "hurtful stalemate" has left the parties ready to stop fighting given the right opportunity.

These things apply to interventions by individual states too, though probably less often. Analysts now know that even interventions by outsiders known to favor one side can work because of the elements just listed, if that party sustains a reputation for being focused on ending the fighting and determined to be fair. It is also *useful* that the intervening state is not seen as seeking its own aggrandizement, though not an absolute necessity. Russians as peacekeepers have this problem in the "near abroad," with Moscow seen as having imperial motives and Russian forces feared as prone to looting and other crimes, but nonetheless have sometimes deterred further fighting. Syrian forces in Lebanon have long helped maintain order despite Syria's blatant desire to dominate Lebanon.

Conclusion

The themes in this chapter can be summarized as follows. Deterrence is a widespread recourse and will continue to be. It can be effective but has difficulties and complications that are unevenly appreciated, understood, and analyzed. The discussions about deterrence after the Cold War have been useful but incomplete. Some fears about deterrence are largely unwarranted, reposing high confidence in it is unwise, and understanding why each is so could stand improvement.

The United States is pursuing a Janus-faced policy. It works hard to get nuclear weapons and nuclear deterrence (plus WMD) deemphasized. It has an enormous advantage, particularly in league with its friends, in conventional forces. It has good reason to doubt the credibility of nuclear deterrence for dealing with anything other than threats of direct nuclear attacks on the US. It has good reason to regard WMD proliferation as awful. But it cannot bring itself to renounce nuclear weapons – other than an on-paper pledge finally extracted from the nuclear powers in 2000. It plans large cuts in strategic weapons but only by stockpiling many of them, pushing the deadline for cuts well into the future, and minimizing the verification. Inside its military establishment, in Congress, industry, and the public there are clusters devoted to finding better living through nuclear weapons, including nuclear testing, plus others devoted by career to seeking security through nuclear deterrence. All are hoping to make nuclear weapons steadily more usable. Another cluster lives for missile defense, whether it is ready or not. An underlying factor on missile defense is an American desire to have plenty of missiles while denying others the benefits of having them – to evade others' deterrence. In the same way the US seeks to have an overwhelming conventional superiority and nearly total freedom from the deterrence of others on using it.

Deterrence is much as it was during the Cold War. It is not greatly changed because of the emergence of supposedly irrational opponents, the disappearance of simple deterrence relationships, the appearance of nuclear powers who cannot control every facet of their nuclear forces with great precision – because all of these things were true in the Cold War. Having opponents not really deterred by nuclear weapons is similarly not new. The US is not crippled by the lack of "usable" nuclear weapons; nor are the US and collective actors unable to confront countries with a few nuclear weapons. Nuclear deterrence still works as it did – it has some effect but not an overwhelming or consistent one. Making nuclear weapons smaller and more precise will not make them more usable, especially when even conventional forces are now expected to avoid unnecessary damage and minimize escalation. The best way to deter the use of WMD now is to offer grave threats on the conventional level, something the US on its own, the US and its allies, and the major collective actors are well equipped to do. But deterrence at the conventional level remains an uncertain activity. It cannot be readily designed to fit the perceptions and fears of each opponent. Without a nuclear threat it is easier for leaders to take the risk because at its worst, a threat often promises unacceptable but not totally unbearable consequences.

The world continues with too many nuclear weapons and too many nuclear powers, and proliferation is an unmitigated evil. Everything nuclear weapons do for the US and its allies can be done without them, the Russians and certain other states are not fully trustworthy in handling nuclear weapons, states that think nuclear weapons will provide a good deal more stature and leverage in world politics are fooling themselves.

Thus we have not entered a "new nuclear age," or the "third nuclear age," or a new age of peril from nuclear weapons – we live with the same peril, just in a far less immediate form. We are, however, approaching a potential shift from offense dominance to defense dominance, at least for states with the most advanced military capabilities. This is an opportunity to see if we can outgrow nuclear weapons, find ways in which to make them irrelevant to security in international politics, particularly by beefing up collective actor deterrence for the general welfare.

As for deterrence, our theoretical grip has never been satisfactory so it remains a difficult policy tool. Accumulated experience suggests it is uneven and notions like the irrationality of decision makers do nothing to refine it. It seems best when used cautiously, with full appreciation of its limitations, and with strong links to conciliation, reassurance, rewards and engagement. In the long run, collective actor security management via (in part) deterrence will get about as much use out of deterrence for the general welfare as we are entitled to expect.

8   **Some conclusions**

People who read a long book deserve a short final chapter. Let me see if I can oblige. Deterrence is a fascinating subject because it is a core relationship among some of the major actors in international politics; for many analysts the nature of international politics is such that deterrence may be its most important interaction. Thus it is odd that it received so little study as a phenomenon in its own right until well into the twentieth century – that is a bit like wanting to study international economic relations without taking a close look at money. Then it began to get intense study. There seemed to be so much riding on it, in the nuclear age, that there was a terrible fear of the consequences if we ever got it wrong because we didn't know what we were doing.

My studies of deterrence have been moved by the following broad concerns. Deterrence came to be a central component of our security so it continues to be very important to understand it and practice it as best we can. But understanding it means facing up to the fact that it is inherently imperfect. It does not consistently work and we cannot manipulate it sufficiently to fix that and make it a completely reliable tool of statecraft. That means it must be approached with care and used as part of a larger tool kit. Not everyone really accepts that; people frequently say they do and then want to carry reliance on deterrence much too far. Deterrence does not readily lend itself to effective study and profound understanding. Nobody can say we haven't given it a good try, but we do not completely understand how it works. The history of the theory and practice of deterrence makes a strong case for concluding that while certain abstract elements of deterrence have something of a universal character, the degree and nature of its challenges and implementation are so uneven and varied, the operational conceptions of deterrence and the specifics of both challenge and response are so elaborate, that it is inevitably lodged in the varying national and political character of conflicts, shaped by the social and cultural details of the motivations, perceptions, and analyses that drive challenges and responses. That's a long way off saying that deterrence, in crucial ways, is not sufficiently consistent to be fully captured by our theoretical apparatus and empirical studies.

For instance, it is hard to believe that in other circumstances, in other hands, after 1945 that the development of the theory, strategy, and military postures of deterrence would have proceeded in roughly the same way and produced approximately what we lived with. If the United States had retired to isolationism and western Europeans had taken up a long-term competitive relationship with the Soviet Union, would civilians have dominated the shaping of a theory of deterrence? Would they have conceived of the nature of a suitable theory in the same way? And would the actors have arrived at the same general strategy, shapes and sizes of nuclear arsenals, concepts of stability and credibility? All that seems very implausible. As a recent illuminating book indicates, there is great variety in the emerging WMD postures around the world today (Lavoy, Sagan and Wirtz 2000).

During the Cold War the imperfections of deterrence and our understanding of it came up against terrible, efficient capacities for death and destruction, capacities which deterrence exploits for maintaining security but with no guarantee of permanent success. As a result it has always been important to study deterrence not just because it could help keep us safe but in order to help figure out what to do to get out of having to rely on it. A good many people find that "peculiar"; some settle on "reprehensible." From their perspective, the way to get out of having to rely on it is to study other ways of dealing with peace and security. But wisdom on this problem, I think, starts by accepting the fact that deterrence has been necessary; it has had to be used as a contributor to getting us from being deterrence dominated to where we can transcend our need for it.

In this connection, the fascination deterrence holds for me derives from three central and interrelated problems that it poses bearing on making that transition. First, we do not want deterrence to work in such a way that it is provocative and produces, rather than prevents, disastrous conflicts – which is the stability problem in its various forms. Second, we do not want deterrence to shape an endless security dilemma, constituting a security arrangement which – despite its imperfections and thus its unreliability over the long run – is highly self-sustaining, placing strong political and psychological obstacles in the way of ever trying to get out of it. Third, and here is where that "reprehensible" label might fit, we do not want deterrence to drive out getting significant attention paid to, and energetic use of, the alternatives that are available for the better management of global, regional, and national security.

I was never comfortable with the way in which the superpowers became so deeply dependent on nuclear deterrence, and on deterrence at lower levels to prevent fighting that could escalate. Chapter 1 reflects my longstanding view that nuclear deterrence was never as critical for preventing another great war as it looked at the time. Deterrence in theory and practice developed in a way that exacerbated rigidity in the Cold War, and helped sustain it for such a long time. Deterrence performed a valuable service in helping to control the impact of the nuclear weapons that made another great war feasible. Chapter 1 reflects the fact that the theory and practice of deterrence made a very fundamental contribution by making people appreciate the interdependence of security via analysis of the stability problem and thus to further appreciate the importance of a cooperative approach to even a very hostile relationship. It is disturbing that this appreciation of interdependence did not extend to many military leaders and political officials who were responsible for getting the superpowers as close to a mutual preemptive war capability as they could. That was flatly contrary to the theory and never officially espoused as policy – it still isn't. But it was a powerful factor in limiting the impact of cooperative approaches to security in the East–West political relationship, which is partly why the commitment to the rivalry remained so profound for so many years. We took far too long to get to a meaningful détente and the maintenance of potentially very destabilizing national military postures did not help. It was crucial that we never again held a crisis quite like the one in October 1962 to test whether these arrangements really were that dangerous.

Thus we managed, however clumsily, to keep the stability problem in check. However, there was another way in which deterrence could create instability, apart from preemption pressures in crises, which was by being subject to human foibles and errors. It could simply be badly done and badly run. Here we let the intellectual challenge of designing deterrence get in the way of fully understanding it in practice. We let the abstract basis on which we approached the design of it excessively dominate our effort to understand how it works in practice. It took decades to fully appreciate what the national military postures really were like. It took years to accumulate enough understanding of the intrinsic logical flaws in deterrence theory (the credibility problem) when applied at the nuclear level – it was appreciated early on but the full implications were not grasped until much later. The true mechanics of arms control, where internal bargaining often precluded successful external bargaining, were not appreciated for years. Neither theorists nor policy makers ever got a firm grip on the details in the development of the nuclear arsenals until the arsenals had assumed their general character, a character which then remained unchanged over decades until the end of the Cold War and which still – in the US – dominates the national strategic posture. The analysis of the credibility problem turned out to have less to do with the actual behavior of states than was anticipated, while nuclear weapons had less existential deterrence capability than was assumed.

Chapter 2 attempts to restate some of these theoretical weaknesses. Chapter 4 then traces a convergence of evidence from three different approaches to the study of deterrence to describe some of the limitations of deterrence in practice and identify the main variables that control its success or failure. It explains the real difficulties involved in carefully studying deterrence and also lays out in some detail the reasons for thinking that deterrence is always difficult and potentially unreliable. This overview culminates in highlighting the conclusion that the strength of challenger motivation is often (when the challenger is not an opportunist) an independent variable that has much to do with deterrence success or failure – it is not consistently a dependent variable which deterrence threats significantly and reliably alter in an appropriate direction to prevent war.

One of the points emphasized in chapter 1 is then raised again in chapter 3, which is that what started out as a highly unilateral approach to national security came to constitute a multilateral approach to global security as well. That was very important to discover, and it has had very strong after-effects with the waning of the Cold War. The chapter takes a first crack at adjusting the concept of general deterrence to better encompass this feature of modern international politics. It is now much more widely appreciated that the Western nations during the Cold War built for themselves a very distinctive international politics, one in which they gradually moved away from a Hobbesian existence in an anarchical system. They resolved the security problems among themselves with a remarkable demonstration of the potential for cooperative security management. That success has overshadowed the impressive degree to which the rivalry and conflict between East and West were driven toward a significant level of cooperative management as well, cooperative management of both the direct relationship and the larger environment in which the competition was conducted. Compare, for example, the degree to which East and West did this on security matters – through rules of the game, the appreciation of crisis instability, arms control treaties, and the direct and indirect exchange of highly sensitive military information – with the very low level of honest, penetrating interchange and cooperation between them economically, politically, and culturally. Who would ever have guessed it? For years people fought hard to promote détente via nonsecurity interchanges in order to build a higher level of cooperation that could then be used to help control the military–security rivalry and build a safer world. But it was the military–security rivalry (once properly understood) that promoted and eventually embraced the greatest degree of effective cooperation.

This capacity, in the intra-Western community and in the East–West relationship, to grasp the centrality of interdependence in and for sustaining security, is a very precious achievement. It contributed a great deal to our ability to avoid the worst pitfalls of the stability problem – we understood, unevenly to be sure, the importance of security interdependence well enough politically to manage the Cold War without total disaster. Being used to this security interdependence, to thinking in system-level terms, also contributed a good deal to our ability to get out of the Cold War as smoothly as we did.

This was the real key to meeting the second of the concerns I outlined above. The dynamics of the arms race itself had a tremendous self-sustaining quality about them, generating huge internal political and other pressures of the sort Eisenhower had briefly hinted at in his farewell address. However, in the end mutual deterrence did not become such a self-sustaining arrangement that we could not get out of it. We did get out of the better part of it in ending the Cold War and fashioning new relationships among the antagonists, but that process is not yet finished. We have also not fully escaped from that passion for a preemption capability – one side had to give that up but the other side has not done so – which could have stood in the way in other political circumstances. Nonetheless, the great-power relationships are in far better shape than they were.

The peaceful demise of the Cold War, combined with the development of a far more relaxed international politics among a large number of Western states, strongly suggests that while we have to treat the security dilemma as a notable concern in international politics, it is not a law, an independent factor that dictates relations among states. It does not automatically arise out of anarchy. Psychological, perceptual, and political factors constitute the contexts in which the security dilemma flourishes or declines. That is comforting if the goal is to safely reduce reliance on deterrence in the years ahead.

Chapters 5 and 6 then take up the two most promising avenues for enlarging interdependent or cooperative security and moving us toward a better basis for security and world order. They are true to the assertion that the best starting point for going in this direction is to appreciate that deterrence is necessary, not least as insurance so that there is room for other approaches to be given serious consideration. Chapter 5 seeks to move toward getting the study of deterrence integrated into the analysis and practice of collective management of peace and security problems for the general welfare. In the broadest sense we want to hold on to the notion of security interdependence and retain the capacity to think in terms of system management from our Cold War experience, and then turn to the use of deterrence to help keep us safe via a growing use of multilateral management. This won't handle all the security problems – in fact it cannot cope with any large conflicts that emerge between the great powers, which are the most consequential and dangerous threats to peace and security. They must find other ways to handle their security relations in an effective multilateral way.

This is not a panacea. It is just a way to keep on applying some of what we learned about security, and security management, during a very long conflict that often did considerable harm, by taking deterrence partly in a new direction. The single most defective element of this collective management, in its various forms and levels, is its underdeveloped and inconsistent ability to apply force when necessary. Some merger of the study of deterrence and compellance, including a sophisticated understanding of their weaknesses and limitations, needs to play a larger role in shaping what is still a very limited, almost atheoretical, effort so far to design and effectively use peacekeeping, peace enforcement, peace imposition, and peacebuilding. What the latter efforts can bring to the merger is a very well-developed emphasis on using many techniques and resources, from conciliation to peacebuilding, to get the job done, filling a gap that critics of deterrence have complained about for decades. Because this is so important, chapter 5 is the one which I find the least satisfying – it does not get very far toward where we ought to be going.

The other promising avenue for moving us in this direction is the emergence of astonishing improvements in conventional forces. They raise the possibility of giving collective actors enough military heft to be really impressive in using force but without levels of harm that contradict the central meaning and objective of having collective security management in the first place. They have already had this impact on several occasions. As a number of analysts have realized, the revolution could transform the deterrence of war by the Security Council and other collective actors, and then transform their ability to deal with the inevitable failures of deterrence in an acceptable fashion.

The revolution in military affairs also raises the possibility that we can begin to outgrow nuclear weapons and other weapons of mass destruction, gradually putting them aside. This seems like the most feasible way to get rid of them – if it works, we can eventually stop pretending that we live a highly civilized existence even though it includes holding hostage so much that is dear to us. It seems more feasible than just unilateral renunciations of WMD; more feasible than trying to negotiate them out of existence too. It can do this, in part, by possibly introducing a defense-dominant world to replace one in which highly destructive military systems face totally inadequate defenses. Here, too, the lessons of the Cold War era on the interdependence of security and the feasibility of collectively arranging it can play a crucial role. It took a long time to get a unilaterally driven race for nuclear weapons and national deterrence transformed into something more multinational in character, and that was a pretty hair-raising period. We should take this to heart and see about moving toward a defense-dominant world in a managed way, through negotiated or informal arrangements that ease security concerns and avoid bad practices.

Chapter 7 then says that we are not going about these matters in all the right ways. The great powers have reduced the salience of WMD in their relationships and their national military strategies – and have finally undertaken substantial WMD disarmament. They are slowly becoming more determined to do something about WMD proliferation. They have revived collective actor security management first through the Security Council and then through NATO. The George W. Bush Administration has led the way in suggesting the need to be thinking about shifting away from a deterrence-dominated world and toward one that is defense-dominated, starting with ballistic missile defense.

Not all the news is good. The US and Russia retain excessively hair-trigger alert arrangements for their strategic forces; the Russians do too little to protect their WMD weapons and materials; China, like Russia, has been too willing to facilitate WMD proliferation for narrow national security reasons; as recent nuclear powers, India and Pakistan are too cavalier about the risks of escalation; and there are several states too de-termined to gain or enlarge operational WMD capabilities. The chapter says that consideration of various shifts in policy rest on reassessments of deterrence that are wrong. Deterrence is not much more unreliable than it used to be – it was never as reliable in the past as it is now de-picted by these analysts and governments and this is not compelling evidence to support many of the steps proposed to deal with the situa-tion now. For instance, steps to make deterrence much more successful by ambiguity about the first use of WMD, or trying to develop much more usable nuclear weapons, or trying to conduct interventions virtu-ally without American and Western casualties, won't succeed. This is not going to make deterrence much better.

Deterrence is not more unreliable in dealing with "rogue" states either. Trying to cite irrationality, for example, does not improve our analysis of the difficulties of deterring an Iraq or North Korea. The United States had a terrible time with North Korea and China and then Vietnam – its nuclear weapons and vast conventional military superiority didn't help much. The Russians had a tough time with the Chinese and the Afghans and the US (over Cuba) – its nuclear weapons and huge conventional forces did not balk military challenges to Soviet power and policy. The Chinese had a bad time with the Russians along the border and with the Vietnamese – their nuclear weapons and very large conventional forces did not make the Russians amenable or the Vietnamese willing to quit fighting. Were these all rogue states? Deterrence is simply not able to consistently bend others to one's will.

Those states are not going to find it easy to deter us (the US, the Security Council, the West, etc.) if they develop WMD – not if they are sufficiently provocative and we are exceedingly determined. In such confrontations the vastly more powerful actor is in a position to threaten that *less* than the worst possible consequences for the regime and its leadership will occur unless that regime resorts to WMD, in which case the worst will indeed happen. The absence of feasible scenarios for a better outcome from escalation is not only a powerful motivator but will invite the conclusion that the opponent (us) really will persist, will not be deterred.

The drawbacks of deterrence have more to do with the fact that it is still deterrence – it remains a sometime thing. It often works, but past studies of its limitations still apply – it is not guaranteed, is hard to do properly, and does not provide total control over what happens. For instance, we are not clear about how credibility comes to be attached to deterrence threats. And now deterrence often rests on threats of unacceptable, but not necessarily unbearable, consequences which leaves more room for mistakes and miscalculations. This was typical of deterrence in the past, and it can often result in what I call "serial deterrence" – you threaten, the other side attacks, you respond, so they respond, so you respond.

The real problem is that, partly in response to the alleged deterioration in the utility of deterrence, Americans have become more willing to try to step back from classic deterrence thinking and policies (a) without trying to make this a sufficiently multilateral endeavor so that it contributes to and does not detract from further development of cooperative global and regional security management, and (b) by trying to ensure that the US is completely invulnerable at home and in any intervention abroad – as I write we feel threatened by the prospect of the new international court!

Part of this has shown up in the form of the Bush administration trying hard to detach the United States from multilateral efforts to manage security – to adopt a more independent and unilateral posture. It came into office pressing for a reduced American involvement in collective actor operations. It has taken a highly unilateral approach to the continued development of the RMA and missile defense. It has opted out of some other formal or unspoken arms control arrangements because its discomfort with the impact of the agreements, in its view, on American interests was the only relevant consideration. Then it conducted the war in Afghanistan in a very unilateral fashion – others were invited to participate but within the American design, to join in by bandwagoning rather than jointly deciding and implementing. It has maintained an enormous level of military expenditures, particularly in research and development, in comparison with even its wealthy friends, much less its poor enemies. It has proposed to make war on Iraq irrespective of the opinions of others.

This started, in many ways, under the Clinton Administration. It is reasonably popular. But it comes close to a failure to understand the value of alternative, multilateral ways to arrange for and then conduct the management of security. On the basis of what deterrence should have taught the US by now, on the basis of its great success, over some decades now, in getting the world to go in directions that it approves of, America should know better.

References

Achen, Christopher H., 1987, "A Darwinian View of Deterrence," in Jacek Kugler and Frank C. Zagare, eds., *Exploring the Stability of Deterrence*, Boulder: Lynne Rienner, pp. 90–105

Achen, Christopher H. and Duncan Snidal, 1989, "Rational Deterrence Theory and Comparative Case Studies," *World Politics* vol. 41 no. 2 (January), pp. 143–169

Adams, James, 1997, "Peril of Primed Nuclear Missiles," *Sunday Times* (London), May 18

Alexander, John B., 1999, *Future War: Non-Lethal Weapons in Twenty-First Century Warfare*, New York: St. Martin's Press

Allison, Graham T. and Philip Zelikow, 1999, *Essence of Decision: Explaining the Cuban Missile Crisis*, 2nd edn., New York: Longman

Amili, Gitty M., 1997, "A Larger Role for Positive Sanctions in Cases of Compellance?" UCLA Center for International Relations Working Paper No. 12, May

Arkin, William M., 1996, "Calculated Ambiguity: Nuclear Weapons and the Gulf War," *Washington Quarterly* vol. 19 no. 4 (Autumn), pp. 3–19

2002a, "The Rules of Engagement," *Los Angeles Times*, April 21

2002b, "Secret Plan Outlines the Unthinkable," *Los Angeles Times*, March 10

Arms Control Today, 1997, "Clinton Issues New Guidelines on U.S. Nuclear Weapons Doctrine," *Arms Control Today* vol. 27 no. 8 (November/December), p. 23

Arquilla, John, 1992, *Dubious Battles: Aggression, Defeat, and the International System*, Washington, DC: Taylor and Francis

Arquilla, John and Paul K. Davis, 1994, "Extended Deterrence, Compellance and the 'Old World Order,'" RAND paper, Santa Monica

Arquilla, John and David F. Ronfeldt, 1996, *The Advent of Netwar*, Santa Monica: RAND

1997, eds., *In Athena's Camp: Preparing for Conflict in the Information Age*, Santa Monica: RAND

Axelrod, Robert M., 1984, *The Evolution of Cooperation*, New York: Basic Books

Bacevich, Andrew J., 1995, "The Use of Force in Our Time," *The Wilson Quarterly* vol. 19 (Winter), pp. 50–63

Bailey, Kathleen, 1995, "Why We Have to Keep the Bomb," *Bulletin of the Atomic Scientists* (January–February), pp. 30–37

Baker, John, Kevin O'Connell, and Ray Williamson, 2000, eds., *Commercial Observation Satellites: At the Leading Edge of Global Transparency*, Santa Monica: RAND

Baldwin, David A., 1995, "Security Studies and the End of the Cold War," *World Politics* vol. 48 no. 1 (October), pp. 117–141

Ball, Desmond, 1984, "U.S. Strategic Forces: How Would they Be Used?" in Steven E. Miller, ed., *Strategy and Nuclear Deterrence*, Princeton: Princeton University Press, pp. 215–224

Ball, Desmond and Robert Toth, 1990, "Revising the SIOP," *International Security* vol. 14 no. 4, pp. 65–92

Baocun, Wang and James Mulvenson, 2000, "China and the RMA," *Korean Journal of Defense Analysis* vol. 12 no. 2 (Winter), pp. 275–304

Bar-Joseph, Uri, 1998, "Variations on a Theme: The Conceptualization of Deterrence in Israeli Strategic Thinking," *Security Studies* vol. 7 no. 3 (Spring), pp. 145–181

Barkenbus, Jack N., 1992, ed., *Ethics, Nuclear Deterrence, and War*, New York: Paragon House, 1992

Beckman, Peter R., Paul W. Crumlish, Michael N. Dobkowski, and Steven P. Lee, 2000, *The Nuclear Predicament: Nuclear Weapons in the Twenty-First Century*, 3rd edn., Upper Saddle River, NJ: Prentice-Hall

Bendor, Jonathan and Thomas H. Hammond, 1992, "Rethinking Allison's Models," *American Political Science Review* vol. 86 no. 2 (June), pp. 301–322

Berkowitz, Bruce D., 1985, "Proliferation, Deterrence, and the Likelihood of Nuclear War," *Journal of Conflict Resolution* vol. 29 no. 1 (March), pp. 112–136

Betts, Richard K., 1987, *Nuclear Blackmail and Nuclear Balance*, Washington, DC: Brookings Institution

   1995, "What Will it Take to Deter the United States?" *Parameters* vol. 25 no. 4 (Winter), pp. 70–79

   1998, "The New Threat of Mass Destruction," *Foreign Affairs* vol. 77 no. 1 (January/February), pp. 26–41

Bevin, Alexander, 1995, *The Future of Warfare*, New York: W. W. Norton

Biddle, Stephen, 1996, "Victory Misunderstood: What the Gulf War Tells US About the Future of Conflict," *International Security* vol. 21 no. 2 (Fall), pp. 139–179

Black, Peter, 1999, "When Melissa Meets Up with Hal," *Los Angeles Times*, March 30

Blainey, Geoffrey, 1973, *The Causes of War*, New York: The Free Press

Blair, Bruce G., 1993, *The Logic of Accidental Nuclear War*, Washington, DC: Brookings Institution

   1997, "Taking Nuclear Weapons off Hair-Trigger Alert," *Scientific American*, November, pp. 74–81

Blair, Bruce, Harold Feiveson, and Frank von Hippel, 1997, "Redoubling Nuclear Weapons Reduction," *Washington Post*, November 12

Blechman, Barry M. and Stephen S. Kaplan, 1978, *Force without War: US Forces as a Political Instrument*, Washington, DC: Brookings Institution

Blight, James G., 1992, *The Shattered Crystal Ball: Fear and Learning in the Cuban Missile Crisis*, Lanham, MD: Littlefield Adams

Blight, James G. and David A. Welch, 1998, "What Can Intelligence Tell US About the Cuban Missile Crisis and What Can the Cuban Missile Crisis Tell US about Intelligence?" *Intelligence and National Security* vol. 13 no. 3 (Autumn), pp. 1–17

Bloch, Ivan, 1998, *The Future of War*, New York: Doubleday and McClure (originally published 1899)

Bobbitt, Philip, 1988, *Democracy and Deterrence: The History and Future of Nuclear Strategy*, New York: St. Martin's Press

Bobrow, Davis B., 1999, ed., *Prospects for International Relations: Conjectures About the Next Millennium*, special issue of *International Studies Review*, Malden, MA: Blackwell

Booth, Ken, 1991, *New Thinking about Strategy and International Security*, London: HarperCollins Academic

Bracken, Paul, 1999, *Fire in the East: The Rise of Asian Military Power and the Second Nuclear Age*, New York: HarperCollins Perennial

Brecher, Michael and Jonathan Wilkenfeld, 1997, *A Study of Crisis*, Ann Arbor: University of Michigan Press

Bremer, Stuart A., 1995, "Advancing the Scientific Study of War," in Stuart A. Bremer and Thomas R. Cusack, eds., *The Process of War: Advancing the Scientific Study of War*, Amsterdam: Overseas Publishers Association, pp. 1–33

Bremer, Stuart A. and Thomas R. Cusack, 1995, eds., *The Process of War: Advancing the Scientific Study of War*, Amsterdam: Overseas Publishers Association

Brito, Dagobert L. and Michael D. Intriligator, 1998, "Deterring Nuclear Weapons Proliferation," UCLA Center for International Relations Working Paper No. 16

Broad, William J., 2000, "We're Ready for Our Close-Ups Now," *New York Times*, January 16

Brodie, Bernard, 1959, *Strategy in the Missile Age*, Princeton: Princeton University Press

Brown, Michael, Owen R. Cote, Jr., Sean M. Lynn-Jones, and Steven E. Miller, 2000, eds., *Rational Choice and Security Studies: Stephen Walt and His Critics*, Cambridge, MA: MIT Press

Brown, Neville, 1992, *The Strategic Revolution: Thoughts for the Twenty-First Century*, London: Brassey's

Bueno de Mesquita, Bruce, 1989, "The Contribution of Expected-Utility Theory to the Study of International Conflict," in Manus I. Midlarsky, ed., *Handbook of War Studies*, Ann Arbor: University of Michigan Press, pp. 143–169

Bueno de Mesquita, Bruce and David Lalman, 1992, *War and Reason: Domestic and International Imperatives*, New Haven: Yale University Press

Bueno de Mesquita, Bruce and William H. Riker, 1982, "An Assessment of the Merits of Selective Nuclear Proliferation," *Journal of Conflict Resolution* vol. 26 no. 2 (June), pp. 283–306

Bundy, McGeorge, 1984, "Existential Deterrence and its Consequences," in Douglas MacLean, ed., *The Security Gamble: Deterrence Dilemmas in the Nuclear Age*, Totowa, NJ: Rowman and Allanheld, pp. 3–13

    1986, "Risk and Opportunity: Can We Tell them Apart?" in Catherine Kelleher et al., eds., *Nuclear Deterrence: New Risks, New Opportunities*, Washington: Pergamon, Brassey's, pp. 27–38

Burr, William, 2001, *Launch on Warning: The Development of U.S. Capabilities, 1959–1979*, A National Security Archive Electronic Briefing Book, available at http://www.gwu.edu/%7Ensarchiv/NSAEBB/NSAEBB43

Butler, George Lee, 1998, "The Risks of Deterrence: From Super Powers to Rogue Leaders," address by General Lee Butler to the National Press Club, Northeast Asia Peace and Security Network Special Report, February 10, available via NAPSNet@nautilus.org

Butterworth, Robert L., 1992, "Space Systems and the Military Geography of Future Regional Conflicts," Report no. 14, Center for National Security Studies, Los Alamos National Laboratory, January

Buzan, Barry, 1991a, "Is International Security Possible?" in Ken Booth, ed., *New Thinking about Strategy and International Security*, London: HarperCollins Academic, pp. 31–55

    1991b, *People, States and Fear: An Agenda for International Security Studies in the Post-Cold War Era*, 2nd edn., Boulder: Lynne Rienner

    1994, "The Evolution of Deterrence Theory: Lessons for Israel," in Aharon Klieman and Ariel Levite, eds., *Deterrence in the Middle East: Where Theory and Practice Converge*, Boulder: Westview Press, pp. 19–33

Buzan, Barry and Eric Herring, 1999, *The Arms Dynamic in World Affairs*, Boulder: Lynne Rienner

Buzan, Barry, Charles Jones, and Richard Little, 1993, *The Logic of Anarchy: Neorealism to Structural Realism*, New York: Columbia University Press

Byman, Daniel, Kenneth Pollack, and Mathew Waxman, 1998, "Coercing Saddam Hussein: Lessons from the Past," *Survival* vol. 40 no. 3 (Autumn), pp. 127–152

Cambone, Steven A., 1996, "The United States, Japan, and the Republic of Korea and Theater Missile Defense," in Tae Hwan Ok and Gerrit W. Gong, eds., *Change and Challenge on the Korean Peninsula: Past, Present and Future*, vol. VI, Seoul: The Research Institute for National Unification, pp. 87–116

Canberra Commission, 1996, *Report of the Canberra Commission on the Elimination of Nuclear Weapons*, Canberra: National Capital Printers

Carus, W. Seth, 1994, "Military Technology and the Arms Trade: Changes and Their Impact," *The Annals* vol. 535 (September), pp. 153–174

Chan, Steve, 1978, "Chinese Conflict Calculus and Behavior: Assessment from a Perspective of Conflict Management," *World Politics* vol. 30 (April), pp. 391–410

Chang, Gordon H. and He Di, 1993, "The Absence of War in the US–China Confrontation over Quemoy and Matsu in 1954–1955: Contingency, Luck, Deterrence?" *American Historical Review* vol. 98 no. 5, pp. 1500–1524

Chellaney, Brahma T., 1994, "Pakistan," in Mitchell Reiss and Robert S. Litwak, eds., *Nuclear Proliferation after the Cold War*, Washington, DC: Woodrow Wilson Center Press, pp. 191–205

Chen, Jian, 1994, *China's Road to the Korean War*, New York: Columbia University Press

Cimbala, Stephen J., 2000, *Nuclear Strategy in the Twenty-First Century*, Westport, CT: Praeger

Clark, Ian, 2001, *The Post-Cold War Order: The Spoils of Peace*, New York: Oxford University Press

Cockburn, Andrew and Cockburn, Leslie, 1997, *One Point Safe*, New York: Anchor Books

Cohen, Avner and Benjamin Frankel, 1991, "Opaque Nuclear Proliferation," in Benjamin Frankel, ed., *Opaque Nuclear Proliferation: Methodological and Policy Implications*, London: Frank Cass, pp. 14–44

Cohen, Stephen P., 2001, *India: Emerging Power*, Washington, DC: Brookings Institution

Commission on Integrated Long Term Strategy, 1988, *Sources of Change in the Future Security Environment*, Washington, DC: Department of Defense

Cooper, Jeffrey R., 1997, "Another View of the Revolution in Military Affairs," in John Arquilla and David Ronfeldt, eds., *In Athena's Camp: Preparing for Conflict in the Information Age*, Santa Monica: RAND, pp. 99–140

Craig, Gordon A. and Alexander L. George, 1995, eds., *Force and Statecraft: Diplomatic Problems of our Time*, New York: Oxford University Press

Cushman, John H., Jr., 2002, "Rattling New Sabers," *New York Times*, March 30

Dao, James, 2002, "Pentagon Study Urges Arms Shift, from Nuclear to High-Tech," *New York Times*, January 9

Davis, Paul K. and John Arquilla, 1991, *Deterring or Coercing Opponents in Crisis: Lessons from the War with Saddam Hussein*, Santa Monica: RAND

Davis, Zachary S. and Benjamin Frankel, 1993, eds., *The Proliferation Puzzle: Why Nuclear Weapons Spread (and What Results)*, London: Frank Cass

Dawes, Robyn M., 1998, *Rational Choice in an Uncertain World*, Fort Worth: Harcourt Brace

Defense Intelligence Journal, 1999, vol. 8 no. 1 (Summer) – on reconnaissance intelligence

Defense News, 1998, September 14–20 – six articles on UAVs

Delpech, Thérèse, 1998, "French Nuclear Disarmament and Restrictions in the 1990s," in Barry R. Schneider and William L. Dowdy, eds., *Pulling Back from the Nuclear Brink: Reducing and Countering Nuclear Threats*, London: Frank Cass, pp. 206–213

DeNardo, James, 1995, *The Amateur Strategist: Intuitive Deterrence Theories and the Politics of the Nuclear Arms Race*, Cambridge: Cambridge University Press

Department of Defense Dictionary of Military and Associated Terms, 1994, Joint Publication 1–02, Washington, DC: Government Publications Office

Deutsch, Morton, 1987, "Going Beyond 'Beyond Deterrence,'" *Journal of Social Issues* vol. 43 no. 4, pp. 149–153

Diamond, John, 1998, "Military Urges U.S. on Nuclear Arms," Associated Press, reported in NAPSNet Daily Report, March 2, available at ftp://ftp.nautilus.org/napsnet/daily reports

Dickson, P., 1971, *Think Tanks*, New York: Atheneum

Doran, Charles F., 1999, "The Structural Turbulance of International Affairs," *Survival* vol. 41 no. 2 (Summer), pp. 146–149

Dougherty, James E. and Robert L. Pfaltzgraff, Jr., 1981, *Contending Theories of International Relations: A Comprehensive Survey*, 2nd edn., New York: Harper and Row

Dowler, Thomas W. and Joseph S. Howard II, 1995, "Stability in a Proliferated World," *Strategic Review* vol. 23 no. 2 (Spring), pp. 26–37

Downs, George W., 1989, "The Rational Deterrence Debate," *World Politics* vol. 41 no. 2 (January), pp. 225–237

    1994a, "The Limits of Deterrence Theory," in Aharon Klieman and Ariel Levite, eds., *Deterrence in the Middle East: Where Theory and Practice Converge*, Boulder: Westview Press, pp. 63–84

    1994b, ed., *Collective Security Beyond the Cold War*, Ann Arbor: University of Michigan Press

Downs, George W. and Keisuke Iida, 1994, "Assessing the Theoretical Case against Collective Security," in G. W. Downs, ed., *Collective Security Beyond the Cold War*, Ann Arbor: University of Michigan Press, pp. 17–39

Downs, George W. and David M. Rocke, 1990, *Tacit Bargaining, Arms Races, and Arms Control*, Ann Arbor: University of Michigan Press

Drogan, Bob, 1999a, "U.S. Scurries to Erect Cyber-Defenses," *Los Angeles Times*, October 31

    1999b, "In Theory, Reality, U.S. Open to Cyber-Attack," *Los Angeles Times*, October 9

Dror, Yehezkel, 1971, *Crazy States: A Counterconventional Strategic Problem*, Lexington, MA: D. C. Heath and Co.

Durch, William J., 1993, "Protecting the Homeland," in Barry M. Blechman et al., *The American Military in the Twenty-First Century*, New York: St. Martin's Press, pp. 197–265

Economist, 1997, "Circles of Fear," January 4, pp. 47–49

Elster, Jon, 1979, *Ulysses and the Sirens*, Cambridge: Cambridge University Press

Erlanger, Steven, 1999, "NATO Was Closer to Ground War in Kosovo than Is Widely Realized," *New York Times*, November 7

Evron, Yair, 1994, "Deterrence Experience in the Arab–Israeli Conflict," in Aharon Klieman and Ariel Levite, eds., *Deterrence in the Middle East: Where Theory and Practice Converge*, Boulder: Westview Press, pp. 98–121

Fallaci, Oriana, 1982, "Galtieri: No Regrets, No Going Back," *The Times* (London), June 12

Farnham, Barbara, 1994, ed., *Avoiding Losses/Taking Risks: Prospect Theory and International Conflict*, Ann Arbor: University of Michigan Press

Fearon, James D., 1994, "Signaling Versus the Balance of Power and Interests," *Journal of Conflict Resolution* vol. 38 no. 2 (June), pp. 236–269

1995, "Rationalist Explanations for War," *International Organization* vol. 49 no. 3 (Summer), pp. 379–414

Feaver, Peter Douglas, 1992, *Guarding the Guardians: Civilian Control of Nuclear Weapons in the United States*, Ithaca: Cornell University Press

Feldman, Shai, 1982, *Israeli Nuclear Deterrence: A Strategy for the 1980s*, New York: Columbia University Press

1994a, "Israeli Deterrence and the Gulf War," in Aharon Klieman and Ariel Levite, eds., *Deterrence in the Middle East: Where Theory and Practice Converge*, Boulder: Westview Press, pp. 122–148

1994b, "Israel," in Mitchell Reiss and Robert S. Litwak, eds., *Nuclear Proliferation After the Cold War*, Washington, DC: Woodrow Wilson Center Press, pp. 67–88

Ferejohn, John and Debra Satz, 1995, "Unification, Universalism, and Rational Choice Theory," in Jeffrey Friedman, ed., *The Rational Choice Controversy: Economic Models of Politics Reconsidered*, New Haven: Yale University Press, pp. 71–84

Fink, Clinton F., 1965, "More Calculations About Deterrence," *Journal of Conflict Resolution*, vol. 9, pp. 54–65

Fischer, Beth A., 1998, "Perception, Intelligence Errors, and the Cuban Missile Crisis," *Intelligence and National Security* vol. 13 no. 3 (Autumn), pp. 150–172

Fischhoff, Baruch, 1987, "Do We Want a Better Theory of Deterrence?" *Journal of Social Issues* vol. 43 no. 4, pp. 73–77

1991, "Nuclear Decisions: Cognitive Limits to the Thinkable," in Philip E. Tetlock et al., eds., *Behavior, Society, and Nuclear War*, vol. II, New York: Oxford University Press, pp. 110–192

Fisher, Cathleen S., 1999, "Reformation and Resistance: Nongovernmental Organizations and the Future of Nuclear Weapons," Report no. 29, Henry L. Stimson Center, Washington, DC

Fitchett, Joseph, 1995, "Nuclear States See Vindication," *International Herald Tribune*, September 12

Fontaine, Andre, 1972, "DeGaulle's View of Europe and the Nuclear Debate," *The Reporter* vol. 27 no. 2 (July 19), pp. 33–34

Frankel, Benjamin, ed., 1991, *Opaque Nuclear Proliferation: Methodological and Policy Implications*, London: Frank Cass

Freedman, Lawrence, 1981, *The Evolution of Nuclear Strategy*, New York: St. Martin's Press

1989, "General Deterrence and the Balance of Power," *Review of International Studies* vol. 15, pp. 199–210

1996, "Does Deterrence Have a Future?" Future Roles Series Papers no. 5, Sandia National Laboratories, New Mexico

1997, "Nuclear Weapons: From Marginalization to Elimination?" *Survival* vol. 39 no. 1 (Spring), pp. 184–189

1998a, ed., *Strategic Coercion: Concepts and Cases*, New York: Oxford University Press

1998b, "Military Power and Political Influence," *International Affairs* vol. 74 no. 4, pp. 762–779

1998c, "The Revolution in Strategic Affairs," Adelphi Paper 318, International Institute for Strategic Studies

Freedman, Lawrence and Efraim Karsh, 1993, *The Gulf Conflict 1990–1991: Diplomacy and War in the New World Order*, Princeton: Princeton University Press

Friedan, Jeffrey A. and Ronald Rogowski, 1996, "The Impact of the International Economy on National Policies: An Analytical Overview," in Robert O. Keohane and Helen V. Milner, eds., *Internationalization and Domestic Politics*, Cambridge: Cambridge University Press, pp. 25–47

Friedman, Jeffrey, 1995a, ed., *The Rational Choice Controversy: Economic Models of Politics Reconsidered*, New Haven: Yale University Press

1995b, "Introduction: Economic Approaches to Politics," in Jeffrey Friedman, ed., *The Rational Choice Controversy: Economic Models of Politics Reconsidered*, New Haven: Yale University Press, pp. 1–24

Friedman, Milton, 1953, *Essays in Positive Economics*, Chicago: University of Chicago Press

Fulghum, David A., 1999, "New Radars Peel Veil from Hidden Targets," *Aviation Week and Space Technology*, January 18

Fursenko, Aleksandr and Timothy Naftali, 1997, *"One Hell of a Gamble": Khrushchev, Castro and Kennedy*, New York: W. W. Norton

Gaddis, John Lewis, 1982, *Strategies of Containment*, New York: Oxford University Press

1991, "Great Illusions, the Long Peace, and the Future of the International System," in Charles W. Kegley, Jr., ed., *The Long Postwar Peace: Contending Explanations and Projections*, New York: HarperCollins, pp. 22–55

1992, "Nuclear Weapons, the End of the Cold War, and the Future of the International System," in Patrick J. Garrity and Steven A. Maaranen, eds., *Nuclear Weapons in the Changing World: Perspectives from Europe, Asia, and North America*, New York: Plenum Press, pp. 15–31

1996, "Nuclear Weapons and Cold War History," in Jorn Gjelstad and Olav Njolstad, eds., *Nuclear Rivalry and International Order*, Thousand Oaks, CA: Sage, pp. 40–54

1997, *We Now Know; Rethinking Cold War History*, Oxford: Clarendon Press

Gaillard, Theodore, 2000, "Successful THEL Tests Raise Warning Flag for U.S. Arsenal," *Defense News*, October 30

Gansler, Jacques, S., 1999, "Technology 2000: Meeting Defense Needs in an Evolving Geopolitical Environment," remarks at the Tech Trends 2000 Conference, April 17, available at wysiwyg://mid.rig.5/http://www.defense-a...e.com/data/verbatum/data/ve19/index.htm

Garfinkle, Adam, 1995, "An Observation on Arab Culture and Deterrence: Metaphors and Misgivings," in Efraim Inbar, ed., *Regional Security Regimes: Israel and its Neighbors*, Albany: State University of New York Press, pp. 201–229

Garrity, Patrick J. and Stephen A. Maaranen, 1992, eds., *Nuclear Weapons in the Changing World: Perspectives from Europe, Asia, and North America*, New York: Plenum Press

Garthoff, Raymond L., 1991, "Assessing the Adversary: Estimates by the Eisenhower Administration of Soviet Intentions and Capabilities," Brookings Occasional Paper, Washington, DC: Brookings Institution

1998, "US Intelligence in the Cuban Missile Crisis," *Intelligence and National Security* vol. 13 no. 3 (Autumn), pp. 18–63

Garwin, Richard, 1994, "New Applications of Nonlethal and Less Lethal Technology," in Arnold Kanter and Linton F. Brooks, eds., *U.S. Intervention Policy for the Post-Cold War World: New Challenges and Responses*, New York: W. W. Norton, pp. 105–131

1999, *Nonlethal Technologies Progress and Prospects*, New York: Council on Foreign Relations Press

Geller, Daniel S., 1990, "Nuclear Weapons, Deterrence, and Crisis Escalation," *Journal of Conflict Resolution* vol. 34, pp. 291–310

Geller, Daniel S. and J. David Singer, 1998, *Nations at War: A Scientific Study of International Conflict*, Cambridge: Cambridge University Press

Gellman, Barton, 1999, "Learning from Kosovo," *Washington Post National Weekly Edition*, June 14

General Accounting Office, 1999, "DOD Efforts to Develop Laser Weapons for Theater Defense," GAO/NSIAD-99–50, March

George, Alexander, D. K. Hall and W. E. Simons, 1971, *The Limits of Coercive Diplomacy*, Boston: Little, Brown

George, Alexander and Richard Smoke, 1974, *Deterrence in American Foreign Policy: Theory and Practice*, New York: Columbia University Press

1989, "Deterrence and Foreign Policy," *World Politics* vol. 41 no. 2 (January), pp. 170–182

Gibler, Douglas and John A. Vasquez, 1998, "Uncovering the Dangerous Alliances, 1495–1980," *International Studies Quarterly* vol. 12 no. 4 (December), pp. 785–807

Gilpin, Robert, 1981, *War and Change in World Politics*, Cambridge: Cambridge University Press

Gjelstad, Jorn and Olav Njolstad, 1996, eds., *Nuclear Rivalry and International Order*, Thousand Oaks, CA: Sage

Glaser, Charles L., 1990, *Analyzing Strategic Nuclear Policy*, Princeton: Princeton University Press

Goertz, Gary and Paul F. Diehl, 1992, "The Empirical Importance of Enduring Rivalries," *International Interactions* vol. 18 no. 2, pp. 151–163

1993, "Enduring Rivalries: Theoretical Constructs and Empirical Patterns," *International Studies Quarterly* vol. 37, pp. 147–171

Goldblat, Josef, 2000, *Nuclear Disarmament: Obstacles to Banning the Bomb*, London: I. B. Tauris

Goldstein, Avery, 1993, "Understanding Nuclear Proliferation: Theoretical Explanation and China's National Experience," in Zachary S. Davis and Benjamin Frankel, eds., *The Proliferation Puzzle: Why Nuclear Weapons Spread (and What Results)*, London: Frank Cass, pp. 213–255

Goldstein, Steve, 2000, "Bill Would Give Push to 'Mini-nuke,'" *Philadelphia Inquirer*, October 16, at http://www.ransac.org/new-web-site/pub/nuclearnews/10.16.00.html

Gordon, Michael R., 2002, "U.S. Nuclear Plan Sees New Targets and New Weapons," *New York Times*, March 20

Gormley, Dennis M., 1998, "Hedging Against the Cruise Missile Threat," *Survival* vol. 40 no. 1 (Spring), pp. 92–111

Graham, Bradley, 1998a, "Pentagon Bolsters Anti-Hacker Defense," *International Herald Tribune*, May 25

1998b, "A Cyberspace Pearl Harbor," *Washington Post Weekly Edition*, June 1

Graham, Bradley and Walter Pincus, 2002, "A Shift in Focus," *Washington Post National Weekly Edition*, March 18–24

Graham, Bradley and Dana Priest, 1999, "'No Way to Fight a War': The Limits of Coalitions," *Washington Post National Weekly Edition*, June 14

Grand, Camille, 1998, "A French Nuclear Exception?" Henry L. Stimson Center Occasional Paper No. 38, Washington, DC

Gray, Colin S., 1990, "The Definitions and Assumptions of Deterrence: Questions of Theory and Practice," *Journal of Strategic Studies* vol. 13 no. 4, pp. 1–18

1992 "Deterrence in the New Strategic Environment," *Comparative Strategy* vol. 11, pp. 247–267

1996, *Explorations in Strategy*, Westport, CT: Greenwood Press

1998, "Nuclear Weapons and the Revolution in Military Affairs," in T. V. Paul, Richard Harknett, and James Wirtz, eds., *The Absolute Weapons Revisited: Nuclear Arms and the Emerging International Order*, Ann Arbor: University of Michigan Press, pp. 99–134

Green, Donald P. and Ian Shapiro, 1994, *Pathologies of Rational Choice Theory: A Critique of Applications in Political Science*, New Haven: Yale University Press

Grey, Stephen and Steven Haynes, 1997, "Police See Knife Carriers at 60 Feet with E-Ray Spy Cameras," *The Sunday Times* (London), May 11

Grigoryev, Sergey, 1999, "Russia's Military Political Trump Card," *Nezavisimoye Voyennoye Obozrenie*, December 17–23, in NAPSNet Daily Report, December 21, 1999 available at ftp://ftp.nautilus.org/napsnet/daily reports

Hagerty, Devin T., 1993, "The Power of Suggestion: Opaque Proliferation, Existential Deterrence, and the South Asian Nuclear Arms Competition," in Zachary S. Davis and Benjamin Frankel, eds., *The Proliferation Puzzle: Why Nuclear Weapons Spread (and What Results)*, London: Frank Cass, pp. 256–283

Hall, Brian, 1998, "Overkill Is Not Dead," *New York Times*, March 15

Halpern, Jennifer J. and Robert N. Stern, 1998, eds., *Debating Rationality: Nonrational Aspects of Organizational Decision Making*, Ithaca: Cornell University Press

Hanson, Martin and Timothy J. Sinclair, 1999, eds., *Approaches to Global Governance Theory*, Albany: State University of New York Press

Harden, Blaine, 1999, "A Long Struggle that Led Serb Leader to Back Down," *New York Times*, June 6

Harvard Nuclear Study Group, 1983, *Living With Nuclear Weapons*, Cambridge, MA: Harvard University Press

Harvey, Frank P., 1995, "Rational Deterrence Theory Revisited – A Progress Report," *Canadian Journal of Political Science* vol. 28 no. 3 (September), pp. 403–436

1997a, *The Future Is Back: Nuclear Rivalry, Deterrence Theory, and Crisis Stability After the Cold War*, Montreal: McGill-Queens University Press

1997b, "Deterrence and Compellence in Protracted Crises: Methodology and Preliminary Findings," *International Studies Notes* vol. 22 no. 1 (Winter), pp. 12–23

Harvey, Frank P. and Patrick James, 1992, "Nuclear Deterrence Theory: The Record of Aggregate Testing and an Alternative Research Agenda," *Conflict Management and Peace Science* vol. 12 no. 1, pp. 17–45

Herek, G. M., I. L. Janis, and Paul Huth, 1987, "Decision Making During International Crises: Is Quality of Process Related to Outcome?" *Journal of Conflict Resolution* vol. 30, pp. 497–531

1990, "Quality of U.S. Decision Making During the Cuban Missile Crisis: Major Errors in Welch's Reassessment," *Journal of Conflict Resolution* vol. 33, pp. 446–459

Hermann, Richard, 1987, "Political Diagnosis and Strategic Prescriptions: The Essential Connection," *Journal of Social Issues* vol. 43 no. 4, pp. 93–97

Heuser, Beatrice, 1997, *NATO, Britain, France, and the FRG: Nuclear Strategies and Forces for Europe, 1949–2000*, Basingstoke: Macmillan

Hewson, Martin and Timothy J. Sinclair, 1999, eds., *Approaches to Global Governance Theory*, Albany: State University of New York Press

Hillen, John, 2000, "Armed and Unready: Why Are We Pouring Money into a Military Designed to Fight Wars of the Past?" *San Francisco Chronicle*, October 15

Hoag, Malcolm W., 1962, "On Stability in Deterrent Races," in Morton A. Kaplan, ed., *The Revolution in World Politics*, New York: John Wiley, pp. 338–410

Hoffman, David, 1998, "Downsizing a Mighty Arsenal," *Washington Post*, March 16

1999a, "When the Nuclear Alarms Went off, He Guessed Right," *International Herald Tribune*, February 11

1999b, "A Weakened Bear: An Impoverished Russian Military Envies NATO," *Washington Post Weekly Edition*, June 21

1999c, "Russia's Nuclear Future Uncertain," *Washington Post*, August 31

Holloway, David, 1994, *Stalin and the Bomb*, New Haven: Yale University Press

Holsti, Ole R., 1989, "Crisis Decision Making," in Philip E. Tetlock et al., eds., *Behavior, Society, and Nuclear War*, vol. III, New York: Oxford University Press, pp. 8–84

Hoodbhoy, Pervez, 2002, "What, US Worry?" *Los Angeles Times*, June 9

Hopf, Ted, 1991, "Polarity, the Offense–Defense Balance, and War," *American Political Science Review* vol. 85 no. 2, pp. 475–493

  1994, *Peripheral Visions: Deterrence Theory and American Foreign Policy in the Third World, 1965–1990*, Ann Arbor: University of Michigan Press

House Armed Services Committee, 1992, "Potential Threats to American Security in the Post-Cold War Era, Hearings Before the Defense Policy Panel of the Committee on Armed Services, House of Representatives, One Hundred Second Congress, December 10, 11, 13, 1991," Washington, DC: Government Publications Office

House of Commons Defence – Fourteenth Report, Session 1999–2000, London, available at http://www.parliament.the-stationery-off. . .cm19900/cmdefence/ 347/ 34702.htm

Howard, Michael, 1991, *The Lessons of History*, New Haven: Yale University Press

Howlett, Darryl, Ben Cole, Emily Bailey, and John Simpson, 1999, "Surveying the Nuclear Future: Which Way from Here?" *Contemporary Security Policy* vol. 20 no. 1 (April), pp. 5–41

Hundley, Richard O., Robert H. Anderson, John Arquilla, and Roger C. Molander, 1996, eds., *Security in Cyberspace, Challenges for Society: Proceedings of an International Conference*, Santa Monica: RAND

Huth, Paul, 1988, *Extended Deterrence and the Prevention of War*, New Haven: Yale University Press

  1999, "Deterrence and International Conflict: Empirical Findings and Theoretical Debates," in Nelson W. Polsby, ed., *Annual Review of Political Science*, vol. II, Palo Alto, CA: Annual Reviews, pp. 25–48

Huth, Paul, Christopher Gelphi, and D. Scott Bennett, 1993, "The Escalation of Great Power Militarized Disputes: Testing Rational Deterrence Theory and Structural Realism," *American Political Science Review* vol. 87 no. 3 (September), pp. 609–623

Huth, Paul and Bruce Russett, 1984, "What Makes Deterrence Work? Cases from 1900 to 1980," *World Politics* vol. 36 no. 4 (July), pp. 496–526

  1988, "Deterrence Failures and Crisis Escalation," *International Studies Quarterly* vol. 32 no. 1 (March), pp. 47–66

  1990, "Testing Deterrence Theory: Rigor Makes a Difference," *World Politics* vol. 42 (July), pp. 466–501

  1993, "General Deterrence Between Enduring Rivals: Testing Three Competing Models," *American Political Science Review* vol. 87 no. 1 (March), pp. 61–73

Hybel, Alex Roberto, 1993, *Power over Rationality: The Bush Administration and the Gulf Crisis*, Albany: State University of New York Press

Ignatius, David, 1992 "Madman's Bluff: Why Deterrence Still Works," *Washington Post*, May 10

IISS (International Institute for Strategic Studies), 1995–6, "Is There a Revolution in Military Affairs?" *Strategic Survey 1995–6*, London: Oxford University Press, pp. 20–40

    1996, "Improvements in Commercial Satellite Imagery," *IISS Strategic Comments* vol. 2 no. 10 (December)

    1998a, "Advanced Military Communication Satellites," *IISS Strategic Comments* vol. 4 no. 3 (April)

    1998b, "The Future of Armored Warfare," *IISS Strategic Comments* vol. 4 no. 8 (October)

    1999a, "Air Power over Kosovo: A Historic Victory?" *IISS Strategic Comments* vol. 5 no. 7 (September)

    1999b, "The Future of Urban Warfare," *IISS Strategic Comments* vol. 5 no. 2 (March)

Ikenberry, G. John, 2001, *After Victory: Institutions, Strategic Restraint, and the Building of Order After Major Wars*, Princeton: Princeton University Press

Inbar, Efraim and Shmuel Sandler, 1995, "The Arab–Israeli Relationship: from Deterrence to Security Regime," in Efraim Inbar, ed., *Regional Security Regimes: Israel and its Neighbors*, Albany: State University of New York Press, pp. 273–297

Intriligator, Michael and Dagobert Brito, 1984, "Can Arms Races lead to the Outbreak of War?" *Journal of Conflict Resolution* vol. 28 no. 1, pp. 63–84

Janis, Irving, 1982, *Groupthink: Psychological Studies of Policy Decisions and Fiascos*, 2nd edn., Boston: Houghton-Mifflin

Jervis, Robert, 1976, *Perception and Misperception in International Politics*, Princeton; Princeton University Press

    1979, "Deterrence Theory Reconsidered," *World Politics*, vol. 39, pp. 289–324

    1982–3, "Deterrence and Perception," *International Security* vol. 7 no. 3 (Winter), pp. 183–207

    1984, *The Illogic of American Nuclear Strategy*, Ithaca: Cornell University Press

    1985, "From Balance to Concert," *World Politics* vol. 38, pp. 58–79

    1989a, "Rational Deterrence: Theory and Evidence," *World Politics* vol. 41 no. 2 (January), pp. 183–207

    1989b, *The Meaning of the Nuclear Revolution: Statecraft and the Prospect of Armageddon*, Ithaca: Cornell University Press

    1994, "Leadership, Post-Cold War Politics, and Psychology," *Political Psychology* vol. 15 no. 4, pp. 769–777

    1997, *System Effects: Complexity in Political and Social Life*, Princeton: Princeton University Press

Jervis, Robert, Richard Ned Lebow, and Janice Gross Stein, 1985, eds., *Psychology and Deterrence*, Baltimore: Johns Hopkins University Press

Job, Brian L., 1992, *The Insecurity Dilemma: National Security of Third World States*, Boulder: Lynne Rienner

Joeck, Neil, 1999, "Nuclear Developments in India and Pakistan," *AccessAsia Review* vol. 2 no. 2 (July)

Johnson, Rebecca, 1998, "British Perspectives on the Future of Nuclear Weapons," Henry L. Stimson Center Occasional Paper No. 37, Washington, DC

Johnson, Stuart E. and Martin C. Libicki, 1996, eds., *Dominant Battlespace Knowledge*, Washington, DC: National Defense University Press

Joseph, Robert G. and John F. Reichart, 1998, "The Case for Nuclear Deterrence Today," *Orbis*, Winter, pp. 7–19

Journal of Strategic Studies, special issue, 2000, "Preventing the Use of Weapons of Mass Destruction," vol. 23 no. 1 (March)

Kahn, Herman, 1961, *On Thermonuclear War*, Princeton: Princeton University Press

  1965, *On Escalation: Metaphors and Scenarios*, New York: Praeger

Kaiser, David, 2000, *American Tragedy: Kennedy, Johnson and the Origins of the Vietnam War*, Cambridge, MA: Belknap Press of Harvard University Press

Kaldor, Mary, 1991, "Rethinking Cold War History," in Ken Booth, ed., *New Thinking About Strategy and International Security*, London: HarperCollins Academic, pp. 313–331

Kanter, Arnold and Linton F. Brooks, 1994, "Introduction," in Arnold Kanter and Linton F. Brooks, eds., *U.S. Intervention Policy for the Post-Cold War World: New Challenges and Responses*, New York: W. W. Norton, pp. 13–41

Karl, David J., 1995, "Enduring Rivalries in the Nuclear Shadow: The Case of the Sino-Soviet Relationship," paper presented at conference on Deterrence After the Cold War: Theoretical Perspectives and Policy Implications of Enduring Rivalries, Monterey

Karp, Regina, 1992, ed., *Security without Nuclear Weapons: Different Perspectives on Non-Nuclear Security*, New York: Oxford University Press

Kaufmann, William W., 1954, *The Requirements of Deterrence*, Center of International Studies Memorandum no. 7, Princeton University

Keaney, Thomas A. and Eliot A. Cohen, 1993, *Gulf War Air Power Survey Summary Report*, Washington, DC: Government Printing Office

Kegley, Charles W., Jr., 1991, ed., *The Long Postwar Peace: Contending Explanations and Projections*, New York: HarperCollins

Kelley, Stanley, Jr., 1995, "The Promises and Limitations of Rational Choice Theory," in Jeffrey Friedman, ed., *The Rational Choice Controversy: Economic Models of Politics Reconsidered*, New Haven: Yale University Press

Khalilzad, Zalmay M. and John P. White, 1999, eds., *The Changing Role of Information in Warfare*, Santa Monica: RAND

Khong, Yuen Foon, 1992, *Analogies at War*, Princeton: Princeton University Press

Kim, Woonsang and James D. Morrow, 1992, "When Do Power Shifts Lead to War?" *American Journal of Political Science* vol. 36 no. 4 (November), pp. 896–922

Kissinger, Henry, 1981, *For the Record: Selected Statements 1977–1980*, Boston: Little, Brown

Klieman, Aharon and Ariel Levite, 1994, eds., *Deterrence in the Middle East: Where Theory and Practice Converge*, Boulder: Westview Press

Knorr, Klaus and Patrick Morgan, 1983, *Strategic Military Surprise: Incentives and Opportunities*, New Brunswick, NJ: Transaction Books

Kolodziej, Edward, 1987, "The Limits of Deterrence Theory," *Journal of Social Issues* vol. 43 no. 4, pp. 123–133

Koster, Karel, 2000, "An Uneasy Alliance: NATO Nuclear Doctrine and the NPT," *Disarmament and Diplomacy* no. 49 (August), http://www.acronym.org.uk/dd/dd49npt.htm

Krepinevich Andrew, Jr., 1994, "Cavalry to Computer: The Pattern of Military Revolutions," *National Interest* no. 37 (Fall), pp. 30–42

Kristensen, Hans M., 1999, "U.S. Nuclear Strategy Reform in the 1990s," Nautilus Institute for Security and Sustainable Development, Berkeley
    2001, "The Matrix of Deterrence," Nautilus Institute for Security and Sustainable Development, Berkeley

Kugler, Jacek, 1984, "Terror Without Deterrence," *Journal of Conflict Resolution* vol. 28, pp. 470–506
    1987, "Assessing Stable Deterrence," in Jacek Kugler and Frank C. Zagare, eds., *Exploring the Stability of Deterrence*, Boulder: Lynne Rienner, pp. 41–68
    1993 "Political Conflict, War, and Peace," in Ada W. Finifter, ed., *Political Science: The State of the Discipline II*, Washington, DC: American Political Science Association, pp. 485–509

Kugler, Jacek and Douglas Lemke, 1996, eds., *Parity and War: Evaluations and Extensions of the War Ledger*, Ann Arbor: University of Michigan Press

Kugler, Jacek and A. F. K. Organski, 1989, "The Power Transition: A Retrospective and Prospective Evaluation," in Manus I. Midlarsky, ed., *Handbook of War Studies*, Ann Arbor: University of Michigan Press, pp. 171–194

Kugler, Jacek, A. F. K. Organski, and Daniel Fox, 1980, "Deterrence and the Arms Race: The Impotence of Power," *International Security* vol. 4, pp. 105–138

Kugler, Jacek and Frank C. Zagare, 1987, "Risk, Deterrence, and War," in Jacek Kugler and Frank C. Zagare, eds., *Exploring the Stability of Deterrence*, Boulder: Lynne Rienner, pp. 69–89

Kupchan, Charles A. and Clifford A., 1991, "Concerts, Collective Security, and the Future of Europe," *International Security* vol. 16 no. 1 (Summer), pp. 114–161

Lakatos, I., 1978, *The Methodology of Scientific Research Programs*, vol. I, Cambridge: Cambridge University Press

Lambeth, Benjamin S., 1996, "Technology Trends in Air Warfare," RAND Reprints Series; reprinted from Alan Stephens, ed., *New Era Security: The RAAF in the Next 25 Years*, RAAF Air Power Studies Centre
    1997, "The Technology Revolution in Air Warfare," *Survival* vol. 39 no. 1 (Spring), pp. 65–83
    2001, *NATO's Air War for Kosovo: A Strategic and Operational Assessment*, Santa Monica: RAND

Langlois, Jean-Pierre P., 1991, "Rational Deterrence and Crisis Stability," *American Journal of Political Science* vol. 35 no. 4 (November), pp. 810–832

Lariokhin, Taras, 1999, "Beijing Learned How to See the 'Invisible' Ones," *The Izvestia*, November 30

Larson, Jeffrey A. and Gregory J. Rattray, 1996, *Arms Control: Towards the 21st Century*, Boulder: Lynne Rienner

Latham, Andrew, 1999, "Re-imagining Warfare: The 'Revolution in Military Affairs,'" in Craig A. Snyder, ed., *Contemporary Security and Strategy*, New York: Routledge, pp. 210–235

Lavoy, Peter R., Scott D. Sagan, and James J. Wirtz, 2000, eds., *Planning the Unthinkable: How New Powers Will Use Nuclear, Biological, and Chemical Weapons*, Ithaca: Cornell University Press

Lebovic, James H., 1990, *Deadly Dilemmas: Deterrence in U.S. Nuclear Strategy*, New York: Columbia University Press

Lebow, Richard Ned, 1981, *Between Peace and War: The Nature of International Crises*, Baltimore: Johns Hopkins University Press

    1984, "Windows of Opportunity: Do States Jump Through Them?" *International Security* vol. 9 no. 1 (Summer), pp. 147–186

    1987a, "Conventional or Nuclear Deterrence: Are the Lessons Transferable?" *Journal of Social Issues* vol. 43 no. 4, pp. 171–191

    1987b, "Beyond Deterrence: Building Better Theory," *Journal of Social Issues* vol. 43 no. 4, pp. 155–169

    1989, "Deterrence: A Political and Psychological Critique," in Paul C. Stern et al., eds., *Perspectives on Deterrence*, New York: Oxford University Press, pp. 25–51

    1994, "The Long Peace, the End of the Cold War and Theories of International Relations," *International Organization* vol. 48 no. 2 (Spring), pp. 249–277

Lebow, Richard Ned and Janice Gross Stein, 1987, "Beyond Deterrence," *Journal of Social Issues* vol. 43 no. 4, pp. 5–71

    1989, "Rational Deterrence Theory: I Think, Therefore I Deter," *World Politics* vol. 41 no. 2 (January), pp. 208–224

    1990a, "Deterrence: The Elusive Dependent Variable," *World Politics* vol. 42 no. 3 (April), pp. 336–369

    1990b, "When Does Deterrence Succeed and How Do We Know?" Occasional Papers No. 8, Canadian Institute for International Peace and Security, Ottawa

    1994, *We All Lost the Cold War*, Princeton: Princeton University Press

    1995, "Deterrence and the Cold War," *Political Science Quarterly* vol. 110 no. 2, pp. 157–181

Lepgold, Joseph, 1998, "NATO's Post-Cold War Collective Action Problem," *International Security* vol. 23 no. 1 (Summer), pp. 78–106

Levy, Jack, 1982, "Historical Trends in Great Power War, 1495–1975," *International Studies Quarterly* vol. 26 no. 2 (June), pp. 278–300

    1989a, "Quantitative Studies of Deterrence Success and Failure," in Paul C. Stern et al., eds., *Perspectives on Deterrence*, New York: Oxford University Press, pp. 241–243

1989b, "The Causes of War: A Review of Theories and Evidence," in Philip E. Tetlock et al., eds., *Behavior, Society and Nuclear War*, vol. I, New York: Oxford University Press, pp. 209–233

1989c, "The Diversionary Theory of War: A Critique," in Manus I. Midlarsky, ed., *Handbook of War Studies*, Ann Arbor: University of Michigan Press, pp. 259–288

1992a, "An Introduction to Prospect Theory," *Political Psychology* vol. 13, pp. 171–186

1992b, "Prospect Theory and International Relations: Theoretical Applications and Analytical Problems," *Political Psychology* vol. 13, pp. 283–310

1996, "Loss Aversion, Framing, and Bargaining: The Implications of Prospect Theory for International Conflict," *International Political Science Review* vol. 17, pp. 179–195

1997, "Prospect Theory, Rational Choice, and International Relations," *International Studies Quarterly* vol. 41, pp. 87–112

1999, "Loss Aversion, Framing Effects, and International Conflict," in Manus I. Midlarsky, ed., *Handbook of War Studies*, vol. II, Ann Arbor: University of Michigan Press, pp. 193–221

Lewer, Nick and Steven Schofield, 1997, *Non-Lethal Weapons: A Fatal Attraction?* London: Zed Books

Lodal, Jan, 2001, *The Price of Dominance*, New York: Council on Foreign Relations Press

Lubkemeier, Eckhard, 1992, "Building Peace Under the Sword of Damocles," in Patrick J. Garrity and Steven A. Maaranen, eds., *Nuclear Weapons in the Changing World: Perspectives from Europe, Asia, and North America*, New York: Plenum Press, pp. 223–239

Lund, Michael S., 1996, *Preventing Violent Conflicts: A Strategy for Preventive Diplomacy*, Washington, DC: United States Institute of Peace Press

Lynn-Jones, Sean M., 2001, "Does Offense-Defense Theory Have a Future?" Working Paper 12, Research Group in International Security, McGill University, Montreal

Mandelbaum, Michael, 1981, *The Nuclear Revolution: International Politics Before and After Hiroshima*, Cambridge: Cambridge University Press

Mann, Jim, 1998, "U.S. Considered '64 Bombing to Keep China Nuclear-Free," *Los Angeles Times*, September 27

Mansfield, Edward D. and Jack Snyder, 1995, "Democratization and the Danger of War," *International Security* vol. 20 no. 1 (Summer), pp. 5–38

Mansourov, Alexandre, 1995, "Stalin, Mao, Kim, and China's Decision to End the Korean War, September 16–October 15, 1950: New Evidence From the Russian Archives," *Cold War International History Project Bulletin* Nos. 6–7 (Winter)

Manwaring, Max G., 2001, ed., *Deterrence in the 21st Century*, London: Frank Cass

Mares, David R., 1996, "Deterrence Bargaining in the Ecuador–Peru Enduring Rivalry," *Security Studies* vol. 6 no. 2 (Winter), pp. 114–147

Markoff, John, 1998, "'Science Fiction' Power for the PC," *International Herald Tribune*, July 16

1999, "Ushering in a Very Tiny Computer Revolution," *International Herald Tribune*, November 2

Martel, William C. and William T. Pendley, 1994, *Nuclear Coexistence: Rethinking U.S. Policy to Promote Stability in an Era of Proliferation*, Air War College Studies in National Security no. 1, Washington, DC: Government Printing Office

Maxwell, Stephen, 1968, "Rationality in Deterrence," *Adelphi Papers* no. 50, London: International Institute for Strategic Studies

May, Ernest and Richard Neustadt, 1986, *Learning in Time: The Uses of History for Decision Makers*, New York: The Free Press

May, Ernest R. and Philip D. Zelikow, 1997, eds., *The Kennedy Tapes: Inside the White House During the Cuban Missile Crisis*, Cambridge, MA: Belknap Press of Harvard University Press

May, Michael D. and Roger D. Speed, 1994, "The Role of U.S. Nuclear Weapons in Regional Conflicts," Stanford: Center for International Security and Arms Control

Mazarr, Michael J., 1997, ed., *Nuclear Weapons in a Transformed World: the Challenge of Virtual Nuclear Arsenals*, New York: St. Martin's Press

McCullough, David, 1992, *Truman*, New York: Simon and Schuster

McGuire, Martin, 1965, *Secrecy and the Arms Race*, Cambridge, MA: Harvard University Press

McGwire, Michael, 1985, "Deterrence: The Problem Not the Solution," *SAIS Review* vol. 5 no. 2 (Summer/Fall), pp. 105–124

McMaster, H. R., 1997, *Dereliction of Duty: Lyndon Johnson, Robert McNamara, the Joint Chiefs of Staff, and the Lies That Led to Vietnam*, New York: HarperCollins.

Mearsheimer, John J., 1983, *Conventional Deterrence*, Ithaca: Cornell University Press

1990, "Back to the Future: Instability in Europe After the Cold War," *International Security* vol. 15 no. 1 (Summer), pp. 5–56

1993, "The Case for a Nuclear Deterrent," *Foreign Affairs* vol. 72 no. 3 (Summer), pp. 50–66

2001, *The Tragedy of Great Power Politics*, New York: W. W. Norton

Mercer, Jonathan, 1996, *Reputation and International Politics*, Ithaca: Cornell University Press

Metz, Steven and James Kievit, 1994, "The Revolution in Military Affairs and Conflict Short of War," Strategic Studies Institute, U.S. Army War College, July 25

Millburn, George, 1991, "New Technologies: An Overview," in Desmond Ball and Helen Wilson, eds., *New Technology: Implications for Regional and Australian Security*, Canberra: Australian National University Strategic and Defense Studies Centre, pp. 2–19

Millot, Marc Dean, 1995, "Facing the Emerging Reality of Regional Nuclear Adversaries," in Peter L. Hays, Brenda J. Vallance, and Alan R. Van Tassel, eds., *American Defense Policy*, 7th edn., Baltimore: Johns Hopkins University Press, pp. 453–470

Milner, Helen V., 1997, *Interests, Institutions, and Information: Domestic Politics and International Relations*, Princeton: Princeton University Press

Mintz, Alex, 1997, "Foreign Policy Decisionmaking: Bridging the Gap Between the Cognitive Psychology and Rational Actor 'Schools,'" in Nehemia Geva and Alex Mintz, eds., *Decisionmaking on War and Peace: The Cognitive–Rational Debate*, Boulder: Lynne Rienner, pp. 1–7

Mintz, Alex and Nehemia Geva, 1997, "The Poliheuristic Theory of Foreign Policy Decisionmaking," in Nehemia Geva and Alex Mintz, eds., *Decisionmaking on War and Peace: The Cognitive–Rational Debate*, Boulder: Lynne Rienner, pp. 81–101

Mitchell, Russ, 2002, "The Pilot, Gone. The Market, Huge," *New York Times*, March 31

Mlyn, Eric, 1995, *The State, Society, and Limited Nuclear War*, Albany: State University of New York Press

Moaz, Z., 1981, "The Decision to Raid Entebbe: Decision Analysis Applied to Crisis Behavior," *Journal of Conflict Resolution* vol. 25, pp. 677–708

Modelski, George and Patrick M. Morgan, 1985, "Understanding Global War," *Journal of Conflict Resolution* vol. 28 (Fall), pp. 391–417

Modelski, George and William R. Thompson, 1989, "Long Cycles and Global War," in Manus I. Midlarsky, ed., *Handbook of War Studies*, Ann Arbor: University of Michigan Press, pp. 23–54

Molander, Roger C., Andrew S. Riddile, and Peter A. Wilson, 1996, *Strategic Information Warfare: A New Face of War*, Santa Monica: RAND

Molander, Roger C. and Peter A. Wilson, 1998, *The Day After . . . In the American Strategic Infrastructure*, Santa Monica: RAND

Molander, Roger C., Peter A. Wilson, David Mussington, and Richard Mesic, 1998, *Strategic Information Warfare Rising*, Santa Monica: RAND

Morehouse, David, 1996, *Nonlethal Weapons: War Without Death*, Westport, CT: Praeger

Morgan, Patrick M. 1983, *Deterrence, A Conceptual Analysis*, 2nd edn., Beverly Hills: Sage

1985, "Saving Face for the Sake of Deterrence," in Robert Jervis et al., eds., *Psychology and Deterrence*, Baltimore: Johns Hopkins University Press, pp. 125–152

2000, "The Impact of the Revolution in Military Affairs," *Journal of Strategic Studies* vol. 23 no. 1, pp. 132–162

Mueller, John, 1988, "The Essential Irrelevance of Nuclear Weapons . . ." *International Security* vol. 13 no. 2 (Fall), pp. 55–79

1989, *Retreat from Doomsday: The Obsolescence of Major War*, New York: Basic Books

1989–90, "A New Concert of Europe," *Foreign Policy* no. 77 (Winter), pp. 3–16

Mueller, John and Karl Mueller, 2000, "The Methodology of Mass Destruction: Assessing Threats in the New World Order," *Journal of Strategic Studies* vol. 23 no. 1, pp. 163–187

Murphy, James B., 1995, "Rational Choice Theory as Social Physics," in Jeffrey Friedman, ed., *The Rational Choice Controversy: Economic Models of Politics Reconsidered*, New Haven: Yale University Press, pp. 155–174

Murray, Williamson, 1997, "Thinking About Revolutions in Military Affairs," *Joint Force Quarterly* (Summer), pp. 69–76

Myers, Steven Lee, 1997, "U.S. 'Updates' Nuclear War Guidelines," *New York Times*, December 8

  1998, "Pentagon Ready to Shrink Arsenal of Nuclear Bombs," *New York Times*, November 23

  1999, "NATO Air War May Have Done Less Damage Than Alliance Thought," *International Herald Tribune*, June 29

Nalebuff, Barry, 1991, "Rational Deterrence in an Imperfect World," *World Politics* vol. 43 (April), pp. 313–335

NATO, 1999, "Press Conference on the Kosovo Strike Assessment," available via natodoc@hq.nato.int

Naylor, Sean D., 2000, "Virtual Deployment: Soldiers Could Train Anywhere," *Defense News*, October 23

Neustadt, Richard E. and Ernest R. May, 1986, *Thinking in Time: The Uses of History for Decision Making*, New York: The Free Press

New York Times, 1997, "When Kennedy Faced Armageddon, and His Own Scornful Generals," *New York Times*, October 5

Nitze, Paul H., 1999, "The United States Ought to get Rid of its Nuclear Weapons," *International Herald Tribune*, October 29

Nolan, Janne E., 1991, *Trappings of Power: Ballistic Missiles in the Third World*, Washington, DC: Brookings Institution

  1999, *An Elusive Consensus: Nuclear Weapons and American Security After the Cold War*, Washington: Brookings Institution

  2000, "Preparing for the 2001 Nuclear Posture Review," *Arms Control Today*, November, pp. 10–14

Noonam, Michael P. and John Hillen, 2002, "The Coming Transformation of the U.S. Military?" Foreign Policy Research Institute, University of Pennsylvania, E-notes, February 4

Norris, Robert and William Arkin, 2000, eds., "NRDC Nuclear Notebook: Global Nuclear Stockpiles 1945–2000," *Bulletin of the Atomic Scientists*, March/April

"Nuclear Posture Review Report," January 8, 2002, excerpts available at wysiwyg://3/http://www.globalsecurity.org/wmd/library/policy/dod/npr.htm

Nunn, Sam and Bruce Blair, 1997, "From Nuclear Deterrence to Mutual Safety," *Washington Post*, June 22

Nye, Joseph S., Jr., 1987, "Nuclear Learning and US–Soviet Security Regimes," *International Organization* vol. 41 no. 3 (Summer), pp. 371–402

Oberdorfer, Don, 1991, "Missed Signals in the Middle East," *Washington Post Magazine*, March 19

Office of Technology Assessment (Congress), 1987, *New Technology for NATO: Implementing Follow-On Forces Attack*, Washington, DC: Government Printing Office

O'Hanlon, Michael E., 1992, *The Art of War in the Age of Peace: U.S. Military Posture for the Post-Cold War World*, Westport, CT: Praeger

2000, *Technological Change and the Future of Warfare*, Washington, DC: Brookings Institution

Oliveri, Frank, 1996, "U.S. Air Force Packs Punch in Mini Bombs," *Defense News*, January 15–21

Organski, A. F. K. and Jacek Kugler, 1980, *The War Ledger*, Chicago: University of Chicago Press

Orme, John, 1987, "Deterrence Failures: A Second Look," *International Security* vol. 11 no. 4 (Spring), pp. 96–124

1992, *Deterrence, Reputation and Cold-War Cycles*, Basingstoke: Macmillan

1997, "The Utility of Force in a World of Scarcity," *International Security* vol. 22 no. 3 (Winter), pp. 138–167

1998, "The Good Theory and Bad Practice of Deterrence in Korea," in Daniel J. Meador, ed., *The Korean War in Retrospect: Lessons for the Future*, Lanham, MD: University Press of America, pp. 65–87

Otsuka, Ryuichi, 2000, "North Korean Missile Base Detailed: US Firms Give Public Clear View of Taepodong Launch Site," *The Daily Yomiuri*, January 9, in NAPSNet Daily Report, January 14, 2000, available at http://www.nautilus.org./napsnet/daily reports

Overy, R. J., 1992, "Air Power and the Origins of Deterrence Theory Before 1939," *Journal of Strategic Studies* vol. 15 no. 1 (March), pp. 73–101

Owens, Bill with Ed Offley, 2001, *Lifting the Fog of War*, New York: Farrar, Straus and Giroux

Pae, Peter, 2002, "Pentagon Flies High on Drones," *Los Angeles Times*, January 19

Panofsky, W. K. H., 1999, "Weapons of Mass Destruction and the Physical Heritage of the Cold War: Two Examples of Adverse Impacts of Technology on U.S. Security," in Charles Hermann, Harold K. Jacobson, and Anne S. Moffat, eds., *Violent Conflict in the 21st Century: Causes, Instruments and Mitigation*, Chicago: American Academy of Arts and Sciences, pp. 37–65

Parker, Geoffrey, 1988, *The Military Revolution: Military Innovation and the Rise of the West 1500–1800*, New York: Cambridge University Press

Paul, T. V., 1995, "Nuclear Taboo and War Initiation in Regional Conflicts," *Journal of Conflict Resolution* vol. 39 no. 4 (December), pp. 696–717

Paul, T. V. and John A. Hall, 1999, eds., *International Order and the Future of World Politics*, Cambridge: Cambridge University Press

Payne, Keith B., 1996, *Deterrence in the Second Nuclear Age*, Lexington: University Press of Kentucky

2001, *The Fallacies of Cold War Deterrence and a New Direction*, Lexington: University Press of Kentucky

Perkovich, George, 1999, *India's Nuclear Bomb: The Impact on Global Proliferation*, Berkeley: University of California Press

Perrow, Charles, 1984, *Normal Accidents: Living with High-Risk Technologies*, New York: Basic Books

Pilat, Joseph F., 1994, "Responding to Proliferation: A Role for Nonlethal Defense?" in Mitchell Reiss and Robert S. Litwak, eds., *Nuclear Proliferation After the Cold War*, Washington, DC: Woodrow Wilson Center Press, pp. 275–289

Pincus, Walter, 1998a, "Ike Delegated Approval for Nuclear Strike, Files Show," *Los Angeles Times*, March 21

1998b, "Whose Finger is on the Nuclear Trigger?" *Washington Post Weekly Edition*, March 30

1998c, "Paying the Price for Nuclear Arms," *Washington Post National Weekly Edition*, July 6

Pincus, Walter and George Lardner, Jr., 1998, "More 1950s Nuclear Secrets Revealed," *International Herald Tribune*, September 3

Pomfret, John, 1999, "Rewriting the Rules of War," *Washington Post National Weekly Edition*, August 16

Post, Gaines, Jr., 1993, *Dilemmas of Appeasement: British Deterrence and Defense, 1934–1937*, Ithaca: Cornell University Press

Powaski, Ronald E., 2000, *Return to Armageddon: The United States and the Nuclear Arms Race, 1981–1999*, New York: Oxford University Press

Powell, Robert, 1990, *Nuclear Deterrence Theory: The Search for Credibility*, Cambridge: Cambridge University Press

1999, *In the Shadow of Power: States and Strategies in International Politics*, Princeton: Princeton University Press

2002, "National Deterrence Theory and National Missile Defense," unpublished paper

Priest, Dana, 1999a, "Divided, They Withstood," *Washington Post Weekly*, October 4

1999b, "Strikes Divided NATO Chiefs," *International Herald Tribune*, September 27

1999c, "Serb Targets: NATO's Conflicting Views," *International Herald Tribune*, September 21

1999d, "The Battle that Never Was," *Washington Post National Weekly Edition*, September 27

1999e, "NATO Secretly Planned an Invasion of Kosovo," *International Herald Tribune*, September 20

Questor, George, 1966, *Deterrence Before Hiroshima*, New York: John Wiley

1986, *The Future of Nuclear Deterrence*, Lexington, MA: Lexington Books

1989, "Some Thoughts on Deterrence Failures," in Paul C. Stern et al., eds., *Perspectives on Deterrence*, New York: Oxford University Press, pp. 52–65

Questor, George H. and Victor A. Utgoff, 1994, "No-First-Use and Nonproliferation: Redefining Extended Deterrence," *Washington Quarterly* vol. 17 no. 2 (Spring), pp. 103–114

Quinlan, Michael, 1994, "The Future of Nuclear Weapons: Policy for Western Possessors," *International Affairs* vol. 70 no. 2, pp. 211–228

Rabin, Yitzhak, 1994, "Deterrence in an Israeli Security Context," in Aharon Klieman and Ariel Levite, eds., *Deterrence in the Middle East: Where Theory and Practice Converge*, Boulder: Westview Press, pp. 6–15

Rapoport, Anatol, 1995, *The Origins of Violence: Approaches to the Study of Conflict*, 2nd edn., New Brunswick, NJ: Transaction Books

Ray, James Lee, 1989, "The Abolition of Slavery and the End of International War," *International Organization* vol. 43 no. 3 (Summer), pp. 405–439

Reed, Thomas and Michael O. Wheeler, 1993, "The Role of Nuclear Weapons in the New World Order," in *Future Nuclear Weapons Requirements, Hearing Before the Defense Policy Panel and the Department of Energy Defense Nuclear Facilities Panel of the Committee on Armed Services, House of Representatives, One Hundred Second Congress* (April 8, 1992), Washington, DC: Government Printing Office, pp. 13–72

Reiss, Mitchell, 1995, *Bridled Ambition: Why Countries Constrain Their Nuclear Capabilities*, Washington, DC, Woodrow Wilson Center Press

Reiter, Dan, 1995, "Exploding the Powder Keg Myth: Preemptive Wars Almost Never Happen," *International Security* vol. 20 (Fall), pp. 5–34

1996, *Crucible of Beliefs: Learning, Alliances, and World Wars*, Ithaca: Cornell University Press

"Report: Russia Used Dummy Missiles," 1998, in NAPSNet Daily Report, November 18, available at ftp://ftp.nautilus.org/napsnet/daily reports

Reuters, 2000, "Military Use of PlayStation 2?" April 15

Revkin, Andrew C., 2001, "U.S. Is Developing Powerful Weapons to Pierce the Deepest Sites," *International Herald Tribune*, December 4

Richardson, James L., 1994, *Crisis Diplomacy: The Great Powers Since the Mid-Nineteenth Century*, Cambridge: Cambridge University Press

Richter, Paul, 1997, "Clinton Orders Revised Nuclear Weapons Policy," *Los Angeles Times*, December 7

1998, "China May Seek Satellite Laser, Pentagon Warns," *Los Angeles Times*, November 28

1999a, "Digging in Useless Against New High-Tech Army Rifle," *Los Angeles Times*, December 23

1999b, "Air-Only Campaign Offers a False Sense of Security, Some Say," *Los Angeles Times*, June 4

Roehrig, Terrence, 1995, "Extended Deterrence in Korea: the U.S. Defense Commitment to South Korea," unpublished Ph.D. dissertation, University of Wisconsin, Madison

Rogers, Clifford, 1995, ed., *The Military Revolution Debate*, Boulder: Westview Press

Rosecrance, Richard N., 1986, *The Rise of the Trading State: Commerce and Conquest in the Modern World*, New York: Basic Books
    1992, "A New Concert of Powers," *Foreign Affairs* vol. 71 no. 2 (Spring), pp. 64–82
Rotblat, Joseph, 1998, ed., *Nuclear Weapons: The Road to Zero*, Boulder: Westview Press
Rotblat, Joseph, Jack Steinberger, and Bhalchanda Udgaonker, 1993, eds., *A Nuclear-Weapon-Free World. Desirable? Feasible?*, Boulder: Westview Press
Russett, Bruce, 1963, "The Calculus of Deterrence," reprinted in John Mueller, ed., *Approaches to Measurement in International Relations*, New York: Appleton-Century-Crofts, 1969, pp. 34–50
    1967, "Pearl Harbor: Deterrence Theory and Decision Theory," *Journal of Peace Research* vol. 4, pp. 89–105
    1987, "Further Beyond Deterrence," *Journal of Social Issues* vol. 43 no. 4, pp. 99–104
    1994, "Between General and Immediate Deterrence," in Aharon Klieman and Ariel Levite, eds., *Deterrence in the Middle East: Where Theory and Practice Converge*, Boulder: Westview Press, pp. 34–44
Russett, Bruce and Harvey Starr, 1989, *World Politics: The Menu For Choice*, New York: W. H. Freeman
Sagan, Scott D., 1985, "Nuclear Alerts and Crisis Management," *International Security* vol. 9 no. 4 (Spring), pp. 99–139
    1993, *The Limits of Safety: Organizations, Accidents, and Nuclear Weapons*, Princeton: Princeton University Press
    1994, "The Perils of Proliferation: Organization Theory, Deterrence Theory, and the Spread of Nuclear Weapons," *International Security* vol. 18 no. 4, pp. 66–107
Sagan, Scott D. and Kenneth Waltz, 1995, *The Spread of Nuclear Weapons: A Debate*, New York: W. W. Norton
Sample, Susan, 1998, "Military Buildups, War, and Realpolitik," *Journal of Conflict Resolution* vol. 42 no. 2 (April), pp. 156–176
Sanger, David E., 2002a, "Bush Finds that Ambiguity Is Part of Nuclear Deterrence," *New York Times*, March 18
    2002b, "Bush and Putin to Sign Treaty to Cut Nuclear Warheads," *New York Times*, May 13
Sauer, Tom, 1998, *Nuclear Arms Control: Nuclear Deterrence in the Post-Cold War Period*, New York: St. Martin's Press
Schell, Jonathan, 2000, "The Folly of Arms Control," *Foreign Affairs* vol. 79 no. 5, pp. 22–46
Schelling, Thomas C., 1960, *The Strategy of Conflict*, Cambridge, MA: Harvard University Press
    1966, *Arms and Influence*, New Haven: Yale University Press
Schmitt, Eric, 2002, "Improved U.S. Accuracy Claimed in Afghan Air War," *New York Times*, April 9

References

Schmitt, Eric and James Dao, 2001, "Use of Pinpoint Air Power Comes of Age in New War," *New York Times*, December 24

Schroeder, Paul, 1972, *Austria, Great Britain, and the Crimean War: the Destruction of the European Concert*, Ithaca: Cornell University Press

1989, "Failed Bargain Crises, Deterrence, and the International System," in Paul C. Stern et al., eds., *Perspectives on Deterrence*, New York: Oxford University Press, pp. 66–83

Schwartz, Stephen I., 1998, "Introduction," in Stephen I. Schwartz, ed., *Atomic Audit: The Costs and Consequences of U.S. Nuclear Weapons Since 1940*, Washington, DC: Brookings Institution, pp. 1–31

Senate Armed Services Committee, 1992, "Military Implications of START I and START II, Hearings Before the Committee on Armed Services, United States Senate, One Hundred Second Congress, 2nd Session, July 28 and August 4, 1992," Washington, DC: Government Printing Office

1994, "Briefing on Results of the Nuclear Posture Review, Hearing Before the Committee on Armed Services, United States Senate, One Hundred Third Congress, Second Session, September 22, 1994," Washington, DC: Government Printing Office

Shapiro, Jeremy, 1999, "Information and War: Is it a Revolution?" in Zalmay M. Khalilzad and John P. White, eds., *The Changing Role of Information in Warfare*, Santa Monica: RAND, pp. 113–153

Simon, Herbert A., 1985, "Human Nature in Politics: The Dialogue of Psychology with Political Science," *American Political Science Review* vol. 79, pp. 293–304

Slocombe, Walter, 1992, "The Future of Nuclear Weapons in a Restructured World," in Patrick J. Garrity and Steven A. Maaranen, eds., *Nuclear Weapons in a Changing World: Perspectives from Europe, Asia, and North America*, New York: Plenum Press, pp. 53–64

Smith, R. Jeffrey, 1997, "Clinton Directive Changes Strategy on Nuclear Arms," *Washington Post*, December 7

Snyder, Glenn, 1961, *Deterrence and Defense: Toward a Theory of National Security*, Princeton: Princeton University Press

1968, "Deterrence and Defense: A Theoretical Introduction," in Mark Smith and Claude Jones, Jr., eds., *American Defense Policy*, Baltimore: Johns Hopkins University Press

Snyder, Glenn H. and Paul Diesing, 1977, *Conflict Among Nations: Bargaining, Decision Making, and System Structure in International Crises*, Princeton: Princeton University Press

Snyder, Jack L., 1984, *The Ideology of the Offensive: Military Decision Making and the Disasters of 1914*, Ithaca: Cornell University Press

Snyder, Jack L. and Robert Jervis, 1993, eds., *Coping with Complexity in the International System*, Boulder: Westview Press

Sorokin, Gerald, L., 1994, "Alliance Formation and General Deterrence: A Game Theoretic Model and the Case of Israel," *Journal of Conflict Resolution* vol. 38 no. 2 (June), pp. 298–325

Spezio, Kim Edward, 1995, *Beyond Containment: Reconstructing European Security*, Boulder: Lynne Rienner

Stein, Arthur A., 1990, *Why Nations Cooperate: Circumstances and Choice in International Relations*, Ithaca: Cornell University Press

Stein, Janice Gross 1987, "Extended Deterrence in the Middle East: American Strategy Reconsidered," *World Politics* vol. 34 no. 3 (April), pp. 382–407

   1991, "Deterrence and Reassurance," in Philip E. Tetlock et al., eds., *Behavior, Society, and Nuclear War*, vol. II, New York: Oxford University Press, pp. 9–72

Stein, Janice and Raymond Tanter, 1980, *Rational Decision Making: Israel's Security Choices*, Columbus, OH: Ohio State University Press

Stein, Janice Gross and David A. Welch, 1997, "Rational and Psychological Approaches to the Study of International Conflict: Comparative Strengths and Weaknesses," in Nehemia Geva and Alex Mintz, eds., *Decisionmaking on War and Peace*, Boulder: Lynne Rienner, pp. 51–77

Steinbruner, John, 1974, *The Cybernetic Theory of Decision: New Dimensions of Political Analysis*, Princeton: Princeton University Press

   1983, "Beyond Rational Deterrence: The Struggle for New Conceptions," in Klaus Knorr, ed., *Power, Strategy, and Security*, Princeton: Princeton University Press, pp. 103–125

Stern, Paul C., Robert Axelrod, Robert Jervis, and Roy Radner, 1989a, eds., *Perspectives on Deterrence*, New York: Oxford University Press

   1989b, "Conclusions," in Paul C. Stern et al., eds., *Perspectives on Deterrence*, New York: Oxford University Press, pp. 294–325

Sullivan, Brian R., 1996, "The Reshaping of the US Armed Forces: Present and Future Implications for Northeast Asia," *Korean Journal of Defense Analysis* vol. 8 no. 1 (Summer), pp. 129–152

Sundarji, K., 1996, "India's Nuclear Weapons Policy," in John Gjelstad and Olav Njolstad, eds., *Nuclear Rivalry and International Order*, Thousand Oaks, CA: Sage, pp. 173–195

Tammen, Ronald L., Jacek Kugler, Douglas Lemke, Carole Alsharbati and Brian Efrid, 2000, eds., *Power Transitions: Strategies for the 21st Century*, New York: Chatham House

Tarr, David W., 1991, *Nuclear Deterrence and International Security: Alternative Security Regimes*, New York: Longman

Taylor, Michael, 1995, "When Rationality Fails," in Jeffrey Friedman, ed., *The Rational Choice Controversy: Economic Models of Politics Reconsidered*, New Haven: Yale University Press, pp. 223–234

Tellis, Ashley J., 2001, *India's Emerging Nuclear Posture: Between Recessed Deterrent and Ready Arsenal*, Santa Monica: RAND

Tetlock, Philip E., 1987, "Testing Deterrence Theory: Some Conceptual and Methodological Issues," *Journal of Social Issues* vol. 43 no. 4, pp. 85–91

Tetlock, Philip E., Charles B. McGuire, and Gregory Mitchell, 1991, "Psychological Perspectives on Nuclear Deterrence," *Annual Review of Psychology*, vol. 42, pp. 239–276

References

t'Hart, Paul, Eric K. Stern, and Bengt Sundelius, 1997, eds., *Beyond Groupthink: Political Group Dynamics and Foreign Policy-Making*, Ann Arbor: University of Michigan Press

Thee, Marek, 1986, *Military Technology, Military Strategy and the Arms Race*, London: Croom Helm

1991, *Whatever Happened to the Peace Dividend? The Post-Cold War Armaments Momentum*, Nottingham: Russell Press

Toland, John, 1970, *The Rising Sun: The Decline and Fall of the Japanese Empire*, New York: Random House

Trachtenberg, Marc, 1985, "The Influence of Nuclear Weapons in the Cuban Missile Crisis," *International Security* vol. 10 no. 1 (Summer), pp. 137–163

Tucker, Robert W., 1985, *The Nuclear Debate: Deterrence and the Lapse of Faith*, New York: Holmes and Meier

Turner, Stansfield, 1997, *Caging the Nuclear Genie: An American Challenge for Global Security*, Boulder: Westview Press

Twigge, Stephen and Len Scott, 2000, *Planning Armageddon: Britain, the United States and the Command of Western Nuclear Forces 1945–1964*, Amsterdam: Harwood Academic

Ullman, Harlan K., 1995, *In Irons: US Military Might in the New Century*, London: Duckworth and RUSI

US Information Agency, 1998, "State Department Noon Briefing," USIA Transcript, Washington, DC, March 16

Utgoff, Victor A., 1993a, "Future Needs for US Contingency Forces," in Barry M. Blechman et al., *The American Military in the Twenty-First Century*, New York: St. Martin's Press, pp. 267–342

1993b, "Military Technology: Options for the Future," in Barry M. Blechman et al., *The American Military in the Twenty-First Century*, New York: St. Martin's Press, pp. 143–195

Van Benthem van den Bergh, Godfried, 1992, *The Nuclear Revolution and the End of the Cold War*, Basingstoke: Macmillan

1996, "The Nuclear Revolution into its Second Phase," in John Gjelstad and Olav Njolstad, eds., *Nuclear Rivalry and International Order*, Thousand Oaks, CA: Sage, pp. 22–39

van Crevald, Martin, 1989, *Technology and War: From 2000 BC to the Present*, New York: The Free Press

1993, *Nuclear Proliferation and the Future of Conflict*, New York: The Free Press

Vartabedian, Ralph, 1995, "The Laser: Air Force's Top Gun," *Los Angeles Times*, November 30

Vasquez, John, 1991, "The Deterrence Myth: Nuclear Weapons and the Prevention of Nuclear War," in Charles A. Kegley, Jr., ed., *The Long Postwar Peace: Contending Explanations and Projections*, New York: HarperCollins, pp. 205–223

Vertzberger, Yaacov, Y. I., 1998, *Risk Taking and Decision-Making: Foreign Military Intervention Decisions*, Stanford: Stanford University Press

320

Von Riekhoff, Harald, 1987, "Methodological and Historical Problems in Determining Deterrence Success," *Journal of Social Issues* vol. 43 no. 4, pp. 79–84

Wagner, R. Harrison, 1989, "Uncertainty, Rational Learning, and Bargaining in the Cuban Missile Crisis," in Peter C. Ordeshook, ed., *Models of Strategic Choice in Politics*, Ann Arbor: University of Michigan Press, pp. 177–205

    1994, "Peace, War, and the Balance of Power," *American Political Science Review* vol. 88 no. 3 (September), pp. 593–607

Wald, Mathew, 1998, "Air-Navigation System: A Jamming Liability?" *International Herald Tribune*, November 24

Wallensteen, Peter, 2002, *Understanding Conflict Resolution: War, Peace and the Global System*, London: Sage

Wallensteen, Peter and Margaretta Sollenberg, 1996, "The End of International War? Armed Conflict 1989–1995," *Journal of Peace Research* vol. 33 no. 3, pp. 353–370

    1997, "Armed Conflicts, Conflict Termination, and Peace Agreements, 1989–1996, "*Journal of Peace Research* vol. 35 no. 3, pp. 339–358

Walt, Stephen M., 1996, *Revolution and War*, Ithaca: Cornell University Press

    2000, "Rigor or Rigor Mortis: Rational Choice and Security Studies," in Michael Brown et al., *Rational Choice and Security Studies: Stephen Walt and His Critics*, Cambridge, MA: MIT Press, pp. 1–44

Waltz, Kenneth N., 1979, *Theory of International Politics*, Reading, MA: Addison-Wesley

    1995, "More May Be Better," in Scott D. Sagan and Kenneth N. Waltz, *The Spread of Nuclear Weapons: A Debate*, New York: W. W. Norton, pp. 1–45

Ware, Willis H., 1998, *The Cyber-Posture of the National Information Infrastructure*, Santa Monica: RAND

Watman, Kenneth and Dean Wilkening, 1995, *U.S. Regional Deterrence Strategies*, Santa Monica: RAND

Weber, Steve, 1992, "Security After the Revolutions of 1989 and 1991: The Future with Nuclear Weapons," in Patrick J. Garrity and Steven A. Maaranen, eds., *Nuclear Weapons in a Changing World: Perspectives from Europe, Asia, and North America*, New York: Plenum Press, pp. 199–221

Weede, Erich, 1983, "Extended Deterrence by Superpower Alliance," *Journal of Conflict Resolution* vol. 27, pp. 231–254

Welch, D. A., 1989, "Crisis Decision Making Reconsidered," *Journal of Conflict Resolution* vol. 33, pp. 430–445

White, Paul C., Robert E. Pendley, and Patrick J. Garrity, 1992, "Thinking About No Nuclear Forces: Technical and Strategic Constraints on Transitions and End-Points," in Regine Cowen Karp, ed., *Security Without Nuclear Wepons? Different Perspectives on Non-Nuclear Security*, New York: Oxford University Press, pp. 103–127

White, Ralph K., 1987, "Underestimating and Overestimating Others' Fear," *Journal of Social Issues* vol. 43 no. 4, pp. 105–109

Whiting, Alan C., 1975, *The Chinese Calculus of Deterrence: India and Indochina*, Ann Arbor: University of Michigan Press

References

Wiener, Malcolm H., 1995, *Nonlethal Technologies: Military Options and Implications*, New York: Council on Foreign Relations Press

Wilkening, Dean and Kenneth Watman, 1995, *Nuclear Deterrence in a Regional Context*, Santa Monica: RAND

Williams, Carol J., 2000, "NATO's Effort in Kosovo Lambasted," *Los Angeles Times*, February 6

Williams, Michael C., 1992, "Rethinking the 'Logic' of Deterrence," *Alternatives* vol. 17, pp. 67–93

Williams, Phil, 1992, "Nuclear Weapons, European Security, and Regional Deterrence," in Patrick J. Garrity and Steven A. Maaranen, eds., *Nuclear Weapons in a Changing World: Perspectives from Europe, Asia, and North America*, New York: Plenum Press, pp. 91–110

Willmer, Stephen J., 1998, "British Nuclear Disarmament and Restrictions in the 1990s," in Barry R. Schneider and William L. Dowdy, eds., *Pulling Back from the Nuclear Brink: Reducing and Countering Nuclear Threats*, London: Frank Cass, pp. 214–217

Windle, David, 1997, "Missile Puts Pilots Clear of Danger," *The Sunday Times* (London), January 12

Winters, Francis X., 1997, *The Year of the Hare*, Athens, GA: University of Georgia Press

Wohlforth, William, 1999, "A Certain Idea of Science: How International Relations Theory Avoids the New Cold War History," *Journal of Cold War Studies* vol. 1 no. 2 (Spring), pp. 39–60

Wohlstetter, Albert, 1959, "The Delicate Balance of Terror," *Foreign Affairs* vol. 37 no. 2 (January), pp. 211–234

Wolf, Barry, 1991, "When the Weak Attack the Strong: Failures of Deterrence," Rand note 3261-A, Santa Monica

Wolfers, Arnold, 1952, "'National Security' as an Ambiguous Symbol," *Political Science Quarterly* vol. 67 (December), pp. 481–502

Wright, Robert, 1999, "Private Eyes," *New York Times Magazine*, September 5

Wu, Samuel, 1990, "To Attack or Not to Attack: A Theory and Empirical Assessment of Extended Immediate Deterrence," *Journal of Conflict Resolution* vol. 34 no. 3 (September), pp. 531–552

Zagare, Frank Z., 1987, *The Dynamics of Deterrence*, Chicago: University of Chicago Press

  1996, "Classical Deterrence Theory: A Critical Assessment," *International Interactions* vol. 24 no. 4, pp. 365–387

  2000, "All Mortis, No Rigor," in Michael Brown et al., eds., *Rational Choice and Security Studies: Stephen Walt and His Critics*, Cambridge, MA: MIT Press, pp. 96–103

Zagare, Frank C. and D. Marc Kilgour, 1993a, "Asymmetric Deterrence," *International Studies Quarterly* vol. 37, pp. 1–27

  1993b, "Modeling 'Massive Retaliation,'" *Conflict Management and Peace Science* vol. 13 no. 1, pp. 61–86

  2000, *Perfect Deterrence*, Cambridge: Cambridge University Press

Zakaria, Fareed, 1998, *From Wealth to Power: The Unusual Origins of America's World Role*, Princeton: Princeton University Press

Zartman, I. William, 1989, *Ripe For Resolution*, 2nd edn., New York: Oxford University Press

Zey, Mary, 1992, ed., *Decision Making: Alternatives to Rational Choice Models*, Newbury Park, CA: Sage

Zhang, Shu Guang, 1992, *Deterrence and Strategic Culture: Chinese–American Confrontations, 1949–1958*, Ithaca: Cornell University Press

Zimmerman, Peter D., 1994, "Proliferation: Bronze Medal Technology Is Enough," *Orbis* vol. 38 no. 1, pp. 67–95

Index of names

Index of subjects

arms control, 10, 22, 96, 97, 226, 253, 288
arms race, 27, 131, 140, 159, 289

balance of power, 12, 85, 87, 88, 89, 97, 130, 140, 154, 158
ballistic missile defense, 17, 30, 95, 112, 222, 228, 291, 293
Berlin crisis, 24, 27n, 28, 145, 240
bluffing, 16, 47, 63, 121, 128, 140, 160, 187, 275

C³I, 20, 255
cheap victory strategy, 6–7, 8, 14, 38, 39, 41, 132, 153, 154, 162, 206, 220
coercive diplomacy, 3, 117
cognitive defects (in decision making), 134–137, 142
cognitive process theory, 67, 163, 165, 169
collective security, xvii, 86, 90, 91, 100, 114, 173–174
commitments, 17, 19, 153, 270
    clarity v. ambiguity, 17, 63
    interdependence of, 50, 153, 241
    reputation for upholding, 50–51
compellance, 2–3, 47, 82, 117, 120, 131, 159, 178, 187, 238, 280
concert, 86, 89, 99, 100, 114, 172, 173
conflicts, *see* wars and conflicts
cooperative security management, 4, 288
counterfactual, 123, 128
counterforce posture, 25, 32, 53
credibility (generally), 3, 8, 23, 24, 46, 134, 176, 177, 180, 187, 190, 193, 194, 198, 220, 221, 238, 286
credibility problem, xvii, 15–20, 47, 48, 49, 50, 51, 53, 86, 101–105, 162, 177, 185, 186, 187, 198, 199, 222, 239, 264, 272, 288

Cuban missile crisis, 16n, 24, 26, 27n, 28, 29, 33, 34, 40, 54, 59, 62, 83, 94, 128, 139, 143–144, 146, 147, 170, 171, 213, 239, 252, 278, 287

democratic peace, theory of, 244–246
détente, 28, 85, 228, 287
deterrence
    among great powers, xvi, 247–255
    among smaller states, 276–279
    as a tactic, 3, 11
    as a tool of statecraft, xx, 42
    as a strategy, 3, 8, 11
    collective actor, xviii, xx, 7, 172–202, 219, 227, 261, 264, 277, 284, 290
    cumulative, 75, 81n, 158
    definition of, 1–3, 44
    designer, 66
    existential, 23, 40, 54, 56, 63, 147, 180, 288
    extended, 15, 17, 19, 49, 89, 98, 153, 157, 177, 221, 247, 259
    general, xvi, xix, 9, 10, 27n, 40, 41, 80–115, 122, 124, 128, 130, 143, 157, 161, 174, 175–178, 193, 239, 250, 288
    immediate, xvi, 9, 10, 11, 41, 80–85, 115, 120, 124, 153, 157, 174, 178–188, 253
    internal inconsistencies of, 46–58
    in intrastate conflicts, 279–282
    in the Cold War era, 238–242
    in the global management of security, 247, 255–269
    in the post-Cold War era, 242–284
    key elements of, 8–22
    lessons of the Cold War for, 26–41
    mutual, 4, 20, 22, 23, 32, 47, 49, 51–53, 241

CAMBRIDGE STUDIES IN INTERNATIONAL RELATIONS